SIR GARNET WOLSELEY

Sir Garnet Wolseley at the Battle of Tel-El-Kebir, 13 September 1882. (*The Graphic*)
'Before leaving England he placed his finger on a map of Egypt at the point now
known to fame as Tel-El-Kebir, and said, "That is where I shall beat Arabi."'

Sir Garnet Wolseley

Victorian Hero

Halik Kochanski

The Hambledon Press
London and Rio Grande

Published by The Hambledon Press, 1999

102 Gloucester Avenue, London NW1 8HX (UK)
PO Box 45674, Rio Grande, Ohio (USA)

ISBN 1 85285 188 0

A description of this book is available from
the British Library and from the Library of Congress

Typeset by Carnegie Publishing, Lancaster

Contents

Illustrations

(between pages 110 and 111)

Maps

Preface

Garnet Wolseley's active fighting career covered many of the small wars of imperial expansion: from Burma, China and India in the east, to Canada in the west, but most of all in Africa. His biographers have tended to concentrate on this part of Wolseley's career and to ignore his work in the War Office and as a colonial administrator. His first biographers, Sir Frederick Maurice and Sir George Arthur, did cover Wolseley's entire life, but it is obvious that they felt that the time he spent as a commander was more important than the period he served at the War Office. Later authors such as Joseph Lehmann, Byron Farwell and Leigh Maxwell have concentrated on Wolseley as a commander. Lehmann devoted only eighteen of 392 pages to Wolseley's career after the Gordon Relief expedition, and Maxwell and Farwell did not even get so far. Adrian Preston edited three of Wolseley's campaign journals and wrote long critical introductory commentaries to them without clarifying Wolseley's opinions on army reform.

Other historians who have written about certain aspects of the late nineteenth century British Army, such as Edward Spiers, Brian Bond, Ramsay Skelley and Gwyn Harries-Jenkins, have all paid tribute to Wolseley's contribution to the reform of the British Army. Adrian Preston argued in the introduction to one of Wolseley's campaign journals that: 'it has been the fault of Wolseley's biographers to claim for him too much rather than to appraise him for what he did, or, perhaps more importantly, for what he was unable to do'. This biography seeks to redress this balance. It is the first since 1924 to cover the whole of Wolseley's life.

Wolseley began writing his autobiography after his retirement in 1900. He only completed two volumes, which took his career to the end of the Asante War. More of his autobiography exists in manuscript in the main Wolseley archive at Hove Central Library but even it does not cover all of his career. The library at Hove contains his private papers, particularly his correspondence with members of his family and his wife, as well as some letters from colleagues and friends. It is by no means a complete archive: some periods are well covered but there are major omissions. Some of these gaps have been impossible to fill. Wolseley's diaries from his early campaigns and family papers were destroyed by fire in 1874. The Ministry of Defence

Library contains a large collection of Wolseley's official papers which has proved extremely valuable. Other official papers exist in the collection of War Office papers at the Public Record Office at Kew.

Apart from these official papers I have used the collections of many of Wolseley's colleagues and contemporaries, both military and political. These are open to the historian at various locations in Britain and Ireland, as well as the collection of letters at Duke University, North Carolina. I was able to gain brief access to the Lansdowne Papers which had recently been donated to the British Museum. These had not yet been catalogued at the time of writing.

I am deeply indebted to a number of librarians and archivists. I would particularly like to thank the staff of the following institutions: the British Library; Devon Record Office; Hatfield House; Hove Central Library; the Institute of Historical Research, London; Kent Record Office; King's College, London, Library; the London Library; the Liddell Hart Centre for Military Archives, King's College, London; the Ministry of Defence Library, Whitehall; the National Army Museum; the National Library of Ireland, Dublin; the Public Record Office, Kew; the Royal Commonwealth Society Library, London; the Royal United Service Institution, Whitehall; the Senate House Library, University of London; the Trustees of the Chatsworth Settlement; and the William R. Perkins Library, Duke University, North Carolina.

Crown copyright is acknowledged for citations from records at the Public Record Office and the Duke of Cambridge papers in the Royal Archives. I wish to thank the Trustees of the Liddell Hart Centre for Military Archives for permission to quote from papers held in the archives.

I am also extremely grateful to Martin Sheppard of Hambledon Press for the comments and suggestions he made on my manuscript.

Abbreviations

BL   British Library
NAM National Army Museum
PRO   Public Record Office, Kew
RA   Royal Archives
WOP Wolseley Official Papers, Ministry of Defence Library
WPP   Wolseley Private Papers, Hove

In Memory of My Father

Introduction

Garnet Wolseley rose from an impoverished background to become the leading soldier of the later nineteenth century. Benjamin Disraeli called him 'our only general'; Gilbert and Sullivan turned him into 'the very model of a modern major-general'; and even the disorderly soldiers in Rudyard, Kipling's stories refer to *The Soldier's Pocket-Book*, Wolseley's pioneering manual of soldiering. The phrase 'All Sir Garnet' passed into the army's common language, the equivalent of the navy's 'all ship-shape and Bristol fashion'.

His career was dominated by the British empire's expansion and the consequent problems. By 1900 the empire covered 13,000,000 square miles and contained 366,793,000 people, the majority of its growth having taken place in the preceding century. Britain had not, at the beginning of the nineteenth century, set out to become an imperial power. Trade was the principal driving force behind initial moves into the Far East and the con- solidation of British rule in India. The conversion to free trade in the 1840s created the impetus to open up new markets for British goods since Britain was then, and remained so until the 1870s when the New World began to take over, the workshop of the world. Free trade needed settled markets and stable governments, and so any interference with friendly governments or reluctance to open markets to British goods was met with swift military intervention.

Although trade may have been the ultimate driving force, imperial policy in the nineteenth century was also largely influenced by moral consider- ations. Britain was seen as a civilising power, bringing modern and superior codes of behaviour to the indigenous population – Britain's success in itself proving the moral superiority of the British way of life. Missionaries were seen as the prime civilising factor, but soldiers, as the expanders of British influence, had a role to play as well. Moreover, if diplomacy failed, only the British army could see off challenges from foreign powers such as France and Germany, when they too began to acquire land in Africa.

Wolseley shared the missionary soldierly zeal of his contemporaries as well as their moral certainty. The wars he was involved in early in his career demonstrate the relationship between trade, the civilising belief of the British

Empire, and settled governments. The campaign in Burma in 1853 was designed to crush a recalcitrant native ruler who was interfering with trade inland. Similarly, the 1860 war with China aimed purely at securing the trading rights and free ports promised by the as yet unsigned Treaty of Tientsin. Wolseley's early experiences as a commander were in punitive expeditions: in 1870, to destroy opposition to the federation of Canada; and in 1873–74 to expel the Asante from the Gold Coast and punish them for their temerity in invading a British protectorate.

Even the Crimean War, the only war that Britain fought against a European power during Wolseley's lifetime, can be seen in an imperial context.[1] When, as a result of a quarrel between the Russian and Ottoman empires, the Russians sank the Turkish fleet at Sinope, the Russian fleet was suddenly free to sail from the Black Sea into the Mediterranean through the Dardanelles. This was a direct threat to British interests, as the free movement of her trade through the Mediterranean to her Far Eastern possessions could be halted by the Russian fleet. French interests were similarly threatened, and the Crimean War was the result.

This introduces a new theme of nineteenth-century strategy and diplomacy: Russophobia. Keeping Russia out of the Mediterranean was a major force behind British policy throughout the century. It led Britain to accept the Turkish gift of the island of Cyprus in 1878 with Wolseley becoming the first British High Commissioner. It also forced Britain to uphold the integrity of the Ottoman empire even when such a policy was morally repugnant, for example, when the Muslim Turks massacred Christians in the Balkans.

Russophobia is linked to another theme of British policy in this period: the debate on how best to defend India. India was the 'Jewel in the Crown', yet a section of its population had risen savagely against British rule in 1857. Wolseley took part in the campaign to crush the Indian Mutiny and shared the sense of betrayal felt by many of his contemporaries; unlike the majority of them, he continued to doubt the loyalty of the sepoy army and advocated defending India away from the country itself, in areas where British troops would be used.

The 'Scramble for Africa' in the last quarter of the nineteenth century secured vast tracts of the continent for Britain. Again, trade was one of the principal driving forces. In the 1870s the European powers and the United States abandoned free trade and introduced protective tariffs. This forced Britain to seek new markets for her goods, and Africa was seen as a largely untapped market. South Africa, in particular, was viewed with interest. British trading interests were already securely established in the region but further expansion inland would bring conflict with both the indigenous black

population and the established Boer republics. Imperialists such as Sir Bartle
Frere and, later, Sir Alfred Milner, wanted soldiers to lead the way for British
trade. British encroachment into black areas led to the Zulu War and, after
initial military disasters, Wolseley took charge and finished off the war, going
on to crush the last threat to white expansion: the Pedi tribe.

Not all white settlers in South Africa were British. Wolseley's first mission
to South Africa, in 1875, was undertaken to impose a new constitution on
the Natal settlers and bring their government into line with other British
possessions in the region. Most importantly, the attempt to create a federation in South Africa led to a war between Britain and the Boer republic
of the Transvaal. The peace that followed this war, in 1881, was an unsettled
one and the two countries went to war again in 1899. Wolseley supported
efforts to secure British dominance in the region because he viewed South
Africa as not only a wealthy trading area but one of vital strategic importance.
South Africa was the key to the British possession of an empire in the Far
East. The Suez Canal was vulnerable to instability in Egypt, and even when,
after a brilliant and short campaign conducted by Wolseley, Britain effectively took over the government of Egypt, the Mediterranean and the Suez
Canal remained vulnerable to interference from continental powers and
could have been closed to Britain in the event of a major European war.

Another factor lay behind Britain's imperial expansion. In 1872 Disraeli
made an important speech at Crystal Palace aimed specifically to appeal to
the newly enfranchised urban working class. He believed that they shared
his belief in the inherent greatness of Britain and her right to rule over the
so-called lesser peoples of the world.[2] Wolseley had no quarrel with that:
indeed he supported Disraeli's policy of imperial expansion, whilst deploring
the methods used which led to two wars in Afghanistan and Zululand. Yet
Wolseley disliked the way in which politicians, Disraeli as well as Gladstone,
began to appeal directly to the electorate for support for party policy.
Disraeli's speech may have influenced the electorate in the 1874 General
Election, although Liberal errors in office probably contributed more to the
victory of the Conservative Party. Certainly it is likely that Gladstone's
Midlothian campaign, launched in 1879 in response to Disraeli's imperial
policy and British military defeats, influenced the electorate sufficiently to
secure a Liberal victory in the following year. Wolseley was not in sympathy
with Britain's move towards democracy. He complained to a friend in 1892,
by which time much of the rural working class had been enfranchised, that:
'Our mob ruled country, where honesty of purpose is now the worst quality
any ambitious man can possess. "Jaw" is now King, and the man who can
flatter the crowd most effectively is he who obtains the privilege of being
its well paid servant'.[3]

To hold its vast empire Britain of course needed an army, but it is an extraordinary feature of the nineteenth century that the British army was tiny in relation to the territory it was supposed to garrison and the populations it was expected to control. Even by the end of the century the total establishment of the army had never exceeded 231,851 officers and men. Throughout his time at the War Office, Wolseley constantly urged politicians to take heed of the fact that the army was dangerously overstretched and needed an increase to its establishment. He met with limited success, and it took the three year struggle in South Africa at the end of the century to bring the politicians to their senses and to accept that either the empire was too large or the army too small.

Political complacency was not entirely surprising given the performance of the British army in the colonial wars. Fighting under-equipped and ill-trained native forces, the victories of the small armies that took part in these campaigns flattered their abilities – although of course colonial campaigning contained its own challenges and inherent dangers. The historian of these 'small wars', C. E. Callwell, rightly described them as 'in the main campaigns against nature'.4 Wolseley was a colonial commander *par excellence.* He led a small force into the thick bush of West Africa to defeat the Asante; concluded the search for Cetshwayo across the wide open veldt of South Africa; and then turned his attention to the destruction of the mountainous stronghold of the robber-baron Sekhukhuni; routed the well-armed Egyptian army by a daring night march and dawn attack on defended entrenchments; and only narrowly failed to rescue General Charles Gordon from a besieged Khartoum, having led his army up the Nile and across the Sudanese desert.

Yet Wolseley was aware that the British army would not necessarily fare so well against well-armed and trained European foes. He worked extremely hard to improve the quality of the British army from its rank and file up to its senior staff officers. He held a number of high positions at the War Office, culminating with the office of Commander-in-Chief. Working within the framework of army reforms made by Edward Cardwell, Secretary of State for War from 1868 to 1874: short-service; the creation of an Army Reserve; linked battalions and the abolition of the purchase of commissions, Wolseley's principal task was to make this new system run smoothly. He encountered great opposition from the Duke of Cambridge, the Queen's cousin and Commander-in-Chief of the Army until 1895; and the army also suffered from the parsimony of successive governments.

Wolseley's limited success in army reform should not detract from his greatness: that any progress at all was made was largely due to him. When, after years of obstruction from the Duke of Cambridge, Wolseley became Commander-in-Chief in his turn, he was too old and often too ill to impose his previously formidable will to batter down opposition to his proposals; but he had set the agenda for future reform. After the Second South African War and his retirement from office, politicians and soldiers alike combined to reform the British army, largely along his lines, so that in 1914 the British Expeditionary Force could surprise the German army with its fighting prowess, if not its size.

1

Early Life and Burma

Garnet Wolseley was descended from an old Saxon family that had been granted one of England's oldest estates at Rugeley in Staffordshire by King Edgar for ridding that county of wolves. The family motto reflected this link: *Homo Homini Lupus* – 'man is a wolf to his fellow man'. King Charles I granted the family a baronetcy in 1628. In the 1690s Brigadier-General the Right Hon. William Wolseley was allegedly rewarded with lands in Ireland for service to King William III during his campaigns against the Catholic James II. This grant of lands was not, however, easy to prove, and in the early 1730s Garnet Wolseley's great-grandfather, Colonel Sir Richard Wolseley, Bart, went to Ireland to attempt to settle the claim. He was unsuccessful, but married and settled in Tullow in County Carlow, thereby founding the Irish branch of the Wolseley family.

Two traditions dominated in the Wolseley family: military service and attachment to the Anglo-Protestant ascendancy in Ireland. Wolseley's grandfather had served with the Royal Dragoons in Germany during the Seven Years' War, and then became a clergyman in northern Ireland. Both Wolseley's father and uncle served with the King's Own Borderers. During the Napoleonic Wars they missed the excitement, glory and chance for prize money offered by the war in the Peninsula. Instead, the Wolseleys were stationed in the West Indies, where the tedium of garrison life was broken only occasionally by brief expeditions against the French on the islands of Martinique and Guadeloupe. Lacking the finance to purchase a promotion and bitterly disappointed with military life, Wolseley's father sold his commission as a major and returned to Ireland to marry. His wife and Garnet's mother, Frances Ann Smith, was the daughter of a pious Protestant Englishman, William Smith. They settled in Golden Bridge House near Dublin, which they rented from her father who returned to England.

On 4 June 1833 Garnet Joseph Wolseley was born, the eldest of seven children. He had three brothers, Richard, Frederick and George, and three sisters, Matilda, Frances and Caroline. Little is known about Wolseley's early life. His father died when Wolseley was seven years old, leaving the family to struggle on his army pension. This poverty was to have a great effect on his life, both immediately and in the future. It meant that he could not be sent to England for his education, like other boys of his class; instead he attended the local day school. At home his mother educated him in her tradition of simple Protestantism with its great emphasis on the Bible. Wolseley wrote of her that she was 'very clever, capable, tactful, of sound judgement, and as a girl had read much'.[1] This love of reading was passed to Wolseley, who enjoyed reading military history and the Latin classics, particularly Caesar's commentaries and Xenophon's *Anabasis*. He disdained the Greek classics and the myths and stories about the ancient gods of Greece because 'my precise and mathematical mind revolted against the unreal nonsense'.[2] At school he excelled at mathematics, history and drawing.

Poverty forced Wolseley to leave school when he was fourteen years old. The young boy took up employment in a land surveyor's office in Dublin to bring money into the family and to further his knowledge of mathematics and surveying. His talents in surveying served him well later in the army. The whole of Ireland was affected by extreme poverty during this period. The successive years of the potato blight in the mid 1840s had led to famine, disease and widespread emigration. In his autobiography, he made no comment on the impression the sight of starving people had on him, although he must have seen poverty-stricken families arriving in Dublin in search of food and work from the devastated areas of west Ireland. If anything he was unsympathetic to their plight. He was a strong believer in the work ethic he saw embodied in Protestantism, and despised the Irish for both their poverty and their Catholicism.

Wolseley loved sports and all outside activities, so it was understandable that he should have been attracted by a military career. Yet his father had been so disappointed by his army service that he wanted his son to enter the church. Wolseley was at first keen on this idea and even planned his first sermon based on the last verse of the 27th Psalm, 'Wait on the Lord: be of good courage, and he shall strengthen thine heart: wait I say on the Lord'. Later, at moments of crisis and worry, he would repeat this verse for comfort.[3] But the purchase of a clerical living required either finance or a wealthy patron, both of which the Wolseley family lacked.

The army seemed, after all, a more attractive proposition, but lack of finance was again a major stumbling-block. There were several ways in which a commission in the army could be obtained. The most common method was to purchase a commission. The regulation price for a commission as an ensign in a line regiment was £400. Above-regulation prices were the norm, and Wolseley could have expected to pay double the amount set out by law. Another means of gaining a commission was to attend the officer cadet school at Sandhurst, but Sandhurst demanded fees and Wolseley's family, with six other children to provide for, could not afford neither the purchase of a commission nor the fees. This left the last method: nomination to a commission by the Commander-in-Chief. In 1847, when he was fourteen years old, Wolseley first appealed directly to the Duke of Wellington, the Commander-in-Chief, stressing his father's twenty-nine years' service in the army. The Duke received many such requests from the sons of impoverished army officers, including sons of his Peninsular colleagues but, despite Wolseley not falling into that category, promised to consider him for a commission when he reached the minimum age of sixteen.

He remained at the land surveyor's office and studied algebra, field fortification, history and geography, French and Latin in the evenings so that he would have the basic educational requirements for a commission.[4] In 1850, when he was seventeen, he wrote again to the Duke asking for a commission. When his request was ignored, he turned his attention to Lord Raglan, the Duke's Military Secretary. The army had recently suffered losses in the latest Kaffir War in South Africa and Wolseley hoped to be nominated as a replacement. He ended his letter that 'I shall be prepared to start at the shortest notice, should your Lordship be pleased to appoint me to a regiment now at the seat of war'. Again he was ignored by Horse Guards. In September 1851 his mother took up his case, writing to the Duke as 'a poor widow of an old officer'.[5] At first it seemed that the Duke had again overlooked Wolseley, but on 12 March 1852 he was gazetted an ensign in the 12th Foot at the age of eighteen.

The British Army in 1852 was near its nadir in terms of efficiency and competency. The army that won at Waterloo had been forced to decline in size drastically, as a long period of peace in Europe was predicted. There was no impetus for reform: tactics had not changed since the Napoleonic Wars and the administrative system was in a dire state, with a confusion of responsibilities between the military and civilian services. The total strength of the army was 140,143 but of these 39,754 were out of sight and mind in remote colonial stations and between 40,000 and 60,000 were stationed in India. The rank and file were recruited from what Wellington had described as the 'dregs of society' and 'scum of the earth'. Army service was seen as an unpopular option and rural and industrial workers looked upon a man who enlisted as a disgrace to the family name. Since most army service was abroad, such a family member usually never returned home. The rank and file were housed in conditions worse than convicts and the death rate from disease far outstripped that in civilian life.[6] Until 1847 soldiers served for twenty-one years and thereafter for twelve years. Long service in hot climates or poor conditions in the home barracks meant that many never lived to the end of their term of service.

Officers were recruited exclusively from representatives of the landed interest.[7] This served the country in a number of ways. For example, officers from the higher classes upheld the principle of social hierarchy at a time when revolutions in Europe frequently upset the social order. It also meant that the government obtained its officer corps cheaply: officers' pay was low and they were expected to maintain a high standard of living at their own expense. Service in the home army was expensive: elaborate uniforms had to be purchased and maintained, mess bills were high and even in line regiments an officer was expected to keep a stable of horses. Promotion in the army at home was entirely dependent on the ability to purchase a higher rank. Therefore the only option for poor officers like Wolseley was to obtain an immediate transfer to a regiment serving in India where the cost of living was lower and the chances of war higher. War brought the opportunity of promotion for valour. As he said much later: 'There is only one way for a young man to get on in the army. He must try to get killed in every way he possibly can'.[8] He set out to do just that by seeking and achieving an immediate transfer to the 80th Foot, later designated the South Staffordshire Regiment, because it was on service in the Second Burma War.

In June 1852 he joined a provisional battalion at Chatham, the depot for men waiting to be sent to join their regiments in India and Burma. He had grown into a man who was 'somewhat under middle height, of well-knit, well-proportioned figure; handsome, clean-cut features, a broad and lofty forehead over which brown chestnut hair closely curled; [and] exceedingly sharp, penetrating blue eyes'.[9] Most of the ensigns at Chatham came from similar backgrounds to himself, poverty sending them to serve in India, but he was unimpressed by his contemporaries, describing them 'as wanting in good breeding, and all seemed badly educated'.[10] He wrote to his mother after his first mess night that many of these men had been drunk halfway through dinner because the champagne had flowed so freely. He reassured her that, despite having consumed a large quantity of wine, he had not been drunk. He concluded that the Commandant of Chatham, Colonel Kelly, was not a gentleman and that 'the fellows here are a wild lot'.[11]

Wolseley was very short of money at Chatham, partly because of the heavy mess bills. The army provided him with a tiny room furnished only with a barrack table and two chairs, leaving him to find the rest of the furniture himself. Corruption was endemic among the non-commissioned officers in charge of the young officers. A cracked pane of glass in a quarter occupied by fifty men would be paid in full by each man with the NCOs sharing the profits. Wolseley had personal experience of this corruption when the barrack sergeant accosted him just before he was about to embark for India, demanding several shillings for a 'lost' latch key. In his innocence he proffered the key which was rejected by the sergeant. After paying up Wolseley, in disgust, threw his key into the river. Fortunately, after only ten days he was sent to Sheerness to join a troop ship, the *Maidstone*, sailing to India.

In the days before the Suez Canal was built the voyage to India took five months, sailing round Africa. At first Wolseley was extremely seasick and remained in his cabin. He recovered just as bad weather hit the ship as it neared the Equator, when he was driven from his cabin to sleep on deck by 'the cockroaches flying about or settling at times on nose or face'.[12] The young and active man was very bored on the voyage and anxious to reach his regiment before the end of the fighting in Burma. He kept himself busy learning Hindustani, shark fishing, sketching the passing islands, and climbing about the rigging for exercise. After fifty days the ship reached Cape Town and officers were allowed on shore. Ten days later the ship set sail for Calcutta using the westerly trade winds. On nearing Calcutta all aboard ship were alarmed to hear the minute gun firing from Fort William, signalling that someone important had died. The firing marked the death of the Duke of Wellington in September 1852 and signalled the passing of an era for the British Army.

The officers and soldiers were all sent up river from Calcutta to Chinsura where the English drafts for regiments in the Bengal Presidency were gathered annually before being dispersed to their respective battalions.[13] Wolseley became even more impatient to join the 80th Foot before its operations in Burma ended, but drafts were only sent onwards slowly. There was no training at Chinsura, and little to keep the young men occupied apart from snipe shooting. Wolseley remembered how they used the clock on the church tower twenty yards from the veranda of their barracks as target practice, eventually stopping the mechanism permanently. He watched a great Hindu festival and procession with interest and visited Calcutta to see its fort and the Government House. He saw little of society but was amazed by the luxurious living of members of the Indian Civil Service. At last the draft for the 80th was ordered to embark on an East India Company steamer for Rangoon.

The First Burma War had broken out in 1824 when two Burmese armies entered Cachar, which was under the protection of British India. The British military operations were successful and Burma ceded the disputed Arakan and renounced its claims on Assam and other frontier regions. However in 1837 the king, Ba-ggi-daw, who had signed the treaty with the British ending the first war, was overthrown by his brother, Tharrawaddi, who in turn was succeeded by his son, Pagan, in 1846. Pagan began making incursions into British territory and interfering with British ships and trade. Therefore in April 1852 military and naval operations began, under the command of Major-General Henry Godwin, and the Burmese army was driven northwards.[14] On 20 January 1853 the lower Irrawaddy valley was annexed to India.

The war was over by the time Wolseley joined his regiment, and therefore the training of the new recruits and officers could begin. Soon after joining his regiment he was ordered to command an outpost outside the British stockade. The immediate problem was that he had no idea of the necessary words of command. A good-natured sergeant helped him but, nevertheless, three privates from the Royal Irish Regiment repeatedly disobeyed his orders and Wolseley sent them back to camp. Their friends took their revenge on him all night by firing on imaginary enemies, forcing the young officer constantly to patrol the line of sentries. Soon, however, Wolseley was well-drilled in the movements of squads and companies.

He took the opportunity to learn something of Burma and its inhabitants. He had known nothing of Buddhism before his arrival in Burma and was pleasantly surprised to see how much there was in common between his simple Protestant faith and Buddhism. Although the British generally regarded the Burmese as heathens and barbarians, he was pleased to note that the Burmese placed a great emphasis on the education of their children.[15]

The war had, however, failed to put an end to the activities of the robber baron Myat-htoon, who had attacked the supplies being transported along the Irrawaddy from Rangoon to the British camp at Prome. He operated from a base deep in the jungle about twenty-five miles from the river. General Godwin relied on naval action to bring Myat-htoon under control, but a naval expedition under Captain Lock in February 1853 met with disaster when it abandoned its boats and took to the jungle. Ignorance of elementary tactics led to the death of Lock and twelve other sailors. A military expedition under Brigadier-General Sir John Cheape was ordered to avenge their deaths at once. Wolseley was overjoyed to hear that he had been selected as the ensign to take a detachment of the 80th recruits to join Cheape at the base of operations near Donabew. He arrived there on 6 March and learnt that the expedition was to start the next day. There had already been one brief expedition against Myat-htoon at the end of February which had lasted a week and had turned back short of the chief's stronghold because supplies were dwindling.[16]

Conditions for campaigning in the jungle were appalling. Wolseley wrote to a family friend that 'I cannot find words to express the sufferings of the troops and indeed of everyone belonging to the force'. The heat and humidity were oppressive, with temperatures reaching 105.5 Fahrenheit in Wolseley's hut. The scarcity of water contributed to an outbreak of cholera which threatened to decimate the small British force: 'a man whom you saw lie down in perfect health at night, you had sometimes to bury before breakfast the next morning'. To make matters worse the officers and men were expected to campaign in the same uniform used on parade in India and England. For example, cloth shell jackets were worn buttoned up to the chin along with white buckskin gloves. In contravention of the Queen's Regulations the men were told that they need not wear the stiff leather stocks normally worn tightly wound round the neck, although Wolseley noted that many of the older soldiers continued to do so.[17] The troops of the East India Company army were dressed in looser fitting clothing, far more suitable for campaigning in hot climates. Little was known of the terrain to be crossed, and no one knew the exact whereabouts of the stronghold, or the number and deployment, of the enemy forces.

The expedition left Donabew on 7 March with six to seven days' provisions. Wolseley was sent to the right wing under the command of Major Francis Wigston. After about three miles the advanced guard surprised an enemy picket and shot two of them. This was the first time Wolseley had fired in anger and the first time he had seen a man killed. He recalled 'I was not at the moment in the least excited, and it gave me an unpleasant sensation'. He was able to cope with seeing bodies torn apart by gunfire, but was unable to pass a butcher's shop without feeling nauseous.[18] The expedition advanced slowly as the guides often led the troops in the wrong direction. There was a delay of five days while a force was sent back to the river to bring up more supplies. Finally on 19 March the force was on the move, with Wolseley commanding the 80th as the advanced guard. Visibility was down to a hundred yards as a thick fog had descended in the jungle, and all around them the troops could hear the Burmese cutting down trees to strengthen their stockade somewhere in front of the force. Suddenly the fog lifted and the advanced guard saw the enemy stockade about a hundred yards in front of them. It was solidly built, and stretched over a width of 400 yards. The enemy had not yet spotted the British, so Wolseley was ordered to advance as far as he could without being seen, and not to fire unless fired upon. Then the alarm was raised and the Burmese opened fire, hitting four of his troops. They fell back into the jungle to join the main force of British and Indian troops to await the arrival of the guns.

After the guns had weakened the stockade a storming party was called for. Wolseley eagerly volunteered for it along with Lieutenant Allan Johnson. While running towards the stockade, he fell into a well-concealed mantrap and was briefly knocked unconscious. On climbing out he found himself alone and was forced to shelter in the pit while the shooting match between the British and Burmese troops continued. He had lost his pistol in the fall and was only armed with a sword, so he made an ignominious retreat back to the British lines. Another storming party was called for and Wolseley again volunteered and, since he knew the ground, was chosen to lead it along with Lieutenant G. C. Taylor. He recorded later that 'I have never experienced the same unalloyed and elevating satisfaction, or known again the joy I then felt as I ran for the enemy's stockades at the head of a small mob of soldiers'.[19] As they reached the pit where he had fallen before he was surprised to see Taylor turn a somersault. No sooner had Wolseley registered that Taylor had been seriously wounded then he too was hit, a large jingall bullet passed through the upper part of his left thigh. Staunching the bleeding as best he could, he continued to cheer the men as they broke into Myat-htoon's stronghold. A doctor soon reached him and saved his life by tourniqueting the wound. Taylor was less fortunate and bled to death before the doctor could reach him. Wolseley received a Mention in Despatches for his valour.

He spent an uncomfortable night in a hut in the stronghold until he was taken down a creek by a boat the following day to Prome. It was common medical practice then to starve wounded men to keep down inflammation. Wolseley recorded his hunger when watching the doctors eating and drinking, unaware of the suffering of their patients. At Prome he was put in a hut where the temperature rose to 109 Fahrenheit in the day. He contracted a kind of choleric diarrhoea and, weakened by the loss of blood, spent some days fighting for his life. Eventually he was deemed fit enough to be sent to Calcutta and then back to England in the steamer *Lady Jocelyn* for convalescence. By the time he reached England he could walk quite well. While convalescing he paid a long visit to Paris, before returning to England where he had been promoted to lieutenant. He transferred to the 90th Light Infantry, then stationed in Dublin. Although the wound appeared to have healed well, his left leg was weakened and caused him trouble in later years particularly after riding for long periods.

Dublin was an exciting station for young officers, since there was an unlimited opportunity for hunting and plenty of balls and dances for entertainment. Wolseley, however, could not share in these pleasures. He could not afford to own a stable full of horses for hunting, and his wounded leg prevented him from dancing. He amused himself by gambling in the two officer clubs in Dublin, the United Service Club and the Victoria Yacht Club, and, although he did not gamble for high stakes, he admitted that the money he lost 'would have enabled him to have kept at least one horse'.[20] He joined the Freemasons and by a special dispensation was raised to a Master's Degree when under age. In the 1890s, when Commander-in-Chief in Ireland, he was to rejoin his first lodge as its master.

Wolseley was serving in Ireland when the Crimean War broke out in 1854. In 1853 Russia had invaded the Turkish Balkans but soon its army got bogged down. The Russians then sank the Turkish fleet at Sinope and Britain responded immediately by sending her Mediterranean fleet to the Bosphorus. Russia did not want a war with Britain and so withdraw her fleet to its base at Sevastopol and later scuttled it. Britain and France were not convinced that the Russian threat to their naval predominance in the Mediterranean was over and, with Turkey, declared war on Russia. Britain sent a large military expedition under the command of Lord Raglan to seize the Russian naval base at Sevastopol and demolish its dockyards and storehouses.

Almost the entire resources of the home army were sent to the Crimea, but these resources were severely limited in terms of manpower, armaments and supplies. The 90th had been recently trained in the use of the new rifles, replacing the old Brown Bess muskets. Their rifles were taken from them and sent to the Crimea. As the sheer scale of the undertaking became apparent, all trained men were rushed out to the Crimea from their home stations. Eventually the 90th was the only regular regiment left in Dublin. Wolseley was extremely impatient for orders to go and join the largest campaign Britain had mounted since the Napoleonic Wars and his prayers were soon answered. The incompetent handling of troops at the three main battles, the Alma, Balaclava and Inkerman, meant that on 12 November 1854 the 90th was sent for. Wolseley would 'have shouted for joy' had he not been in church when he heard the news.[21]

2

Crimea and Indian Mutiny

On 19 November 1854 the 90th embarked on the Cunard paddle steamer *Europa* at Kingstown. Wolseley was subaltern of the day and commanded the regimental guard. In his party he had eight or nine prisoners, who excited the sympathy of the local crowd and were given money by some. Wolseley caught sight of his mother sitting on a grassy bank near the Royal St George Yacht Club, crying as her son marched past to war.[1] It was a swift voyage, broken only by a day's break at Malta. All the soldiers aboard were anxious to reach the Crimea before Sevastopol fell. On 3 December the 90th arrived at Balaclava, disembarked and were sent straight to the trenches in front of Sevastopol.

The rank and file in the Crimea suffered appallingly. The incompetence of their military leaders had led to an inconclusive battle on the Alma on 21 September 1854. Then the Russians were able to surprise the allied camp at Balaclava; the battle for which is remembered chiefly for the brave though futile charge of the Light Brigade against the Russian guns. After the battle of Inkerman the allied troops settled down to besiege the Russians in the port of Sevastopol. Soon after his arrival in the Crimea Wolseley purchased a pony and toured the battlefields to see for himself what had gone wrong. He gained some idea of the flaws in the high command when observing two Russian men-of-war bombarding the French defences, unhampered by British naval intervention because the admiral in charge had not expected an attack.

He was unimpressed by the performance of the British Commander-in-Chief, Lord Raglan. He blamed him for the basic strategic errors that had allowed the Russians to retreat into the strongly defended town of Sevastopol. He felt that Raglan's real mistake was to have accepted the command at all after having led a purely sedentary life in London for forty years. Wolseley's criticism was reserved chiefly for General John Burgoyne, Raglan's adviser on siege warfare. Burgoyne appeared to have learnt nothing of strategy since the sieges of the Peninsular War. His strategy had been seriously flawed: instead of moving straight against the weakly defended northern part of Sevastopol, Burgoyne's strategy had led to heavy allied losses as the armies made their way round to the better-defended southern side. Indeed Wolseley saw few able officers in the Crimea: Sir Richard Airey, the Quartermaster General, and General Sir Colin Campbell were exceptions.[2]

The junior regimental officers were little more competent than their seniors. Wolseley was appalled at their lack of interest in military craft and their overwhelming concern with their own comforts. Officers in the rear were well-supplied with food and tents. Wolseley's brother Dick served as a regimental doctor and, when Wolseley visited him, he noted that Dick had managed to gather a supply of wine and preserved meats.[3] The officers at the rear had little knowledge of or care about the conditions in the trenches. There even officers suffered during the brutal Russian winter: Wolseley recalled how one officer was forced to part reluctantly with the planks from his bed in order to build a fire for cooking and warmth. One officer who did impress him with his concern for the men under him was Colonel Charles Gordon.[4] A friendship was struck up between the two men and Gordon later told him that he was one of the two men for whom he prayed daily. In 1884 Wolseley would command an expedition to rescue Gordon from Khartoum.

Although life for Wolseley and his fellow officers in the trenches was harsh, it was nothing compared to the suffering of the rank and file. Wolseley could afford to buy a warm jacket and long boots from a sailor to keep out the snow and wind but the troops were dressed in their parade uniforms which were soon reduced to rags. He recalled later, after a visit to the Crimea, that: 'the worn and hungry expression on the faces of these gallant fellows often haunts me still, and I can well remember how I hated myself and my brother officers for being better fed and better clothed than they were'.[5] Most of the camp equipment dated from the Napoleonic Wars and was rotten.[6] A storm in Balaclava harbour in mid November had sunk a number of ships carrying winter clothing and an adequate supply of blankets did not reach the Crimea until the summer. Ill-clad and under-fed, the fighting strength of the British army in the Crimea dropped by 30 per cent. Wolseley wrote later, 'What killed our men most was the want of firewood. The consequence was that we all soon began to eat our salt pork and red navy-junk in a partially uncooked state, and this brought on diarrhoea, which too frequently ended in dysentery'.[7] Wolseley and his fellow subaltern, Lieutenant James Wade, attempted to brighten the troops' Christmas by making a pudding. They visited Balaclava to find figs and some suet, albeit rather rancid suet, and set to work creating the pudding. They were ordered to the trenches that night for duty before the pudding was fully cooked. Wolseley ate some of it and spent a very uncomfortable night doubled up with severe stomach ache.[8]

The suffering of the troops in the trenches was due largely to incompetent staff work in the rear. The Admiralty succeeded in bringing respectable quantities of supplies to Balaclava harbour. There a confusion of military and civilian agencies was responsible for getting the supplies to the front. The narrow muddy track from the harbour to the trenches slowed supplies and much rotted unused at the harbour. The French Army was better organised and built a railway from its harbour to the front. Men and horses died and food and fodder ran out: indeed so many pack animals died that their corpses could be used to give directions in the area. The despatches of W. H. Russell for *The Times* brought home to the British public for the first time the sheer incompetence of its army administration. The government began an enquiry into the system and unfairly, in Wolseley's opinion, blamed Sir Richard Airey for the failure to get the supplies to the trenches. The high death rate from disease in the military hospitals led to Florence Nightingale going out to Scutari to attempt to bring about an improvement in conditions.

In January 1855 Wolseley, eager for action, volunteered to serve as an assistant engineer. This took him to the front line and he was promoted to captain. The winter forced a temporary cessation of operations while the allies and Russians alike struggled to survive, but patrolling and the clearing of mud, slush and snow from the trenches continued. On one such patrol Wolseley had a narrow escape. Blinded by the driving snow on his way to visit a gun battery near Middle Ravine, he lost his way. Pausing by a large boulder to regain his bearings, he was startled to hear three Russian soldiers talking on the other side. Unarmed, he had little choice but to flee back to the British trenches before the Russians could open fire.[9] On 9 April the allied artillery opened a great bombardment of Sevastopol, firing over 130,000 shells into the town. The Russians replied forcefully and Wolseley was kept extremely busy repairing the trenches while under fire from shells and Russian snipers. He was calm under fire, encouraging the troops in their work, and had several narrow escapes from shells bursting nearby.

In early June the British and French commanders devised a complex plan for a simultaneous assault on the defences of Sevastopol. The British were to take the Quarries and the Redan, the French the Mamelon. Wolseley was ordered to connect the Quarries, when taken, with the existing British trench line. The bombardment opened on the morning of 6 June and continued till the evening of the next day, when the infantry assault was ordered. While working to extend the trenches that day Wolseley was hit on the right thigh by a bullet that did not penetrate but nevertheless caused heavy bleeding. He refused to go to the rear. The assault failed and the British flooded back to the old lines. Wolseley and his sappers continued working through the night, strengthening the trenches against the anticipated Russian counter-attack the next morning. The historian of the Crimean War, Alexander Kinglake, noted that 'the loss of blood caused by a wound at an earlier hour did not slacken his powerful energies'. By the next morning Wolseley and his men were exhausted after working for thirty-six hours without a break. The Russians counterattacked and Wolseley and Colonel Robert Campbell of the 90th stood on top of a trench rallying the tired troops to beat off the attack. Wolseley received another Mention in Despatches for his work. After the attack was defeated, he collapsed and slept for twenty-four hours.[10]

On 18 June, Waterloo Day, the British and French began a complex attack on the Russian positions. The two attacks should have begun simultaneously, but the French began too early. Despite all chances of success having evaporated, Raglan ordered the British to advance and the troops soon fell back with heavy casualties. Wolseley observed later: 'You can ask too much from even British soldiers. Upon this occasion what we asked from them was beyond the power of men to give'.[11] British naval operations in the Sea of Azov had cut the Russian supply lines but they made a last desperate attack on the allies at the battle of Tchernaya which began on 16 August.[12] On 30 August Wolseley was in a forward sap repairing the damage done by the Russian assault when the working party came under heavy fire from the approaching Russians. Soon twelve of the sixty-five strong party were casualties. Wolseley, a sergeant and two sappers continued work at the head of the sap. A Russian shell landed on the group: both sappers were killed and Wolseley hit in the head. The sergeant dragged his badly wounded young officer back to a doctor. There it was discovered that he had a large piece of jagged rock sticking out of his jaw, his left cheek was badly split, and his right eye seriously damaged. He was soon transferred to a hospital set up in a Russian monastery near Balaclava.

While in hospital he kept abreast of the news of the renewed allied attacks on Sevastopol. He was well looked after and provided with fresh milk, eggs and fruit. When Sevastopol was evacuated by the Russians, on 8 September, He resigned his post as assistant engineer because he had no desire to build roads and camp sites, the usual duties of the Royal Engineers. In October, while still in hospital, he received a letter from the Military Secretary, who wrote of the Commander-in-Chief's pleasure at Wolseley's bravery, but regretted that he could not be promoted to the rank of major, as he deserved, because he had only served for three years and seven months in the army.[13] The doctors recommended that he should return home to gain further advice about his eye. Wolseley was preparing to do so when he received a message from General Airey who wanted him to join his staff. He was appointed Deputy-Assistant Quartermaster General and worked on the military survey of the Crimea. His immediate superior was Major the Hon. Hugh Clifford who later, in South Africa, served on Wolseley's staff under his former junior. His second winter in the Crimea was far more comfortable winter than the first. The troops were now all housed in huts and there were sufficient supplies of food and firewood. He stayed in the Crimea until the Treaty of Paris ending the war was signed in April 1856. After a short period of leave, he rejoined the 90th at Aldershot, but he never regained sight in his right eye.

In February 1857 Wolseley was at Portsea with the 90th Regiment when it was ordered to prepare for a war in China to be followed by service in India. Britain's relations with China had broken down again over the issue of trade. Three wars were fought in 1839, 1856 and 1860 to force the Chinese to accept more British trade and to grant treaty ports and naval bases. After the first China War in 1842, Britain had obtained Hong Kong on a lease until 1997; a British representative at Peking was permitted and five ports opened up to foreign trade. But in 1856 the Chinese offended both the British and the French by trying and executing a French missionary, and by seizing twelve Chinese seamen from a Hong Kong registered vessel and trying them for piracy. This began the Second China War and the forts outside Canton were bombarded and captured. The 90th Light Infantry was to form part of the expeditionary force to compel the Chinese to sign a new treaty.[14]

Most of the troops embarked in HM Troopship *Himalaya*, but Wolseley and three companies were sent on HM Troopship *Transit*, which left Portsmouth on 8 April 1857. On board were about 650 troops. The first night was spent at anchor in the Solent and Wolseley was wakened the next morning by his servant with the news that the ship was sinking because its bottom had been pierced by its anchor. The ship returned to Portsmouth for repairs. Bad weather later forced the captain to make for the harbour of Corunna. Wolseley gratefully accepted the opportunity to visit the area where Sir John Moore had died conducting a retreat from the French army in 1808. As the ship was leaving the Cape rumours were heard of the outbreak of the Indian Mutiny. Wolseley was the only officer aboard who had been in India and was prepared to believe the rumours. On 9 July, as the *Transit* entered the Straits of Bangka between Sumatra and the islands of Bangka, Wolseley was on deck after breakfast lighting a fellow officer's cigar 'when I was shot forward upon him by the ship having suddenly stopped dead'. The *Transit* had hit a rock. He returned below to organise his company and remained with them in the darkness as the ship began sinking by the stern. Finally, they were ordered on deck and in the ship's boats made for a long, low coral reef lying about three quarters of a mile from the foundering ship.[15]

Every man aboard was saved and reached the reef safely. From there they sailed to the large island of Bangka. Fresh water was available and the men lived on pineapples which were found near the beach. There was no sign of man and no animals except monkeys, which they ate. A boat had been sent to Minto, a Dutch settlement, and a Dutch gunboat soon appeared to give the troops aid. Some belongings were rescued from the wreck: Wolseley's servant brought him eighty sovereigns, some watches and trinkets from his father's dressing case; and a sailor found his dressing gown floating in the ship and returned it to him. After ten days a British gunboat from Singapore arrived with the news that the Indian sepoys had mutinied and that the 90th would now be sent to Calcutta to take part in the suppression of the revolt. HMS *Actæon* landed them at Singapore on 23 July and a week later HMS *Pearl* carried Wolseley's company to Calcutta.

The Indian Mutiny had complex roots. The Indians feared that Britain was attempting to force Christianity on them by underhand methods. It was rumoured that the cartridges of the newly issued Enfield rifle were greased with a blend of beef and pork fat and that the powdered bones of pigs and cows had been added to the ration flour, thereby offending both Muslim and Hindu sensibilities. The sepoys in the Bengal Army had been offended by the introduction of promotion by seniority which paid no attention to the traditional rights of the Muslims and high-caste Hindus to important regimental positions. Finally, the sepoys from Oude were angry at the annexation of the province in 1853 by the Governor-General, Lord Dalhousie, which ignored the rights of the nawab's adopted heir, Nana Sahib.

The mutiny began in the last week of May 1857 at Meerut, where one sepoy cavalry and three infantry regiments rebelled and attacked the European cantonment, killing several officers and their families. It spread swiftly to Delhi, which was seized by the rebels. There were only 45,000 British troops spread across India and 232,000 Indian soldiers. Most were concentrated in the newly annexed Punjab and there were only four white battalions spread across the rebellious areas. The British therefore withdrew to three large towns, Agra, Cawnpore and Lucknow, and attempted to disarm the sepoys of doubtful loyalty. The rebellion spread and within six weeks British authority had been destroyed throughout the upper Ganges and northern areas of central India. The rebels then concentrated on the British defences at Agra, Cawnpore and Lucknow.[16]

British reinforcements were rushed from Burma and Mauritius, as well as from the China Expeditionary Force. The massacre of over one hundred

British women and children at Cawnpore after they had been allegedly promised safe conduct along the river to Allahabad by Nana Sahib deeply shocked the British at home and in India. The British public felt betrayed. In their eyes British rule in India had brought an end to various barbarous religious practices and had modernised and unified the backward country. The cry for revenge was strong. Wolseley wrote to his brother soon after his arrival in India that 'my sword is thirsty for the blood of these cursed women slayers'.[17] Showing the typical racist attitudes of the time, the white troops deplored the idea that native hands had touched their womenfolk. The depth of British disgust was apparent when a mutineer was caught, tried and sentenced to be hanged. Normally bribes had be offered before a soldier would volunteer to be a hangman; on this occasion every man in Wolseley's company volunteered for the job.

Before Wolseley's party could begin making its way towards where Generals Sir Henry Havelock and Sir James Outram were fighting their way to Cawnpore and Lucknow it had to be first re-equipped. The result was that, apart from their helmets and boots which they had worn during the shipwreck, no two soldiers or officers were dressed alike.

At the end of August the three companies of the 90th embarked on the long journey to Cawnpore. They travelled first by railway to Raneegunge after solving a problem with the six pounder gun they had been given. It could not pass through the station to the platform: it was only after much argument with the station official that Wolseley issued a certificate acknowledging his responsibility for pulling down part of the station to get the gun on the train. He half expected to be billed by the East India Company for this destruction but never heard anything more about it. Because the level of the Ganges was too low for river transport, the troops were forced to make their way overland by the Great Trunk Road connecting Calcutta and Delhi. Wolseley's force was the first to travel this route since the beginning of the mutiny and the attitude of the natives was uncertain. The 90th travelled in a column of wagons dragged by bullocks which could cover only two or three miles in an hour. A third of the force marched on foot, regularly relieved, to guard the lengthy column. Determination to join Havelock's column fighting towards Lucknow led the men to embark of a series of forced marches, averaging twenty to thirty miles a day, marching mostly at night. It was the rainy season and the advance was slowed down by swollen streams and rivers. Apart from the intervention of nature the march was largely uneventful, except for a close encounter with a tiger which stampeded the bullock train. The force reached Benares on 10 September and Allahabad on the 13th. Wolseley's company then marched to Futteepore, a civil station, forty miles from Cawnpore. Within a few days the three companies of the 90th were reunited under Major Roger Barnston. Havelock ordered them to stay at Futteepore, which came as an immense disappointment to Wolseley and his men. Nevertheless they spent their time fruitfully, strengthening the defences of the small outpost.

When Havelock crossed into Oude to relieve Lucknow, the 90th was ordered to march into Cawnpore. Lacking tents, they were forced to bivouac in the open near the building where the women and children had been massacred. Evidence of the massacre were visible and the well into which the bodies had been thrown was still uncovered. Wolseley picked up more than one handful of human hair which had been torn from the butchered women before realising what it was. He recorded that 'a more sickening, a more maddening sight no Englishman has ever looked upon. Upon entering those blood-stained rooms, the heart seemed to stop'.[18] Revenge had already been meted out on many of the participants in the massacre. At first, captured mutineers had been forced to lick clean a patch of bloodstained floor before being executed. Even after Sir Colin Campbell put an end to the practice, blowing from the mouth of guns remained a common form of execution.

During September the force under Havelock and Outram reached Lucknow and forced its way into the Residency. Unfortunately the relieving force was too small to carry off the civilian population of Lucknow and the wounded: all it could do was to strengthen the defences and await final relief by a stronger force under Sir Colin Campbell. This army, with Wolseley among its numbers, relieved Lucknow in November.

On 21 October the 90th and remnants of other regiments were ordered to take a convoy of carts to the Alum Bagh, a palace on the outskirts of Lucknow where Havelock had left a small garrison guarding his sick and wounded, plus the baggage and the elephants, while making the final advance. Life at the Alum Bagh was extremely boring for Wolseley. He had expected to return to Cawnpore and had left his baggage and reading material there. Furthermore the old officer in command, Major Duncan McIntyre, would not allow the young officer to lead an attack on the enemy who was close enough to fire an occasional artillery round at the palace. While at the Alum Bagh Wolseley met a Irish clerk, Henry Kavanagh, who had escaped from Lucknow and come to the Alum Bagh carrying a plan of the city, on which Outram had marked a suitable route for Campbell to follow. On 4 November the advanced guard of the main force arrived at the Alum Bagh to collect the plan but Major McIntyre refused to hand it over, stating that Kavanagh (who had already returned to Lucknow) told him to give it to Campbell personally. When Campbell arrived soon afterwards, he executed a war dance of fury round the obstructive major, to Wolseley's vast amusement.

The column under Campbell soon began the final march on Lucknow using the route outlined by Outram. The column consisted of 700 cavalry, 3800 infantry and twenty-four guns. It skirted Lucknow to the south and east with the enemy retreating before it, abandoning both the Dil Khoosha and the Martiniere College. From the college the column turned north west and rested for the night in a garden near Haidar's Canal, which formed part of the south-east boundary of Lucknow, in order to give the supply column time to catch up.[19] Wolseley's company was left on picket duty for that night and during the next day, with no shelter from the sun and constant fire from the enemy at anyone who showed himself. There were no casualties. Wolseley's company and the other two from the shipwreck missed the review held by Campbell that day, but the commander paid them a special visit and advised them to use the bayonet as much as possible when they reached the narrow streets of Lucknow.

On 16 November the column set off at noon with Wolseley's company forming the advanced guard, followed closely by the 9th Lancers and 93rd Highlanders and the guns. The next enemy positions, the Sekunder Bagh and the Shah Najif mosque, were known to be strongly defended. The Sekunder Bagh, formerly the garden of Alexander the Great, was about a hundred yards square surrounded by thick, twenty feet high walls with turrets at each corner and a high gate in the middle of the southern wall. During the advance Wolseley's excellent sergeant Newland, who was later commissioned, was wounded in the mouth and forced to retire from the campaign – much to Wolseley's regret. Eighty yards from the enemy his company halted to allow the heavy gun to be brought to the front. The force had been travelling along a deep hollow road and the gunners needed the assistance of Wolseley's men to drag the gun onto level ground where it could fire on the Sekunder Bagh. There were many casualties before the gun was in a position to open fire. The moment a large hole had been blown in the wall the 93rd Highlanders, the regiment following Wolseley's company, attacked through it, while the Sikhs attacked the gate.

He was then ordered to advance with his company towards the Shah Najif mosque. They reached the cover of the ruins of the old native quarters near the mosque only to find that, although they were now sheltered from enemy fire, British shells were falling short and peppering his force with splinters and bullets. His commander, Major Barnston, was badly wounded in the thigh by one such shell burst. Wolseley decided to attempt to break into the mosque. A corporal in the 93rd Highlanders described what happened next. Wolseley and his troops 'made a most determined attempt to get into the place, but there were no scaling ladders, and the wall was still almost twenty feet high'.[20] The infantry was therefore forced to abandon the honour of taking the mosque to the artillery who bombarded it for three hours. Then the Highlanders were able to advance and by the evening the mosque was in British hands.

After the fighting stopped Wolseley went in search of Major Barnston, one of the few regimental officers he admired.[21] He had wrongly been told that the wounded had been taken into the Sekunder Bagh. There, instead of finding the British wounded, he saw the consequences of the British thirst for revenge on the mutinous sepoys: about 2000 bodies were piled up in an archway. He was woken the next morning by the smell of burning flesh. On investigating the source, he found a dead sepoy was hanging across the wall, his greatcoat smouldering slowly. That morning the British buried the enemy dead in two deep trenches on either side of the road to Lucknow.

The next enemy position was the officer's mess house belonging the 32nd Regiment. The mess house stood on high ground in the middle of a large garden. High though rather dilapidated walls, and a ditch with two drawbridges, encircled the garden. It looked a strong position and was strongly held by the enemy. Campbell selected Wolseley to lead the infantry attack after the artillery had bombarded the position. He was ordered to take cover by the walls, should the first attack fail, and to await reinforcements. He gained the impression that Campbell did not expect him to succeed, and wanted to send the Highlanders in to finish the job. The attack succeeded easily: the troops were both surprised and delighted to find a drawbridge down and the 90th rushed into the mess house, firing on the retreating enemy.

Wolseley had no further orders and the enemy opened fire on his troops from two nearby buildings. By then some of the 53rd Regiment under Captain Leonard Irby had joined him in the mess house. Wolseley suggested that Irby should take the very large building on the left, the Tara Kothee, while he took the one on the right, the Moti Mahul palace. This was surrounded by a twenty foot high thick masonry wall. In front of the entrances the sepoys had built well-loopholed walls to strengthen the defences. However, the wall had been built so recently that the troops could attack the soft mortar with spades and pickaxes to make a hole. Kavanagh suddenly appeared and led Wolseley round to another entrance to the Moti Mahul. This proved to be just as strongly defended, so he returned to the original position where he found that one very brave ensign of his company had managed to squeeze part of his body through the hole while the other soldiers were working hard to widen it.

The troops scrambled through the hole into the courtyard which the enemy had virtually abandoned. The few remaining sepoys fought hard and Wolseley was nearly scalped by one. He lost a number of men in this skirmish, including his servant Andrews. Wolseley recommended him for the Victoria Cross but did not expect to be awarded one himself 'as the butcher's bill was not large enough and I escaped myself without being wounded'.[22] Suddenly there was a loud explosion from the opposite side of the courtyard. As the dust settled, a British officer and several soldiers emerged. The officer was Captain William Tinling of the 90th who had been part of Outram and Havelock's column and had then been besieged in Lucknow. So it came to be that companies of the 90th relieved the rest of the regiment. Soon afterwards Generals Outram and Havelock emerged from the Residency and met Campbell.

Wolseley was strongly advised by his brigadier, Colonel Adrian Hope, to stay out of Campbell's way because 'he is furious with you for pushing on beyond the Mess House, for the capture of which his orders to you alone extended'. Campbell had hoped to use the 93rd Highlanders, his old regiment, to reach the Residency. Exhausted and elated by the events of day, Wolseley took Hope's advice and marched his men off towards the Shah Najif to sleep. During the night he was disturbed by someone lying down next to him. When he woke at dawn he discovered that the newcomer was Campbell, the very man he had been advised to avoid. However Campbell merely shook his fist at him in a friendly manner and with a smile told him, 'If I had but caught you yesterday!'. He was then extremely complimentary about Wolseley's conduct and promised him promotion. Campbell did not know that he had already been promised this promotion in the Crimea as soon as he had completed the necessary six years in the army.[23]

Campbell now faced a dilemma. He had to lead the Lucknow garrison and about 500 British women and children and 1000 sick and wounded soldiers to a place of safety. But the situation at Cawnpore had deteriorated in Campbell's absence. The mutinous Gwalior contingent had seized the city and the stores. Therefore the only option was to abandon Lucknow temporarily until Cawnpore could be secured. Wolseley was on picket duty when the line of women and children began their trek from Lucknow. He wrote 'their faces bespoke the privations, bad food and illness, and their careworn features told us not only of bodily suffering but of sorrow bravely endured'.[24] Many of the women and children were the widows and orphans of the men who had defended the Residency. Campbell then marched off towards Cawnpore, leaving behind a weak division under Outram of 3395 British troops and 1047 loyal sepoys near the Alum Bagh to represent British rule in Oude. This division, which Wolseley joined, faced an estimated 100,000 mutinous sepoys in the neighbourhood.

Life in the Alum Bagh was monotonous, although the British soon organised race meetings. Shortly before Christmas Wolseley was forced to reconsider his previous poor opinion of Major McIntyre. He was on outpost duty a mile from the camp when he was joined on the flat roof of a village house by McIntyre, who was inspecting the outposts. Wild geese flew overhead and McIntyre shot one. That afternoon, back in camp, Wolseley received the goose and a bottle of port from the major along with a note saying it was for his Christmas dinner. It was gratefully received.

At the beginning of March 1858 Campbell returned to the Alum Bagh to begin the final push to relieve Lucknow. The enemy had almost encircled the city with a double line of substantial defences using the Kaiser Bagh palace as the citadel. These defences were manned by 30,000 mutinous, well-armed sepoys and 60,000 men from Oude. In contrast Campbell had only ten infantry battalions, one cavalry regiment and most of the Bengal artillery. He was forced to rest the native regiments but was strengthened by the arrival from home of fresh but untried British battalions. Despite the apparent disparity in strength Lucknow fell for the second time on 14 March without any serious fighting. Much to Wolseley's disapproval, because of the adverse effect on discipline, the British soldiers then began looting.

A few days later Campbell selected Wolseley for a staff appointment as Quartermaster General to Major-General Sir Hope Grant, who had recently been given command of the Oude division.[25] This appointment marked the end of Wolseley's service as a regimental officer. Thereafter he would either serve as a staff officer or as a commander on campaigns. He wrote home proudly that 'I am now a great swell'.[26] He also was also promoted to the rank of major, the highest rank his father had reached. Wolseley greatly admired Hope Grant, writing that 'he had all the best instincts of a soldier [and] was liked by every good man who knew him'. He later wrote a memorial article on Hope Grant for the *United Service Magazine*.[27]

The task before the division was the reconquest of the province of Oude. This entailed a vast amount of 'marching, fighting and skirmishing through its plains, and the crossing of many rivers'. Oude was a flat, rich and well-cultivated province interspersed with many mango groves and some coconut trees. Scattered throughout the province were tanks which Wolseley and the other officers used for bathing. On one occasion he had a close encounter with a yellow snake which shook its head near his face. He fled the scene, despite the fact that the snake was harmless, because he was frightened by all reptiles. The columns suffered greatly marching along seemingly endless dusty roads under the hot sun. Wolseley recalled that, 'I had a good helmet with an unusually long turban wound round it, yet the sun seemed to gimlet a hole through it into my brain. My very hair seemed to crackle from the burning heat, and the nails of one's fingers became as if made of some brittle material that must soon break'.[28] Hope Grant wanted to rest the men during the hot season but was under great pressure from the civil authorities. Wolseley was shocked by the callous nature of these civil officials, who thought nothing of asking an infantry column to march under the burning sun to punish some rajah who had not paid his taxes or had disobeyed government orders. Even ten mile marches caused a large number of casualties from heat-stroke.

In September 1858 a major campaign was launched to clear the whole of Oude. Wolseley feared that he might get killed and wrote to his younger brother George, who had just joined the 84th Regiment and was on his way to India, with friendly advice. He urged George to 'serve God, and honour your Queen', always remember the debt he owed to his mother for their upbringing, not to get into debt, not to speak ill of any men and defend friends from slander, and not to marry unless 'you can make your marriage a stepping stone to advancement'.[29] His well-meant advice fell, however, on deaf ears. As he wrote to Dick, George was 'one of the damnedest young fools I have ever known let loose upon the army, and I never expect anything brilliant or noble from him'.[30] Dick also ignored Wolseley's advice on marrying a heiress for advancement and in 1859 married a charming but not rich woman called Mary.

Wolseley's main duties on campaign were to reconnoitre the route of the march and to draw a plan after an action, showing the movement of the troops, to accompany Hope Grant's despatches to headquarters. Early in 1859 he was able to take a few days' leave to go to Cawnpore to visit his brother George, who was passing through there on his way to join his regiment in the Punjab. No sooner had Wolseley arrived in Cawnpore than he was ordered back to Lucknow because Hope Grant had been ordered to retake the field. He had time only to say a quick greeting and farewell to his brother. The new operations were to cover the district between the Ganges and the Nepal frontier. It was a very rough region where the practice of thuggee was rife.[31] The column was forced to cross the Nepal frontier in May to fight the leader of the rebels in the foothills of the Himalayas. These skirmishes were to be the last of the Indian Mutiny. On 4 June 1859, Wolseley's twenty-sixth birthday, the field force returned to Lucknow for a long rest. He received the best possible birthday present, the brevet of lieutenant-colonel. This made him the youngest colonel in the British army and the fastest promoted officer of recent years.

With British rule fully restored in India, Lucknow became a leading centre

of social life in India. The season officially began at the end of October
with the arrival of the Governor-General Lord Clyde with Lady Canning,
accompanied by the families of British officers and civilian officials. Following them were a number of young women from Britain in search of a
husband. Wolseley became a prime target for their attentions, because of
his rank, but he was too poor to consider marriage seriously. Nevertheless,
he and two fellow officers rented a large country house in a park to make
the most of the opportunities on offer. Their idea was to have as much fun
as possible without becoming seriously entangled in a permanent relationship. They made an agreement that anyone who married would immediately
be ejected from the house.

Wolseley had strong views on the subject of marriage. While in the Crimea
he had come to the conclusion that marriage and army service did not mix
well: 'Should the misfortune of Wedlock ever befall me I shall convert my
sabre into that agricultural implement into which swords are generally said
to be transferred in times of peace'. He had no intention of marrying himself
because 'I am too poor to marry a fortuneless girl, and too proud to owe
affluence to a wife'.32 Time would show Wolseley that love of a good but
not wealthy woman could force him to change his opinions on marriage.
In the meantime, while in Lucknow, 'I manage to console myself with an
Eastern Princess and find she answers all the purposes of a wife without
giving any of the bother'.33

As a result of the mutiny the Crown took over the rule over India from
the East India Company. The East India Company lost its separate army:
the European artillery became batteries of the Royal Artillery, and the
European infantry became British line regiments. The native regiments were
put under royal control with British officers. The transfer of East India
Company regiments to Crown control was not a smooth process. There
were protests, which were termed the 'White Mutiny'. No unified system
of command was established in India: the army remained divided into three
presidencies: Bengal, Madras and Bombay.

3

China

Wolseley was soon called upon to campaign again. An expedition was to be sent to China to accompany British and French representatives to Peking to obtain the ratification of the Treaty of Tientsin that had been agreed after the bombardment of the forts outside Canton in June 1858. The naval force under Admiral James Hope could not pass the mouth of the Peiho to sail up river to Peking; military intervention was requested. Britain did not wish to destroy the Chinese government, merely secure its trading interests. Under the terms of the Treaty of Tientsin foreign diplomatic missions were to be given the right to reside in Peking, missionaries were protected and the number of treaty ports increased to sixteen.[1]

The British expeditionary force consisted of 11,000 men under the command of Sir Hope Grant. To act alongside them, the French sent 6500 troops under General Montauban. Wolseley was still Quartermaster General of the Oude Division and Hope Grant wanted to appoint him to the same post for the China force. Lord Clyde however disagreed, arguing that Wolseley lacked the necessary experience for such a position. Therefore Colonel Kenneth Mackenzie of the Gordon Highlanders was appointed Quartermaster General, with Colonel Robert Ross as his second-in-command and Wolseley as the third member. The staff embarked on the steamer *Fiery Cross* at Calcutta and arrived at Hong Kong on 13 March 1860. During the voyage they read everything they could about China as, 'the war upon which we were entering, was to be carried on in a country regarding the resources of which we knew literally nothing, so provision had to be made against all possible contingencies, and supplies of everything provided, just as if we were about to start upon a desert campaign'.[2]

The British expeditionary force was drawn from all over the empire. British troops arrived from India along with sepoys and native cavalry and mule drivers from Madras and Bombay. Muleteers were recruited from Manila in the Philippines, and a contingent of coolies was raised locally to supply land transport. The staff found that Hong Kong was too small to accommodate a large military force, so Wolseley was sent to Kowloon to find a suitable camping ground. He was kept very busy at first arranging the accommodation and supplies for these troops, but still found time to visit Canton, which was under British military occupation. The Chinese mandarin who had governed the town had been captured by the British but not before he had beheaded 60,000 of his Chinese opponents. Wolseley was disgusted to see many walled-in yards filled with their skulls.[3]

On 8 March the British Minister at Shanghai sent an ultimatum to the Chinese government demanding the right to land at the mouth of the Peiho river and travel to Peking for the ratification of the Treaty of Tientsin. This request was refused, so the home government ordered Hope Grant, and the French ordered Montauban, to begin operations with the occupation of the island of Chausan. This island had been occupied by the British during the Opium War in 1848–49. Wolseley felt this was a pointless exercise as the Chinese attached little importance to the place. Nevertheless, an infantry brigade along with some artillery and engineers were landed along with a few hundred French marines under the command of Hope Grant to take control of the island. There was no opposition to the landing. There was a quarrel between the British and French troops over the height of the flagpoles displaying the Union Jack and the French tricolour, the British having accidentally erected a higher one than the French. Wolseley explored Chausan and was impressed to find that virtually every patch of land was cultivated and growing vegetables, barley and rice. The staff, including Wolseley, also visited the sacred island of Poo-too nearby on 24 April. They were shown temples and gardens which Wolseley found very attractive. He spent some time watching a Buddhist priest who was so deep in meditation that, although he watched closely for over five minutes, he never saw the priest blink or move any other muscle.[4]

In the middle of May the main operations began. At Hong Kong the British contingent of 14,000 men embarked for the British base at Talien-whan on the Gulf of Po Hai. It was comprised of two infantry divisions, one cavalry brigade, four batteries of field artillery, one of horse artillery, one of mountain guns and a siege train of heavy artillery. The French force was expected to camp independently on the other side of the gulf at Chefoo. On arrival there the French decided that the water was too shallow for their transports and requested permission to join the British at their landing ground. Thereafter the British and French embarked on combined operations. Wolseley regretted this development: he confessed privately that 'I have always hated the French, and I see no likelihood of my feelings changing as regards them'. He never doubted the bravery of individual French soldiers, but deplored the lack of preparation of the French force and wrote later 'that our army was hampered throughout its course by the French contingent we had to act with'.[5]

On 1 August the allied army made an unopposed landing at Peh-tang and advanced towards the Taku forts. They were welcomed at Peh-tang by the Chinese population who told the interpreter, Harry Parkes, that they had been harassed by Tartar patrols which they hated as 'stinking more than you English do'.⁶ On 9 August Wolseley began reconnoitring the route of the advance which began three days later. Heavy rain slowed progress as the guns became bogged down in the mud. Near the village of Sin-ho, six miles from Peh-tang, the columns were attacked by two or three thousand Tartar cavalry. The artillery opened fire and a charge by the Indian cavalry finally routed the enemy. There was another brief action near Tang-Koo, where the columns were forced to halt for six days to allow the French and the supplies needed to attack the Taku forts time to catch up.

The difficulties of allied operations were apparent when Wolseley witnessed an argument between the two commanders, Hope Grant and Montauban, on how to attack the Taku forts. Hope Grant prevailed, despite receiving a written protest from Montauban. At 5 a.m. on 21 August the artillery opened fire on the north Taku forts. Despite the explosion of several magazines Chinese resistance lasted for two hours before their guns fell silent. An allied infantry assault followed and the fort was taken. It proved to be the key to the whole Taku defence line and the other forts fell without resistance. The Chinese defending them were allowed to go free. The rain continued falling and Wolseley returned to camp to find his tent had been flooded in his absence and most of his belongings underwater. Since he was already soaked through, he had been hoping to change into dry clothes and footwear, but it was even too wet to light a fire to dry out.

The next morning he heard that the Chinese Governor-General had surrendered all the southern Taku forts and all the country up the Pei-ho as far as Tientsin, including that city. Wolseley mistakenly assumed the war was over and wrote home on 27 August narrating the British success.⁷ The army pushed forward to Tientsin. When two imperial commissioners arrived there all the soldiers thought that peace was certain. However, the commissioners had no instructions to deal with the British, so Lord Elgin, the British Ambassador, decided the force would advance to Tung-chow and hoped that an imperial messenger would meet him there with more satisfactory news. This move began on 8 September and Wolseley, as the only officer on the staff who could sketch well, was kept very busy reconnoitring and mapping the country during the advance. He was escorted by a small party of Punjab cavalry and some mule carts with Chinese drivers. During one heavy thunderstorm every mule driver fled except his. When he asked the duffadar of cavalry why this was, he received the reply that he had put all the drivers in his tent and tied their pigtails together so that they could not flee.

At Ho-see-woo, halfway between Tientsin and Peking, new imperial messengers arrived with letters stating the terms upon which the Chinese government would make peace. It was agreed that the allied armies would advance as far as Chang-kia-wan, sending a thousand men to Tung-chow to wait for the treaty to be signed. Wolseley again operated ahead of the main force, sketching the route it should take. On one such reconnoitring expedition on 18 September he was nearly cut off from the army by the sudden appearance of a large force of Tartars. He crammed his pockets with his surveys and sketches and prepared with his small party to make a run for it before they were completely cut off. Fortunately the Tartars did not see him and he reached the headquarters safely, only to find that a large Chinese force was blocking the road ahead of the allies. It was now clear that the assurances of the Chinese government, negotiated by Parkes, of the safe conduct of the ambassador to Peking were untrue, and that more fighting was to be expected. The advance of the Chinese troops into Tung-chow led to the capture of the British negotiators, including Parkes and some soldiers. Two battles followed in the neighbourhood of Tung-chow, one at Chang-chia-wan to the south and one at Pa-le-chiao bridge just west of the town. Three days later the Chinese army had been completely routed.

Speed was now essential because winter was approaching and the river, upon which much of the allied transport travelled, would be frozen over. There were two options open to Hope Grant: he could advance directly to Peking, with the one division left under his command, or wait at Tung-chow for the Second Division to join it from Tientsin. The first option would succeed only if the Chinese did not oppose the allied entry into Peking, since the siege guns needed to blast a way in were still far in the rear. The second option would take precious time. There was also the need to obtain the release of the prisoners without delay. On 23 September Lord Elgin sent the Chinese an ultimatum stating that if the prisoners were not returned within three days and the demands previously made were not met, then the British would advance on Peking, a move which it was thought might lead to the downfall of the Manchu dynasty. No answer was received, so the allied advance was renewed as soon as the Second Division arrived with the siege guns.

During the advance in the early days of October, contact was broken between the British headquarters and the French contingent and the British cavalry brigade. Wolseley was sent with a squadron of cavalry on 7 October to find them. He found the French at the Yuen-ming-Yuen palace, the Imperial Summer Palace, which the French troops were busy looting. The French general was unwilling to allow Hope Grant and Lord Elgin to witness such a breakdown in discipline. Despite his disapproval of looting, Wolseley was amused to see how many gifts were pressed upon the French general, Baron Jomini, to whom he was chatting. A French soldier pressed Wolsley to take a French enamel from the period of Louis XIV, which he accepted. Later his wife, Louisa, pressed him to have it examined by an expert because she thought that it was by the great miniaturist Boileau as, indeed, it proved to be. British officers were doing so well from the looting but neither the men nor the NCOs were allowed the opportunity. Hope Grant therefore ordered that all loot should be passed to prize agents and the proceeds divided between the members of the force. The amount received by each man depended on his rank: such was the wealth of the booty that every private soldier received nearly £4 as his share.[8]

Negotiations continued with the Chinese and the prisoners began to be returned, and by 14 October nineteen of the thirty-nine men taken prisoner had been returned. It was revealed that they had been tortured while in captivity. The Chinese authorities were ordered to surrender the north-eastern entrance to Peking, the Anting Gate, immediately so that Lord Elgin's safety when entering the city to negotiate could be guaranteed. The Chinese population was warned of an imminent bombardment and the deadline was noon on 13 October. The British were in fact playing a dangerous game of bluff; their ammunition supply was too low to enable a breach to be blown in the walls. It proved unnecessary to open fire because shortly before noon the Anting Gate swung open and Peking surrendered. Wolseley and the troops were disappointed with the appearance of Peking, 'all had imagined it to be something very wonderful'.[9]

Soon after the surrender Wolseley was reconnoitring to the west of Peking when he met a group of Tartars with five carts, each bearing the coffin containing the remains of a tortured British soldier. They were buried with full military honours in the Russian cemetery. Lord Elgin, still trying to negotiate peace with Prince Kung, added a demand for the payment of £100,000 to be given to the families of the murdered men. This payment was made. Prince Kung was also told that, to mark the horror of the murders, the Yuen-ming-Yuen palace, the site of many of the tortures, would be totally destroyed. The ashes from the fire littered the streets of Peking, reminding the population of allied power. A proclamation was issued giving the reasons for the destruction.

The British suspected that the Chinese might attempt to prevent the signing of the peace treaty. Wolseley was ordered to inspect the palace in advance and a British division was distributed along the route Lord Elgin would take through Peking. No disruption occurred and the peace treaty was signed by Lord Elgin and Prince Kung on 24 October in the Hall of

Audience. Wolseley liked the appearance of Prince Kung: 'he looked a gentleman amidst a crowd of bilious, bloated, small-pox-marked faces of the mandarins around him'.[10] After the peace was signed Wolseley was kept busy drawing and surveying and had little time to write letters home. He wrote to his sister Matilda that he was suffering from the consequences of his severe wound in the Crimea: 'my sight is so weak that even to read for five minutes by lamp or candlelight pains me and makes me temporarily blind'. He would lie in the dark making plans for his future: he hoped to be able to spend some time in Paris in order to become really proficient in French, a language he could not speak but could read well.[11]

It was agreed that the army would remain at Peking until 8 November to await the arrival of Frederick Bruce, Lord Elgin's brother, who was to be the British representative at Peking. The army would then have to leave, because any later and the army could not be sure of reaching the Taku forts before the Peiho had been closed to navigation by ice. Winter set in fast as the army prepared for its departure and there were several days of heavy rain and hard frosts which caused great suffering, particularly among the Indian troops. Two and a half British battalions were left at Tientsin to guard the British embassy established there, while Hope Grant and his staff with the remainder of the troops left Tientsin at the end of November, reached the mouth of the Peiho and embarked for Shanghai. Small garrisons of British and Indian troops remained in China to guard the treaty ports. 'Thus ended the China War of 1860, the shortest, most brilliant, and most successful of all that we have waged in that country.' [12]

During the winter of 1860–61 twelve officers of the headquarters staff, including Wolseley and Hope Grant, hired a P & O steamer to make a trip to Japan. This country was only recently emerging from centuries of isolation; the visit took place only six years after the United States Commodore Perry had forced Japan to open her ports to western trade, and the Shogunate was on its last legs. The group visited the treaty ports, Tokyo and Yokohoma. Wolseley was amused to read an inscription in English at the entrance to some extensive and beautiful gardens: 'For the amusement of foreigners: no dogs or Chinamen admitted'. While at Tokyo there were several minor earth tremors every day, showing Wolseley why no building in Tokyo was higher than two low storeys.[13]

While the allies had been occupied in forcing the Chinese government to sign the peace treaty, Chinese authority had been threatened from another source: the Taiping rebellion. A former groom to an American missionary, styling himself the Tien-wan or Heavenly King, had gathered around him a large army of followers and adventurers. They had sacked the wealthy city of Soochow and established an alternative government at Nanking.

Wolseley was curious to meet the self-styled ruler and set off from the British headquarters at Shanghai to Nanking to meet him. He was allowed complete freedom of movement around Nanking and saw at once that the rebels were a weak force, remaining in power solely because of the still weaker state of the imperial government. He noted the consequences of rebel rule: 'the river near the rebels is a great deserted highway' while further away, where the imperial government still ruled, 'it is well covered with trading craft; highly cultivated farms stretch down to the water's edge, whilst neatly-built and snug-looking villages and hamlets are scattered along both sides'.[14] He never met the rebel ruler. The Taiping rebellion was eventually crushed by Wolseley's friend, Charles Gordon, in 1863. Wolseley also managed to visit Hankow before returning to Shanghai in March 1861 to sail home via Suez. When the steamer reached Hong Kong, he heard news that would affect his future career: the first shot of the American Civil War had been fired at Fort Sumter.

My dearest Mother

I always told you that the first person that I intended to announce the news of my intention to marry should be you — I now sit down to do so, and the only cloud that dims my happiness is that it may be unwelcome to you — I have been for some time past engaged to Miss Erskine, but I have postponed carrying out that happy event until I shall obtain some new good Appointment.

Wolseley's letter to his mother, announcing his engagement.

4

Canada

On his return from China, Wolseley was given eighteen months' leave. He went first to Paris where he enjoyed himself as an 'idler', spending the money he had saved through several years campaigning. He then began visiting friends and relations in England and Ireland. At the house of a friend, Tom Fortescue, as he confided to his brother Dick, 'I fell most dreadfully in love, indeed by far the most serious affair of the heart that I have hitherto had'.[1] The lady in question was Louisa Erskine or Loo as she was more commonly known. Louisa Erskine was probably illegitimate but was brought up as the niece and ward of her actual father, Alexander Holmes. She had been living in Ireland with her grandmother since babyhood and was eighteen years old when she met Wolseley.[2] She was not very tall, but then neither was Wolseley, but was attractive with a fair complexion, delicate features and golden hair which she wore piled on top of her head. He later wrote to one of his sisters Matilda that: 'I would marry Miss Erskine if I had a fortune: you may all rest assured that I shall never marry to live in poverty and as that lady is as poor as I am there is not much chance of her being Mrs Garnet Junior'.[3] His shortage of money threatened to constrain his future.

Although he had been given little opportunity to spend his pay while on campaign, his family imposed heavy financial demands on him. The main culprit was Fred, who went to Australia to seek his fortune in 1860. Garnet gladly lent him £1000 to help him set up a business but in early 1861 was forced to lend him another £500. Fred's many schemes failed to make him a fortune and, although he repaid hardly any of his debts to his eldest brother, the latter continued to send money to him. George was little better: in February 1863 Garnet was unable to take leave because George had not repaid the £100 he had borrowed. In 1865 George had got into such financial difficulties in India that he threatened to resign his commission. Garnet wrote to a friend at Horse Guards to prevent this from happening, though he did suspect that George might be better out of the way in Australia. Even Dick, usually the most reliable of the brothers, borrowed a small sum from him, but he at least always repaid the money borrowed.[4]

At the beginning of the winter of 1861–62 he went to Ireland to stay with one of his married sisters in County Cork. He hunted virtually every day on the horses she had bought for him, but felt that he needed a third mount. On his way to view the prospective purchase, he collected his post from the village post office. Among the bundle of letters he found a telegram from the War Office ordering him to embark in four days' time for service in Canada as Assistant Quartermaster General.[5]

The international press was following the events of the American Civil War closely. The British commander in Canada, Lieutenant-General Fenwick Williams, was convinced that as soon as the Union forces had routed the Confederates they would turn their attention to Canada. In a flurry of letters to the Commander-in-Chief of the British Army, the Duke of Cambridge, he urged the immediate despatch of reinforcements and artillery guns to strengthen Canadian defences. Little was done until it became clear that Britain might be drawn into the American Civil War following the *Trent* Incident in November 1861.

In that month a Union frigate stopped a British steamer the *Trent* and removed two Confederate representatives from the ship despite their apparent protection under the British flag. A similar violation of the rights of a neutral nation on the seas in 1812 by Britain against the United States had led to war then. The *Trent* Incident was viewed very seriously by the British government because the captain of the Union frigate was thanked by Congress. Britain demanded an immediate apology and the release of the Confederate envoys. The country was actually in no position to fight a land war against the United States in Canada. There were only approximately 4500 British troops in Canada spread across the country. In addition, there were about 10,000 uniformed and armed but poorly-trained Canadian volunteers. The Duke of Cambridge promised Williams that reinforcements were being sent and urged him to concentrate his existing defences on the towns of Quebec, Montreal and Kingston.[6] The reinforcements being rushed to Canada included a brigade of Guards, and by February 1862 there were 18,000 British troops in Canada.

Wolseley left for London on the evening of the day he received the War Office telegram. In London he met his immediate superior, Colonel Kenneth Mackenzie, who was to be Quartermaster General in Canada. Mackenzie told him that the staff was to embark from Woolwich on the following day in the steamship *Melbourne*. This ship had been condemned during the Crimean War as unfit for further service and was known to be very slow. Mackenzie argued with the authorities that the Quartermaster General's department should travel on the fastest ship available so as to allow the staff time to reach Montreal ahead of the troops. He failed to make his case and the staff suffered an extremely slow and uncomfortable voyage, finally reaching Halifax on 5 January 1862.

At Halifax several items of news awaited the Quartermaster General's staff. The first was that President Abraham Lincoln had apologised for the *Trent* Incident and that the immediate crisis was over. The second was that the Prince Consort Albert had died. The final piece of information was that ice had made the St Lawrence River impassable. The troops were therefore travelling along the snow road from New Brunswick. The staff would have to travel overland to join them at Montreal. The Governor of Nova Scotia and commander of the troops there, General Sir Hastings Doyle, thought it would be fastest if the staff travelled to Montreal through the United States via Boston. In view of the recent crisis in Anglo-American relations, all military titles were erased from their baggage for the crossing of United States territory. Wolseley travelled by steamer to Boston, and was shown the sights of the American War of Independence by an American whom he had met in China. From Boston the staff travelled by rail to Montreal.

Wolseley was then sent to Rivière de Loup, the eastern terminus of the Grand Trunk Railway, to arrange the housing of troops on their way to Montreal. No one in the village could speak English, so he was forced to learn some Canadian-French patois in order to communicate. There was little to amuse him once the transfer of troops had begun to run smoothly, but he learned to skate and to walk on snow shoes. As a child he had read stories of life in the Canadian backwoods and of the battles of the pioneers with the Indians. An acquaintance offered him the chance to meet an old Indian chieftain, but Wolseley was bitterly disappointed: instead of the dignified figure wearing furs and feathers he had expected, the chief proved to be 'a watery-eyed old rascal, without any glimmer of distinction', who only came to Rivière de Loup to drink whisky.[7] Finally, in March, when the last of the British troops passed through the village on their way to Montreal, Wolseley was allowed to follow them to rejoin the headquarters of the British Army in Canada.

Montreal provided him with many amusements and little work. He bought horses and a sleigh and drove many Canadian and American women on sightseeing expeditions. There was ample opportunity for skating and many plays were acted by the garrison troops. He wrote of this period: 'Altogether, it was an elysium of bliss for young officers, the only trouble being to keep single. Several impressionable young captains and subalterns had to be sent home hurriedly to save them from imprudent marriages'.[8] Wolseley was still in love with Louisa Erskine and made no attempt to seek a wife in Canada.

British officers stationed in Canada watched the operations of the American Civil War with great interest. In general, British sympathies lay with the secessionists, not out of any sympathy for the institution of slavery, which Britain had led the world in abolishing, but rather out of a desire to see the great potential power of the United States diminished. Several officers had visited the Union armies but little was known of the state of the Confederate forces. Wolseley avidly followed the movements of the southern armies on maps, and was particularly struck by the audacity of General Robert Lee's invasion of Maryland. He was determined to visit the Confederate armies and took two months leave to do so, without telling his superior of his intentions. Supplied with letters of introduction to American acquaintances in Baltimore, a southern town in its sympathies but held by the Union army, he travelled south, hoping to discover the means of crossing the Union lines into Virginia. He met Frank Lawley, *The Times* correspondent who had recently arrived from London where he had been Gladstone's private secretary. The two men agreed to travel south together along the so-called 'Underground Route', used by smugglers between Maryland and Richmond, the Confederate capital. They were stopped many times by Union patrols and, on one occasion, Wolseley had to divert the attentions of a suspicious Union officer by offering to light his cheroot. The real challenge was to cross the Potomac but, after several uncomfortable nights in verminous quarters, the two men found a smuggler willing to row them across the river.

Soon after arriving in Virginia, a Confederate cavalry patrol arrested them and took the two men to their camp at Fredericksburg. There they were released and allowed to travel by train to Richmond. The journey stunned both men, especially Lawley, who had no previous experience of warfare. The train was full of wounded soldiers from the recent battles of Manassas and Antietam. Wolseley admitted later that: 'Though well inured to the sight of human suffering, I never remember feeling so moved by it as during that short railway journey'.[9] At Richmond, he was introduced to the Confederate Secretary of State for War, General George Randolph, who supplied him with an officer to escort him around the recent battlefields. The trail of military debris showed him the movements of the two armies and how, though heavily outnumbered, Lee had managed to hold his own and capture enough Union armaments, equipment and clothing to supply his own forces.

Wolseley was naturally keen to meet the great man himself, and asked permission to visit Lee's headquarters at Winchester. General Randolph issued him a passport with a note stating that Wolseley had not been asked to take the usual oath of secrecy because he was a British officer. He was immediately struck by the informality of Lee's camp; he noted that Lee preferred to camp with his army rather than to use a nearby house for his quarters. The camp itself showed little of the pomp of British or European armies: there were few staff officers evident and no military bands. Lee impressed Wolseley immediately. Later in his life, even after meeting such great men as General von Moltke, the architect of victory in the 1870 Franco-Prussian War, he still maintained that Lee 'was one of the few men who ever seriously impressed and awed men with their natural, their inherent greatness'.[10] Lee's only weakness appeared to be a dislike of offending people, which led him to retain officers in positions of responsibility beyond their abilities. He also visited Lee's two corps commanders: 'Stonewall' Jackson and James Longstreet. Jackson impressed Wolseley, who believed that 'with such a leader men would go anywhere, and face any amount of difficulties'.[11] He saw Longstreet's division march past and noted that, although most of the men were shabbily dressed and many badly shod, 'all rifles were clean and serviceable'. Longstreet later told him that the worst-clad of his corps had refused to march past a British officer. He concluded that 'This southern army interested me beyond any army I ever saw before or since'.[12]

On his return to Canada Wolseley made his first excursion into the field of journalism and wrote an article on his visit to Lee's headquarters for *Blackwood's Magazine.* Although he wrote extensively and effectively, his spelling let him down, for example 'fur trees'. He sent the draft article to his sister Matilda who rewrote it for him and 'put in some such dreadfully long words that I had to haul down a dictionary to find out their meaning'.[13] After their marriage his wife would take over this task. He received a cheque of £40 for the article. Later he wrote biographical sketches of the Union General William Sherman and the Confederate General Nathan Forrest.[14]

The American Civil War was the only major war Wolseley ever witnessed at first hand, as he was in Canada during the Franco-Prussian War. He believed that the British Army could learn many lessons from the war. The first was 'that no great military success can be achieved quickly by an improvised army'.[15] This was relevant to Britain because her army was small and recruited on a voluntary system, unlike the conscript armies of the European powers.[16] Should Britain become embroiled in a European war, she would have to create a mass army quickly, and ought to bear in mind the mistakes of the American Civil War. Wolseley highlighted the problems caused by the American practice of ninety days' enlistments and the election of officers. He stressed the importance of discipline when putting volunteers into the field 'without any knowledge of drill or any proper number of officers to teach it'.[17] Volunteers could be turned into valuable soldiers only if there were enough experienced officers to teach them drill and enforce discipline. He believed that the readiness to use entrenchments by both armies demonstrated the unwillingness of inexperienced officers and men to take the offensive. He, like many officers until the end of the century, would not accept that the new technology of warfare was fast making the offensive obsolete.

In 1889 Wolseley wrote a series of six articles reviewing an article 'Battles and Leaders' in Century Magazine's *History of the American Civil War*. He drew attention to several items of relevance to the British way of warfare. The first was the value of army-navy cooperation. He believed that the end of the Confederacy had been signalled when joint Union army and naval operations in the Mississippi split the Confederacy in two, allowing the Union generals to defeat each southern army in turn. The value of combined operations was clear to Britain which, as an island nation, would nearly always have to use the navy to thrust the army into the seat of war. So was the importance of harbour defences: Wolseley cited the defence of Charleston harbour as an example of the value of using the most modern defences against an invading force. Home defence was a major issue in Britain at the time he was writing these articles. He also examined the issue of civil-military relations of which, by 1889, he had had considerable experience. He pointed out that both General McClellan and General Lee had suffered from political interference: McClellan had been put under pressure by Lincoln to achieve a victory before he was ready to take the offensive; Lee had been forced to defend too much territory, the defence of Richmond being a prime example of political expediency overriding military requirements.[18]

On the tactical front, the American Civil War also had some lessons to teach Britain, but many were misunderstood at the time. In 1862 Wolseley still believed in the value of regular cavalry in large-scale operations. He believed that both sides had resorted to irregular cavalry, or mounted infantry, for two reasons. One was that neither side possessed enough experienced cavalry officers to train the men to charge the enemy, and the Union, in particular, suffered from a lack of good horsemen. The second reason was that the countryside of Virginia and Maryland was too wooded to permit the full application of the *arme blanche*. Later he revised his ideas and became a prime exponent of mounted infantry. He realised that for home defence mounted infantry was more suitable than cavalry, as the terrain of southern England resembled that of Virginia. In this field he was also influenced by the opinions of General Havelock and Colonel George Denison, who both served in Canada at the same time as him. Havelock had gained experience of the value of irregular cavalry in India in 1858, and Denison wrote a book *Modern Cavalry* which emphasised the value of mounted infantry in areas unsuitable for regular cavalry.[19]

Wolseley returned to Canada, to a desk job. After years of activity and rapid promotion, he felt frustrated by being stuck in a backwater. He was in a great deal of pain from the old wound in his leg and, after an operation to remove a splinter of bone, it refused to heal. He could only sleep by keeping the leg outside the bed clothes. In September 1863 the doctors in Canada recommended that he should go home for a more major operation on the leg. The doctor he consulted in England did not see the need for an operation and the leg healed apparently of its own accord. By November 1863 he was able to walk two or three miles a day. Although he had been given six months' leave, he was too short of money to keep an establishment in Canada while living in England and so returned to Canada that winter.[20]

Back in Canada he became extremely frustrated. He was seriously short of money which meant that he could not purchase a promotion. No wars seemed likely in which he could prove himself again in battle and be promoted in that way. He began to believe that his career had stagnated and he wrote to Dick in 1864 that the recent years 'have pushed away the ladder from under me and I am left hanging here without any prospects. I am of no use to anyone and all my visions of being able to advance have all vanished'.[21] He considered leaving the army to become a civil engineer. This career change might at least provide him with enough money to marry Louisa Erskine, whom he still loved. Wolseley did, however, take the opportunity to cultivate important friendships, such as with General Sir Patrick MacDougall, Adjutant General in Canada from 1865 to 1869, in the hope of gaining better opportunities in the future.[22]

The surrender of the Confederate forces in April 1865 reawakened the fear that the United States might turn its attention to its northern neighbour. Even when the number of British troops in Canada had been raised to 18,000, they were insufficient to defend the long frontier with the United States, so schemes were established to improve the organisation and training of the Canadian militia. MacDougall was very active in this respect, and in 1865 appointed Wolseley as commandant of the new militia officer camp of instruction at La Prairie near Montreal. The camp was attended by 1100 cadets for three week periods of instruction. Wolseley 'found there young gentlemen delightful to deal with, all being seriously anxious to learn a soldier's work'.[23] He was greatly assisted by the commander of troops in the province of Quebec, General James Lindsay, who would occasionally march the Montreal garrison of infantry and field artillery to La Prairie for a field day with Wolseley's two battalions of cadets.

The United States showed little interest in invading Canada: instead she turned her attention to the resettlement of the south and the conquest of the west. For Wolseley and the British forces stationed in Canada there was, however, a glimmer of an opportunity for further action in Canada due to other events in the United States. In 1859 the Fenian Brotherhood was set up in New York with the ultimate aim of establishing a republic, independent of Britain, in Ireland. Its activities were curtailed by the outbreak of the American Civil War, and its cause damaged by an unsuccessful rising in Ireland. After the war the Brotherhood met in Philadelphia to establish a republic, along with a president and a senate, but with no territory. The Irishmen looked to Canada for land. They were tacitly supported by both political parties in the United States. The Republicans hoped to embarrass the Democratic administration of President Johnson, and the Democrats looked to the Irish vote at the next election. During 1865 and 1866 there were many Fenian scares in Canada: British troops were pushed westwards to occupy new positions, and Wolseley spent some time visiting them. In March 1866, when a Fenian invasion seemed imminent, the British government rushed two regiments to Canada. The Canadian government called for 10,000 volunteers and got 14,000.

In May 1866, 1500 Fenians under an Irish former Union cavalry officer, Colonel O'Neil, crossed the Niagara river from Buffalo into Canada and occupied a deserted British fort, Fort Erie. The military authorities reacted with incredible incompetence. The Canadian government had been warned in advance of the invasion of the Niagara Peninsula but had made no provision for its defence. The commander of the province of Ontario, General George Napier, who Wolseley described as 'useless for any military purpose', sent out contingents of ill-trained and under-equipped Canadian volunteers to defeat the Fenians, most of whom were seasoned soldiers who had fought in the American Civil War.[24] Colonel Peacock was put in charge of the Niagara peninsula but demonstrated his incompetence by exhausting his men by marching them along a road running parallel to the railway and then taking a wrong turning. This meant that the troops under Colonel Booker were left to face the Fenians alone. There was a brief skirmish before the inexperienced Canadian volunteers turned and fled. Wolseley was sent by the commander of British forces in Canada, General Sir John Michel, to coach Napier 'and prevent him from doing anything very foolish'.[25] He found Napier extremely willing to accept his advice. He travelled towards Fort Erie to assess the situation for himself. On reaching the river, he was surprised to see a United States gunboat towing a barge full of Fenians away from Canada. On boarding the ship and speaking to the captain of the *Michigan*, Wolseley learned that the American government had decided to arrest the Fenians and would later release them on parole, on the condition that any schemes for the invasion of Canada were abandoned.

The Canadian government realised that it had had a narrow escape and set up more camps of instruction. That summer Wolseley was appointed commandant of a camp in the Niagara peninsula at Thorold on the Welland Canal. He trained the Canadian troops hard, and held several field days a week, including several using live ammunition. He wrote of this period, 'It is capital practice for me, as I am so little with troops and I now have such opportunities by learning how to handle men'.[26] He was aided by the presence of a battalion of the Bedfordshire Regiment and a field battery of the Royal Artillery. This period was therefore important to his future career as the commander of military expeditions and was a very happy time for him. But it did not last long: in the winter the Canadian government decided to close the camp and Wolseley returned to his duties in Montreal. There was another brief Fenian scare in January 1867, when he was sent to Toronto to organise a brigade there with a promise of command if invasion should occur; in the event it was only another scare, and in the spring Wolseley's term of office as Assistant Quartermaster General ended. He returned to Ireland to await further orders on his future. By July even Sir John Michel acknowledged the fact that the Fenian threat had passed and accepted the request from London for the return of two infantry regiments.[27]

While in Ireland Wolseley fell more deeply in love with Louisa Erskine. In April 1867 he wrote a long, rather confused letter to his mother announcing his intention to marry her. Wolseley had seen his mother the previous week but, fearing her disapproval of him getting married before he had gained 'some good new appointment' and because he had so often preached against marriage, had not mentioned his plans, feeling it easier and preferable to write. He explained that his marriage would not detrimentally affect his mother's lifestyle since Wolseley would continue to provide for her. Louisa 'is not a millionaire, [but] she is very comfortably provided for, so the arrangement about my pension which I have settled upon you shall not in any way be interfered with'.[28] There is no evidence to suggest that his mother disapproved of his decision but Dick did. In September Wolseley wrote to him making his disappointment at Dick's reaction clear. He promised Dick that he would continue to finance his mother and unmarried sister Caroline.[29]

The wedding was due to take place in the autumn of 1867 but had to be postponed when another Fenian scare caused Wolseley to be recalled to Canada to serve as Deputy Quartermaster General. He managed to escape for two months in 1868 and on 4 June, his thirty-fifth birthday, they were married in Ireland. He then returned to Canada and Louisa followed him that October. They made a strong partnership, unendangered by infidelity by either partner and were fiercely loyal to each other. Wolseley's nickname for Louisa was Loo or Runterfoozle. They corresponded with each other virtually every day when apart. Louisa was well-educated and able to assist her husband when he was writing articles or papers. Though strong-willed, she was also extremely tactful and diplomatic, and used these talents to calm the waters that Wolseley's outspokenness often muddied.

With Louisa still in Ireland, Wolseley occupied himself by writing *The Soldier's Pocket Book for Field Service*. This was a veritable vade mecum of information on every aspect of practical campaigning. It was a guide designed to cover warfare, from the field operations of the various arms to the minutiae of life on campaigns. *The Soldier's Pocket Book* was above all a manual for colonial warfare, an area in which Wolseley had some experience and would become expert in his later career. It was designed to fill the gap left by the two existing army manuals, the *Queen's Regulations* and the *Field Exercise Book*, particularly, as he wrote to Dick, 'nearly all the military books lately published in England are from the pens of men who have never seen a shot fired'. He hoped to make money from the book because he needed money to pay off his debts and had discovered that Loo's money was mostly tied up in investments.[30] *The Soldier's Pocket Book* was later adopted by the War Office and issued to every officer. Wolseley regularly updated the text when experience demanded amendments.

The Soldier's Pocket Book also brought Wolseley to the attention of the military authorities at the War Office and gained him a reputation as an advanced forward-thinking young officer, not least because of controversial statements contained in the text. Of these, perhaps the most startling were his ideas on the relationship between officers and the rank and file, written in the light of his experiences in the Crimea.

> Let us sink as far as possible the respective titles of officers, sergeants, and privates, merging them into the one great professional cognomen of soldier, causing all ranks to feel that it is a noble title of which the general as well as the private may well be proud. Let us give up the phrase 'officer' and 'gentleman', substituting that of 'soldier' for it.[31]

This statement greatly offended general belief in Victorian society of the necessity for a rigid social hierarchy. It also appeared to undermine the importance of hierarchy in the maintenance of military discipline. Officers were recruited primarily from the aristocracy and gentry, and the rank and file from the lowest orders of society. Most civilians and officers believed that the lower classes should treat their 'betters' with the greatest respect and unquestioned obedience. Wolseley accepted this, but was arguing that the soldier was a man not a machine and should be treated accordingly in order to preserve the social hierarchy.

He stressed that the rank and file should be treated as individual soldiers.

The mechanical movements laid down in the drill book were designed for men of low intelligence and, furthermore, had no place on the modern battlefield. The increased firepower of rifles and breech-loading artillery required the services of men capable of both obedience to orders and of acting on their own initiative. This in turn required education. Here his requirements were to be assisted in part by the passage of the 1870 Education Act, which made primary education compulsory. At the War Office he fought for a drill book relevant to the conditions of the modern battlefield.

He also emphasised the value of military intelligence. It was essential to learn as much as possible about the strength, tactics and deployment of the enemy. It was just as important to maintain camp security so that the enemy would not learn where and when it would be attacked. Wolseley saw war correspondents as a threat to this need for secrecy. It had been alleged during the Crimean War that the despatches of W. H. Russell had given information to the Russians. Wolseley attacked war correspondents as a 'race of drones [who] eat the rations of fighting men, and do no work at all'.[32] They should be kept under careful supervision and their despatches monitored. He was accompanied on most of his expeditions by numerous journalists and generally disliked them. In South Africa he would try to get officers on his staff appointed as correspondents in order to control the information reaching Britain. But journalists could serve a useful purpose: they could spread false information. Wolseley did this in Egypt in 1882 to divert attention away from where the British expeditionary force was really planning to land.

The Soldier's Pocket Book also marked the start of Wolseley's long campaign to improve the quality of senior regimental and staff officers. In the Crimea and in India he had been largely unimpressed by the quality of his superiors. He wrote that 'the Staff is to an army what steam is to a locomotive'.[33] No matter how good the soldiers were or the commander, bad staff work could lead to disaster. The root of the problem lay in the method of appointing men to important posts: seniority. Wolseley advocated the selection of officers for particular positions. He fought the battle to achieve this on two levels: first, by creating his own ring of trusted officers; and, secondly, by pressing his arguments while working at the War Office.

The detail contained in *The Soldier's Pocket Book* is remarkable. Part One covers the formation, numbers, duties and equipment of every branch of the army from the three fighting arms to the support services. The details are meticulous, down to tables giving the amount and weight of equipment a wagon can carry. Part Two covers the composition of an army, its transport by sea to the seat of war, and how to set up a camp. Again the details supplied are impressive, from the design of horse stalls aboard ship to the diet of the men, with recipes. Part Three covers the army in action from marching to fighting. The final section details how to build bridges, operate railways, and the use of the telegraph. Wolseley even designed his own code for use in the field. This proved essential during the Gordon Relief Expedition when he discovered that Gordon had lost his cipher books. Gordon was immediately advised to base his communications on the code in *The Soldier's Pocket Book.*

Wolseley was soon given the opportunity to put into practice many of the principles he had expounded in *The Soldier's Pocket Book,* when he was appointed to command the Red River expedition to crush a rebellion in western Canada. In 1867 the Canadian government had begun a scheme for the federation of the provinces of Canada. The Red River valley, in the heartland of Manitoba, became the centre of controversy. The land was held by the Hudson's Bay Company, who had a monopoly of trade with the Indian tribes.[34] The company's resistance to the incorporation of its territory into the Canadian government was overcome with a payment of £300,000, but the settlers in the region were less amenable to change. The British settlers were prepared to await the publication of the Manitoba Bill, but the *métis*, or French-Canadians, were not, and rose in revolt in November 1869. They set up a provisional government at the largest settlement in the area, Fort Garry, under their leader Louis Riel. Admittance was refused to Canadian surveyors, and to the newly appointed Lieutenant-Governor, William McDougall, whom Wolseley described as 'a cold-blooded man, destitute of geniality and of sympathy in dealing with men'.[35] This unfortunate appointment worsened the situation. Riel court-martialled and shot a loyal British settler called Thomas Scott, adding the crime of murder to that of rebellion.

Various other influences were thought to be operating against the Canadian government in the region. The head of the government, Sir John McDonald, feared that the United States might attempt to annex the fertile territory. Wolseley suspected that the Roman Catholic priesthood tacitly supported the rebellion in the hope for the establishment of another French province. The Canadian government was determined to show its authority and so, aided by the recent arrival of General Sir James Lindsay to command the British Army in Canada, prepared to send out a military expedition to crush the rebellion. On 5 April 1870 Wolseley was appointed to the command.

He was delighted with the appointment: 'This was my first independent command, so I was on my mettle, and felt that if I possessed any genius for such practical work, the time had at last arrived for me to show it'.[36] The expedition was no mean undertaking, since Fort Garry lay 1200 miles from Toronto across largely unmapped country. The route can be divided into four stages: the first ninety-four miles from Toronto to Collingwood on Lake Huron would be covered by train; then the force would be transported for 524 miles by steamer across Lakes Huron and Superior to the base of operations at Thunder Bay; from there the soldiers would travel by road for forty-eight miles to Lake Shebandowan, before taking to boats for the final 600 miles to Fort Garry. Wolseley was given 1200 men for his expedition. The British contingent consisted of the 1st Battalion, 60th Rifles, a battery of Royal Field Artillery with four seven-pounder guns, a detachment of Royal Engineers, and various departmental troops. The Canadian government supplied two militia battalions: the 1st Ontario Rifles, and the 2nd Quebec Rifles.

Preparations were crucial to the success of the expedition, especially since the last 600 miles would be covered by boats passing through a wilderness where few supplies could be obtained. Wolseley was involved in every aspect of the preparations. He paid especial attention to the design of the boats which had to be strong and light enough to withstand being carried or dragged over the estimated forty-seven portages en route.[37] The boats also had to be large enough to carry fifteen men – eleven or twelve soldiers and two or three voyageurs – and four tons of supplies to last sixty days.[38] The boats were between twenty-five and thirty feet long with masts, sails and oars, and two hundred were specially constructed in Canada. Wolseley even tried out the equipment. He discovered that the regulation issue axe was useless at cutting brushwood, and ordered double-edged axes of the United States design. These were later adopted by the whole British Army.

His careful calculations were upset by the conduct of some members of the Canadian government: 'A large outlay of money was to be made, and they wished to spend as much as possible amongst their political supporters'.[39] Wolseley had gone to Collingwood to organise the steamers for the transportation of the force to Thunder Bay. He then learned that contracts had been awarded on political grounds, and the reduced capacity of the steamers which resulted delayed the start of the expedition for two weeks. Another serious difficulty arose because of the attitude of the United States. The normal route to Red River was through the United States, where the railway ended at St Paul in Minnesota, only 100 miles from Fort Garry. Obviously this route could not be taken by a British-Canadian military expedition, but American acquiescence was needed on the Great Lakes. Three miles of the St Mary River between Lake Huron and Lake Superior were impassable for steamers; but the Americans had built a canal bypassing the rapids. Wolseley planned to disembark the men and military equipment and march round the obstruction, sending the unladen steamers through

the canal. During the American Civil War the Canadian government had
turned a blind eye to Union operations on the St Lawrence River and the
Great Lakes, so it was reasonable to assume that this favour might be
returned. Wolseley, being a cautious man, planned a trial run, and sent
one unladen steamer through the canal. The United States promptly closed
the canal and ignored the protests of the Canadian government. The situation was saved when Wolseley succeeded in chartering a United States
steamer already on Lake Superior. The American captain had to swear to
the United States authorities that he had nothing to do with the Red River
expedition. Later the embargo was lifted and supplies allowed through the
canal.

The expeditionary force reached Prince Arthur's Landing at Thunder Bay
on 21 May. A recent fire had devastated the region and Wolseley wrote that
'I have never looked upon a drearier or less inviting prospect in any of my
many wanderings'.[40] This was to be the main supply depot for the force
taking the road through the forest. A hospital was set up, and a stockade
built around the settlement to protect the company of Canadian militia left
behind with two guns to guard the base against threatened Fenian intervention. Wolseley went forward to inspect the corduroy road being laid
out by the Public Works Department under Mr Dawson.[41] He was appalled
by what he discovered. The Canadian government had promised that the
road would be ready by the end of May, but Wolseley found that the last
eighteen miles were still virgin forest, and, that many stumps and large
boulders remained on the existing road. He suspected sabotage because
most of the men working on the road were French-Canadians who might
be secretly supporting Riel. The expeditionary force had no choice: it had
to work on the road in the heat, plagued by swarms of mosquitoes and
other flies. The men had been supplied with the means to ward off the flies
but preferred to put them to other purposes: the veils were used to strain
the stagnant water of the Lake of the Woods and the mosquito oil was
burned in lamps.

Although he was careful to appear always cheerful in front of the men,
Wolseley became very depressed with the slow progress he was making.
He was dissatisfied with the quality of the men of the Land Transport
Company, who were mostly idlers, although he felt that Dawson was making
the best of the poor material. The Iroquois Indians worked better, but had
to be promised an extra day's pay to get them to work on Sundays.[42] One
fortunate discovery saved a considerable amount of time. The Kamaristiqua
River ran from the Shebandowan Lake to Thunder Bay, falling over 800
feet and with many waterfalls along the route. It was thought impassable
by boat, but an intrepid party under Captain John Young of the 60th made

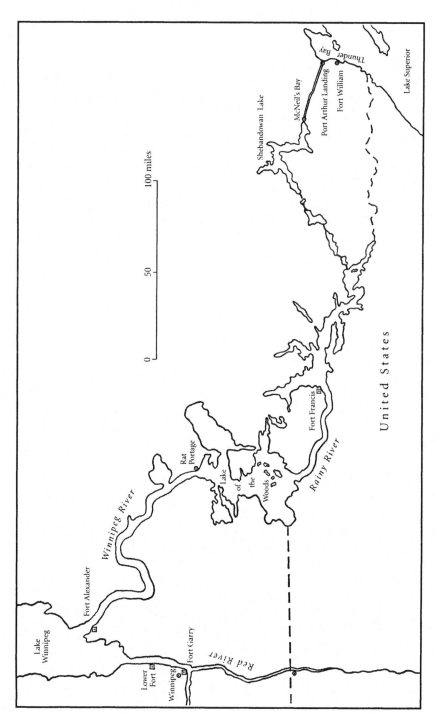

The Red River Expedition 1870

an attempt. It was found passable and many supplies were sent along the river as well as the road. This saved the expedition about six to eight weeks.

Thunder Bay lived up to its name: it rained for twenty-three days from the end of May to mid July and there were exceptionally violent thunderstorms on the nights of 11 and 15 July. The last was particularly alarming because the departure date for the boat expedition had been fixed for 16 July. Fortunately the day broke warm and sunny, and that evening the first three companies of fifty men each from the 60th Rifles, the Royal Artillery and Royal Engineers left McNeill's Bay to cross Lake Shebandowan. On each subsequent day six to eight boats left until the last departed on 1 August. By this time the first boats had covered 150 miles. Wolseley left on 23 July in a swift bark canoe manned by eight voyageurs. He was rowed up and down the column of boats, sometimes leading and marking the trail, sometimes falling back to iron out some problem.

A routine was soon established. The force would set out at first light and row until 8 a.m., when they would halt for an hour for breakfast, before working again until 1 p.m., when there was another hour-long break, finally stopping for the night at 6 or 7 p.m. Bell tents were carried in each boat but there was never the time or energy to pitch them. Instead the soldiers slept wrapped in blankets on the soft mossy ground. Each boat carried the rations for the men: salt port, beans, preserved potato, flour, biscuit, tea and sugar. No alcohol was allowed on the expedition, and Wolseley attributed the lack of sickness to this fact. During the journey to Fort Francis on the far side of Rainy Lake there was a headwind and the men had to row most of the way, but at least the west wind kept the rain away. At each portage the boats would be unloaded. Then the men would don the harness attached to each boat and drag or carry it over the portage. The supplies also had to be carried, and often ten trips per man were needed to get them across. Wolseley put into practice his advanced views on officers and men: the officers were expected to carry the same loads as the men. The wear and tear on clothing was severe, and by the time the expedition reached Fort Francis most men had been forced to patch their clothing using sacks which had earlier contained beans.

On the nineteenth day, 4 August, the expeditionary force reached Fort Francis. This was a Hudson's Bay Company post rather than a military fort. Wolseley now hoped to receive accurate intelligence about the state of affairs at Fort Garry from his spies. He had sent a British officer, Captain William Butler, from Toronto to Fort Garry via the United States to spy out the situation and report back at Fort Francis. Butler arrived on 24 July and reported that panic had set in among the settlers. The aspirations of most of them had been achieved by the Manitoba Bill but Riel still had a hard

core of supporters ready to resist Wolseley's little army. Riel also wanted
an amnesty for the murder of Scott. A loyal half-breed who Wolseley had
sent to Fort Garry arrived at Fort Francis on 31 July. He carried letters from
the Protestant bishop and loyal settlers urging haste because the French
and British settlers were at each other's throats. He also reported that Riel
was moving his loot into the United States. He then learned that the road
between the north-west corner of the Lake of the Woods and Fort Garry,
the shortcut he had hoped to take, was impassable and consequently the
expedition would have to take the Winnipeg River.

At Fort Francis, Wolseley also heard that war had broken out between
France and Prussia. He suspected that the French army, despite being widely
viewed as the best in Europe, might be defeated when he learned that
General Montauban, of China fame, was the French Minister of War. Later
on the expedition he received a telegram imparting the news of the French
defeat at Sedan and the abdication of Napoleon III. He translated it into
French for the voyageurs, who refused to believe such appalling news.

The appeals for haste were answered by Wolseley as he pressed his troops
up Rainy River after leaving a company of the Ontario Rifles at Fort Francis.
On reaching the Lake of the Woods, he pushed ahead without a guide and
soon got lost. He later wrote that to get lost 'where no sound was to be
heard but the dip of the oars at regular intervals, or the distant or weird-like
whistle of the loon, is to experience the exquisite sensation of solitude in
all its full intensity'.[43] Two days later his party reached Rat Portage at the
mouth of the Winnipeg River in a state of collapse. There he found further
appeals for speed, and a flotilla of Hudson's Bay Company boats to help
transport the men along the Winnipeg River.

Wolseley had feared having to use this river, which was known to be full
of fast-running and dangerous rapids and waterfalls. He wrote later that
'no one who has ever descended the Winnipeg River in boat or canoe is
ever likely to forget that experience' and 'there is no more deliciously
exciting pleasure in the world than that of running a really large and
dangerous rapid in a canoe'.[44] In fact he nearly foundered when his voyageurs
sent the canoe down the centre of a steep rapid rather than take the safer
route near the river bank. In the end no men were lost and only two boats
were smashed. At Fort Alexander, where the Winnipeg River ran into Lake
Winnipeg, Wolseley learned that Riel had called his men to arms and had
about six hundred followers. Three days later, on 21 August, the expedition
left Fort Alexander for the mouth of Red River which they entered on the
following day. This river proved difficult to pass because the boats kept
grounding in the shallow stream. It was also very hot, although the nights
were cold. When the force reached Lower Fort, twenty miles from Fort

Garry, on 23 August the soldiers were greeted with cheers from the loyal settlers and the Indian chiefs: no one had expected them so soon.

Surplus supplies were then unloaded and horses, ponies and carts commandeered so that a mounted company could be organised under Captain Nesbit Wallace to reconnoitre the route. The Canadian militia were left behind to guard the stores, and the remainder of the force returned to the lightened boats. 'Our advance up the river had much of a triumphal procession about it', as church bells rang out and crowds cheered the men on from the shore.[45] Strong currents, however, prevented them from reaching Fort Garry that day and they halted for the night six miles away from it. That night the weather broke and there was a torrential downpour which forced a change of plan on 24 August. 'Instead of advancing upon the Fort in all the pride, pomp and circumstance of war' by foot, the boats were used again until Point Douglas, two miles from Fort Garry by road and six by river, was reached.[46] There Wolseley was warned that Riel was still in the fort, had run out the artillery guns and was clearly ready to fight. The force was 'like drowned rats' after the heavy rain but the news that there might be a battle soon cheered the troops.[47]

The little army swept round the village of Winnipeg to approach the fort from the west to cut off Riel's escape route. The approach of the troops was masked by the continuing rain. They found the north gate closed and could see gun muzzles extending from the walls. No shots were fired by either side. Wolseley sent some officers round the fort to investigate and they reported back that a gate was open. Riel had fled, and the fort was deserted apart from one extremely drunk Indian. Riel had abandoned the fort on hearing the troops' bugles, his breakfast half-eaten, and had swum across to the United States. Wolseley wrote 'our victory, although bloodless, was complete'. He regretted only that the Canadian militia had not arrived in time to witness it.[48]

He formed up the troops in the fort's square. The Union flag was run up, the fort's guns fired a royal salute, and three cheers rang out for the Queen. There now followed a period of chaos as soldiers, voyageurs and settlers tried to drink Winnipeg dry. For a whole day military discipline broke down before Wolseley and the officers could restore order. Nevertheless problems still continued because Wolseley had not been given any civil powers, and consequently could not punish the townspeople. In the interval before the arrival of the new civil governor, he persuaded the senior representative of the Hudson's Bay Company, Donald Smith, to accept responsibility for civil affairs. On 28 August the first companies of the militia battalions reached Fort Garry, where they were to spend the winter, and on the following day the British troops departed along the route they had just come, back to Toronto and then on to Britain. Britain's garrison in Canada was being reduced, on financial grounds, to a presence at Halifax. This was the first tacit acknowledgement that Britain could not afford to guard her entire empire. Wolseley sailed home in the same steamer as General Sir James Lindsay.

He was satisfied with his first experience of independent command. There had been no casualties, and he refused to recommend the senior doctor for promotion on the grounds that he had had nothing to do. Many Canadians had expected the expedition to fail and Wolseley remembered that 'we were looked upon as men whom the gods having doomed to destruction had first made mad'.[49] He had proved them wrong and western Canada was opened up for further settlement. A post at Hungry Hall on Rainy River was renamed Fort Louisa in honour of Wolseley's wife; it became an important staging post until the railway was built. Above all, he was proud that the expedition had been cheap, costing only £100,000, of which only a quarter was paid for by the British taxpayer. He attributed 'this economic result chiefly to the fact that it was planned and organised far away from all War Office influence and meddling'.[50] The events of the Red River expedition were little known in Britain – 'no home newspapers cared to record its success, nor to sound one single note of praise in its honour'.[51] This was understandable because the Franco-Prussian War had captured the attention of Britain and Europe. Wolseley was, however, made a Knight Commander of St Michael and St George. No medal was issued for the Red River expedition until the survivors received one on 25 December 1909.[52]

The Red River expedition marks the origins of the so-called 'Wolseley Ring', which soon became a contentious issue in the politics of the late Victorian army. This Ring can be defined as a select group of officers personally chosen by Wolseley for their abilities and loyalty to serve on his staff on the various campaigns he commanded. He believed that he was justified in his actions: 'I had always been in the habit of keeping a list of the best and ablest soldiers I knew, and was always on the look-out for those who could be safely entrusted with any special military piece of work'.[53] He would claim that there were very few officers in the British Army worthy of selection for staff duties. Only the nucleus of the Ring emerged from Red River, and many would argue that the Ring only really emerged as a coherent entity after the Asante War.[54] Wolseley had little say in the selection of staff officers for Red River, since the choice was limited to those already serving in Canada. Two of them, Colonel John McNeill and Captain G. L. Huyshe, were noted by him for use in the future. Other members had either been noticed in the past, like Lieutenant William Butler, or impressed Wolseley by their performance on the expedition, like Captain Redvers Buller and Lieutenant Hugh McCalmont.[55]

Lieutenant Butler had met Wolseley briefly in Montreal in 1868 when the former was hoping for an appointment as a military surveyor of the frontier with the United States. He was unable to offer him employment at that time, but was impressed by Butler's keenness and his reputation within his regiment for cleverness and versatility. Therefore, when Wolseley was preparing to leave for Red River, the arrival of a telegram 'Remember Butler, 69th Regiment' did not surprise him. The staff positions were all filled but he sent Butler to Red River as an intelligence officer. Butler's success in this area led Wolseley to earmark him for future employment. Another officer drawn to Wolseley's attention for his abilities was Captain Redvers Buller. Buller was only a regimental officer on this expedition but became famous during it for his axe-wielding and strength: he could carry a barrel of pork weighing 100 pounds unaided. He described Buller as 'full of resource, and personally absolutely fearless, those serving under him always trusted him fully'.[56]

Lieutenant Hugh McCalmont also made his mark on the Red River expedition – but not entirely favourably. He made his own way to Canada, taking leave from the 9th Lancers, when he heard of the prospect of a campaign and begged Wolseley to take him along. Wolseley refused his services, but eventually was persuaded when McCalmont threatened to come along anyway in his own canoe, and when Louisa, who had met him on the steamer crossing Lake Superior, pleaded on his behalf to her husband. He was so satisfied with McCalmont's performance on the expedition that he gave him the honour of taking home the despatches. Returning home via the United States, McCalmont entrusted the precious despatches to the American postal system before leaving for Britain from New York. Wolseley was outraged and refused McCalmont the promotion that was normally awarded to the bearer of despatches. Nevertheless, he was later to forgive the young man's error and to employ him on later campaigns.

5

War Office

In May 1871 Wolseley was appointed Assistant Adjutant General under Sir Richard Airey, the Adjutant General. This appointment marked the beginning of a fourteen-year period when Wolseley combined his talents as an administrator at the War Office with those of a commander in the field. It coincided with a period of rapid and fundamental reform of the organisation of the British Army. The Liberal Secretary of State for War appointed in 1868, Edward Cardwell, was determined both to modernise the army and to make it more economical.[1] He set about completing the piecemeal reforms in progress since the Crimean War, creating a new system which became known as the 'Cardwell system' or the 'Cardwell reforms'. Cardwell's task was made difficult by the Commander-in-Chief, the Duke of Cambridge, who was the head of the military side of the War Office.[2] The Duke has been justly described as 'a thorough-going representative of the old school, [who] for more than twenty years was destined to impose the weight of his authority against all change'.[3] The Duke had a powerful ally in Queen Victoria, his cousin, and was never slow to appeal for her assistance. Cardwell needed allies among the young reforming officers and selected Wolseley for promotion. He was ready for the challenge: 'I was impatient and in a hurry: my nature would not brook the sapping of a regular siege: I wanted to assault the place at once, and I did so'.[4]

Wolseley's credentials as a reformer were strong. He had already written *The Soldier's Pocket Book* and his thoughtful analysis on Lee's headquarters, and in August 1871 an article appeared in *Macmillan's Magazine* in which he set out his programme for further reforms. In this article he repeated his opinions on the private soldier:

> It is by no means desirable that his individual intelligence should be stifled by the process [of discipline], for of all things it is essential that he should possess sufficient common sense to tell him when, and how, he should in front of the enemy make use of the rules he has learned.

He then courted controversy by referring to politicians as 'clap-trap orators', who had little idea of the complexities of military policy. His basic thesis was that no organisation of the army could create a truly efficient fighting body unless the purposes for which the army existed were clearly set out. He attempted to address this problem by identifying four basic purposes: home defence; the defence of coaling stations abroad; the retention of India and the colonies; and the requirement to send out an expeditionary force to Europe in case of war. Home defence was a particularly topical issue: it caught the attention of the public when, in January 1871, the former Prime Minister Lord John Russell stated that England was open to invasion. He argued for the retention in Britain of a force of 200,000 troops, regular and auxiliary. The consequences of the failure to do this were set out in a literary form when, in May, Lieutenant-Colonel Sir George Chesney published 'The Battle of Dorking' in *Blackwood's Magazine*. This proved so popular that it was reprinted as a 6d. pamphlet a month later: over 80,000 copies had been sold by the end of the summer.[5]

Wolseley joined the War Office too late to influence the content of the Cardwell reforms, which were already essentially complete. Nevertheless, since he was to devote nearly thirty years to the implementation and defence of the Cardwell system it is necessary to examine why the reforms were needed, what they set out to achieve, and what were their flaws. The government was influenced in its reforms by the example of the all-conquering Prussian army, whose unexpected success in the wars of German Unification over the long-service Austrian and French armies had sent a shock wave through the war departments of Europe. The main lesson appeared to be that success was dependent on the possession of a highly efficient small body of fighting men forming the nucleus of an army organised on a territorial basis, which could be expanded in times of need by the influx of trained former soldiers serving in an Army Reserve. The twin advantages of the system were economy and efficiency. Cardwell had already achieved economies (in the event short-lived) by recalling a number of battalions from Canada and from remote colonies of little strategic value. He now set about introducing as much of the German system as possible into the British Army.

The most important change was introduced in the 1870 Army Enlistment Act. This inaugurated a short service system whereby soldiers enlisted for six years in the colours, then six in the newly-established Army Reserve. The Army Reserve would consist of trained soldiers liable for recall to the colours in emergency, but working in civilian occupations. From the government's viewpoint three main reasons stood out for the formation of this system: first, economy; secondly, to improve recruitment; and thirdly, to improve the ability of the army to fight anywhere in the world at short notice. Economy was to be achieved by short service because fewer soldiers would serve a full twenty-one years and draw pensions. Recruitment was a major problem throughout the nineteenth century: government advisers suggested that long service in inhospitable climates, such as India and most of the colonies, was unpopular; and that the introduction of short service might stimulate recruitment. As for fighting efficiency, there was little doubt (especially after the Crimea) that the early Victorian army had to struggle to defeat even under-equipped opponents. Furthermore, it was unsupported, and once the main body of soldiers had been despatched on a campaign, the capability for reinforcement or even the replacement of casualties was severely limited. The Army Reserve was set up to remedy this defect.

The debates in Parliament on the Army Enlistment Bill revealed a number of likely problems. Questions were asked about the efficiency of the short service soldier, who would be on average much younger than his long service predecessor. Cardwell replied that the long service soldier would still have a place in the army: 'We regard him as the centre and the pivot of the service; but we wish to have the young soldier combined with him'. Three-quarters of the army would be recruited for short service.[6] Lord Strathnairn feared that the uncertain employment future of a soldier in the reserve would detract from recruitment unless the government did something to guarantee that employers would engage reservists.[7] The biggest challenge would be to find the required number of recruits: early estimates suggested that approximately 32,000 recruits would have to be found annually if both the establishment of the army and the Army Reserve were to be up to strength. Wolseley indeed spent much of his career at the War Office attempting to overcome recurrent manpower crises.

The establishment of the Army Reserve was linked inexorably with the introduction of short service. There was confusion over the purpose of the Reserve. Wolseley was quite clear on this issue: 'the maintenance of an army strong enough to meet our military requirements is only possible by having about two-thirds of it in a reserve employed in civil life'.[8] Economy was a reason for this: the rank and file were paid a shilling a day in the colours but only 4d. a day in the Army Reserve. Efficiency was another factor. In the event of a major war or invasion, Britain would have a reserve from which men could be taken to bring the ranks of the battalions up to their war establishment, with men left over to act as reinforcements and drafts to replace casualties. This at least was the theory. In practice the efficiency of this system depended on several unknown factors. Would the government provide the funds for the army reserve to be trained regularly? Would the men return to the colours when called? How well would they fight? Would there be enough men to fulfil all the purposes of the army reserve? The constitution of the army reserve also contained a serious flaw. In imitation of the German system, it could only be called out in the event of invasion or a major war abroad; it could not be called out for the many small wars fought by the Victorian army.

The abolition of the purchase of commissions and promotions was a long overdue measure. Above-regulation prices were the norm, and the government faced the problem of how to buy the officer corps for the country. If it paid the regulation prices as compensation there would be immense and justifiable public outrage from the officers, many of whom would resign from the army. If the government compensated the officers at the above-regulation prices they had paid, it would be acknowledging an illegality. The Duke of Cambridge was particularly opposed to the abolition of purchase. Cardwell only gained his acquiescence by threatening to change the tenure of the post of Commander-in-Chief to a five-year term in line with the other senior positions at the War Office. The House of Lords proved even more intractable and purchase eventually had to be abolished by Royal Warrant on 20 July 1871.[9] A new problem then emerged: how to ensure fair and regular promotion for officers. Wolseley never became closely involved in this question, although he made controversial comments on the quality of the officer corps on many occasions.

The Duke of Cambridge was especially sensitive to political challenges to his independence following the 1870 War Office Act. Under the terms of this Act the organisation of the War Office had been revamped to confirm the Secretary of State as the Minister responsible for the army with all the military and civil departments of the War Office under him. The Commander-in-Chief was the Minister's principal military adviser, and would supervise the military departments which had also been reorganised. The Duke was unhappy with these changes because he believed that he was, and should remain, the representative of the Queen, the head of the army. He appealed to the Queen for help but she advised him to give in to the government on this issue. The Duke was also furious that the organisational changes forced him to move from his offices at the Horse Guards to the War Office in Pall Mall. He stoutly resisted the move for as long as possible but eventually moved his office, with bad grace, after Cardwell promised that he could still head his letters 'Horse Guards, Pall Mall'. Wolseley remained outside this dispute but there is no doubt where his sympathies lay. He wrote of Cardwell, 'no British War Minister ever responded more readily to demands made upon him by his military advisers'.[10] In contrast, Wolseley rarely agreed with the Duke's opinions. He, the young upstart, constantly threatened the Duke's leadership, position and values.

The 1872 Localisation Act linked two battalions, one serving abroad and one at home. The home battalion was allocated to a brigade district, with

a depot centre for recruitment and training. It would provide its linked
battalion abroad with drafts and periodically replace it. Two Militia battalions and some Volunteers were to be attached to each depot. This radical
reorganisation of the British Army was complex, as England, Scotland,
Wales and Ireland had to be divided into military districts, sixty-six in all,
and the location of the depots agreed upon. A committee was set up under
Major-General Patrick MacDougall, the Deputy Inspector-General of the
Auxiliary Forces, with Wolseley a member, to decide the division. This
committee issued two reports in 1872, its recommendations being mainly
adopted with little resistance from the local authorities.[11] It was his second
experience of committee work, one made more agreeable to him through
his friendship with MacDougall with whom he had worked with previously
in Canada.[12]

The concept of the linking of two battalions was arguably the most flawed
of the Cardwell reforms. Time would tell whether localisation would have
the desired effect of stimulating recruitment, but one major flaw should
have been evident at once. The establishment of a balance of battalions at
home and abroad implied that British military requirements abroad would
remain constant. This was perhaps a naive hope, as the British empire had
expanded greatly over the last fifty years and the rate of expansion showed
no sign of abating. Consequently, troops would have to be found in the
future to garrison new areas. Furthermore, despite Britain's avowed
disinclination to become embroiled in the complexities of European politics,
there was a danger that a war in Europe could force Britain to become
involved. This had nearly happened in 1870 when there seemed a likelihood
that either France or Germany might infringe Belgian neutrality, which
Britain was bound by treaty to defend.[13] Cardwell had allowed for the
possibility that, on occasion, both battalions might be stationed abroad. In
such circumstances the depot was to expand to form the home battalion.
This, however, would be an expensive measure, and it became clear that it
was one no government was prepared to adopt.

His early period at the War Office imbued Wolseley with an even greater
determination to make his mark as an army reformer. He was always a
great admirer of the Secretary of State. He learned a great deal about the
political manoeuvres of Westminster when accompanying Cardwell to the
House of Commons, ready to supply any information the Minister required.
Some politicians, such as Lord Northbrook, the Under Secretary, impressed
Wolseley with their willingness to accept advice from their military advisers,
but in general he was unenthusiastic about the machinations of party politics.
He also had the opportunity to pursue friendships with senior military
officers. He often rode in Richmond Park with Sir Richard Airey, whose

career had recovered from an attempt by the Palmerston government to blame him for the shortage of supplies during the Crimean War. His ultimate superior, the Duke of Cambridge, never became a friend. They got on well enough personally, but the Duke was constantly reminded that Wolseley was an army reformer attempting to change the system the Duke desired to retain.

During this period he also gained further experience of the practical side of war. For sixteen days from 26 August 1871 large-scale manoeuvres of all arms were held near Aldershot. Wolseley was appointed the Chief of the Staff of the 2nd Division under Major-General Sir Charles Staveley. The three divisions taking part learned many important lessons. Cardwell wrote to the Prime Minister, William Gladstone, 'no doubt there have been many mistakes, but these it was our object to discover, and will be our business to rectify'. In his report on the manoeuvres the Duke of Cambridge highlighted the various weaknesses of the infantry: poor outpost duty, failure to use ground cover, and exposure to enemy fire before being fully deployed.[14] It was essential for these mistakes to be rectified immediately if disaster was to be avoided on the battlefield.

In 1872, when large-scale manoeuvres were again held, Wolseley was on the staff of General Sir John Michel. The Duke reported that the staff work was much improved on the previous year. Wolseley disagreed with him, and wrote in an article:

> Judging from our selections made for our operations of both years, a stranger would be led to think that England was not rich in talented generals. With a few brilliant exceptions, it will be generally admitted that the great majority of generals and brigadiers employed this year were not men to whose care the lives of soldiers could be entrusted in war.[15]

He also noted that regimental officers disliked the discomforts of living in camp, and complained in a letter to Louisa that too many officers were attempting to leave the manoeuvres on entirely spurious grounds.[16] He agreed with the Duke that regular manoeuvres were essential for the training of the home army. Unfortunately large-scale manoeuvres were very expensive. There was also a shortage of land large enough and suitable for the infantry, cavalry and artillery. Furthermore, members of the auxiliary forces, the Militia, Volunteers and Yeomanry, could not afford to be away from their civil employment for several weeks every year. Consequently it was decided in 1873 to exercise each arm separately: on Dartmoor, at the Curragh in Ireland and on Cannock Chase in Staffordshire. Thereafter, until the government purchased a large area on Salisbury Plain in 1898, no further large-scale manoeuvres were held.

In August 1871 an advertisement appeared in *The Times* and other news-papers announcing a prize of £100 for the best essay on 'The System of Field Manoeuvres Best Adapted for Enabling our Troops to Meet a Continental Army', to be known as the Duke of Wellington Prize. Wolseley entered the competition and wrote an essay covering the whole subject in considerable detail. He began by describing how columns on marches should be organised when hostile action was likely. He then turned his attention to the question of how best to protect marching troops. He urged the formation of a well-organised field intelligence department, as well as the use of mounted infantry to scout ahead of the main body of troops. This corps of mounted reconnaissance troops would require a special set of regulations and the opportunity to practise their manoeuvres.

Wolseley then discussed the method of forming, combining and employing the different arms for the offensive. Modern massed rifle firepower meant that special precautions had to be taken on the battlefield. The artillery had to be well entrenched to protect the men from rifle fire, while the infantry needed to adopt a loose order of skirmishers when coming into contact with an enemy force after the artillery had prepared the way by a prolonged bombardment. As modern firepower operated against the mass frontal offensive, Wolseley argued that flank attacks, as illustrated by the Franco-Prussian War, were more likely to succeed. This placed an emphasis on the cavalry's ability to scout the flanks and to act as the ears and eyes of the army. He argued 'the days of the grand imposing charges of horsemen in masses are past': rifle power could pick off the cavalryman before he was within sabre or lance range of the enemy. He urged that the new manoeuvres should be included in a revised drill book and practised regularly.

He also noted that modern weapons made the defensive more favourable than the offensive. But he argued that this should not mean a passive defence: a defensive position should be chosen with the possibility of a future counter-attack constantly in mind. Entrenchments should be dug by the defending force primarily to protect the guns and the flanks of the position. He pointed out that the value of entrenchments was as yet unknown on the European battlefield since neither side had used them significantly in 1870. Nevertheless, it was possible that entrenchments 'when first practised in earnest will surprise the world as much by its astounding effect as did the breech-loading rifle in 1866'.[17] With this statement Wolseley was remarkably prescient: at the end of the century the British Army would struggle to overcome Boer entrenchments in South Africa. The real value of strong defensive positions was, however, not fully realised until 1914.

Wolseley did not win the competition: an officer in the Royal Artillery, Lieutenant Frederick Maurice, was the victor.[18] Wolseley was pleased, however, to note that in his essay Maurice had frequently quoted from *The Soldier's Pocket Book:* he regarded this as 'not only a compliment but a good advertisement for the *great work*'.[19] In 1872 six of the best essays were published, including Wolseley's contribution. This essay was to be his last competition entry, and his only serious writing on the tactical challenges of European warfare. Thereafter he left the subject of tactics to skilled writers, including Robert Home and George Henderson, although he did argue for the adoption of a drill book containing movements suitable for the modern battlefield. Wolseley noted Maurice's name for the future, selecting Maurice to be his private secretary on his next campaign because 'I felt that the man who possessed the thinking and reasoning power which his essay displayed should be given the chance of adding practice to precept'.[20] Neither man had to wait long for a military campaign.

Lord Northbrook, the Governor General designate invited Wolsley to accompany him to India as his military secretary. He declined the appointment because Louisa was pregnant. This was a great loss to him since the British army in India needed major reform. The units of the former East India Company army had been absorbed into the Crown forces, but there was a great deal of work to be done to implement and assess the impact of the Cardwell system in India. Service in India at this point in time would have provided Wolseley with a perfect opportunity to make his mark as an army reformer, under a sympathetic master, in a position largely independent of interference from the Duke of Cambridge and the War Office.

Loyalty to his wife, however, ensured that Wolseley remained in London to continue his work at the War Office. On 15 September 1872 he became a father and the baby was christened Frances. Wolseley did not record his feelings on fatherhood but a letter to his aunt from the Crimea gave his opinion on a baby he had seen:

> who is neither exactly biped or quadruped, who cannot crawl or talk, who with large unmeaning eyes has no nose, but a weakly supported bald head, who bawls and screams by the hour and is only quiet when asleep, and who, pardon me, smells high. I know of no more unpleasant insect, and would prefer fondling a young crocodile to taking into my arms a newly-born embryo of humanity.[21]

Frances proved to be an only child, although Wolseley had hoped for sons in whom he could instil the same sense of nationhood he felt.[22] He was very fond of his daughter, though not outwardly affectionate, and brought her presents from his journeys and campaigns. When she was old enough to read, he wrote to her when he was campaigning abroad.

6

Asante

The Asante were the most cultivated tribal grouping on the west coast of Africa. They were excellent craftsmen in wood, gold and silver. They also had a fearsome reputation as fighters and had formerly been prolific slave owners and traders. In 1824 they had attacked the British fort, Cape Coast Castle, in the British protectorate on the Gold Coast. The British governor, Sir James McCarthy, was defeated by the Asante army, committed suicide, and his skull was sent back to the Asante capital Kumasi where it was used as a drinking cup.[1] The Gold Coast was an area which the British had controlled during the period of the slave trade and, after the abolition of the slave trade, as a base to stop slave traffic. It was now an area of no great strategic interest. In 1867 a Portuguese trading post on the coast, the town of Elmina, was ceded to Britain. The Asante wanted to control this outlet to the ocean, and in 1873 the king of Asante, Kofi Karikari, ordered an attack on the British protectorate.[2] The tribes in the protectorate, including the Akim and Fanti, proved no match for the Asante army commanded by Amankwa Tia and valuable hostages were taken back to Kumasi. The British were in no position to protect the tribes because the garrison at Cape Coast Castle was too small.

The Gladstone government, while determined to uphold the integrity of the protectorate, was understandably reluctant to despatch an expedition to such an unhealthy region. West Africa was a black man's country where disease, humidity and the heat combined to give it a reputation as a white man's graveyard. Malaria was rife in the region and, although quinine was known to give protection from fever, the mosquito was not identified as the carrier of malaria until 1898.

Nevertheless, the government believed that the Asante should be driven back to their own country and on 2 August 1873 sanctioned the expenditure for a naval captain, Captain William Glover, to raise a native force and advance along the Volta river. The Colonial Secretary, Lord Kimberley, and Cardwell were in favour of a military expedition and invited Wolseley to submit a plan to expel the Asante from British territory.[3] Wolseley's plan was for the immediate despatch of a group of special service officers under his command to investigate the strength of the British garrison at Cape Coast Castle. They would then attempt to raise native armies under British officers to drive the Asante back over the Prah into their own territory. He predicted that the services of at least two white battalions from home might be required. In that case, a road to the Prah would be constructed by the natives, with regular stopping places along the route to protect the health of the white troops.

The plan was accepted by Cardwell and Kimberley and on 13 August Wolseley was given the command: 'I was allowed to select whatever officers I required for the native regiments it was my intention to raise locally, and also those whom I wanted for staff duties'.[4] The chief of the staff was Colonel John McNeill, who had served in the same position on the Red River campaign. He was seriously wounded in an early skirmish and had to be replaced by Colonel George Greaves, who had shared an office with Wolseley at the War Office. His military secretary was Captain Henry Brackenbury, 'a profound reasoner with a strong will and logical mind', whose reputation as a military thinker and teacher at Woolwich had brought him to Wolseley's attention.[5] His private secretary was Lieutenant Frederick Maurice. Other appointments of men from the Red River campaign included Captain Hugh McCalmont as an aide de camp and Captain Redvers Buller as the chief of intelligence. Lieutenant-Colonel Evelyn Wood was appointed a special service officer by a lucky chance: he happened to visit Wolseley at the War Office while he was preparing his plan of campaign and was promised a place on the expedition.[6] Captain William Butler acted on his own initiative: he was in Ottawa when he heard of the expedition, sent a telegram to Wolseley that he was on his way, and took a fast steamer from New York to Liverpool. He missed the start by eight hours but found a message telling him to follow by the next boat.[7]

These selections mark the real origins of the Wolseley Ring. Buller, Wood, McNeill, Butler, Brackenbury, and Maurice were all known to Wolseley before this campaign. They would all be used again in the future. The Ring also gained new members. Foremost among these was Major George Colley, who had passed out first from the Staff College at Camberley and was serving on the teaching staff there. He arrived in December to take over the transport arrangements for the home regiments. Wolseley considered him 'the ablest officer then in our army, and in all respects as the man most fitted to be a general'.[8] Two field commanders impressed him on this campaign and would be used again later: Brevet Major Baker Russell and Brigadier-General Sir Archibald Alison. The latter had been thrust on Wolseley by the Duke of Cambridge. He was not at first pleased by this, 'as I don't care much for him and don't think he is the man I want'.[9]

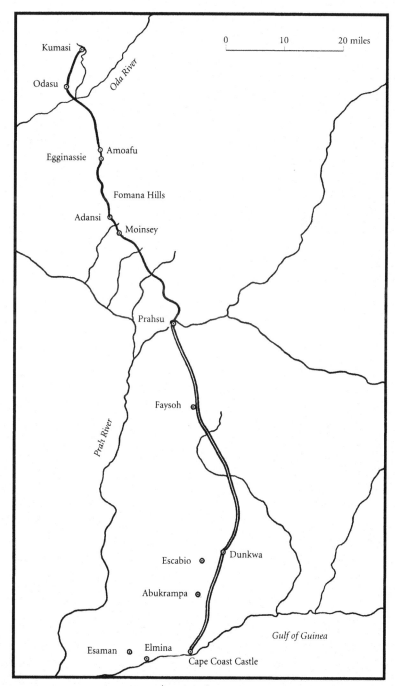

Asante, 1873–74

The appointments were criticised by the MP Augustus Anson as 'using the finest steel in our army to cut brushwood'.[10]

A high quality staff was essential for success because, except for some little information gleaned from the few survivors of the expedition of 1864, Wolseley's sole knowledge of the country, when he started his mission, was derived from works written more than fifty years ago.[11] On board ship, which left Liverpool on 12 September, the staff studied the history and geography of West Africa. Each day Brackenbury and Captain Huyshe lectured on the tribes and the terrain of the Gold Coast. With the assistance of the medical officer, Dr Howe, Wolseley drew up some notes on how to cope with the climate. His fears on this front were well founded: on arrival at Cape Coast Castle on 2 October he found that, of the 130 British soldiers stationed there, only twenty-two were fit for duty. Worse still there were only four days' supplies and only nineteen Snider and 400 Enfield rifles in store. Ignorance of the terrain to be crossed became apparent early: because it had been thought that the first thirty miles inland were flat, the construction of a small railway had been planned and traction engines sent out from England. Instead the staff discovered that there were numerous small hills intersected by deep gullies.[12]

The expedition was accompanied by war correspondents representing all the major newspapers. Among them were Winwood Reade for *The Times*, G. A. Henty for the *Standard*, Melton Prior for the *Illustrated London News* and Henry Stanley for the *New York Herald*. Despatches from correspondents accompanying military expeditions had become common since the work of W. H. Russell during the Crimean War. Wolseley may have despised correspondents but he was well aware that their reports could influence his future career. Consequently he gave every facility to the journalists and earned Melton Prior's gratitude by letting him send home his sketches from Kumasi with the military despatches. Many of the correspondents later wrote books on the campaign; they generally praised Wolseley's leadership and conduct of operations.[13]

The Asante king, Kofi, was informed of the terms for peace on 13 October 1873. He was to withdraw the Asante army from the protectorate by 12 November; release the native prisoners held in the capital Kumasi; and supply an indemnity of gold. Should the king not accept the conditions, Wolseley's plan, accepted by Kimberley and Cardwell, was first to expel the Asante from the protectorate, then to invade Asante territory and destroy Kumasi. Gladstone hoped that operations would be limited to the protectorate itself, but his ministers took care to keep him ignorant of Wolseley's full instructions.

He had been promised that two home regiments, the 23rd Royal Welch

Fusiliers and the second battalion of the Rifle Brigade, would be held in readiness in England in case he needed them. The 42nd Highlanders were to be the reserve. Wolseley hoped to raise sufficient native troops under the command of his special service officers to drive the Asante from the protectorate. Accordingly he sent Russell and Wood to raise men from the Cape Coast militia and Hausa police.[14] He also arranged to meet the chiefs and kings on 4 October. They had not been willing to come: Wood recalled that one chief wrote 'Come and get me if you dare', while another sent back a message, 'I have got smallpox today, but will come tomorrow'.[15] Wolseley harangued the chiefs 'telling them that the Queen would only help those who helped themselves', and gave them two days to agree to his proposals to gather native troops to be commanded by British officers.[16] He was not hopeful of success: he wrote to Louisa that the kings admitted that they had little power over their men.[17]

On 13 October Wolseley decided to attack the Asante-controlled villages on the coast. He used deception to conceal his plans by announcing that he was going to assist Captain Glover on the Volta. He sent ninety soldiers of the 2nd West India Regiment in a gunboat to give credence to his announcement. Then Wolseley and his staff, with Wood in command of the native troops, embarked for Elmina. The idea was to discover the fighting value of the native tribes, to learn about fighting in the bush, and to convince the Asante that the British were serious in their determination to force them back across the Prah. The villages of Essaman, Amquana and Ampenee were to be destroyed to prevent them from supplying food to the Asante camp at Mampon. The path to Essaman led through a knee-deep swamp, then a very narrow path through the thick jungle. Wolseley was carried in a wicker Madeira sedan chair because his leg, wounded in the Crimea, was not strong enough to withstand the march over difficult terrain. The attacks were successful chiefly due to skilled British leadership but Wolseley soon realised that the natives were not good fighters. The Fanti were dismissed as cowards, the Hausa 'have heaps of pluck but they are wild to a degree and expend their ammunition in a way that is dreadful to contemplate'.[18]

In a later article Wolseley compared the fighting performance of the Asante with that of the Fanti and Hausa. He stated that the West African negro was 'a cowardly, lazy fellow' into whom courage could only be instilled by a 'dread of bodily punishment'. In contrast, he admired the bravery of the Asante, and quoted a refrain from their war song:

> If I go forward I die,
> If I go backward I die;
> Better go forward and die.[19]

Short of trustworthy soldiers and faced by a brave enemy he informed Cardwell that the service of white troops would be essential to reach Kumasi.

Before the three home battalions could reach the Gold Coast and be deployed in the bush, many preparations had to be made. Wolseley tried to alter the composition of the force being sent out. Extraordinarily for a defender of short service, he argued that the battalions full of growing lads were unfit for the fatigues of a tropical campaign. He wanted the best men in each battalion to be formed into strong companies. The Duke of Cambridge resisted this proposal, fearing that it would damage regimental esprit de corps. Wolseley felt that the opposite was the case: 'far from hurting regimental feeling; my experience teaches me that this plan of taking companies from each of several battalions serves to intensify it'.[20] The Duke won the dispute and the battalions at the head of the roster for foreign service were sent out with all their companies.

Wolseley had promised Cardwell that great attention would be paid to the health and welfare of the battalions during the campaign. A special loose-fitting fighting dress of grey homespun was designed. Cork helmets were issued to all ranks to protect them from the heat and sun. Baggage was cut to a minimum and carriers appointed, each to carry the supplies for three soldiers. Instructions on health were issued and doses of quinine given before each day's march. A road was to be constructed to the Prah with many resting places on the way. At all of these, huts were to be built on stilts and fires lit beneath them, because it was believed that dampness contributed to fever. Several hospitals were to be built along the road.

While the battalions were on their way to the Gold Coast operations against the Asante continued. At the end of October the Asante camp at Mampon was broken up and the Asante began to retreat across the Prah. The skirmishes at the beginning of November reinforced Wolseley's belief in the unreliability of the Fanti and Hausa troops. Nevertheless, at the beginning of December the Duke of Cambridge was able to congratulate him on his success at reaching Prahsu, a large village on the Prah: 'If one takes into account the very small reliable force at your disposal, and the wretched conduct of the natives, whether under your command or allies, it is only extraordinary that you have been able to accomplish as much as you have done'.[21] Wolseley also learned that the West African sun should be treated with respect: after marching in the heat of the day he fell seriously ill with a high fever. He was forced to spend eight days abroad a ship off Cape Coast Castle, where he was nursed by Maurice, before he recovered. On 17 November he was able to write to Louisa that he had been very ill with fever, 'my head was so bad that during one whole night I thought not that I was going, but that I had gone mad'. He admitted that he was 'still a little weak in the loins'.[22]

In other letters home Wolseley expressed his love for his daughter Frances. He regretted that she missed her nurse, Miss Cart, who had been dismissed, 'for I am sure no one else in our great establishment grieved at her departure'. On another occasion he described a little bush deer that had been shown to him. It was prettily spotted and about the size of a rabbit and he thought 'it would make such a nice plaything for Miss Frances if only I could get it home, but that is out of the question'.[23]

Wolseley had promised Cardwell not to keep the British battalions on the Gold Coast for a day longer than necessary. Accordingly when the first troop ships began arriving in the middle of December he sent them away for a cruise until the end of the year, when he would be ready to advance. Brackenbury described Wolseley's dilemma:

> The European troops whom the Government had sent out with such unexampled rapidity, arrived on the Gold Coast too late, and yet too soon. They arrived too late to take advantage of the proximity of the Ashanti army to the coast, and of that splendid strategical position which the Major-General had held while the enemy was at Mampon, and he was in possession of a fortified post on their main line of retreat at Mansu: they arrived too late to enable Sir Garnet Wolseley to destroy the whole Ashanti army, as he might have done had they been in his hands by the first or second week of November. On the other hand, they arrived too soon for an immediate advance upon Coomassie.[24]

The British troops arrived too soon because the road was not yet complete to Prahsu.

The reason for this was that desertion among the native carriers was so rife that not only was the completion of the road delayed but also the arrival of supplies at Prahsu was well behind schedule. Wolseley kept a close eye on progress, travelling up the road in an American buggy drawn by six natives, which he called the 'Chariot of the Sun'.[25] Responsibility for transport and supply was withdrawn from the civilian Control Department and put under military control. The new controller, Colley estimated that 8500 carriers would be needed for the expedition: 3000 to transport the baggage of the main force and another 5000 to carry supplies and the wounded. He reorganised the transport companies according to tribe and divided the road to Prahsu into four stages. The villages where the carriers had deserted were destroyed. This treatment worked but the expedition fell a week behind schedule.

Wolseley planned an assault on Asante territory with four independent columns. He would lead the main column with all the white troops and the West India Regiment.[26] Captain Glover was to operate an independent column, made up of 18,000 Hausa, and advance from the Volta; Butler was to raise a force of Akim and invade east of Wolseley's route; and Captain William Dalrymple was to raise an army from the Wassaw and invade from the west. All four columns were to cross the Prah on 15 January. The plan was against the rules of war, which stated that an invading force should never be divided in the face of the enemy, because it could be attacked and defeated in turn. Wolseley's strategy was later criticised by Winwood Reade who argued that 'His main body was quite strong enough to fight all the Ashanti in the kingdom; and by dangling a weak body of men as bait to draw off part of the Ashanti army he imperilled the lives of the officers concerned'.[27] Nor was it a successful strategy. Glover made it clear to Wolseley on 31 December that he could only raise about 700 Hausa.[28] Dalrymple only raised fifty Wassaw, while Butler found only 1400 Akim ready to join him. Butler's force later refused to cross the Prah: 'the sight was certainly a curious one: three white men and six native policemen carrying baggage had invaded Ashanti'.[29]

Transport difficulties made Wolseley all the more hopeful of finding a peaceful solution to the crisis. It seemed likely that desertion among the carriers would increase as soon as the force crossed the Prah. Therefore he was relieved to hear, on 2 January, that messengers from the king were on the way to his camp at Prahsu. King Kofi's letter made it clear that he had little idea of Wolseley's position, strength or intentions. He replied, repeating the terms for peace and warning the king that his territory was about to be invaded from four directions. To drive home the message, Wolseley kept the messengers in his camp for four days so that they could report on the strength of the British force. The Gatling machine gun was demonstrated to them and one messenger was so depressed at his future that he shot himself that night. The messengers were finally sent back to the king over the newly constructed bridge over the Prah, passing through companies of Russell's and Wood's Regiments stationed on the north bank. Despite all this show of strength, Wolseley was desperately worried about the future of the expedition. Continuing transport difficulties forced him to halt the disembarkation of the 23rd Regiment because all their carriers had deserted. The West India Regiment was temporarily converted into carriers.

On the morning of 20 January Wolseley's column crossed the Prah and moved slowly but steadily into the bush. The conditions were difficult as a letter from a rifleman revealed: 'we cut our way right to left into the jungle with our cutlasses but the foliage was so dense that it was like being in a net, and the farther we went the thicker it seemed to get'.[30] Malaria hit the force and by the time Fomena was reached on 24 January the Naval

Brigade had lost forty men from 250 and the Rifle Brigade fifty-seven from 650. The special service officers suffered the most since they had been in West Africa the longest: five died and another eight were invalided home. The Asante gave little resistance to the British advance, but prisoners revealed that the king was gathering his army of 5000 men at Amoafu for battle. The king also sent more messages begging Wolseley to halt. On 29 January he replied that he had halted at Fomena for four days, to give the king time to consult his chiefs and arrange for the fulfilment of the terms, but had learned that the king had merely used the delay to build up his army. In fact, he had halted because he needed time to bring up more supplies. Enclosed in this letter from the king was a message from a trader held prisoner, Mr Dawson, who urged Wolseley to read 2 Corinthians 2.11. On consulting a Bible, Wolseley read the verse: 'Lest Satan should get advantage of us: for we are not ignorant of his devices'. He interpreted this as meaning that the king was prepared to fight.

On 30 January the column reached Dechiasu, near Amoafu, and prepared for battle. Wolseley noted in his journal that 'we shall have our grand fight tomorrow and eagerly looked forward to by all here. I have left nothing undone to obtain a peaceable solution to this war, but Mr Koffee in the folly of his barbarous pride had decided upon war'. He issued orders for the composition of the fighting force. The 42nd Highlanders would lead, followed by the Naval Brigade, the 23rd Regiment and the Rifle Brigade. They would adopt the square formation because it was known from previous experience that the Asante tactics were to envelop the advancing force and attack from all sides.[31] The baggage would be left in the rear under guard. The troops were ordered to 'fire low, fire slow and charge home'.

The battle of Amoafu on 31 January lasted all day and 'the enemy fought like men'. The British column of 134 officers, 1375 men and 708 natives engaged approximately 5000 Asante over a two and a half mile stretch of the road to Kumasi. The Asante deployed in a horseshoe fashion and attacked strongly. They made many rushes directly at the British force but often stayed hidden in the bush and attacked the rear of each advancing battalion. Alison noted that 'we were in the midst of a semi-circle of hostile fire, and we hardly ever caught sight of a man'.[32] The square inevitably broke cohesion because of the thickness of the jungle, but the skill of the officers and men meant that the initiative was never passed to the enemy. At one point the headquarters came under threat and newspaper correspondents, including Henry Stanley and Winwood Reade, grabbed rifles to assist in its defence. By mid afternoon the impetus of the Asante attack had begun to fade away as they turned their attention to attacking the baggage column in the rear. They succeeded in stampeding the native carriers, whose mass desertion meant that Wolseley could not continue the advance on the following day. By evening the Asante had withdrawn with heavy casualties including three dead chiefs. The British lost twenty-one officers and 173 men wounded, and one officer and three men killed. Although the British losses may seem low, Wolseley was concerned that, if the Asante continued to resist his advance and forced more battles, he would begin to fall short of men. However, he described Amoafu as 'a brilliant affair'.[33]

The Asante appeared demoralised by the superiority of British rifle and artillery fire over their muskets. They continued to attack the baggage at the rear and again succeeded in stampeding the native carriers. Wolseley decided to gamble on an advance to Kumasi with a flying column. Each soldier would carry rations for two days, and regimental carriers would take supplies for a further four. The advance was contested by the Asante, although Wolseley noted that they appeared less willing to come close to the column. On the evening of 3 February the force reached the Oda river. Wolseley had hoped to reach Kumasi, now only eight miles away, that day but the river needed to be bridged. It was also evident that the Asante were preparing for one last battle to defend Kumasi. The night was spent building the bridge. King Kofi sent a last message pleading for a halt, but Wolseley was not prepared to stop now so close to his goal. A heavy thunderstorm that night warned him of the probable consequences of delay: it was essential to reach the coast before the rains broke, bringing with them more fever and making the country impassable.

On 4 February the Asante attacked as soon as the column crossed the river. It took three hours to cover the few hundred yards to the village of Odasu. During the battle Wolseley was hit on the head by an Asante bullet which struck the thick leather band on his helmet but did not penetrate. After six hours the force had only advanced two miles and Kumasi was still six miles away. Wolseley decided to take a risk and sent Colonel John McCleod to lead the Highlanders in a rush on the capital. At 5.30 p.m. they entered Kumasi. Wolseley and the rest of the column arrived shortly before dusk. 'This entry into Coomassie is in its circumstances unrivalled in the annals of war. In the great street hundreds of armed men were collected to observe the entry, yet not a single shot was fired'.[34] Instead the demoralised but still armed Asante began dispersing into the bush.

Three cheers were ordered for the Queen and the town was searched. King Kofi had fled with members of his family into the bush. Dawson and the Fanti prisoners were located and released. Wolseley then issued a proclamation, saying he would punish with death anyone caught looting. Nevertheless the night was lit by fires caused by the native troops rampaging through the town. Messages were sent to the king asking him to come to

Kumasi to make peace, but by the afternoon of the next day it was clear that the king was not going to come. Wolseley was alarmed by the continuing heavy rain and feared that the rivers and streams crossed by the expedition on the way to Kumasi might become impassable for their return if he did not leave soon. He accordingly gave orders for the mining of the palace and the burning of the town before the troops began their return journey on the following day. Prize agents worked through the night gathering the king's valuables.

Early the next day eight fuses ignited the 125 kegs of gunpowder spread around the palace and the town was set on fire. Wolseley later wrote, 'In my heart I believed that the absolute destruction of Koomassee with its great palace, the wonder of Western Africa, would be a much more striking and effective end to the war than any paper treaty'.[35] His fears on the state of the road back were soon to be realised: the Oda bridge was already two feet under water, and the last troops in the column had to swim across. Fever hit the column hard and, after Amoafu, so many men needed to be carried that there was a shortage of hammocks. Should the Asante have massed for another attack, the small British force would almost certainly have been wiped out. As the column retreated it burnt all the villages on the way. On 9 February another messenger arrived from the king. 'I sent him back saying that I would forego the question of hostages, and that I would halt at Fommanah until the evening of the 12th instant, and that if by that time the king had sent me an accredited chief to treat who would bring with him 5000 ounces of gold (£20,000) I would make peace'.[36]

On the evening of 12 February a chief arrived but Wolseley made him wait until the following morning before beginning negotiations. At the same time he was joined by a Russian prince, Leonid Wiasemosky, who had tried to join the campaign as an observer but had been prevented by Wolseley, who had no time for camp followers. He entertained the prince royally before urging him to join Glover. In his private journal he made scathing comments about dilettante princes.[37] As soon as the prince left the camp, Wolseley ordered Glover to halt his advance up the Volta.

By then he was in such a hurry to leave the bush and reach the coast that he was prepared to be lenient. Therefore when the king's negotiator brought only 1040 ounces of gold saying that the king could not afford to pay more, Wolseley knew it was a lie 'but I am too anxious to get a treaty to stick out for money'.[38] Another reason for his haste was that he had heard that Gladstone had resigned. He was not sure whether this was from ill-health, or whether the government had resigned and there was to be a general election. If the latter was true, Wolseley feared a repeat of his return from Red River, when the public had overlooked his achievements because of more interesting events elsewhere. The peace treaty was signed with the Asante which forced King Kofi to renounce his claims to suzerainty over the Adansi, Akim, Assim, the Denkyera tribes and Elmina.

On 19 February Wolseley reached Cape Coast Castle where he was received by the whole population, and where the fleet and the castle fired a royal salute. He was accompanied by only one member of staff, Brackenbury, because the others were all ill. The loot collected by the prize agents at Kumasi was auctioned at the castle and prices exceeded expectation. Wolseley had asked a member of his staff to bid £16 for a group of fifty gold figurines but it went for £100. His staff officers gave him the king's sword. Wolseley bought the king's crown and orb and a Georgian silver teapot for himself, and the king's state umbrella for the Queen and a stool for the Princess of Wales. The total raised by the sale of loot was £5000.[39] On 4 March he boarded a ship bound for England leaving the Gold Coast forever: 'never did I leave a spot upon earth with such pleasure'.[40]

As Wolseley travelled by train from Portsmouth to London he received a depressing piece of news. There had been a major fire at the Pantechnicon, the large warehouse in which all his belongings had been stored. These were not insured. He wrote, 'no insurance money could replace them, for amongst other things that I regretted extremely were old family papers, reminiscences of my boyhood, and old letters, my Burmese, Crimean, Indian and Red River journals'.[41] The destruction of these records is just as great a loss to the historian as it was to Wolseley.

The Asante War was a great success. British troops had proved an earlier king of the Asante wrong: 'the white man brings his cannon to the bush but the bush is stronger than the cannon'.[42] The Asante had been met and decisively beaten on their own ground. The cost to the British was a total of sixty-eight dead and 394 wounded. The bush had proved the greater danger: 71 per cent of the white troops had fallen sick at some point during the two months spent on the Gold Coast and 43 per cent had been invalided home.[43] Wolseley had shown his abilities as a commander in the first campaign he had led in which the enemy had accepted battle.

Wolseley need not have been concerned that the government would ignore the achievements of his campaign. He himself was promoted to the rank of Major-General and nearly every officer who took part was promoted. Medals were also showered on the participants. At a review of the troops in Windsor Great Park on 30 March, Wolseley was invested with the Grand Cross of St Michael and St George and made a Knight Commander of the Bath by the Queen. The Queen described him as 'thin and grey, but well, and is a very smart, active, wiry-looking man, full of energy, and calm and decided-looking'.[44] He also received the unanimous thanks of both Houses of Parliament and was given a personal grant of £25,000. He apologised to his mother, in a letter on 23 March, for not having written earlier but 'I have been like a hunted hare for the last thirty six hours and have had no time for anything'.[45] He refused to bow to political pressure to accept a baronetcy, arguing that the honour had been reduced by its award to Sir Joseph Paxton, the Duke of Devonshire's gardener.

The public lauded Wolseley as the victor of Kumasi. When, in 1879, George Grossmith appeared on stage in Gilbert and Sullivan's *The Pirates of Penzance* as the 'very model of a modern Major General', imitating Wolseley's mannerisms and dress, the allusion to Wolseley was recognised by the audience. The man himself took no offence at the caricature.[46] The army also acknowledged Wolseley's success in campaigning in such a hostile climate: the epithet 'All Sir Garnet' came to signal that all was in order. With his reputation so firmly established in the public's mind, Wolseley could return to the War Office secure in the knowledge that if the new Conservative government under Benjamin Disraeli were to falter in the pursuit of army reform, his voice would be recognised when, and if, he made his case public.

7

War Office and Natal

Wolseley returned to the War Office from the Asante campaign with mixed feelings. While it was true that his reputation as a commander had been firmly established in the eyes of the public, much work remained to be done to further the cause of army reform. Here Wolseley was less certain of his position. Following the 1874 election, the Conservatives under Benjamin Disraeli had been returned to office and Gathorne Hardy appointed Secretary of State for War.[1] Wolseley was apolitical: indeed, he missed so many elections during his career that it is impossible to know for which party he would have voted since he disliked both equally.[2] His concern centred on the fact that Hardy knew little about the army and would have to rely on his advisers. The question was whether Hardy would turn to young officers, like Wolseley, or to the Duke of Cambridge. Hardy's attitude became clear early: Wolseley recorded that, 'HRH seems now under Mr Hardy's regime to do what he likes with the Army'.[3] Consequently, he had to look elsewhere to further the reform of the army.

The obvious area was India. In India, Wolseley could hope both to reorganise the British army on the basis of short service and, given the threat to India posed by Russia's advances southwards and the continuing unrest on the Indian border with Afghanistan, hope for further command in the field. Indeed a letter from Major-General William Earle, the Governor-General's private secretary in June 1874, suggested this very course to him. Earle urged him to accept the post of Adjutant General in India, should it be offered to him, because 'there is a great deal to be done, and no chance of getting it done unless a Commander-in-Chief and his Adjutant General set to work seriously'. Furthermore, unlike the War Office in London, there was very little political interference from Lord Northbrook, the Governor-General. In the event, Wolseley was not offered the post in India: instead he was appointed the Inspector-General of the Auxiliary Forces in June 1874.

Wolseley's principal task was to extend the Cardwell scheme for localisation to cover Britain's part-time soldiers – the Volunteers, Militia and Yeomanry. Under the scheme, two Militia infantry battalions and a certain quota of Volunteers were to be based in each military district. In the event, Wolseley spent only eight months as Inspector-General of the Auxiliary

Forces before he was appointed to a quasi-military-civil post in Natal. He only had time to prepare the plans for this organisation.

There was also concern over the efficiency of the auxiliary forces, whose main purpose was to support the regular army in the event of an invasion. The Volunteers had been raised in 1859 by the Lords Lieutenant of the counties, but in 1871 the War Office took over responsibility for them. It was now hoped that the Volunteers would become more efficient when trained frequently at a regimental depot alongside the Militia and the regulars. The level of the capitation grant, paid by the War Office for equipment, would henceforward depend on the number of efficient soldiers in each corps. The Militia was treated as a reserve to the army and trained alongside it regularly. The Yeomanry, the cavalry component of the auxiliary forces, remained a largely neglected force until the end of the century. Wolseley's contribution to the efficiency of the auxiliary forces was to produce a special version of *The Soldier's Pocket Book for Field Service* for them.

The *raison d'être* of the Volunteers was to assist in the defence of Britain against invasion, not to serve abroad; but, as the Army Reserve was not growing at the rate Cardwell had anticipated, in 1878 a War Office departmental committee under the Under-Secretary of State for War, Lord Bury, met to discuss whether the Volunteers should be made liable for foreign service. Wolseley opposed this proposal, arguing that the Volunteers were a patriotic force formed solely to defend the homeland. The chance of foreign service might destroy recruitment because employers would be unwilling to engage men subject to such a liability.[4] The Militia was recruited under different rules: at least three-quarters had to be prepared to be sent overseas in an emergency. In the event, before the Second South African War in 1899, only five Militia infantry battalions were embodied, during the war scare in 1885. Despite the short period Wolseley spent in direct contact with the auxiliary forces, in the 1880s, he was a popular speaker at battalion annual dinners when he encouraged them to become efficient enough to take over duties such as signalling from the regular army.[5]

On the issue of the slow growth of the Army Reserve, Wolseley had a clear recommendation to make: 'it should be made an established rule that in every arm of the Service all men found each month in excess of establishment of that arm, should be allowed to enter the Reserve monthly, irrespective of whether other arms were or were not below their respective establishments'.[6] The intention behind this recommendation was good: the conservative elements within the army were indeed trying to retain as many experienced men as possible in the ranks rather than recruit inexperienced men or send the best to the Reserve. However, his proposal was also a reflection of a major fault in military affairs during this time: it showed a lack of long-term planning. No yearly plan was drawn up in the various units of the army to establish whether an excess one month or year might not become a deficit in the following month or year. This fault is evident on examination of the General Annual Returns of the army, which show that the establishment of the army swung periodically between being in excess and being in deficit.

One of the reasons for introducing short service had been to stimulate recruitment, but there was growing concern that this was not happening. Wolseley believed that the only solution would be to double the daily rate of pay to the rank and file from one shilling to two shillings. This, he hoped, would encourage better-educated men to enlist, who could then be drilled in movements relevant to modern war which required more initiative, leading to an improved performance on the battlefield. The politicians were not prepared to take such a step. Not only would an increase in the basic pay lead to a rise in the Estimates for the army but, of greater concern, the army would be put in a position where it competed with trade for the better-educated men and might then affect Britain's industrial growth. The debate over pay continued for the rest of the century.

Rather than increasing pay, the government were more interested in stimulating recruitment by improving the conditions of service and by enhancing the chances of the reserve soldier of finding civilian employment. The first was done by an ongoing series of improvements to the conditions in the barracks, the second by the introduction of deferred pay. This measure had been recommended by a committee under the Inspector-General of Recruiting, Major-General Richard Taylor, in 1875. Under its terms, put into practice on 1876, 2d. a day of the soldier's pay would be withheld until his discharge from the colours into the Army Reserve. The resulting lump sum would enable him to set himself up in civilian life. Although Wolseley supported this measure when it was introduced, later, when Commander-in-Chief, he took part in a debate over its retention because it was beginning to be seen as a hindrance to re-engagement.

In 1876 Wolseley gave evidence to the Royal Commission on Army Promotion and Retirement, and in 1878 to the Committee on the Reserve of Officers. These committees attempted to address the problem of promotion which had slowed considerably since the abolition of the purchase of commissions. It was necessary to decide the ideal age for a given rank, and to devise a fair method of encouraging officers who had no chance of further promotion to retire from the army. Wolseley appears to have held no strong convictions on the length of time an officer should spend in each rank nor on the ideal age of an officer at a given rank. He was in favour of a reserve of officers because he shared the Duke of Cambridge's concern that, should a major war break out, there would be an insufficient number of officers to supervise the reserves and the new recruits.[7]

In March 1877 a debate began on the tactical organisation of a battalion. The German army operated on the system of four large companies per battalion, while the British Army still retained the old system of eight small ones. Therefore the War Office reviewed the advantages of each system. Wolseley was adamant that the German model should not be adopted in this area. He was in favour of the retention of the eight company system on the grounds that 'the maximum strength of the company can in fact be almost mathematically determined by the physical laws controlling the powers of the human sight and voice'. He pressed for an increase in the number of junior officers per battalion so that no fighting unit should contain more than a hundred men, the number Wolseley believed was the maximum one man could control. In the event Britain retained the eight company system since there was no overwhelming evidence against it. As the Adjutant General, Sir Charles Ellice, wryly pointed out: the whole debate had arisen as a means of placing a company under a major and therefore 'simplifying certain questions as regards the promotion and retirement of officers'.[8]

On 16 February 1875 Wolseley was given his first civil post when he was appointed to succeed Sir Benjamin Pine as Lieutenant-Governor of Natal. He was placed on secondment to the Colonial Office, which paid his salary, under the Secretary of State, Lord Carnarvon. Carnarvon held a wide vision of the future of South Africa. He had created a federation in Canada in 1867 and now he wanted to create a confederation of all white-controlled areas in South Africa, including the then independent Boer republics of the Transvaal and the Orange Free State. Natal occupied an important position on the eastern seaboard sandwiched between native areas, the Transvaal and Orange Free State. In order to facilitate confederation the government of Natal had to be brought into line with other British interests in the region, Cape Colony and the newest Crown Colony in the area, Griqualand West. Wolseley's mission was to persuade the colonists of Natal to abandon many of their constitutional privileges, particularly control of finance, granted by royal charter in 1856. Carnarvon did not confide his plans to Wolseley before the latter's departure for Natal but, on 30 April, Wolseley was sent an outline of the confederation proposals to be discussed at a future South African conference.[9]

There was also another important factor at work: native affairs. The home government forced its colonial counterparts to pursue a benevolent policy towards the indigenous people, allowing them their own areas in which to farm. This did not accord with the Natal colonists' desire for land and cheap labour. The clash between the colonists' interests and those of the natives came to a head in 1873 when the Hlubi clan of Zulus, resident in Natal, rebelled under their chief Langalibalele. The rebellion was crushed and Langalibalele was tried and imprisoned on Robben Island, off Cape Colony. His cause was championed by the Bishop of Natal, John Colenso, who, in Wolseley's words, set himself up as the 'supreme chief of the natives'.[10]

An external danger to Natal existed from the Zulus. The Zulus were the most militarily advanced of the native tribes: since the early nineteenth century they had been organised on military lines under a single autocratic chief and, more recently, had begun importing rifles from Natal. The danger from the Zulus, who 'mourned their unbaptized assegais', helped Wolseley persuade the colonists that the loss of their constitutional privileges was a price worth paying for the presence of British regiments in Natal.[11]

Before leaving for Natal Wolseley studied the situation there with great care. He concluded that war with the Zulus was likely in the near future and asked Carnarvon to grant permission for four selected officers to accompany him. These men would not be called special service officers, in case that suggested war, but instead would form part of a large staff. Carnarvon agreed to his request and the four officers accompanied Wolseley to Natal to assist in civil or military matters as required. Captain Lord Gifford was appointed his private secretary, and the other three men were all members of the 'ring': Colonel George Colley, Major Henry Brackenbury and Major William Butler. Wolseley also requested that he be given a military command independent from the Officer Commanding in the Cape, Lieutenant-General Sir Arthur Cunynghame, and that he should be able to call upon British troops stationed in the Cape and Mauritius if the need arose.[12] This was not settled before his departure. On 27 February, he wrote to Carnarvon that the orders he had received from the Duke of Cambridge made no mention of the independent command, although Wolseley was under the impression that this was what Carnarvon had expected. On his arrival at the Cape, he discovered that Cunynghame had published a General Order creating such a command despite the fact that the instructions from the War Office to both men had not made this clear.[13]

Wolseley arrived in Durban on 26 March and then proceeded to the Natal capital Pietermaritzburg. Louisa and Frances remained in London because Wolseley was only planning to be away for a few months and Louisa was a poor sailor. Government House, where Wolseley and his staff lived, was 'a pretty cottage-like building with small but well laid out grounds round it'. He had a place levelled so that in the evenings the staff could play tennis for exercise.[14] On 2 April, he was sworn into office and held his first Executive Council meeting. He soon realised that his mission was not a simple one: 'it is no easy matter to induce men to vote for their own political death'. He compared the colonists' position to that of the Irish Parliament voting for Union with England in 1801.[15] His tactics were to entertain the colony into submission. He had purchased a large quantity of champagne in Cape Town, which he did not drink himself after hearing that it was made from coal oil. He held dinners and balls on virtually every night and his first month's bill exceeded £1400. The dull existence of the hard-working colonists was transformed by this lavish entertaining: 'there is the greatest excitement over the prospects of our coming ball; every yard of silk and every pair of white shoes have been bought up'.[16] Butler recorded the results of all these parties: 'within a fortnight the ladies were all on the new governor's side'.[17] Yet their husbands were likely to pose a more serious problem. By June four members of Wolseley's staff, Brackenbury, Butler, Gifford and Mandeville, were having affairs.[18]

Wolseley devised various tactics to overcome the opposition of the colonists to abandoning their independence. First he hoped to offer them inducements: he asked Carnarvon to offer an imperial guarantee on a loan Natal was raising to build railways. He hoped that this bribe, worth £10,000 a year, would persuade the Legislative Council to vote for the required changes. Carnarvon, however, refused to give the guarantee, forcing him to adopt another method of persuasion. He was disappointed with the attitude and quality of some members of the Executive Council, and encouraged two of them, Barter and Foss, to take a long leave in England. Their posts were then given to Colley and Butler. He attempted to woo the editors of the four newspapers published in Natal with varying degrees of success. The *Maritzburg Times* became a government journal and Wolseley's staff produced four articles a week for it.[19]

On 5 May 1875 Wolseley addressed the Legislative Council and presented the Natal Bill to modify the constitution. The main purport of the Bill was to add eight members to the Legislative Council. Previously there had been five official members, who also formed the Executive Council, and thirteen elected members. Under the new law there would be fifteen members of the Legislative Council among whom eight, selected by the governor, would be unpaid. Therefore the Executive Council would be able to rely on thirteen votes and be certain of a majority on all legislative matters. Finance was to be treated slightly differently: no new tax could be imposed without a two-thirds majority. After three days of heated debate, the Natal Bill passed its second reading on 20 May. One opposition member was so overwrought that he mistakenly voted for the Bill. On 28 May the Bill emerged from the committee stage with one compromise which Wolseley agreed to: the number of members was reduced from fifteen to thirteen. Wolseley was heartily relieved with the success of this part of his mission. The impact on the future of Natal was great:

> It transformed a remote and parochial South African colony into an indispensable constituent of Empire which no government could thereafter treat lightly: and, for good or ill, it gave it an influence in the politics of imperial defence out of all proportion to its intrinsic strategic importance.[20]

There were still other matters to settle in Natal before he could return home.

In June and July Wolseley and his staff toured Natal. Colley was sent to the Transvaal to gain an opinion on the amount of support for confederation and Butler was sent to the Orange Free State on a similar mission. Wolseley was the first governor to visit the Drakensburg range and the Tugela valley, the borderlands of Natal. The remoteness of these areas from the centres of government and commerce, Durban and Pietermaritzburg, had been demonstrated when none of their members had voted for Wolseley's Bill. On his way, he also inspected British garrisons and was appalled by what he found. In Pietermaritzburg the married soldiers' quarters resembled 'very bad Irish hovels': about 120 men had to live under canvas because the barracks were in such poor condition and too small. He felt that it would be better to withdraw the garrison than to shame the British army in this way. In August he inspected a half battalion of the 13th Light Infantry. He saw for himself the effect that short service had had on the age of the rank and file: 'the recruits I saw would not be of much good for the active work of a campaign: in another year when they have had two years good feeding they will be physically good soldiers'.[21]

While in Natal, Wolseley received plenty of evidence on the conditions in Zululand. He believed that the absorption of the country as part of Natal would solve the native question because then the Zulu 'squatters' in Natal would return north, secure in a belief in British justice. It was claimed that the chief of the Zulus, Cetshwayo, was killing his subjects without trial and that 'the barbarity and cruelty of his reign is a disgrace to humanity'.[22] Theophilus Shepstone, Secretary of Native Affairs in Natal, who had lived among the Zulus from childhood, advised Wolseley on the likely conduct of the Zulus. He estimated their army to number 30,000 ready for war. There were three possible targets for them: Natal; the border tribes whose cattle the Zulus wanted; or the Boers. Wolseley hoped for war between the Zulus and Boers because it might destroy Cetshwayo's power if he lost; it would be expensive for the Transvaal, and might make the Boers more amenable to Carnarvon's plan for a confederation of South Africa.[23] Despite the apparent size of the Zulu army, few had rifles. Shepstone advised him that it would only take 1000 British soldiers to take over the country. Wolseley transmitted this information to Carnarvon and the figure became the basis of future British policy towards Cetshwayo; something which led to disaster in 1879.[24]

He returned to Pietermaritzburg in August to complete his mission before the arrival of his successor, Sir Henry Bulwer, at the end of the month. He had to nominate members of the Legislative Council but encountered some difficulty when three men refused his appeal. There were also twenty-five Bills to get through the council touching all aspects of internal affairs. On 27 August Wolseley met Bulwer at Durban and then boarded a ship to take him to the Cape and back to Britain. He confessed that, 'I feel like a school boy just told that I may go home for some holidays'.[25] He had completed the mission given to him but was nevertheless aware that many problems remained in South Africa. Back in England, he was frequently consulted by Carnarvon on South African affairs, such as advising him to consider the annexation of Delagoa Bay which had been granted to Portugal in July 1875 after arbitration by the French President.[26] He recommended that Shepstone should be given a KCMG before the South African Conference opened, since his opinions were respected in South Africa. Wolseley served as Vice-President of the conference when it finally opened in 1876. In September 1876 he would have been sent back to South Africa, instead of Shepstone, to oversee the annexation of the Transvaal, had he not been otherwise occupied.

Wolseley returned to London and bought a house in London. Previously he and his family had rented a house in Belgrave Road but, in November 1875, he purchased a large house with a coach house and good stables in Portman Square. He had managed to buy it for £8000, £2000 less than had been asked. The family did not move in until March 1876 because the lease in Belgrave Road lasted till that date.[27]

The main issue under discussion at the War Office when Wolseley returned to his post as Inspector-General of the Auxiliary Forces was the new mobilisation plan. The 1875 plan was an over-optimistic document. It envisaged the distribution of all military units in Britain into eight army corps which would be called out, in their numerical order, should war be imminent. Only the First Army Corps would be composed entirely of units from the regular army: the remainder were to be a combination of regular units and Militia battalions. The Yeomanry was to supplement the regular cavalry in two corps. The crucial problem was that there were not enough troops to fill all the corps. For example, there was only sufficient artillery for the first three army corps and engineers for the first corps and some divisions of the second. In order for the plan to become real, the government would have to invest greatly in the artillery and engineers, the specialist troops, but it was not prepared to do so. Therefore the 1875 mobilisation plan remained little more than a paper suggesting an ideal, and it was ignored during the mobilisation for the 1882 campaign in Egypt. Nevertheless, it did serve to demonstrate the need for such a plan and to give the broad outlines on which a more practicable document could be drawn up. In the late 1880s Wolseley supervised the formation of the mobilisation plan, with the division of the home establishment into army corps, which would remain in place for the remainder of the century.[28]

8

India Office

Wolseley had been back at the War Office for little over a year when a new position was offered to him. The Secretary of State for India, Lord Salisbury, invited Wolseley to accept a seat on the India Council to give advice on the effect of the Cardwell reforms on India. Hardy and Cambridge were quite happy for him to accept this secondment. Wolseley was equally content: it meant that he was paid £1200 a year instead of £1000 as he had been paid in the War Office. He understood that 'I was offered it as a stepping stone to high command in India'.[1] He was also keen to leave the War Office because he was disappointed with the slow progress of army reform since Hardy had come to office. In an article published in 1877, he complained that Cardwell 'laid the foundations for a great structure; but not only has it never been built, but the foundations which he laid in some instances have been used for purposes altogether different from those for which the master mason intended them'.[2] He referred in particular to the slowness in linking battalions and establishing localisation. One major test for the success of the Cardwell system would be whether it could produce a sufficient number of well-trained and mature troops for India. Should the short service system fail to produce an adequate defence force for Britain's greatest possession, its future would have to be reconsidered.

The report of Lord Cadogan's committee on short service with reference to India recommended various measures to be adopted to increase the average age of the private soldier and non-commissioned officer serving in India from twenty-three years to twenty-six and a half. The committee reported in favour of allowing a quarter of all men to re-engage so as to serve eight years in India. Eight years was generally recognised as the maximum time a soldier could spend in a hot climate before his health deteriorated. On re-engagement the soldier would receive an extra penny a day. The Military Secretary, Major-General T. T. Pears, reacted angrily to these recommendations. He argued that, along with the revised rates of good conduct pay and pay increases to certain departmental officers which added £565,500 to the amount the Indian taxpayer had to pay for the British army, an extra £200,000 would have to be found. It was clear from Pears's letter that he was in favour of a return to long service. Wolseley produced a blistering reply. He emphasised the poor quality of the men of the former East India Company regiments and argued that a return to long service would lead to an overall deterioration in the quality of British battalions in India. He was, however, prepared to accept that eight years was the best length of service for India on grounds of efficiency – the average age of soldiers would increase; and economy – fewer battalions would have to be sent out from England during each trooping season. The debate over the ideal length of service in India continued for years.[3]

Indian defence was very much to the fore at this time. Russia was building strategic railways linking her newly-conquered southern Muslim provinces with the heartland. This brought the Russian frontier closer to India and also meant that, should Russia decide to invade India, she would be in a better position to do so. The main route of the Russian army was likely be from the Caspian Sea along the valley of the Atrek towards Sarakhs, Merv and Herat in Afghanistan, skirting the northern frontier of Persia. British policy towards Persia and Afghanistan was therefore crucial to Indian defence. In 1873, when the Shah of Persia had visited Britain, Wolseley had written an article urging an alliance between Britain and Persia and the creation of a Persian army officered and commanded by the British.[4] His efforts came to nothing, Britain failing to take full advantage of the Shah's friendliness towards Britain. Afghanistan was a more complex problem. Advocates of the 'forward school' of Indian defence, including Major-General Frederick Roberts, the Quartermaster General in India, argued that India should hold the Himalayas and the passes between India and Afghanistan.[5] Others, like Wolseley, viewed the Indus as the more practicable frontier until Russia had at least built railways to an advanced base in Turkestan. In the meantime the policy of Britain and India should be to keep Russia out of Afghanistan.[6] A greater likelihood than military intervention was that Russia would undermine the British position by supporting anti-British elements in Persia and Afghanistan. This dissatisfaction might spread to India where the Native Army hugely outnumbered the British battalions. British rule in India might be lost from internal rebellion – Britain had already had one warning of this possibility in 1857.

Finding a solution to the growing Eastern Crisis proved to be Wolseley's first task at the India Office. Since the defeat in the Crimean War, Russia had sought to restore its status as a great power by setting itself up as the protector of all Slavs. In 1871 Russia had unilaterally torn up the provisions of the 1856 Treaty of Paris which forbade it to station any military naval units on the Black Sea, while the rest of Europe was preoccupied with the consequences of the Franco-Prussian War. This placed Russia in a position to threaten Turkish control of the Dardanelles, the outlet into the

Mediterranean from the Black Sea. Once in the Mediterranean, Russia could support its fellow Slavs in the Balkans, and threaten British and French naval dominance in the region. As one military commentator later wrote: 'To acquire Constantinople is the traditional policy of Russia. To keep her out of it is the traditional policy of England'.[7] Turkey was believed to be in no position to stop such actions as it was seen as the 'Sick Man of Europe' with a corrupt and inefficient government.

In 1875 three Balkan provinces, Bosnia, Herzegovina and Bulgaria, revolted against Turkish rule. The rebellion was crushed with great brutality and in 1876 Gladstone began a public campaign to draw attention to the atrocities being committed by the Turks in Bulgaria.[8] The crisis nearly split both political parties in Britain. Lords Granville, Hartington and Harcourt were alarmed at Gladstone's attacks on Turkish policy, whereas Lords Salisbury, Derby and Carnarvon were equally startled by Disraeli's unstinting support of Turkey and talk of war should Russia pledge support for its fellow Slavs and bring about a major war between Russia and Turkey. Disraeli believed that Russia should be kept out of the Mediterranean at all costs. The interests of trade and the security of India outweighed all humanitarian considerations. At this stage he lacked public support: reports of the massacre of Christians in the Balkans appalled Britain.[9]

Ten days after his arrival at the India Office Wolseley produced his first memorandum on the Eastern Crisis. It revealed much about the narrowness of his political outlook, and represents an almost diametrically opposite view of the question of war with Russia to what he would express later in his career. He accepted the long-held political and military view that 'with the Russians in occupation of the Hellespont how impossible it will be for us, if at war with Russia, to maintain our long lines of communication with India, via Egypt, no matter how strong our fleets may be'. He went on to urge the adoption of a defensive policy in European Turkey and a vigorous offensive in Asia.[10] It was here that Wolseley's political naivety showed itself: Britain had no naval base in the eastern Mediterranean, and Turkey's closure of the Bosphorus to Russian warships was the only means Britain had of maintaining the freedom of the Suez Canal for British commerce to India and Australasia. He, however, proposed to abandon Turkey to its own devices while Britain, in alliance with Afghanistan, conducted a campaign against the Russian provinces of Tashkent and Samarkand. The memorandum was clearly unacceptable to his political superiors. The Assistant Under Secretary, Sir Ralph Thompson, wrote to him that, although Disraeli had read the memorandum, he did not want it circulated to the Cabinet and 'thinks it should be kept as quiet as possible'.[11]

Although this memorandum showed some political shallowness, it did demonstrate that Wolseley had a clear idea of what was militarily achievable. He had no great opinion of the fighting qualities of the Turkish army and, like many other commentators and observers, was to be pleasantly surprised by the vigorous defence Turkey made at Plevna during the war. He recognised that in 1876 Russia's southern provinces were vulnerable to attack since they were relatively recent conquests and the construction of strategic railways connecting them with the rest of Russia was in its early stages. He suggested that the Crimean War had set Russia back fifty years and was convinced that a war in Asia at this point would 'put her back 100 years in her struggle for sovereign rule over the whole of Asia'.[12] He hoped that by demonstrating British power in Asia now Russia would pose less of a threat to India in the future. The theme of war while the enemy is weak was one to which Wolseley would return when considering the aftermath of the First South African War and operations in the Sudan after the fall of Khartoum.

In April 1877 the Russo-Turkish war broke out. Wolseley was not a member of the confidential mobilisation committee and did not play a major role in determining the British response. This was not through lack of trying. In a new memorandum on the subject he now accepted the need to provide support directly for Turkey and advocated the stationing of some British troops on the Gallipoli peninsula to help the Turks defend the Bulair lines.[13] This was in direct contradiction to his usual view of the role of the army: at this time and in the future Wolseley was opposed to the stationing of small bodies of British troops abroad for an indefinite period. However, on this occasion he advocated supporting Turkey on Gallipoli because he predicted, as did all the other military authorities, that the Russians would advance much faster than they in fact did, and that a British expedition to the Balkans would be too late to stop them reaching the outskirts of Constantinople.

Public opinion swung behind Disraeli and talk of war with Russia became commonplace in Britain. In the music halls the audiences sang of war:

> We don't want to fight, but, by Jingo if we do,
> We've got the ships; we've got the men; and we've got the money too!

The truth was, however, somewhat different. Britain had the ships: HMS *Devastation*, the most modern battleship in the fleet, led a flotilla into the Dardanelles. The money could be found, should Parliament vote for war, but the men was the crucial stumbling point. The crux of the matter was the question of whether Britain was prepared to despatch only a limited number of troops to boost the Turkish defence of Gallipoli, or whether it was ready to engage in a major war with Russia. The Cardwell system, which allowed the use of the Army Reserve only in the event of a major war, paradoxically made the latter policy easier to implement than the former. A limited campaign of uncertain duration would strain the resources of the army, whereas a full-scale war would justify the recall of the Army Reserve and, in theory at least, place less of a strain on the army organisation.

The government appeared to have no clearly thought out approach to the subject. In December 1876 the Duke of Cambridge wrote to the Secretary of State, Gathorne Hardy, asking for a policy statement so that military preparations could be started. No such statement was forthcoming and indeed the politicians so misunderstood the military authorities that they thought them obstructive. As Disraeli complained to the Queen:

> It is they who have opposed every military move, that has been suggested from the beginning – Mediterranean garrisons, expeditions to Gallipoli, and so on. What they want, and what they have ever tried to bring about, is a great military expedition, like the Crimean.[14]

Furthermore, the politicians had good grounds to mistrust the military authorities. The command of British military forces was given to General Robert Napier, who had successfully commanded the British expedition to Abyssinia in 1867 but was now old, with Wolseley as his second-in-command.[15] On 27 March 1878 Disraeli wrote to the Queen that he had seen Napier's plans and thought them meagre.[16] Napier planned limited landings near Salonika, Smyrna and St Jean d'Acre; none of these places being near enough the Straits or Constantinople to offer any direct assistance to the Turks.[17] Parliament granted a supplementary estimate of £6,000,000 for the army and navy to enable preparations to be made.[18] Indian troops were stationed on Malta in readiness for war against Russia.

The crucial issue was that Britain could not afford to increase her army by recalling the Army Reserve unless war was imminent and could not undertake occupation of foreign territory for unlimited periods of time without severely disrupting the efficiency of the home army. The Reserves were recalled to the colours on 1 April 1878 but doubts remained about the wisdom of this recall. In an article Wolseley stated that when the Reserves had been called out a few years earlier for drill, 'it was then found than in many instances the men who responded to the call lost their situations in civil life'.[19] This concern was echoed in the House of Commons with questions being asked of the Secretary of State for War, Colonel Frederick Stanley, and the Under Secretary, Viscount Bury.[20] In July, Stanley replied that he believed that 'in a very large number of instances, the men have had their employment kept open for them'. In August, Bury replied that it was still too early to know how many had lost their jobs because of reserve service.[21]

Wolseley viewed the prospect of war with Russia with mixed feelings. It could be the greatest opening he could face in the field but, being known to be ambitious, he had to be cautious when arguing for a war with Russia. He wrote to his brother George:

> I do not dare say this openly, for being a soldier, the curs of England would sneer out, oh he wishes for war from personal motives. In my own heart I know this is not the case: I wish it because I love my country before all earthly things, and am prepared [to] give up my life for her.[22]

At the same time he feared the consequences of a land war between Russia and Britain because of the vast difference in their military resources. This fear is shown in a memorandum Wolseley produced shortly before his appointment as Chief of Staff under Napier. His proposed solution was to bring about a grandiose scheme of alliances. In this case the projected alliance was even less realistic than acquiring the Amir of Afghanistan's support for a campaign against Russia in Asia. He now proposed a grand Muslim alliance of contingents from all the North African states, along with the Turks and Albanians, to fight alongside half a million British and Canadian volunteers.[23] Wolseley would never have achieved this alliance: Britain knew little about the people of North Africa and, apart from holding a financial stake in Egypt, had no interests in the region. The only common bond between the Arabs of North Africa and Turkey was religion. However, he might have been able to raise half a million men from Britain and Canada – given the popular feeling for war.

The Eastern Crisis was brought to an end by the Congress of Berlin in July 1878. Throughout the crisis, as Britain's freedom of action had been restricted by her lack of a naval base in the eastern Mediterranean, the question of a suitable site had started to be explored. In his memorandum of November 1876, Wolseley recommended the acquisition of Crete from Turkey. Crete had several good harbours but, as the Inspector-General of Fortifications, General Lintorn Simmons, pointed out in his memorandum in April 1877, these would be difficult to defend. Simmons added that Cyprus and Rhodes were both unsuitable as coaling stations because of the small size of their main harbours. Therefore he recommended the acquisition of the small island of Scarpanto, which lay between Crete and Rhodes.[24] It was 350 miles from Port Said and 600 miles from Malta and had a small land-locked harbour which would be easy to defend. His recommendations were ignored. In his journal Wolseley noted that, in meetings with Disraeli, Cyprus had often been mentioned but only as a reserve proposal to the principal aim of acquiring a base on the eastern seaboard of the Mediterranean, preferably Alexandretta or somewhere on the Gulf of Iskanderoon.[25]

Wolseley was therefore somewhat surprised to be informed that Turkey had ceded Cyprus to Britain at the Congress of Berlin and that he was to be its first British High Commissioner. He had expected to be appointed to replace General Stavely in the Bombay Command later that year. His appointment was announced in Parliament on 8 July 1878. It met with the approval of Napier, who wrote to the Duke of Cambridge that he did not think that a better appointment could have been made.[26] Wolseley was to communicate directly with the Foreign Office, now under the Marquess of Salisbury. The appointment was made without the knowledge or consent of the Duke of Cambridge, who was visiting Malta when the question arose. The Duke was furious that, not only had he not been consulted about the appointment, but also that Wolseley had been given a free hand in selecting staff officers to accompany him. Wolseley's list included tried and tested men: Colonel Greaves as the Chief of Staff; Brevet Lieutenant-Colonel Baker Russell as Military Secretary; Brevet Major Hugh McCalmont and Captain Lord Gifford as the aides-de-camp; and Brevet Lieutenant-Colonel Henry Brackenbury as an additional staff officer. Only St Leger Herbert was a new appointment, acting as Wolseley's private secretary. The new Secretary of State for War, Colonel Frederick Stanley, took some of the heat off Wolseley by rewriting his list in his own hand before showing it to the Duke of Cambridge. Wolseley was pleased with the work of all his staff officers except Baker Russell, whom he described as unsuitable for staff work but ideal for a field command.[27]

Wolseley and his staff crossed the Channel and made their way overland to Brindisi and then by ship to Malta. There he made arrangements with the governor for the transfer of three battalions to Cyprus, to be followed by three Indian battalions which had been stationed in Malta at the height of the Eastern Crisis. On 22 July 1878 Wolseley landed at Larnarca and swore himself in as High Commissioner. Butler, who visited him at the end of the year, described the island:

> Here in Cyprus it was the East again, the East with the Turk added on: the ragged squalor, the breast of the earth dried up and desolate, the old glory of Greek, Roman, Norman and Venetian civilisation lying in dust and ashes under a thing that was itself a dying force in the world.[28]

Wolseley then travelled to the capital, Nicosia, to establish his government.

He was appalled by conditions on the island, which had been long neglected by Turkey. Everything and everywhere was filthy. He planned to ask Louisa and his six-year-old daughter Frances to join him but could not do so until he found suitable quarters. The heat of the summer drove Wolseley and his staff from Nicosia to a camp in the mountains near an old monastery. The sickness rate among the troops left below began to grow alarmingly: on 15 August the correspondent for the *Daily News*, Archibald Forbes, wrote home that a quarter of the whole force was affected by fever. The Indian troops were sent home and a new healthier camp was found for the remaining troops at Dali in the highlands. By December conditions had improved sufficiently in Nicosia for Wolseley to be joined by his family. Government House was, however, less than salubrious: the nights were so cold that fur coats had to be worn for dinner. The Wolseleys, however, entertained many visitors, including the artist Tristram Ellis and the traveller Sir Samuel Baker.[29]

Financially he was far better off living in Cyprus. He sold the house in Portman Square for £10,550, along with most of the furniture and fittings. This did not represent a vast profit on the £8000 he had paid for the house because he had spent £700 on the furniture and had undertaken substantial redecoration. Life in Cyprus was cheap but Wolseley was still being called upon to pay his brother's debts. In February 1879 Fred was nearly bankrupt and his brother sent him £3000 to bail him out. This brought Fred's total debt to Wolseley to £8500; George owed £1800. Wolseley admitted to Dick that he was thoroughly annoyed by the inability of these two brothers to live within their means. He had a family to support in Cyprus and wanted to be able to spend any extra on supporting his mother.[30]

Wolseley faced two main tasks on Cyprus: the first was to establish British rule, the second to discover whether Cyprus was the suitable military and naval station the politicians expected it to be. The workload was heavy:

> Minutes to be written upon every subject under heaven – petitions from peasants, declaring they have been beaten and ill-treated by the police or someone else, and a thousand other things, one after another, until my poor brain goes round like a humming-top. This is a filthy hole.[31]

On 14 September an Order in Council established Executive and Legislative Councils. The land question proved the most testing, as Wolseley had to determine what lands were held personally by the Sultan of Turkey. This was a potentially serious matter because the Sultan made extravagant claims which, if granted, would have made the establishment of British rule more difficult. The issue was settled by a mixed commission which included two Muslims. The British set to work to improve the state of the island: locusts were exterminated, health care extended throughout the island and British currency introduced. Wolseley also began a programme of planting 20,000 eucalyptus trees.

Finance was a major problem. Under the Convention ceding the island to Britain, a stipulation stated that England would pay Turkey the excess of revenue over expenditure. Turkish statisticians determined the figures, and it was agreed that Britain would pay £92,686 annually. The true state of Cypriot finances was discovered too late to change this and, as a result, Britain was forced to pay £92,000 a year herself to compensate for what Cyprus could not supply. The financial state improved gradually when Wolseley instituted a new tax system. Tax farming and the sale of tithes had led to widespread corruption. He abolished the farming of taxes and appointed new customs officials: for the first time in living memory the entire tithe was collected.

Wolseley faced the task of governing an island in which three-quarters of the population was Greek but all the official offices had been held by Turks. The Greeks petitioned Wolseley for union with Greece and to make Greek the official language. He opposed both measures and tended to support Turkish administration. He continued to keep many Turkish officials in office and Turkish civil and criminal law was retained for the time being. He wanted 100,000 Muslim refugees from the Balkans to be relocated to Cyprus. As this proved impossible, he and Salisbury began work on a scheme to encourage immigration from Malta. This plan came to nothing before the Disraeli government fell in April 1880.

Disraeli had told the Queen that 'Cyprus is the key of Western Asia', but it was clear that few agreed with this opinion.[32] Wolseley himself thought that Egypt would have been a better choice for a British base in the eastern Mediterranean. The government was forced onto the defensive in Parliament where many questions were asked about the value of Cyprus. The Under Secretary of State for the Colonies, A. F. Egerton, was forced to admit that 'technically speaking, there is no harbour; but there were three very fair anchorages'. Sir Julian Goldschmid wanted to know why, if Cyprus was to be turned into a great military and naval base, Wolseley had been placed under the Foreign Office rather than the War Office or Admiralty.[33] It quickly became apparent that Famagusta was not suitable as a coaling station and Wolseley made this clear to Stanley and the First Lord of the Admiralty, W. H. Smith, when they visited Cyprus in November. The two politicians were forced to agree with him that Cyprus could not hold many British troops because the climate was unhealthy, although he convinced them that reports of the severity of illness had been exaggerated. Nevertheless, there was general agreement that, unless it could be exchanged for Port Said in Egypt, Cyprus was worth retaining if only as a place from which to obtain transport animals for expeditions in the region. This prediction was proved correct when, in 1882, transport animals were purchased in Cyprus for the war in Egypt.[34]

Although Wolseley told Butler that 'I have put my hand to the Cypriot plough and must hold it until the furrow is finished', he was keen for a command in the field.[35] A glimmer of hope arose because of events in Afghanistan. In 1876 Lord Lytton was made Viceroy and attempted to persuade the Amir of Afghanistan, Sher Ali, to accept a military mission in Kabul, from where an eye could be kept on Russian movements. Sher Ali refused but in July 1878 admitted a Russian military mission into his capital. Britain attempted to send a mission which was turned back at the Khyber Pass.

In September Wolseley heard this news. He believed that shortly a military expedition would be sent to escort the mission through the Golan Pass to Kandahar. He reflected with some regret that, had he gone to Bombay as Commander-in-Chief instead of to Cyprus, he would have been given the command of the expedition. He telegraphed his friend George Colley, asking him to inform the Viceroy, Lord Lytton, that he was ready to leave Cyprus immediately to take command. He sent a similar telegram to Salisbury in London. Wolseley was unsuccessful: the command was given to the Commander-in-Chief at Madras, General Sir Neville Chamberlain, who was sixty years old. He was disappointed since 'all through my career I dreamt of an Afghan war: the "disasters"!! of our last one are about the first public events I can remember'. As the war progressed, Wolseley continued to regret that he had not been sent out: 'I feel like an eagle that has had his wings clipped'.[36]

The British adventure in Afghanistan led initially to disaster. Lytton issued an ultimatum to the Amir demanding the admittance of a British military mission before invading Afghanistan with three armies. Sher Ali was over-thrown and his son accepted the military mission in May 1879. In September the members of the mission were all killed in Kabul. Major-General Sir Frederick Roberts made his reputation as a commander by a daring high-speed march from Kandahar to Kabul to restore order.

Wolseley's attention was soon diverted by news from South Africa. The new Colonial Secretary, Sir Michael Hicks Beach, was preoccupied with events in Afghanistan and had left the High Commissioner in the Cape, Sir Bartle Frere, to pursue the policy of confederation begun by Lord Carnarvon.[37] During 1878 Frere and Theophilus Shepstone wrote reports to the Colonial Office suggesting that the Zulus posed a serious threat to the security of Natal. They emphasised the size of the Zulu army and its readiness for war. Neither man admitted that their real reason for wanting the destruction of the Zulu nation was to provide a source of cheap labour for farmers and mining companies in Natal.[38]

Frere's aggressive policy towards the Zulus led to an invasion of Zululand under Lord Chelmsford on 11 January 1879.[39] Disaster soon struck: on 22 January the Zulus attacked the British camp at Isandhlwana and left 895 British soldiers dead from a force of 950, and later that day attacked Rorke's Drift which was stoutly held by men of the 24th Regiment. Britain was appalled at the scale of the casualties and there was a call for Lord Chelmsford to be replaced by a more competent general.

9

South Africa

On 27 April 1879 Wolseley was recalled to London to join the committee on short service about to convene. He was happy to leave Cyprus because it would mean missing the hot weather and the trouble of moving his family and household into the mountains for the summer. In contrast Louisa was disappointed to leave Cyprus because she had enjoyed life there. Wolseley was a little concerned because, other than serving on the committee, his future was uncertain: 'What becomes of me when I return home I know not'. He still wanted to go to India but would have to wait for over a year before the post of Commander-in-Chief there became free.[1]

Service on the committee on short service was just the pretext for Wolseley's recall from Cyprus: in reality the Cabinet wanted him to advise them on the Zulu War. Back in February he had sent the Secretary of State for War, Colonel Stanley, 'a few ideas extracted from notes I made on the subject of a war with Cetewayo, when I was in Natal'.[2] Therefore it was not a total surprise that, on 23 May 1879, Disraeli wrote to the Queen proposing that Wolseley should be appointed High Commissioner and Commander-in-Chief for Natal, the Transvaal and territories adjacent including Zululand. Lord Chelmsford was to be retained as the second-in-command. Wolseley's appointment was announced in the House of Commons before the Queen gave her sanction for it, and Disraeli was forced to apologise to her for this oversight. The Queen disliked Wolseley for his forthright opinions and self-esteem: Disraeli admitted that, 'it is quite true that Wolseley is an egoist, and a braggart. So was Nelson'. The Duke of Cambridge had wanted Napier sent out instead of Wolseley, but was forced to admit that the former was really too old for active service and the latter had the advantage of local experience.[3] The press greeted the news of the appointment with loud approval, and *Punch* even broke into verse playing on the similarity between Wolseley's name and that of the Duke of Wellington:

> When Wolseley's mentioned, Wellesley's brought to mind;
> Two men, two names, of answerable kind:
> Call to the front, like Wellesley, good at need,
> Go, Wolseley, and like Wellesley, greatly speed.[4]

Wolseley attended the Cabinet on 28 May to learn the policy of the government towards South Africa. He was to be sent out to make peace with the Zulus and to safeguard existing British territories, not to add to them. In other words, no annexation of Zululand was planned.[5]

Wolseley angered the Duke of Cambridge by criticising Chelmsford's exercise of command. He claimed that Chelmsford had made some elementary errors and wrote:

> To have divided his fighting Army, as he did, into two independent bodies seperated [sic] one from the other beyond mutually supporting distance, in the face of a concentrated enemy, stamped him as a General who was ignorant of his business. To say, he did not know the enemy's concentrated Army was close by only serves to strengthen this description of him as a commander in the field.[6]

Although the Duke of Cambridge attempted to defend Chelmsford, arguing that 'he had evidently a bad Staff', the Cabinet was unanimous in agreeing that Wolseley should be sent out to supersede both Chelmsford and Frere. A court of enquiry sat on the Isandhlwana disaster and concluded that Chelmsford had dangerously underestimated the size and power of the Zulu army.[7]

Again controversy surrounded the staff appointments Wolseley made for the Zulu War. The Duke of Cambridge was furious that he had been given permission to take out with him whoever he wanted. Again members of the 'ring' featured prominently: Brevet Lieutenant-Colonel Henry Brackenbury was appointed as the Military Secretary; Brevet Major Hugh McCalmont was an aide-de-camp; St Leger Herbert was the private secretary, and among the special service officers were tried men such as Major Baker Russell and Captain Frederick Maurice. Wolseley was given the local rank as Full General to emphasise his seniority to Lord Chelmsford. George Colley was promoted to the rank of Brigadier-General and served as Chief of Staff, but Wolseley lost the battle to have Colley confirmed as his second-in-command in place of Major-General Hugh Clifford. The Duke of Cambridge confirmed the latter as Wolseley's deputy because 'no army could stand these sorts of preferences without entirely dampening the energies of senior officers'. Wolseley's somewhat caustic reply was that he 'naturally assumed it would be the object of the Government that the ablest and most fitting man should succeed me'.[8] He was very anxious to have the best men with him because 'I shall not have time to act on my own plans or to alter Chelmsford's arrangements, and because many of the tools I shall have to work with, are not of my own selection, but are men chosen by HRH and the Horse Guards party'.[9]

Wolseley's departure for South Africa was a highly public occasion and a very emotional one. After three years of virtually unbroken life with Louisa, he was reluctant to leave her:

> What a brave woman you are and how manfully you bore up all yesterday and indeed I may say ever since the news arrived that I was to leave for the Cape. My own throat and my eyes were very full as I said goodbye to you, and I had to stay in the little dining room a little to collect myself before appearing before the public downstairs.[10]

He was seen off at Paddington by a large crowd of well-wishers and many others lined the stations on the route to Dartmouth.

Wolseley and his staff reached Cape Town on 23 June 1879. There he received two pieces of important information: the first was that the Zulus had killed Louis, the Prince Imperial and son of Napoleon III, and there was to be a court of inquiry into the incident; the second was that, after months of relative inactivity, the news that he was about to be superseded had spurred Chelmsford into action.[11] Chelmsford now planned to advance on King Cetshwayo's kraal at his capital Ulundi on 1 June with three times the number of men that had accompanied him on the first invasion of Zululand in January. Wolseley was appalled by both pieces of news. He wrote to his wife expressing his sympathy for Empress Eugénie, the mother of the Prince Imperial. He was also dismayed to find that although Chelmsford was now invading Zululand with only two columns – one under Chelmsford himself and one under Major-General Henry Crealock – instead of the four of the January invasion, the columns were again operating independently and with no means of communicating and supporting each other.[12] Disaster appeared imminent so Wolseley made all haste to reach Durban as quickly as possible and travel overland to the seat of the war. He sent orders to Crealock and Chelmsford, ordering them to stop all operations and not to communicate directly with England or South Africa without his permission. Chelmsford received his telegram on 2 July when he was only four miles from Ulundi.[13]

Wolseley arrived at Durban on 28 June and travelled immediately to Pietermaritzburg where he was sworn in as High Commissioner. Two days later he met seventy native chiefs from Natal to win their support for the transport of supplies. Reliance on ox-drawn transport seriously slowed the progress of the columns and Wolseley wanted the natives to act as bearers. At Pietermaritzburg, he heard that Chelmsford was only seventeen miles from Ulundi and Crealock's column was much further away. Wolseley therefore rushed back to Durban to board a ship that would take him to Port Durnford, on the Zululand coast. The sea was so rough that a landing was impossible and a frustrated Wolseley was forced to return to Durban and to travel overland to Port Durnford. There he met John Dunn who had lived among the Zulus and whom he heard was 'a power in Zululand and I intend making as much use of him as possible'. He envisaged giving Dunn an important role in the settlement of Zululand, once Cetshwayo's power had been destroyed.[14] While he was attempting to reach Zululand, Chelmsford, in complete disobedience to Wolseley's orders, reached Ulundi with 4000 British soldiers and 1000 native allies. On 4 July he attacked and defeated the Zulu army of an estimated number of 20,000.

Wolseley received the news while still at Durban and seems to have been delighted. Telegrams were sent home proclaiming that the war was over. The reinforcements on their way to Zululand were either turned back while still at sea or retained at Cape Town. However, the war was not over. Chelmsford made no attempt to hold Ulundi nor to capture Cetshwayo, who had escaped when it was clear the Zulus would be defeated. Chelmsford was censured by Wolseley for these failures, although he argued that Wolseley had given him no orders on what to do after the battle had been won. That was true, but only because Chelmsford had been ordered not to fight a battle until Wolseley's arrival. Chelmsford met Wolseley at St Pauls mission station on 15 July while travelling back to Durban and then back to Britain, leaving him to undertake the reoccupation of Ulundi, the capture of Cetshwayo – who Chelmsford had expected to surrender after the battle – and the settlement of Zululand. The two men 'studiously avoided all subjects upon which there could be any difference of opinion'.[15]

Wolseley spent the next month assessing the states of affairs in Zululand and planning the capture of Cetshwayo. He could not undertake operations immediately because of the state of the troops and the quality of the commanders. Dunn informed him that the withdrawal from Ulundi had strengthened Cetshwayo's position and that, far from being ready to surrender, the king was gathering about three or four hundred troops around him. Wolseley concluded that 'Cetewayo must either be killed or taken prisoner or driven from Zululand before this war is considered over and before the country can ever be restored to peace and order'.[16] Many of the troops who had marched with Chelmsford and Crealock were too exhausted for further active service and Wolseley sent many of them home. This caused alarm in Parliament where some members felt that this was evidence that Wolseley planned to kill Cetshwayo rather than to capture him. The Duke of Cambridge was also anxious that he was sending too many troops home and had not even landed the Royal Marines who had been sent out at great expense.[17] He had been forced to send home Major Redvers Buller and Brigadier-General Evelyn Wood, who had 'been the life and soul of this war', because they admitted to being too exhausted to continue. This left him short of experienced commanders. He wrote to the Duke of Cambridge, 'For want of really good leaders here, I am forced to give the command of columns I am about to operate with to officers holding the rank of only Lieutenant-Colonel'.[18]

By mid August, most of the Zulu chiefs had met Wolseley at Ulundi to surrender. Cetshwayo was thought to have sought refuge in the thick Ngome forest thirty miles north of Ulundi. Wolseley set up the main camp at Ulundi and established fortified posts throughout Zululand from which patrols would go in search of Cetshwayo. Gradually more and more of the king's supporters came in to surrender but it was not until 28 August, the seventieth day of the search, that Cetshwayo was captured by Lord Gifford. On 31 August he reached Wolseley's camp: 'He has a very wise countainance [sic] and is quite the King in his bearing and deportment. He is very fat, but as he is tall he carries it off: he is very black, and wore round him a coloured tablecloth'.[19] Cetshwayo was sent to be imprisoned in Cape Town but left Wolseley a necklace of lion's claws. He sent it home to be broken up, instructing his wife to have some claws engraved 'Cetewayo, 28th August 1879', and then give them to various female friends whom he listed.[20]

Wolseley believed that the capture of Cetshwayo marked the end of the Zulu War but the War Office disagreed. In March 1880 he was furious to discover that the clasp for Zululand was to be awarded for service between 11 January and 4 July, the date of the battle of Ulundi. He claimed that 'I, and I alone brought the Zulu war to an end', and threatened to resign if the dates were not changed.[21] The War Office gave in and the capture of Cetshwayo was accepted as the real end of the Zulu War.

The government had made it clear that there was to be no annexation of Zululand nor interference in the administration of the country beyond what was necessary to secure peace and safeguard the interests of its neighbours. The settlement of Zululand divided the country into thirteen provinces under chiefs drawn from ruling houses of the pre-Chaka era. Every chief was required to sign a statement promising to abolish the Zulu military system, not to import arms or make war, and not to seize land. The most important frontier territory, neighbouring Natal, was given to John Dunn. The settlement has been described by one historian as 'an act of scuttle'.[22] However, Wolseley described it as based on expediency because it was important not to add to the 'already serious and heavy responsibilities of Empire in South Africa'.[23] This was undoubtedly true: one feature of Wolseley's pronouncements on imperial policy was his desire to restrict

the size of the British forces needed to defend each area. But the settlement
ignored local factors. The High Commissioner at the Cape, Sir Bartle Frere,
was not consulted in advance on the settlement and was greatly disturbed
by its contents. He believed that British Residents should have been imposed
on each chief to oversee internal affairs, otherwise there was the danger of
Zulu rule falling into disrepute, leaving the way open for one powerful
chief to unite the country.[24] Nevertheless, the home government was pleased
with the settlement. Disraeli noted of Wolseley: 'All he has promised and
proposed he has fulfilled. I entirely approve of everything he has done
and look upon him as a first-rate man'.[25]

The settlement of Zululand fundamentally altered the balance of power
in South Africa. The destruction of Zulu military power meant that the
white colonists were totally dominant in the region with one exception,
the area in the north-east corner of the Transvaal controlled by the Pedi
robber-baron Sekhukhuni. Yet the white population was not united: the
Boers in the Transvaal were deeply unhappy about the annexation of January
1877 and were agitating for the restoration of their independence. So long
as the Zulus had been a power on their borders, the Boers were willing to
await the constitution promised them by Theophilus Shepstone in 1877.
With the end of Zulu power and no external threat to their country, the
Boers began to talk of war. Therefore in September 1879 Wolseley visited
the Transvaal to meet the Boer leaders. On 19 September he met Petrus
Joubert and informed him that annexation was 'irrevocable' but that he
was willing to hear Joubert's suggestions on the interests and welfare of the
population. He found Joubert unwilling to consider any cooperation with
the British government.[26] Wolseley pressed ahead with his plan to secure
the British position: on 4 October he published a proclamation forming a
new Executive Council whose members would be selected by the governor
to replace the former Volksraad. A Legislative Council would be established
at a later date. This system of government was similar to the one Wolseley
had set up in Natal and Cyprus. It was done without the sanction of the
Colonial Office and the Letters Patent were not promulgated in Parliament
until 8 November 1879.

He judged that the Boers should be content with the Executive Council
and the promise of a Legislative Council and left the Transvaal to its own
resources while he turned his attention to the last native chief capable of
causing the white population difficulties: Sekhukhuni, who was leading the
Pedi on raids on local Boer farms, massacring the inhabitants and seizing
the cattle. A Boer expedition under Thoms Burgers had failed to dislodge
him in 1876 and, in 1878, a weak British force under Colonel Hugh Rowlands
was equally unsuccessful. Sekhukhuni's stronghold, the Fighting Kopje, was

situated in steep mountains, honeycombed with caves and strengthened by dug-outs and zarebas.[27] It was guarded by 6000 warriors of whom two-thirds were armed with rifles.[28] It was therefore not a simple position to attack and capture.

Two officers, Major Charles Carrington and Captain Charles Clarke, were sent to reconnoitre the area in September and to offer Sekhukhuni peace terms, which were rejected on 27 October. Therefore Wolseley designed an attack on the Fighting Kopje. The first difficulty was how best to approach the mountain. The route from the north, which Burgers had taken, was suitable for wheeled transport but well defended by outlying kopjes. The route from the east taken by Rowlands was less well defended but only suitable for pack transport and there was a shortage of water in the area. Wolseley decided to take this route for the approach, but to move round the mountain to attack the Fighting Kopje from the north. This route would be taken by the main fighting force of British infantry, the 21st and 94th regiments, and the Swazi auxiliaries. The eastern part of the mountain would be simultaneously attacked by Bantu auxiliaries with a few British infantry. The total number of the so-called Transvaal Field Force was 1400 British infantry, 400 colonial cavalry and nearly 10,000 natives, of whom the Swazis formed the vast majority.

Wolseley had wanted to use the Swazis against the Zulus but had abandoned this plan on the grounds that 'I have to think of the howling Societies at home who have sympathy with all black men whilst they care nothing for the miseries inflicted on their own kith and kin who have the misfortune to be located near these interesting niggers'.[29] The Swazis were known not to take prisoners: this did not appear to matter when it was a question of destroying Sekhukhuni but was of concern when it was hoped to effect a peaceful settlement on a country like Zululand. His belief was that, after the losses in the Zulu and Afghan wars, the British public would not stomach heavy losses among white troops. In contrast, Swazi losses would be discounted in most circles.

Meticulous plans for transport and supply were made by the acting Chief of Staff, Henry Brackenbury. Detachments of the Royal Engineers were employed building roads approaching the stronghold. The command of the actual assault was given to Lieutenant-Colonel Baker Russell, whose orders for immediate departure for India Wolseley conveniently ignored. Wolseley arrived at Fort Albert Edward on 23 November and decided that sufficient supplies had been collected to allow the march into the valley to the south of the Fighting Kopje to begin. He accompanied the main column and on 27 November rode up to within 800 or 1000 yards of the Fighting Kopje and was not fired upon. That night the Swazis, who were to form the main part of the assault, moved into position at the foot of the mountain. In the early hours of the morning Wolseley was disturbed to hear from their commander, Bushman, that they refused to climb the mountain in the dark. At first light the Swazis advanced, but along a path east to the one planned for their ascent. They were nevertheless in position to assault the upper part of the Fighting Kopje and to slaughter the Pedi fleeing from the British infantry attack below them. Explosives were thrown into the caves and the town set on fire. Wolseley watched the battle from a short distance away and was impressed by the fighting prowess of both sides: 'the enemy fought with great pluck to the last, and sounded their horns all through our fire on the koppie'.[30] During the night Sekhukhuni escaped from the Fighting Kopje and on the following day the town surrendered. He was captured on 2 December and taken to Pretoria.

Wolseley was both relieved by his success, 'I have cracked the nut, thank God, and Sekukuni's Town is now a thing of the past', and proud of the fighting abilities of the young soldiers under his command. He was furious that the war correspondent W. H. Russell, for the *Daily Telegraph*, who had joined him in September, had written articles criticising the conduct of the young soldiers alleging, in particular, that they had engaged in farm burning. Wolseley sent home 'a most crushing answer' and put down Russell's attitude to sour grapes after Captain Hugh McCalmont had terrified the old man by putting a baby ape in his bed.[31] The Sekhukhuni campaign was also, as Wolseley pointed out in letters to the Duke of Cambridge, the first time that British troops had gone on the offensive in battle in South Africa.[32] The Queen telegraphed her congratulations from Windsor Castle. The government, beleaguered at home over its disastrous policies in South Africa and Afghanistan, was also overjoyed at his success. Disraeli wrote to his friend Lady Bradford: 'Sir Garnet has not disappointed me. He is one of those men who not only succeed, but succeed quickly. Nothing can give you an idea of the jealousy, hatred, and all uncharitableness of the Horse Guards against our only soldier'.[33] The losses had been remarkably low: the British lost three officers dead and seven wounded, four rank and file dead and thirty wounded; the Swazis lost about 600 men. The campaign had also been cheap: it cost £383,000, far less than the Zulu War.[34]

Pretoria greeted the victor over Sekhukhuni with great enthusiasm, but behind the scenes the Boers were continuing to agitate for the restoration of their independence. Wolseley was extremely dismissive of the Boers. He described them as 'the only white race I know of that has been steadily going back towards barbarism' and rated them as below the Zulu in intellect.[35] At the request of the British resident in Pretoria, Colonel Owen Lanyon, Wolseley concentrated all available troops in the area while he himself was preparing to move against Sekhukhuni, 'hoping by a display of military strength to overawe the turbulent, and to impart some courage into the hearts of the desponding and demoralised'.[36] Yet he largely dismissed the strength of the Boer opposition to confederation and compounded this error by deriding the military strength of the Boers. His opinion was that the Boers were cowards who 'go on playing at soldiers and blustering, knowing in their hearts they would bolt at the sight of the first troop of Dragoons they saw'.[37] This belief was strengthened by the failure of the Boer meeting held near Potchestroon on 10 December to achieve anything. However, it can be argued that it was British weakness that was demonstrated during this meeting: Andries Pretorius, chairman of the People's Committee, and William Bok, the secretary, were arrested by British troops for treason. It seemed unlikely, however, that a trial in Pretoria would succeed in convicting them so they were released.

Wolseley was determined that the Transvaal should remain a part of British South Africa. Unlike Zululand, which was of little value, the Transvaal 'is rich in minerals; gold has already been found in quantities, and there can be little doubt that larger and still more valuable goldfields will sooner or later be discovered'. Therefore, he continued in this letter to the Colonial Secretary, Sir Michael Hicks Beach, the British government should not weaken in its resolve for confederation, because the exploitation of the gold fields would bring a large British population into the Transvaal and the Boers would eventually become a small minority. Consequently, it was worthwhile bearing the cost of a garrison of two to three hundred troops in the country until that situation came about.[38] But the Conservative government was losing faith in its South African policy in the face of increasing Liberal opposition to it, particularly in Gladstone's Midlothian campaign. Wolseley became increasingly morose about the prospects of his ever leaving the region: 'the present Ministry are in a funk about their South African policy, and my presence here is supposed by them to be a help, so I am kept doing next to nothing to serve the exigencies of party'. His journal reveals a similar depression and anger with Hicks Beach whom he now renamed Higgs-Bitch.[39] He had no desire to be linked with any policy of withdrawal in South Africa and was anxious to leave before such a policy was put into practice. Finally, on 5 May 1880, he was recalled home and his friend Major-General George Colley succeeded him in the command in South Africa.

In England, he made it clear that he was very keen to resume the reform of the army either at the War Office or in India. In February 1879 he wrote to the Secretary of State for India, the Marquess of Salisbury, that he was interested in being appointed Commander-in-Chief in India:

I believe that great reforms are possible in the Indian army, and I should like
to carry them out before I turn into a cut and dry old general to who [sic]
reforms are an abomination. All the young school of soldiers are well aware that
considerable reforms are required in our home army also, but as I am known
to hold these views I can never hope for any great military position in England
under the existing regime at the Horse Guards. My only opening therefore is in
India.[40]

He was not appointed to replace General Sir Frederick Haines as Commander-
in-Chief in India: General Frederick Roberts, the victor of the Second Afghan
War, was appointed instead. Thereafter the supporters of Wolseley and
Roberts clashed over the subject of army reform, since Roberts was more
conservative than Wolseley. The consequent divisions in the Victorian army
damaged its reform.

Later, Wolseley wrote on why he believed he failed to get this command:
the Duke of Cambridge's

dislike for me was so great at that time that, whilst he was very anxious to get
me away from Army Head Quarters, he feared to give me any high post abroad,
lest it should add to my influence in the Army, and make me so powerful that
I might possibly oust him from his own position which he had come to regard
as permanently his. His interest was to keep all high military positions in the
hands of creatires [sic] who would do his bidding.[41]

His reputation had been enhanced by his successful work abroad, both in
Cyprus and in South Africa. He was highly regarded by many politicians
but was viewed with suspicion by the Queen and the Duke of Cambridge.
Yet Wolseley did not mean to offend these august personages. He was
horrified to be informed by Sir Henry Ponsonby, the Queen's Private
Secretary, that the Queen had been upset by a letter he had written to her
in which he had praised the Prince Consort for having been an advocate
of army reform. He had meant this as a compliment, whereas the Queen
took it as an insult because 'the Queen very naturally adopts the Duke of
Cambridge's outlook'.[42] Wolseley was equally anxious not to offend the
Duke: while in South Africa, he wrote an article on army promotion but
suppressed it because it was 'too plainspoken for publication' and might
make all future cooperation between the Duke and himself impossible.[43]

He was offered the post of Quartermaster General at the War Office, in
February 1880, but did not accept the offer immediately because he was
still hoping to be appointed to the command in India. He changed his
mind in April when it was clear that the Conservative government had lost
the election and that Gladstone and the Liberals had been returned to
power. This change of government was of importance to Wolseley in several

ways. The Liberals had been returned to power largely because of dissatisfaction with the imperial policy of the Conservatives. During the winter of 1879–80 Gladstone toured southern Scotland – the Midlothian campaign – denouncing Conservative imperial policy as immoral. Wolseley thought that 'these professors who are now coming into office are less disposed to fight than the Tory party', and therefore there would be less likelihood of an active field command. Furthermore, the pace of army reform had slowed during the term of the Conservative government, 'whereas the Liberals will probably take it up, and if they do, will look to me for advice'.[44] Consequently, he hoped that he could effect some great reforms of the army under the new government. He was, however, aware of a major difficulty: 'I cannot pull with the Duke and we shall have continued rows and he will hate me more than before if indeed that be possible'.[45]

Wolseley arrived back in England on 24 May 1880 and, after a period of leave, took up his appointment as Quartermaster General on 1 July. He received no reward for his service in South Africa other than a GCB. His local rank of Full General was not confirmed by the War Office. A greater disappointment was that he received no command in India despite the reinforcements being sent there: 'All the swells have left this but I presume there is no chance of my being sent out or I should have heard of it by this time'.[46]

10

Quartermaster General

Wolseley took up his appointment as Quartermaster General under a new government and a new Secretary of State, Hugh Childers.[1] He looked forward to a further period of army reform because Childers had previously been successful in reforming the Admiralty. He later wrote that Childers 'was a very keen Army Reformer, but first of all he was a devoted follower of Mr Gladstone'.[2] The qualifying clause was necessary because Gladstone was the dominant force in his own government. While Wolseley had no quarrel with Gladstone's domestic policies until the end of 1885, when Home Rule for Ireland became an issue, he was at odds with the Liberal imperial policy, which he believed damaged Britain's prestige abroad. Gladstone had come to power largely because the electorate had turned against the Conservatives' imperial policy, which had led to war in Afghanistan and war and crisis in South Africa, and wanted cuts in government expenditure.

Wolseley left South Africa believing that he had settled the Transvaal, and that the Boers were prepared to wait for future discussions on the whole question of confederation. His friend and successor in South Africa, Major-General George Colley, agreed that the Transvaal was quiet. On 24 August 1880 he recommended a reduction in the British garrison there.[3] However, the Boers were waiting to see what the new Liberal government would do. During his Midlothian election campaign Gladstone had spoken in favour of restoring self-government to the Boers but showed no great hurry in honouring his pledge. This statement, coupled with the military weakness of Britain in the country (Colley commanded approximately 5000 men), led the Boers to pursue a bold policy. On 19 December 1880 Colley shocked the Colonial Office by telegraphing that 5000 Boers had occupied the town of Heidelberg and established a government there. A week later he reported that the rebellion was spreading; and that the British High Commissioner in the Transvaal, Sir Owen Lanyon, had been ordered to give up the keys of office. Furthermore, a British column sent to strengthen the Transvaal garrison had been ambushed en route at Bronkhurst Spruit and had suffered high casualties. The Colonial Secretary, Lord Kimberley, reacted quickly, and Childers agreed to the despatch of a regiment to South Africa.[4]

Events now moved rapidly beyond the British government's control. The Boers crossed into Natal at the beginning of January 1881 and, on 21 January, Gladstone told the House of Commons that Britain would fight to reestablish its authority in the Transvaal before making a settlement with the Boers. No one, however, had bargained for the superior rifle shooting of the Boers, whose tactics were to remain concealed and snipe at the British who, advancing in close formation, were highly visible in their red uniforms and white helmets. On 28 January Colley was defeated at Laing's Nek: the Colonial Office then informed him that he should either defeat the Boers quickly or end hostilities before the war spread. This was a very real danger since British troops were already engaged quelling a native insurrection in Pondoland which threatened to cross Natal and infect the Zulus. Britain also feared that the Boers of the Orange Free State might be tempted to join their Transvaal kin. Colley's reaction was to attack again, at the Ingogo River on 8 February, even though he knew that the Boer commander, Piet Joubert, was ready to negotiate peace terms. The Boer offer was repeated even after Colley's defeat at the Ingogo.[5]

During February the Colonial Office repeatedly urged Colley to negotiate peace with the Boers but Colley was determined to restore his reputation and that of his troops. On 21 February he wrote to Wolseley: 'I am afraid I have not fulfilled your expectations. I am now getting together a force with which I could command success but the Home Government seems so anxious to terminate the contest'.[6] That day Colley sent the Boer President, Paul Kruger, an ultimatum with the terms for negotiation but gave him only forty-eight hours in which to reply. Kruger could not be contacted within the time limit so Colley attacked Majuba Hill, the high ground overlooking the Boer positions, on 26 February. He, and a mixed force of 554 men taken from the 58th, 60th and 92nd regiments, reached the summit without difficulty.[7] There they committed two basic errors: they did not dig in, 'a crime, not so much against the science of war as against the art of war', and they did not reconnoitre the position. The result was that the Boers were able to advance uphill, using dead ground Colley did not realise existed, and attack the British party. Colley was killed and 'a panic seized all the troops concerned, and this ended in a disaster without any real loss to the attacking party'.[8]

The news of Majuba reached London on 28 February. Wolseley mourned his dead friend, and later asked another member of the ring, Frederick Maurice, to publish Colley's letters because Colley was 'the ablest man I knew in any walk of life, and although I am well aware that he under estimated the fighting power and strength of his enemy, I still think so'. Evelyn Wood, Colley's immediate successor in South Africa, echoed this

1. Wolseley in 1880, painting by Paul Besnard (*National Portrait Gallery*)

2. Wolseley as an ensign in the 80th Foot.

3. The young Garnet Wolseley

4. The sinking of HM Transport *Transit*, July 1857, a contemporary sketch.

5. Storming Myat-Toon's stronghold, Burmah, February 1853. 'Impetuously eager to distinguish himself in this, his first serious fight, the young officer was rushing forward, well ahead of his men.'

6. In the trenches before Sebastopol, 1855. 'A shell had fallen on the magazine … and an explosion was momentarily expected. At the risk of being blown to atoms, Peel and Wolseley jumped into the trench, pulled down the sand-bags, and thus prevented a disaster which would otherwise have been inevitable.'

7. General Charles Gordon's departure from Charing Cross Station. The Duke of Cambridge is shaking hands with him. Wolseley stands between them.

8. Wolseley going up the Nile.
Caricature by 'Assus'

9. Staff officer in full Sudan uniform

10. George, 2nd Duke of Cambridge (1819–1904), Commander-in-Chief of the army. Pencil drawing by Frederick Sargent, *c.* 1880 (*National Protrait Gallery*)

11. Redvers Buller

12. On campaign in Egypt

13. Louisa Wolseley, miniature by
Turrell

14. Frances Wolseley, Wolseley's only
child

15. Garnet and Louisa Wolseley, *c.* 1890

16. The War Office, Pall Mall, 1885

17. The Ranger's House, Greenwich Park, 1888

18.   Garnet and Louise Wolseley at Hampton Court Palace, 1904

sentiment: 'For him success was impossible, no smaller mind would have attempted to achieve it with the totally inadequate means at hand'.[9]

At first it appeared that the government was determined to fight and defeat the Boers: on 3 March reinforcements were sent out under Major-General Frederick Roberts, who had recently returned from Afghanistan. However, before Roberts arrived in South Africa, the government had changed its mind. It ordered Evelyn Wood to negotiate an armistice with the Boers, which he did on 6 March. At the end of March a peace treaty was signed and the Boers dispersed to their homes. Under the terms of the Pretoria Convention the full independence of the Boers, as enshrined in the 1852 Sand River Convention, was not restored; instead the Boers received self-government under British suzerainty. A British Resident would remain in Pretoria and Britain would control the Transvaal's foreign relations and native affairs.[10]

The terms of the peace treaty horrified many people in Britain. The Queen felt that is was a 'humiliating' peace. Gladstone's private secretary, Edward Hamilton, was surprised that no revenge had been taken for Majuba before Britain surrendered 'what we had no business ever to have taken'. Wood was criticised in the press for the weak treaty, and Childers attempted to reassure him that 'everyone knows you are guided by Instructions from home, which the telegraph makes now more detailed than ever'.[11]

Having been indignant about the vacillating policy of the government towards the Boers, Wolseley furious with Wood for signing a peace treaty 'that has injured our national renown most seriously abroad'. He wrote later:

> I feel sure we should never have relinquished our hold over the Transvaal. If we were to have a fight upon the question, how much better it would have been to have had it when the Boers possessed no artillery, were only armed with bad sporting rifles, had very little ammunition and still less money than in 1899.[12]

His argument was that the 1881 settlement had allowed the Boers to remain a strong force capable of challenging British supremacy in South Africa at any time of their choosing. British awareness of this challenge is demonstrated by the fact that the pre-war establishment of four battalions in South Africa was now raised to twelve infantry battalions and four cavalry regiments. It became a great point with every Colonial Secretary from 1881 until 1895 to avoid provoking another Boer challenge and another war.[13]

The government's withdrawal from the Transvaal was matched by its policy towards Afghanistan but, on this point, Wolseley supported the government. The Second Afghan War ended when Roberts routed the Afghan army near Kabul on 3 September 1880. There followed a debate on future policy in the region which turned on whether or not the Afghan town of Kandahar should be retained. The Queen, the Duke of Cambridge and the two generals of the war, Sir Donald Stewart and Roberts, argued for retention, on the grounds that Kandahar gave Britain and India a forward post from which it could advance against an invading Russian army. The Cabinet was unanimous in favour of withdrawal, seeking to reduce the military commitment in a foreign country. The new Viceroy, Lord Ripon, was also in favour of withdrawal but his council in India was not. The government had its way: in April 1881 Kandahar was transferred to the new Amir, Abdur Rahman. Roberts was extremely disappointed. He heard the news when he was on his way back from South Africa, seeing it as a further insult on top of the poor treatment he felt had been meted out to him after the war.[14] Wolseley was delighted with the withdrawal from Kandahar. He had feared that the retention of the British garrison there would lead to a demand for more troops from Britain which, in turn, would place further strain on the short service system.[15]

Wolseley was right to fear for the future of short service. The two wars fought simultaneously, without the aid of the Army Reserve, had placed an immense strain on the Cardwell system because of the demands for drafts and extra battalions to be sent abroad. Furthermore, a Land War was being waged in Ireland and the garrison there had to be reinforced. Worse still, the fighting qualities of the short service soldier had come under attack from Roberts and the Duke of Cambridge. The Duke had spoken out for the long service soldiers when he told Wolseley that the best regiments in South Africa were the 13th and 57th, composed mostly of long-service troops. The Duke cast doubts on the stamina of the two short service battalions in South Africa, the 58th and 60th, which had suffered heavily at Laing's Nek and the Ingogo. In response to this criticism, Wolseley was relieved to note that the troops who had fled Majuba Hill had been seasoned long service troops fresh from service in India.[16]

In 1878 a committee was appointed under the presidency of General Sir Richard Airey to examine the organisation of the army. The pretext for Wolseley's recall from Cyprus had been to give evidence to this committee; instead he went to South Africa. The committee was formed largely of conservative officers, whom Wolseley termed 'Wellington's men', who sought to turn back the clock and undo much of the Cardwell system. In its report the committee recommended enlistment for eight years in the colours, in order to provide India with a sufficient number of well-trained, physically mature men. This was not controversial since many senior officers, including Wolseley, had accepted that six years did not achieve this goal. It was the committee's other recommendations which caused more controversy. By proposing the abolition of the linked battalion system, and the amalgamation of the brigade depots into larger depots serving more regiments, the Airey Committee called for the abolition of the main tenets of the Cardwell system.[17]

After reading the report published in March 1880, Wolseley sprang to the defence of the system. He argued that it had not received a fair trial, and that blame for its failures should be placed on the politicians who had failed to provide the funds to raise the establishment of the depots to compensate for the despatch abroad of both battalions of a regiment. In direct contradiction to his 1876 proposal, he now announced that he was opposed to extending service to thirteen or fourteen years because, 'if you so increase the period of service, you will create the idea that the soldier who has given you the best years of his life should be allowed to serve on until he has earned a pension'. Now in a senior position at the War Office, he was hostile to India's demands, claiming that service of eight years in India would seriously damage the formation of the Army Reserve unless the Secretary of State was prepared to allow more men at home to join the Reserve after three years in the colours.[18]

His alarm was unnecessary because Childers bravely ignored the recommendations of the Airey Committee. He did increase service in the colours to seven years, the half way point between Cardwell's six years and the eight proposed by the Airey Committee; but, far from abolishing the linked battalion system, Childers completed Cardwell's work and, following the recommendations of the 1872 MacDougall Committee on localisation, worked towards the territorial reorganisation of regiments including the controversial task of renaming them. A War Office committee under the Adjutant General, Charles Ellice, considered how to convert linked battalions into double-battalioned regiments. The task was not easy because of the hostility of the Queen and the Duke of Cambridge and of the battalions concerned, but was eased by the loyal support of Wolseley. In December 1880 the Queen thought she had won a victory when her private secretary, Sir Henry Ponsonby, wrote to the Duke that Childers had promised that 'in the formation of the double-battalioned territorial Regiments the numbers and special designations of the old single-battalioned Regiments and as far as possible any other valued territorial peculiarity, shall be preserved'. Childers and his assistants at the War Office were, however, aware that this would not always be possible because, unless both battalions of a territorial regiment wore the same facings, the transfer of drafts and officers between them would be difficult. The complexity of the task was demonstrated when it was proposed to put all the Highland regiments into the Royal Hunting tartan, at which the Queen made her objections known.[19] Although the regiments were allowed to retain their numbers as well as their new titles, eventually the numbers fell into disuse: regiments such as the 92nd became known thereafter as the Gordon Highlanders and the 99th as the Wiltshire Regiment.

Although recruitment had been stimulated by the prospect of war since 1878, there was still a great deal of concern over the quality of the recruits coming forward.[20] Wolseley acknowledged this problem, and in 1881 wrote an article defending the new short service soldier. In it he argued that in 1863 the average age of recruits had been twenty years and three months, and that in 1877 it had been twenty years and seven months, thereby suggesting that the short service soldier should be no worse than his long service predecessor.[21] The article deliberately ignored the fact that, under short service, the recruits and freshly-trained soldiers formed a far higher proportion of the establishment of the army as a whole than under long service, when the inexperience of the young troops could be hidden behind the ranks of the seasoned soldiers. He was ready to accept that the figures he had quoted were probably not the exact truth, since it was impossible for recruiting officers to confirm the age a recruit had given on enlistment because 'our population is so migratory that recruits are seldom enlisted in the parishes they were born in'.[22] Wolseley was therefore keen to recruit older and physically more mature men to the army. This could best be achieved by increasing the basic rate of pay: however, this course was as politically and financially unacceptable in 1880 as it had been earlier.

Instead, Childers attempted to attract men to the army by improving the conditions of service and the chances of employment while in the Army Reserve. Flogging had been largely abolished in the peacetime army in 1868, but flogging on active service was only abolished in 1881. The Queen questioned the wisdom of this: 'the Queen hates the system of flogging, but sees no alternative in extreme cases on active service'. There was also concern expressed by senior officers that under the new laws the only punishment for serious offences on active service was shooting the offender after he had been found guilty by a court martial. The law did, however, allow for the use of imprisonment and keeping the prisoner in a fixed position for a period of time as an alternative.[23] Wolseley, who wanted flogging retained, would become the first commander in the field, in Egypt in 1882, to experience the effect on discipline of its abolition. Other measures Childers hoped to introduce achieved less success: the rise in the pay of non-commissioned officers did not increase the number of suitable men coming forward for re-enlistment, and the government did not assist Childers in his attempt to ensure that all future messengers in government departments should be ex-soldiers or in the Army Reserve.

Conversely, the government also considered a proposal that would damage the chances of employment of the Army Reservists. In 1881 the Financial Secretary, Henry Campbell-Bannerman, put forward a proposal to make reservists liable for recall to the colours during the first year of their reserve service. This proposal was strongly approved of by the Adjutant General and the Duke of Cambridge, both of whom viewed it as a means of avoiding a repetition of the difficulties of 1879 when two small wars were fought simultaneously without the Reserve. Wolseley argued strongly against the proposal. He did not believe that the time had come for such a definite move away from the spirit of the Cardwell reforms, and that, as the Reserve was still growing in size, no action should be taken to stop this growth. He wanted the practice of calling for volunteers from the Army Reserve for service abroad to be continued. He was supported in this by the Surveyor General of Ordnance, General Sir John Adye.[24]

Wolseley found too little to occupy his active mind in the Quartermaster General's office. The work was mostly routine, dealing with supplies to the troops, the issue of stores and equipment, and the garrison movements and the transport of troops abroad. Therefore he had plenty of free time in which to use his fame to publicise his opinions on army reform. This brought him into conflict with the Duke of Cambridge and eventually led to a government crisis. He justified his outspoken support of the army reforms on the grounds that, 'were I to hold any other language in public, or to be entirely silent, on what my experience tells me are points of vital importance to the State, I should not feel that I was acting honestly by the Army or by my country which pays me'.[25] The Duke of Cambridge, on the other hand, felt strongly that if an officer opposed the Duke's own views he was insubordinate, but a powerful position and the public's readiness to listen were of no real consequence if an officer voiced the Duke's own opinions.

At no point does this become clearer than when considering the different treatment accorded to Roberts by the Duke of Cambridge. Roberts returned to England in November 1880 as the victor of the Second Afghan War and, as a result, was invited to address a large and illustrious body at the Mansion House on 14 February 1881. Here the Duke, in introducing Roberts to his audience, which included Wolseley, gave Roberts leave to speak the truth about the state of the army as he saw it. Like Wolseley, Roberts made clear his reasons for speaking: 'it will not be possible to avoid treading upon debatable ground [but] I am actuated simply by a sincere and honest desire to place my countrymen in possession of the truth about their army'. He went on to make several points which demonstrated that his views were at variance with those of the government: he claimed that the linking and localisation of regiments was contrary to *esprit de corps*; that men were

being moved from one regiment to another with little or no concern for
their personal wishes; and that the Second Afghan War had demonstrated
that the army needed men not boys. He further made clear his opinion
'that we are sacrificing our army to obtain a reserve', and spoke in favour
of creating two armies, one for long service abroad, and a short-service
quasi Militia for home service and the production of a reserve.[26]

All these views were in direct contradiction to the spirit and substance
of the Cardwell system and the ongoing Childers reforms. No controversy
arose from these public statements and no known reprimand was given to
Roberts by the Duke. Criticism must, however, have come from some
quarter, probably the government, because Roberts felt obliged to explain
and amplify his views in an article in the November 1882 issue of *Nineteenth
Century*. He wrote 'it never occurred to me that the old system of long
service could be reverted to. What I desired to show was, that no trial,
however lengthened, could be satisfactory, unless due consideration were
given to the results of practical experience in the field.'[27] Roberts also gave
a definition of what he considered to be an 'old' soldier as 'a man of
between five and twelve years' service', and admitted that once a man was
over thirty years old he was of little good as a private soldier. Wolseley
would certainly have agreed with this definition but, at the War Office, he
was concerned with the problem of how to obtain enough recruits; Roberts,
in India, was concerned only about how to use them.

The difference between the official treatment of Roberts, who returned
to India to become the Commander-in-Chief there, and that accorded to
Wolseley's article 'Long and Short Service' in the March 1881 issue of
Nineteenth Century is very marked. In his article Wolseley set out to be
deliberately controversial. He started his article by saying that 'all armies
and navies are naturally conservative in their tendencies, and consequently
view with great suspicion any changes effected by a Liberal Government'.
After listing the failings of the long service system, and outlining the benefits
of short service, he made a spirited attack on regimental officers: 'in en-
deavouring to account for the dislike with which short service is generally
viewed in the army, the fact that it adds very considerably to the daily work
of regimental officers must not be forgotten'. These officers must now
become instructors, as in the German Army, and 'many hours of idleness
daily, the long periods of leave, must be abandoned'. Wolseley admitted
that the need for volunteers from a number of regiments to make one up
to full strength for active service was a problem but voiced the hope that
once the Reserve was fully established the problem would disappear because
volunteers would be called upon from it and not from regiments of the
line.[28]

An article in the May 1881 issue of *Blackwood's Magazine* contrasted Roberts's speech with Wolseley's article and, with a degree of truth, suggested that 'Sir Frederick looks at the point from within, Sir Garnet views it from without, the profession; and it must be said that if the army hangs on the words of Sir Frederick with delight the words of Sir Garnet are nevertheless more likely to prevail'. Furthermore, this author and others suggested that Wolseley's real crime was less his defence of a flawed system, more that he treated 'the profession to which he has the honour of belonging with very considerable scorn'.[29]

While still in South Africa, Wolseley expressed his resentment at lacking a patron who could advance his career, since patronage was a fact of Victorian life:

> Throughout my life I have always felt myself heavily weighted in the race for power, and I often think, if I had had for my father a Lord Chancellor, as Chelmsford had, instead of being a poor Major in a marching Regiment, what could now have been my position! How many times in my life might not the authorities have pushed me on.[30]

But his career was now about to take an unexpected turn as the Liberal government itself became his patron. The Conservatives in the House of Lords had been vociferous in their opposition to the Cardwell reforms, and Childers wanted to ensure that his reforms would not encounter a similar rough passage. He therefore asked Gladstone to seek the Queen's permission to raise Wolseley to a peerage so that he could act as the government spokesman for army reform in the House of Lords. In March 1881 Gladstone asked the Queen to make Wolseley a peer. He had no doubt that it would prove a controversial request: in conversation with his private secretary, Edward Hamilton, Gladstone described the proposal as 'a nasty pill for Her'. It was one which the Queen was not prepared to swallow without a fight. There was a precedent for Gladstone's action: when in 1870 he had asked the Queen to make Sir William Mansfield a peer, Lord Sandhurst, specifically to assist in the process of army reform, she had done so.[31]

There were two main arguments against raising Wolseley to the peerage: first, the Duke of Cambridge did not want him in the House of Lords at all; and, secondly, there was the danger that by making the Quartermaster General a peer it might become a political office. The Duke based his opposition to Wolseley on the charge that he was insubordinate, and that his use of the press and his public speeches were undermining the Duke's role as head of the army. If he were admitted to the House of Lords, where the Duke sat and spoke as the Commander-in-Chief, who could predict what mischief he could get up to when speaking to such a body? The matter did not simply stop with the threat of Wolseley himself, but extended into a general dispute over who was actually the head of the British Army. The Queen's private secretary, Ponsonby, wrote to Childers that the Queen accepted without question the Duke's charge that Wolseley was insubordinate. Gladstone received a similar missive, and described it to Earl Granville, the Foreign Secretary, as 'a "no surrender" – "non possumus" – nail the colours to the mast, break the bridges and burn the boats, letter!' [32] On 4 March 1881 Childers replied that he had 'watched Sir Garnet Wolseley's conduct narrowly since I became Secretary of State' and had found 'his behaviour has been most becoming both to myself as the Head of the Department, and to his Royal Highness as his immediate superior'. On the same day he further pointed out to Gladstone, when forwarding Ponsonby's letter and his own reply, that 'if His Royal Highness had any complaint against a subordinate officer to which he wished Her Majesty's attention to be drawn, he should have submitted the matter to me'.[33] He had not done so but had instead made use of his connection with the Royal Family. Therefore, Childers concluded that the differences between the Duke and Wolseley rested on personal grounds and that the charge of insubordination had no foundation.

On the question of whether Wolseley should continue serving as Quartermaster General while a peer, Childers had little sympathy for the position of the Duke of Cambridge and the Queen. He reported to Gladstone on 7 March that he had warned the Duke that the imposition of such a condition would be 'a very dangerous precedent as it would mean that no Peer could be employed at Head Quarters'.[34] Gladstone made the same point in a memorandum to the Cabinet, in which he pointed out that many senior officers were rewarded with peerages for services rendered, and that to forbid them to hold high positions at the War Office would have the effect of dangerously reducing the size of the pool from which such appointments could be made. The Queen, while refusing to take a step that might politicise the army, was prepared to accept that the government needed support in the House of Lords and therefore suggested that Sir Neville Chamberlain might be a suitable man to assist the government.[35]

The real trouble was that, if Wolseley were admitted to the House of Lords and remained in the office of Quartermaster General, the members of the Lords and the public would be in a position to judge for themselves the opposing positions on army reform held by a senior officer and the Commander-in-Chief. The Duke was naturally very concerned that the public might side with Wolseley against him. The matter dragged on into May, leading Edward Hamilton to conclude that the whole proposal had been a mistake 'and it is worth considering whether the admission of a mistake would not be better than pursuing a matter which the Sovereign strongly disapproves, which the Army would resent, and which the House of Lords would not welcome'.[36] Gladstone was deeply committed to the peerage question and even threatened to resign if the Queen refused to accept his recommendation. Granville urged caution over the use of this threat because more serious issues might arise in the future, 'and threats of resignation ought not to be frequent'.[37]

The depth of Wolseley's commitment to army reform and his recognition of the importance of mobilising the public are at no point clearer than when considering the proposal he put forward after the government had all but abandoned the idea of making him a peer. On hearing of the postponement of the matter, he indicated to Childers that, if the argument still centred round the inadvisability of having the Quartermaster General sit in the House of Lords, he was prepared to resign his position and accept a peerage and the position of Governor-General of Gibraltar in succession to Lord Robert Napier. He would then be able to support the government in its programme of reform; the Quartermaster General had, in any case, virtually become 'a sinecure' since the changes of 1871–72.[38] This proposal was declined on the grounds that he had not realised that Napier still had another year to serve in Gibraltar, and that such a posting would effectively end his career as an active fighting general. Rather than send him to Gibraltar, Childers suggested to Gladstone that John Morley might be promoted from his existing position as Under Secretary for War, and a seat found for Wolseley to replace him.[39] With his attention distracted by Ireland, Gladstone preferred to let the matter rest as it was. Nevertheless, the proposal demonstrated that Wolseley was prepared to abandon his attempts to reform the army from within the War Office and instead to concentrate his attention on publicising the cause of reform in the House of Lords, where he would get more publicity. He believed that if he held such a minor position as that of Governor-General of Gibraltar the Duke of Cambridge would have less ground for complaint.

The government backed down on the peerage issue because it was finding its second period of office more challenging than the first. The greatest problem was in Ireland which had exploded into an often violent Land War. Over 10,000 tenants were evicted in 1880 and the leader of the Irish Nationalist party, Charles Stewart Parnell, challenged the government to find a solution. He urged public protests against landowners and their agents carrying out evictions until a fairer method of assessing rents was established. The word 'boycott' entered the language when Captain Boycott became the first victim of social ostracism. Order was restored temporarily to Ireland with the suspension of the Habeas Corpus.

A few months later, in September 1881, the government put forward Wolseley's name to succeed Charles Ellice as Adjutant General; and this time, following their earlier defeat by the Duke of Cambridge and the Queen, they were prepared to fight. As Edward Hamilton noted in his diary:

> Mr G. thinks that where there are personal objections and recommendations only; much weight may be given to reason, or even unreason of the Sovereign; but when there are reasons of public policy closely involved, then he holds that for a Prime Minister to give way is an abandonment of duty and a commencement of the process of sapping the constitution.[40]

That 'reasons of public policy' were involved there can be little doubt. One method of securing a slowing down of the reform process was for the Duke to surround himself with like-minded conservatives in high office. Childers, in replying to the Duke's refusal to accept Wolseley as Adjutant General, pointed out that the two last appointments to the War Office, of Deputy Adjutants General of the Royal Artillery and of the Royal Engineers, had both been given to men of the old school opposed to short service.[41] Again the Duke mobilised the royal family in his defence. The Queen was, at least to begin with, willing to throw her weight behind the Duke and, when the Duke threatened resignation over the issue, the Prince of Wales gave him his wholehearted support.[42]

The Duke of Cambridge fought hard to oppose the appointment. He put forward the argument that Wolseley was not the best qualified for the post and proposed Sir Lintorn Simmons instead. Simmons was unacceptable to the government because he had allied himself with the conservative officers by pressing for retrograde measures while sitting on the Airey Committee. The Duke argued that the new Adjutant General should be a man he could trust, and said of Wolseley that 'I could never feel that confidence in him, which is essential in the interests of the Public Service as well as to my own comfort and even usefulness as a public officer, should exist between the Commander-in-Chief and his right hand man the Adjutant General'. Childers could only repeat the arguments put forward earlier: 'that the Adjutant General should be an officer known to the Army to be of the new, and not of the old school'.[43]

The Duke of Cambridge complained to the Queen that Wolseley's use of the press would be a danger to himself, the Duke, and to the army because it would become politicised. The Queen sympathised with this argument, and closely questioned every visiting Cabinet Minister in order to find a solution to the problem which would be acceptable to both the Duke and the government. Sir William Harcourt, the Home Secretary, wrote to Gladstone from Balmoral that 'She is quite conscious that the Duke has put himself out of court by the ground he has taken up and the reasons he has given for his objection to Sir Garnet's appointment'. Gladstone replied to Harcourt that the Queen was making things worse 'by multiplying channels of communication'. One suggestion was taken seriously: that Roberts should become Quartermaster General and Wolseley Adjutant General in order to have representatives of both schools in the War Office.[44]

Before he could be confirmed as Adjutant General, two points remained to be cleared up: first, the exact relative roles of the Adjutant General and the Commander-in-Chief; and secondly, Wolseley's habit of speaking in public. The first point was only raised because of an article in *The Times* in early November announcing Wolseley's appointment as Adjutant General, and hinting strongly that there would be a change in the relationship between the Adjutant General and the Commander-in-Chief, giving the former more power.[45] There was no foundation for such an announcement and, after an agitated correspondence with the Queen, the government was forced to issue the official appointment of Wolseley as Adjutant General accompanied by a disclaimer denying that any change in the roles was planned.

The question of public speaking and writing was less easy to solve satisfactorily. When Wolseley's peerage had been under discussion, the Duke of Cambridge had sought an assurance from him that he would not speak in public, citing the case of Lord Tenterden who as Permanent Under Secretary had never taken his seat in the House. Wolseley's reply on that occasion was indicative of his whole approach:

> the case was in no way analogous: he could not speak without taking a party side with me it was different, for I should speak only upon military subjects, which were entirely removed from the sphere of politics. That if I spoke in favour of breechloaders and supposing His Royal Highness did not approve of them, it could only be the expression of two opinions upon a professional matter, and that no scandal could possibly arise from any such difference of opinion.[46]

The Duke disagreed, probably fearing that the voicing of any difference of professional opinion in public might lead to his opinion being disregarded with fearful consequences for his authority as the Commander-in-Chief. Before his appointment as Adjutant General was confirmed, Childers was forced to exact from Wolseley a promise that he would not 'write articles in the press or magazines, or make speeches on military affairs opposed to the Duke's views'.[47] This was an oral assurance and did not satisfy the Duke, who asked Childers to demand that he should put his promise in writing. Time would show that Wolseley had absolutely no intention of obeying this injunction; in fact, his future position could best be described as in accordance with the promise he had made to Childers in April 'that he would be as reticent on subjects in which he differed from His Royal Highness as the Duke is on subjects in which he differs from the Government'.[48]

11

Adjutant General

Wolseley took up his appointment as Adjutant General on 1 April 1882, and remained in that post until 1 October 1890. During this period he was absent from the War Office for two periods of active command in the field: from July to October 1882 in Egypt; and from August 1884 to July 1885 in the Sudan.[1] The post of Adjutant General was very important: it effectively made Wolseley the Duke of Cambridge's deputy and representative on War Office Councils in the absence of the Commander-in-Chief. His department was responsible for the discipline, training and education of all ranks, the design of clothing and equipment, the statistics of the army and recruitment. After a disappointing period as Quartermaster General, when his proposals for army reform had been weakened by the Duke of Cambridge and the previous Adjutant General, Charles Ellice, Wolseley relished the challenges of this responsible office.

The first important debate he was involved in was over the desirability of a Channel Tunnel. In 1875 the chairman of the London, Chatham and Dover Railway, Sir Alfred Watkin, had introduced a Private Member's Bill in Parliament which proposed the construction of a railway tunnel under the English Channel from Dover to the French coast. The French government was consulted and agreed to the scheme. Parliament granted permission for the company to begin experimental tunnelling and the first shafts were sunk in 1880.

In December 1881 Wolseley wrote his first memorandum on the Channel Tunnel. He announced that the construction of the tunnel could:

> be fairly described as a measure intended to annihilate all the advantages we have hitherto enjoyed from the existence of the 'silver streak', for to join England to the Continent by a permanent highway, will be to place her under the unfortunate condition of having neighbours possessing great standing armies. The construction of the tunnel would place us under those same conditions that have forced the Powers of Europe to submit to universal service.[2]

He made the same point in a speech to the debating society of University College London: conscription was unnecessary so long as the English Channel remained 'neither bridged over nor tunnelled under by a band of speculators'.[3]

In this memorandum, he also introduced a theme he would refer to again later, the speed with which an enemy could open hostilities. He asked his friend Frederick Maurice to provide the evidence for this belief. Maurice responded by writing *Hostilities without Declaration of War* in early 1883, which listed the occasions in the past when wars had begun without a formal declaration. The production of this pamphlet not only provided the War Office with some of the evidence it needed to oppose the tunnel, it also served in the future to remind politicians of the speed in which countries could move from peaceful relations to war.[4]

Wolseley was urged by the Duke of Cambridge and the Secretary of State for War, Hugh Childers, to make his hostility to the tunnel known to the public.[5] Initially Childers arranged for Wolseley's views to be published by Lord Dunsany, in an article which appeared in the February 1882 issue of the *Nineteenth Century*.[6] The public response was immediate: the windows of the offices of the Channel Tunnel Company were smashed by angry Londoners, and in April 1882 a mass petition opposed to the tunnel was organised by the editor of the journal *Nineteenth Century*, James Knowles, and was signed by many important public figures including fifty-nine generals and seventeen admirals.[7] In Parliament two conflicting points of view quickly became apparent. Lord Brabourne, who had an interest in the tunnel company, drew attention to the fact that the French felt no threat from the tunnel and that, having agreed with France that the scheme was possible, drawing back at this stage gave a clear message to the French 'that we thought them dangerous neighbours who were not to be trusted'. Lord Strathnairn introduced an issue that Wolseley fully recognised: the danger of Fenian action against the tunnel given the acute disaffection in Ireland in the early 1880s.[8]

The government was forced to take action and set up a Joint Parliamentary Select Committee chaired by Lord Lansdowne to examine the arguments. The War Office formed a Military and Scientific Committee under Lieutenant-General Sir Archibald Alison for the same purpose.[9] In April the Board of Trade ordered the Channel Tunnel Company to stop boring operations until the War Office committee had reported. Wolseley was not made a member of the Scientific Committee. Indeed membership of the committee would have been of no benefit to him: it was purely concerned with an examination of the means of defending the tunnel. In its report, issued on 17 May 1882, the committee discussed the matter under two headings: the first, surprise from within, by treachery; and secondly, attack from without. The report detailed plans for fortifications, closure or temporary obstructions such as a portcullis and the closing of the air shafts, explosion by mines or charges, and either temporary or permanent flooding of the tunnel.[10] While the committee's brief had not been to recommend whether or not the tunnel should be constructed, a recommendation against the tunnel's construction was implicit in its conclusions.

Childers was prepared to go even further in his support of Wolseley, and asked him to prepare another memorandum based on the conclusions of the Scientific Committee. He urged him to 'take care that it is sent to the public printers for publication in the shape of an official protest. I am quite prepared to put upon it officially that I fully concur in the views therein expressed, having already done so on your Confidential minute'.[11] Childers's actions demonstrate that, despite the concern over Wolseley's use of publicity when his appointment as Adjutant General was under consideration, when the Secretary of State and the Commander-in-Chief felt publicity to be a useful tool, Wolseley was seen as the ideal man to wield it.

In his memorandum of 16 June 1882, Wolseley described his views on the subject at length. While agreeing with the conclusions of the Scientific Committee, he went further into the question than the committee's remit had permitted them, and entered into the question of the desirability of the tunnel per se. His principal objection to the tunnel was that Britain had been saved from the cost of maintaining huge standing armies on a continental scale by having the natural protection of a 'great wet ditch' protecting her from aggressive neighbours. As early as 1871, he had estimated that it might be possible for 100,000 enemy soldiers to land on the southern shore of England.[12] Other commentators put the figure for a likely invasion force at nearer 40,000. In this memorandum Wolseley argued that the construction of a tunnel would reduce the numbers needed for a successful invasion to 20,000. These soldiers would hold the entrance, enabling reinforcements to be brought over quickly through the tunnel. He estimated that 'the seizing of the tunnel by a coup de main it is in my opinion a very simple operation', provided no advance warning had been given. He summed up his fears thus:

It must be remembered that the works at our end of the tunnel may be surprised by men sent through the tunnel itself, without landing a man upon our shores. A couple of thousand men might easily come through the tunnel in a train at night, avoiding all suspicion by being dressed as ordinary passengers, or passing at express speed through the tunnel with the blinds down and fully armed.[13]

In his memorandum on the subject, the Duke of Cambridge agreed with Wolseley's views on the threat of a *coup de main* by drawing attention to the fact that the Fenians had in the past attacked Chester Castle, and that no guarantee could be given that they would not attack the Dover fortifications to coincide with a French attempt on the tunnel.[14]

Despite the support of the Duke of Cambridge and Childers, Wolseley still needed to convince the parliamentary committee of the dangers of the Channel tunnel scheme. In his evidence before the Joint Select Committee he played a very cunning political game. He pointed out that all the precautions recommended by the Scientific Committee would be essential to safeguard the tunnel in times of peace but might not be sufficient in time of war. These plans were costly, though no estimates had been drawn up. Further expenditure would be essential on a regular basis as 'Dover was by no means a first-class fortress; indeed, it could only be put into the third-class category'. Its armament was outdated, and its garrison only a fraction of what would be essential to guard the mouth of the tunnel.[15] Given the cost of building fortifications for the tunnel itself, strengthening the fortifications of Dover Castle, installing new modern armament, building barracks for and maintaining a larger force in the garrison, it is perhaps unsurprising that the government rejected the idea of the construction of a tunnel under the Channel. Indeed, it is more than likely that the cost of providing security was the principal deciding factor in the rejection of the scheme, not Wolseley's somewhat far-fetched fears of trainloads of French soldiers pretending to be civilians passing through the tunnel.

The Joint Select Committee surprisingly reported in favour of the tunnel, even though the committee was badly divided on the issue. Only three members were prepared to sign the report, while six submitted separate minority reports outlining the reasons for their hostility to the scheme. In July 1883 the government decided to stop the construction of the tunnel permanently. Alfred Watkin was not easily deterred from his great project and made numerous attempts to win support for it. Watkin reintroduced his Channel Tunnel Bill in 1883 but it was swiftly rejected by 222 votes to 84. Subsequent reintroductions met with the same fate, although the majority against the Bill fell steadily, until in 1887 it was defeated by only seventy-six votes. In 1893 the War Office was again asked for its opinion and the Adjutant General, Buller, reported that no military man was in favour of the tunnel. In 1894 Watkin finally abandoned his project.[16] Wolseley and his colleagues had created so much doubt on the security of the tunnel that no government was prepared to announce to the public that it had dismissed military opinion on the vital issue of home defence.

The government was more prepared to ignore military opinion on other issues. The establishment of the Army Reserve was a cornerstone of the Cardwell system yet the government did little to ensure its efficiency. Under the law establishing the Reserve, the Secretary of State for War had the power to call out the Reserve for twelve whole days or twenty drills a year.

This was never put into practice, and the Army Reserve was not trained apart from small numbers of men who volunteered to take part in the autumn manoeuvres. The Airey Committee recommended that the Reserve should be called up for a month at a time, 'provided that the whole amount of training did not exceed the aggregate twelve days for every year of his reserve service'. The Committee believed that training was only necessary for men in the third and fourth year of their Reserve service, but these recommendations were not put into practice.[17]

Until 1882, the men of the Army Reserve had to present themselves to the paying officers four times a year, only receiving their reserve pay once it had been proved that they were effective. The system was altered in 1882, so that the reservists were now paid by Post Office orders and were only seen by the medical and military officers once a year. Wolseley and the Duke of Cambridge were alarmed by this development. Wolseley wrote to the Under Secretary of State, the Earl of Morley, that:

His Royal Highness is of opinion that an inspection of the Army Reserve men by a military officer every three months, and an annual inspection by an Army Surgeon, would be the very smallest amount of inspection that we could depend upon to serve the objects for which the Reserve exists, and that this should be regarded as a temporary measure, for as soon as it reaches its normal size, His Royal Highness would urge most strongly that regulations be issued for insuring that every Reserve man undergoes some amount of periodical drill and of musketry instruction.[18]

As he repeated in 1883, the annual medical inspection, which cost £6000 a year, was money well spent since it ensured that all men receiving Reserve pay were efficient.[19]

The two principal objections to the regular training of the Reserve were cost, and the attitude of employers to the Army Reserve. Childers was bombarded by a series of memoranda from Wolseley on the subject of training, and in 1882 he set up a committee under Wolseley's chairmanship to examine the means by which reservists could receive some form of annual training. The sittings of this committee began in June 1882, were interrupted by Wolseley's trip to Egypt, then reconvened in February 1883. The committee's principal concern was to cause the least inconvenience to the reservist so that his employment would not be affected. To this end, the reservist was to be given a free year to settle down in civilian life before being asked to select one of four systems of training for the remainder of his service with the Reserve. The options open to the reservist were: enrolment as supernumerary members of the Volunteers and qualifying as efficients therein; joining the headquarters of a regimental district or regular battalion for eight consecutive days' training; or joining a Militia battalion and training with it. For cavalrymen and Royal Horse Artillerymen, there was the additional option of joining Yeomanry regiments.[20] These options formed the basis of all discussions on the training of the Reserve for the remainder of the century.

Progress on the issue was slow. Throughout 1883 memoranda were passed between Wolseley, the Marquess of Hartington, Childers's successor as Secretary of State for War, the Surveyor General, General Sir John Adye, and the Duke of Cambridge on the subject of annual medical inspections.[21] The result was that four districts in England, two in Scotland and one in Ireland were called out for medical inspection in January 1884.[22] In January 1884 Wolseley drew the attention of the Parliamentary Under Secretary, Ralph Thompson, to the fact that the question of the training of the Reserve had not yet been settled. He pointed out that the actuaries' report on the proposals of his committee had concluded that, for 1884, the cost of training would be £34,356, and that when the Reserve reached its estimated maximum size training would cost £83,014 annually, figures which he described as a 'small price to pay for efficiency'.[23]

The occupation of Egypt after the campaign in 1882 placed a further strain on the army as many regiments had both their battalions abroad, yet their depots were not increased in size in compensation. In October 1883 Wolseley wrote a long memorandum on the state of the army to draw the attention of the Secretary of State for War to the serious difficulties facing the army. He pointed out that 26.5 per cent of the cavalry and 42.8 per cent of the infantry were men with less than one year's service. These men could not be used in time of war, nor could they be sent to India as drafts. Some battalions, including the Northamptonshire and the Argyll and Sutherland Highlanders, were barely able to function at all. Consequently, he asked that 8000 men be added to the establishment of the army immediately because, 'until this is done our military machine will go from bad to worse until it breaks down altogether'.[24] In December 1884 the Duke of Cambridge, in his annual report on the state of the army, drew Hartington's attention to this memorandum.

The government was not prepared to sanction the necessary expenditure to raise the establishment to such an extent, nor was it convinced that the recruits would be forthcoming. Instead, the War Office was forced to resort to a number of short-term expedients to keep the establishments abroad and at home to the determined level. The Foot Guards, whose strict physical standards had led to a shortfall in recruits, were allowed to enlist men for three years' service in the colours before being transferred to the Reserve. Wolseley applauded the success of this scheme, ignoring the fact that three years was deemed barely sufficient to train a soldier, and that the more rapid turnover of poorly-trained men would necessarily have an adverse effect on the efficiency of the Foot Guards in time of war. Similar schemes to move men to the Reserve early merely reduced the average age of soldiers on the home establishment further, making it less efficient. Enlistment bounties had been abolished in 1870 but, in 1883, the War Office was forced to offer bounties of £2 to men in India, whose period of colour service was about to end, to encourage them to extend their service to twelve years. The scheme met with little success. Another expedient was to control recruitment by altering the physical standards required: from 1883 to 1889 the height requirement of infantry recruits was reduced from five feet six inches to five feet three inches. Minimum chest measurements and weight were also reduced. The 1883 Anthropometric Committee considered that the average stature of an eighteen-year-old boy was five feet seven inches, weighing 137 pounds, and with a chest measurement of thirty-four inches. The army was forced to accept recruits weighing 115 pounds with a chest measurement of thirty-three inches.[25] This problem of undersized men worsened over the remainder of the century.

The condition of the rank and file was not the only concern: Wolseley was not impressed with the quality of the officers. He was deeply concerned to make the officer corps of the British Army both a profession and professional. The officer corps had been offended by Wolseley's comments in his 1881 article 'Long and Short Service'. He continued to cause offence: in a speech to the Institution of Civil Engineers in December 1882, he highlighted the excellent performance of officers from the professional corps, the Royal Artillery and the Royal Engineers, in Egypt. This earned him a reprimand from the Queen, who argued that all her officers were of equal value. Wolseley replied that the newspaper reports of his speech had been 'very poor and inaccurate'. In fact, he had praised the conduct of all the officers in Egypt: 'we had splendid soldiers commanded by splendid regimental officers'. He was criticised by W. E. Montague, in an article in *Blackwoods Magazine*, for this apparent change of heart.[26] He had not changed his opinion: he argued consistently that when the officers had something interesting to do, as when campaigning, they worked hard; it was their poor attitude to training while in garrison to which he objected.

Wolseley's experience of fighting in hot climates led him to campaign for practical fighting uniforms. In 1873 he had succeeded in dressing the men for the Asante campaign in more comfortable clothing. After the Second Afghan War, the Indian army had begun the process of introducing khaki uniforms for field service, but the British army lagged behind. Wolseley was appointed president of the Colour Committee which, in 1882, recommended the introduction of grey for service dress but the retention of red or the traditional regimental colours for full dress.[27] The Egyptian campaign, fought in the heat of the summer, lent urgency to the question. The British army suffered more casualties from heat-stroke than from enemy action. Wolseley found an ally in the Queen's son, the Duke of Connaught, who had participated in the campaign:

> The clothing supplied to the men – viz., red serges and blue serge trousers – was thoroughly inappropriate to this climate, and the men suffer terribly from the want of a cooler and more comfortable dress. Khaki is the only sensible fighting dress for our men, and had they been dressed in it like the troops from India, it would have been an inestimable boost to all.[28]

The opposition to change was strident.

The Duke of Cambridge objected to the introduction of grey because 'it is a convict colour'. The only reason grey had been recommended rather than khaki was that there had been a problem with khaki dye for serge clothing, but this was swiftly overcome and khaki was adopted in preference to grey.[29] In a speech at the Mansion House the Duke also gave other grounds for his opposition to the introduction of khaki:

> I should be sorry to see the day when the English Army is no longer in red. I am not one of those who think it at all desirable to hide ourselves too much. I must say I think the soldier had better be taught not to hide himself, but to go gallantly to the front. In action the man who does that has a much better chance of succeeding than the man who hides himself.[30]

Wolseley did not believe that the ability to conceal himself would make any difference to the soldier's willingness to fight, but neutral coloured uniforms would prevent unnecessary casualties caused by being conspicuous and would reduce the likelihood of heat-stroke. The Queen also added her objection to the change: 'the Queen thinks the Kharkee clothing hideous and hopes she may never see it in England'. Her private secretary, Sir Henry Ponsonby, added, rather oddly, that he thought that khaki was more visible than red.[31]

In May 1883 Wolseley was invited to accompany the Duke and Duchess of Edinburgh to Moscow, where they were to represent the Royal Family at the coronation of Tsar Alexander III. He was very interested by what he saw in Russia but found the length of the coronation service exhausting: 'for nearly eight hours we were on our legs, and my poor wounded limbs are aching in every nerve'.[32] His wife was not totally sympathetic, writing to him from her holiday on the Isle of Wight:

We laughed more than you can imagine over the *Times* account of the coronation. I dare say you thought we were impressed by all your grandeur, but not a bit of it. The 'conqueror of Tel-el-Kebir appeared (or disappeared) eclipsed behind a pillar, and could not change his base of operations as from Alexandria to Suez'; but I hope you peeped round your pillar and saw something.[33]

Wolseley and the Edinburghs also visited St Petersburg before returning to England.

While working at the War Office, Wolseley settled in a house in Hill Street, Mayfair, with his wife and daughter. Louisa took great pleasure in decorating the house with wallpapers in soft blues and greens. She also began collecting Queen Anne and Chippendale furniture. Frances liked being close to her father and they rode together on Wimbledon Common every Sunday. Her father, however, showed little understanding of the needs of children. When she was ten years old he mounted her on his old sixteen hand mare and showed no alarm when the mare more than once bolted across the common with his frightened daughter clinging on hard.[34]

He made several visits to Ireland to visit those members of his family still living there. On one such visit to his mother, in October 1883, he found her dying. He wrote to his friend the Duchess of Edinburgh: 'her death makes a gap in my existence, in my thoughts, which can never be refilled; it is a blow to me that I reel under, feeling that the world has now lost its greatest charm to me'.[35] The effect of his loss was to draw him even closer to his wife, Louisa. Wolseley continued to provide financial support for his unmarried sister Caroline. Their mother had died intestate so her assets would have to be divided between her seven children but Wolseley and Dick made it clear that they wanted Caroline to have everything. Until this matter was settled, Wolseley would pay all Caroline's bills but needed to know the true state of her affairs: 'You will hurt my feelings very much unless you take me entirely into your confidence about your money matters'.[36]

Egypt

Britain's interest in Egypt rested on the fact that the country bordered the Suez Canal, which was vital to British trading interests in the east. The government of the Khedive, Ismail, was extremely corrupt and inefficient. In 1875 he had been forced to sell his shares in the Suez Canal Company, which Disraeli promptly purchased on behalf of Britain. In 1876 the Khedive was bankrupt and dual Anglo-French control was established over Egyptian finances. This did little to help Ismail's government and, in 1879, his overlord, the Sultan of Turkey, lost patience and deposed Ismail in favour of Ismail's son Tewfik. The Anglo-French financial management of Egypt led to a nationalist uprising in the army and among the impoverished peasantry, the fellahin. Its leader was Colonel Ahmed Urabi.

The Liberal Party had espoused high-minded abstract principles on foreign and imperial policy during the 1880 election campaign. It had been forced to return self-government to the Boers and now faced a serious challenge to its principles in Egypt. At first, Gladstone was sympathetic towards the concept of 'Egypt for the Egyptians', so long as neither European financial interests nor the Suez Canal were threatened.[1] He hoped that Turkey would intervene to restore order, leaving him free to cope with Ireland. Sultan Abdul Hamid was not prepared to uphold the financial interests of Britain and France: Gladstone had insulted him over the Bulgarian massacres and the position of Greeks at Smyrna; France had seized Tunis from him in 1881.

During the first half of 1882 the Egyptian government gradually collapsed. In April the British Consul-General in Cairo, Sir Edward Malet, reported that the soldiers were taking over the government now that Urabi had been appointed Minister of War. Malet was right: in May Urabi deposed the Khedive and the nationalists took over the government. Britain was particularly anxious to restore order to Egypt quickly. The Suez Canal was an important link with the empire in the east and 80 per cent of the traffic through it was British. In the absence of any sign of Turkish intervention, Britain and France were forced to act. Both countries sent warships to Alexandria harbour to guard the interests of the 100,000 Europeans living in Alexandria and throughout Egypt. This angered the nationalists and on 11 and 12 June there were anti-European riots in Alexandria causing fifty deaths. On 23 June a conference opened of the European powers to decide a policy towards Egypt but, without Turkey's participation, seemed unlikely to reach any conclusions. Finally, on 24 June, the British and French Controllers were informed that they were no longer welcome to sit in on Egyptian Council meetings. Egypt had effectively been taken over by the Egyptians.[2]

Pressure for Britain to take the initiative in Egypt built up in the Cabinet. Gladstone, though personally unwilling to intervene, was forced to give way to his Cabinet colleagues because he needed the assistance of a united Cabinet to push through the important Irish Rent Arrears Bill. The British admiral at Alexandria, Sir Beauchamp Seymour, informed the Admiralty that Urabi was building shore batteries in the harbour which could threaten his ships. Two infantry battalions were ordered to move from Malta to Cyprus to protect the Suez Canal in case of need. Wolseley, at the War Office, was asked to prepare a return showing the number of horses, mules and carts on the transport establishment at home and on the Mediterranean bases. The transport was to be sufficient for 24,000 men, thereby indicating that Britain intended to seize Egypt back for the Khedive.[3]

Wolseley was not entirely happy with the prospect of armed intervention: in March 1882 he had talked to a supporter of Egyptian nationalism, Wilfred Blunt, who had told him that the Egyptians would fight, and that a British expedition would need at least 60,000 men. Wolseley was not convinced that the Egyptians would fight, but told Blunt that 'nobody wanted to intervene, that the occupation of Egypt would be most unpopular with the army, and that he himself should be very sorry to have to go there'.[4] He was most concerned that the Navy would intervene prematurely before there were sufficient troops in the area to provide support. His fears were realised when, on 11 July, the guns of the Royal Navy ships in Alexandria opened fire on the gun emplacements. Damage was done to the town, but no troops were on hand to take over control.[5] This futile action served only to anger the nationalists.

The bombardment did at least force the British government to develop a coherent policy towards Egypt. In the House of Commons, on 12 July, Wilfred Lawson complained that the government was:

> drifting into war, and they had been drifting with their eyes open. The system had been to ask some Question of a Minister, who declined to give an answer; and then, next day, to ask another Question of some other Minister, who again referred to the Minister who had before refused to answer.[6]

Eight days later, on 20 July, Childers announced the appointment of Wolseley to command a British expedition to Egypt to the House of Commons.

The Duke of Cambridge had advised the Queen to sanction this appointment because his responsibilities as Adjutant General could be taken over temporarily by someone else, and the public would approve of the appointment. On 24 July Gladstone clarified the British position: 'our purpose will be to put down tyranny and to favour law and freedom'. A vote of credit of £2,300,000 was obtained for the army, and 12,000 men of the 1st Class Army Reserve were recalled to the colours by an Order in Council.[7] India provided one infantry brigade and three native cavalry regiments.

By the end of July it was apparent that Britain would have to intervene in Egypt without assistance. France had been keen to crush Urabi in order to protect the Suez Canal and to prevent the spread to nationalism across North Africa to France's recent acquisition, Tunis, but now the Khedive had been deposed, the French Chamber of Deputies refused the Freycinet government the necessary vote of credit and the ministry fell from office. Turkey showed neither willingness nor the ability to intervene, seeming content to watch British actions from the wings.[8]

A mobilisation committee had been sitting at the War Office under Wolseley's presidency since 30 June. It considered the two possible routes to Cairo. The first, which Napoleon had taken, was the 120 miles from Alexandria to Cairo. This was ruled out on the grounds that the Nile Delta was now intersected with numerous irrigation canals which, during the period of the high Nile in August and September, would be inundated. There were no roads of any consequence and Urabi's army could easily block the railway by blowing up the bridges over it. The second route, the seventy-five miles from Ismailia to Cairo, seemed a better prospect. Acting from Ismailia, the Suez Canal would immediately be protected, troops could be conveyed along the railway, while the Sweetwater Canal would provide drinking water for the troops and the animals. Furthermore, unlike the sand of the Nile Delta, in this part of the desert the sand was hard enough to allow men and animals to progress with relative ease.[9]

Wolseley saw the campaign as a logistical challenge rather than one of strategy or tactics, since he was not convinced the Egyptians would put up much resistance, despite the large army camp at Tel-el-Kebir, thirty-nine miles from Cairo. Detailed preparations were essential to ensure the smooth running of the campaign once the expeditionary force arrived in Egypt. The army would be marching through the heat of the summer and the shorter the time they spent in Egypt the less damage would be done to their health. Furthermore, the expedition virtually denuded Britain of troops: the Queen even allowed her bodyguard, the Household Cavalry, to go out. Obviously Britain wanted her army back as soon as possible. Arrangements were made for locomotives, a hundred open goods wagons and ten miles of rails to be sent from Britain in case the Egyptians destroyed the rolling stock. Transport carts and animals were gathered from all over Britain and the Mediterranean stations. Plans were made to establish hospitals at Malta and Cyprus. Gladstone's private secretary noted that the government had gained kudos for the way the expedition had been prepared: 'there has been no hitch, no bustle, no flurry, and great expedition'. Wolseley later disagreed, complaining that his army had been 'thrown together without cohesion between its component parts and no organised transport'.[10]

The expeditionary force was the largest Britain had mounted to date: 16,400 men came from home stations and a further 14,400 from India and the Mediterranean stations. Wolseley was not free to choose his chief commanders as he had been in most of his previous campaigns. Instead, the divisional commanders were those who had been designated to command in the autumn infantry manoeuvres. Lieutenant-General Frederick Willis was given the 1st Division and Lieutenant-General Sir Edward Hamley the 2nd Division, but neither man had seen active service since the Crimean War. Hamley had been teaching at the Staff College, where he had a great reputation as a strategist and tactician.[11] Wolseley did, however, manage to take along most of the members of his 'Ring': Major-General Evelyn Wood was given the command of an infantry brigade; Colonel Redvers Buller worked in the intelligence department; Colonel Baker Russell commanded the 1st Cavalry Brigade under the cavalry divisional commander, Major-General Drury Lowe. Lieutenant-Colonel William Butler and Major Frederick Maurice received junior appointments on the headquarters staff; and Brevet Lieutenant-Colonel Herbert Stewart and Lieutenant-Colonel Hugh McCalmont joined the staff of the cavalry.[12] The Duke of Cambridge was furious with Wolseley for making Baker Russell a brigadier but Wolseley's only comment was that 'when it can be asserted that I have appointed a bad man to an office, it will be time to find fault with my selections'.[13]

The War Office was effectively stripped of its most able administrators. The Surveyor General of Ordnance, General Sir John Adye, was appointed Chief of the Staff. The head of the Intelligence Department, Major-General Sir Archibald Alison, joined the 2nd Division to command the Highlanders, and six of his deputies also joined the expedition. Questions were asked in Parliament about the wisdom of sending the holders of high staff appointments abroad but Childers replied that it was for a short time only. In fact all the officers were back in their offices by the end of October, with the exception of Alison, who remained in Egypt as Wolseley's successor.[14]

Everyone who was anyone wanted a place on the expedition. The Prince of Wales, as Colonel-in-Chief of the Guards, wanted to accompany them

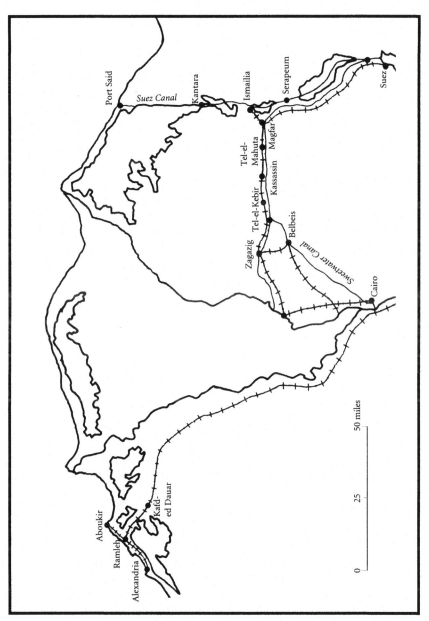

Egypt 1882

50 miles

0   25

on their first campaign since the Crimea but, much to Wolseley's relief, the Queen refused permission.[15] The Queen's favourite son, the Duke of Connaught, was more successful and joined the 1st Division as a brigadier.[16] Wolseley was forced to take along the Duke of Cambridge's son, Major George Fitzgeorge, and also the Queen's cousin, the Duke of Teck. Neither man made a favourable impression on him. Men soon started to appear in Egypt who had no official role in the expeditionary force. The Duke of Cambridge ordered Wolseley to send them home. He mostly obeyed this order and, for example, refused to employ Captain Charles Beresford RN, who had taken part in the bombardment of Alexandria, on the Khedive's staff or as a newspaper correspondent. He did manage to find a place for St Leger Herbert, but only as a private in the mounted infantry.[17]

On 28 June all the generals of the expeditionary force had an audience with the Queen at Osborne on the Isle of Wight. On his way back to London, Wolseley caught a cold which developed into erysipelas. His doctors insisted that he should travel by sea all the way to Alexandria rather than take the overland route to Brindisi, and he left London on 2 August.[18] He was very well cared for on board and complained to Louisa, 'If this goes on long I shall be like a prize pig: I am fed every three hours, and take no exercise'.[19] The troops had begun leaving on 27 July. Wolseley arrived in Alexandria on the evening of 15 August and found the situation in the town much improved. After the bombardment, General Alison and two infantry battalions had been rushed to Alexandria to restore order there. They were ordered to probe the Egyptian positions to discover the depth of resistance after the Egyptians had fallen back to their camp at Kafr-ed-Duer. Wolseley vetoed Alison's plan to seize Ismailia at once because he feared that this would lead Urabi to cut the Sweetwater Canal and attack the Suez Canal before there were sufficient troops in the area to protect it.[20]

The maintenance of secrecy was a paramount concern for Wolseley because Alexandria was full of war correspondents and Egyptian spies. It was also known that the French designer of the Suez Canal, Ferdinand de Lesseps, was hostile to British intervention. He controlled all the Canal pilots, so the task of guiding the transport ships through the Canal was given to Captain Jacky Fisher, RN.[21] Wolseley therefore devised an ingenious plan to divert attention away from his true goal of Ismailia, letting it be known that Aboukir and the Kafr-ed-Duer lines would be the first point of attack. Hamley was ordered to prepare plans for this attack, which Wolseley duly approved. On 19 August the expeditionary force set sail for Aboukir harbour and anchored there for the night. Wolseley was reluctantly forced to leave Wood's division at Alexandria to defend the town because Wood was the junior Major-General commanding the junior brigade.

Secretly, naval landing parties advanced towards the Canal to begin seizing strategic points along its length. On 20 August the force set sail again and only then was Hamley permitted to open his orders. To his great anger he discovered that the plans to attack Aboukir were a ruse and that he was ordered back to Alexandria to wait there until Willis's 1st Division had been landed at Ismailia.[22] Hamley never forgave Wolseley for this slight.

Landing at Ismailia on 21 August, Wolseley took up residence in the governor's house. De Lesseps put up a feeble resistance to the first landing party, then retired to his house to sulk. Wolseley managed to meet him on the following day, when the two men were civil towards each other. De Lesseps left for France after being caught telegraphing Cairo with the news of the British arrival in force. By 22 August the whole length of the Suez Canal was in British hands after the landing parties had seized the locks to the inland canals and the railway. The railway from Suez to Ismailia had been damaged and repair work was begun immediately by the Royal Engineers. Their work was urgent because the port at Ismailia was primitive: there was no railway track between the port and the town, so the locomotives and rolling stock had to be unloaded at Suez, and only one narrow road bridge linked the port to the town. Nonetheless, by the evening of 23 August 9000 men had been landed at Ismailia.[23]

The level of water in the Sweetwater Canal was falling noticeably and intelligence revealed that the Egyptians had built a dam at Magfar, six miles from Ismailia. On 24 August General Drury Lowe, with a mounted force consisting of three squadrons of the Household Cavalry, a detachment of the 19th Hussars and some mounted infantry, set out to seize Magfar. Wolseley and Willis accompanied them and Major-General Gerald Graham led the York and Lancaster Regiment. The Egyptians had been taken by surprise and were still expecting the main attack to descend from Aboukir. Wolseley's ruse had worked. Consequently there was no opposition at Magfar. The prisoners taken revealed that there was another dam at Tel-el-Mahuta guarded by a large force of infantry.[24]

Wolseley pushed ahead to make a reconnaissance of the Tel-el-Mahuta position. It was clear that the prisoners had spoken the truth: trains were seen arriving at the station laden with supplies for about 8000 troops. He faced a difficult decision because he needed to advance to Kassassin Lock as soon as possible to secure the water supply in the Sweetwater Canal. Once in Kassassin a base could be built up for the assault on the main Egyptian camp at Tel-el-Kebir, nine miles away. Any delay would give the Egyptians time to strengthen the position at Tel-el-Mahuta and turn what might be little more than a major skirmish into a full-blown battle. Wolseley did not have enough troops with him to be sure of success.

He decided to gamble and attack Tel-el-Mahuta that day. Graham's force was ordered forward and a message was sent back to Ismailia ordering the Guards to advance with all speed. The cavalry and the mounted infantry protected the small infantry force but the Egyptians would not come close, so the battle became little more than an artillery duel. The Egyptian shells did little damage because they were fitted with percussion fuses and many of them did not burst on hitting the sand. One shell did hit a horse but 'its rider was on his feet in a moment, calling out, "Three cheers for the first charger of the Life Guards killed since Waterloo!"'.[25] The heat did the real damage to the British: Willis collapsed and the Guards, who arrived in the early evening, were too exhausted after their long march through the hottest part of the day to be able to fight.[26] Wolseley suffered too: he watched the battle with Butler while in considerable pain from a desperately tight riding boot. After the battle the two men rode off into the desert and Wolseley dismounted and Butler cut the offending boot. He had not wanted this done earlier in case any of the troops spotted them and feared that their commander had been hit.[27] That night he returned to Ismailia, while the two forces remained in close proximity, ready to fight again on the morrow.

On the morning of 25 August, when it was discovered that the Egyptians had abandoned their positions during the night, the British occupied Tel-el-Mahuta without any opposition. Wolseley, back at the front, then ordered the cavalry and horse artillery to advance to cut off the enemy's retreat. The horses had suffered a long voyage and had been given no time to acclimatise to the heat of the desert and were scarcely capable of such a movement. Nonetheless, the cavalry advanced slowly and found no opposition until the heights over Mahsama were reached. There a large infantry force was drawn up protected by artillery and eight to ten squadrons of cavalry. Drury Lowe attacked and the Egyptians retreated until the British captured the camp at Mahsama. The Egyptian camp was full of a wealth of supplies and war matériel, including seven Krupps guns. Originally Wolseley had planned for Mahsama to be captured and then abandoned after the destruction of the supplies but, on hearing the amount of supplies found, he ordered Drury Lowe to remain in position and sent Willis forward with his infantry to support the cavalry. At dawn on 26 August General Graham arrived at Mahsama and, after a reconnaissance force under Lieutenant-Colonel Herbert Stewart had reported Kassassin Lock abandoned by the Egyptians, sent his force forward to occupy it. Thus by the morning of 26 August the whole of the Sweetwater Canal and railway between Kassassin Lock and Ismailia was in British hands, a week earlier than Wolseley had anticipated.[28] He wrote to the Duke of Cambridge that 'our extraordinary success has forced my hand'.[29]

Yet Wolseley was not in a strong position. Although the ground up to Kassassin had been taken with little loss, five killed, twenty-eight wounded and forty-one cases of sunstroke, he had few forces in the front line. The cavalry was at Mahsama and the Guards at Tel-el-Mahuta. Now he needed time to sort out the chaos in the rear. By 26 August not all of the troops had even arrived at Ismailia: General Hamley's division was still at Alexandria; most of the artillery was still at sea; and most of the Indian contingent under Major-General Herbert Macpherson, including Wolseley's brother George, was still at Suez.[30] The railway between Suez and Ismailia was not completely repaired until 27 August. Only then could the long and slow process of bringing the stores up the railway to Kassassin begin. Working parties from the troops were detailed to remove the dam at Tel-el-Mahuta so that supplies could be sent along the canal all the way to Kassassin. The conditions for this work were appalling and Butler noted: 'the heat had become simply outrageous, the sun stood straight overhead, the yellow sand glowed like hot coals, not a breath of air stirred over these hot hillocks'. Wolseley suffered too, writing home to his wife that 'my poor nose has blossomed into a sort of half fungus, half cauliflower'.[31] At one point the men were down to a pint of water a day.

On 28 August the vulnerability of the British position was amply illustrated when the Egyptians, now under the direct command of Urabi, attacked Graham's position at Kassassin. Graham commanded only a weak brigade and was so short of supplies that the only ammunition for his two guns was carried in their limbers. He immediately asked the cavalry brigade at Mahsama for support and it began advancing. Willis also sent some of his cavalry from Tel-el-Mahuta to assist. The advancing forces kept in communication with Graham by means of the mounted infantry, since mirages made the use of the heliograph ineffective. This nearly led to confusion when a verbal message by Graham's aide-de-camp suggested that Graham's force was in greater danger that it actually was. This news gave Wolseley, still at Ismailia, some uncomfortable moments that evening, particularly when a message arrived that Graham had been defeated. It was only at 1 a.m. that Lagden, the correspondent for the *Daily Telegraph*, reported that Graham had won a victory after the Household Cavalry had made a brilliant charge. The British losses were sixteen killed and seventy-nine wounded. The Egyptians withdrew back to the Tel-el-Kebir lines. Wolseley visited Graham's camp on the following day and wrote of his good impression of the Household Cavalry: 'they can be laughed at no longer; I believe they will owe the continuance of their existence to my bringing them here and pushing them well to the front'. The Queen's bodyguard were now to be seen as more than just theatrical troops.[32]

During the first week of September there appeared to be a lull in operations and the press and the government at home began to put pressure on Wolseley to attack soon. He could not hurry because the supplies were still processing up the line slowly and, until sufficient supplies had been concentrated at Kassassin, he could not order the entire force there. Various reconnaissances revealed the strength of the lines at Tel-el-Kebir: the Egyptian defences were four miles long, running north into the desert, with redoubts mounting seventy-five guns covering the Sweetwater Canal and the railway. Unknown to the British, there was also an advanced post outside these entrenchments, 100 yards ahead and 1600 yards north of the railway, which held four guns and an infantry battalion. Two British reconnaissances had spotted this work but, due to the line of observation and mirages, thought it was part of the main lines. This was a serious error which nearly caused disaster. The Egyptians were commanded by Rashid Pasha, although Urabi was present, and he had approximately 18,000 regulars and 7000 irregulars at his disposal.[33]

On 8 September Wolseley ordered the army to concentrate on Kassassin, to which he moved his headquarters on 10 September. Before the army could do so the Egyptians attacked on 9 September, because the Bedouin had reported the British to have only a weak force there. In fact, Graham had recently been reinforced and had 8000 men, including the cavalry division, to assist him in the easy task of routing the Egyptians. The pursuit took the British to within 5000 yards of the Tel-el-Kebir lines. The advance was halted because, even if Tel-el-Kebir had been captured then, probably with heavy losses, there would not have been enough men to pursue the Egyptians into Cairo and another major battle might have been necessary. Wolseley had anticipated having to fight two battles in any case, because he thought the Egyptians might run from the first, but he wanted to devise some tactic to achieve more in the first battle and to reduce the chances of a 'disquieting "butcher's bill", over which Mr John Bull rather gloats, and thinks, when the list is a long one, that he has had something for his money'.[34] The final advance to Tel-el-Kebir would have to be made across open desert with no cover. Such an advance would have presented little danger against primitively-armed troops, but the Egyptians were armed with Remington breech loading rifles and were therefore equal in firepower to the British.

Wolseley therefore devised a daring plan for a night march and a dawn attack on Tel-el-Kebir, because 'I am so weak that I cannot afford to indulge in any other plan'.[35] Adye and Hamley were both alarmed at this plan, distrusting the ability of the young soldiers to maintain order during a night march. Night marches had taken place during the Peninsular War but had not been practised since in peace time. Wolseley was taking a huge gamble. On 12 September he outlined his dispositions to his divisional commanders. The 1st Division would be on the right with Graham's brigade leading and the Guards behind. The 2nd Division would be on the left with Alison's Highlanders in front. The Indian contingent would be to the south of the Sweetwater Canal, the field artillery would be in the centre with the horse artillery covering the flanks. The cavalry would cover the extreme right flank. The force was to be guided by Lieutenant Harry Rawson, Wolseley's naval aide-de-camp, who had plenty of experience in navigating according to the stars.[36] A total of 17,401 troops would attack Tel-el-Kebir at dawn on 13 September like a 'gigantic bolt of flesh, steel and iron shot westward into the darkness'.[37]

The main advance moved off at 1.30 a.m. Wolseley himself followed the Highland Brigade. All equipment had been tied up to prevent any rattling breaking the silence of the night. The quiet was only broken at one point by a drunken Highlander; but his fellow soldiers quickly silenced him.[38] Frequent halts were made to check the direction and alignment of the march. As the stars set to the north west the British line accidentally veered slightly to the right. This error meant that the left flank passed the advanced Egyptian redoubt 1100 yards away, rather than the 400 yards if the true course had been followed. By this lucky chance the advance escaped detection. The night march was designed to carry the British force to within 300 yards of the Egyptian trenches, within charging distance for the infantry, as dawn came up.[39] At 4.50 a.m. a light shone in the east earlier than Wolseley and his staff had anticipated. It was not, however, the first light of dawn but a comet streaking through the sky. Five minutes later the Egyptian sentries spotted the Highlanders and opened fire. The Highlanders immediately began the charge and then the whole force charged forward into the trenches. The Egyptians were given no time to awaken or form up before the British attack descended upon them. Most of the killing was done by bayonet rather than bullet. Nevertheless, the enemy fought hard: 'the black Sudanese fought like blazes and our men like Trojans, and the Gypies ran like hares'.[40] The artillery drove the enemy out of the trenches only for them to be slaughtered by the cavalry which was cutting off their retreat. By 6 a.m. the battle was over and the Egyptians were in full flight back towards Zagazig and Cairo.

By 7 a.m. the whole of the Tel-el-Kebir lines, the camp and the railway station were in British hands. Wolseley sat on the bridge over the canal to write his despatch for the War Office. The total British casualties were fifty-seven killed, 382 wounded and thirty missing: the Egyptian dead numbered thousands.[41] He was well satisfied with the work of that night and morning. He had tried a risky strategy because 'troops are seldom steady in the dark, and are so liable to panic', but had succeeded. He wrote to Childers of his pride in the soldiers under his command: 'after a trial of an exceptionally severe kind, both in movements and in attack, I can say emphatically, that I never wish to have under my orders better Infantry Battalions than those who I am proud to have commanded at Tel-el-Kebir'.[42] Not everyone agreed with Wolseley: Wilfred Blunt called the battle 'a mere butchery of peasants, too ignorant even to know the common formulas of surrender'. Butler, though proud to have been a member of the expedition, wrote a moving tribute to the Egyptians: 'Peace to them, lying under these big mounds on the lone desert – ten thousand it is said. They did not desert the desert, and Egypt will not forget them'.[43]

As the infantry battle ended, Wolseley ordered to Indian contingent to capture the station at Zagazig to prevent any Egyptian troops from reaching Cairo from Alexandria. The cavalry was ordered to pursue the Egyptian forces to Cairo and, on the evening of 14 September, General Drury Lowe led the cavalry into Cairo and received the surrender of the capital. Ten thousand Egyptian troops surrendered their weapons without resistance and Urabi and Toubla, who had commanded at Kafd-ed-Duer, surrendered their swords.[44] On 15 September Wolseley reached Cairo and telegraphed to Childers that the war was over.

On the afternoon of 25 September the Khedive re-entered Cairo to the acclamation of the crowd and was driven in a carriage between the ranks of the British army. At the Queen's request Wolseley relinquished his right, as the commander of the expedition, to sit next to the Khedive to the Duke of Connaught. Instead he sat with his back to the horses next to the British Consul, Sir Edward Malet. On 30 September there was a parade of all British troops for the Khedive and a salute of 101 guns. The sickness rate among the British troops had been rising alarmingly since the battle, mostly due to opthalmia and diarrhoea, and the ranks of the Guards were noticeably diminished for the parade. Race meetings were held and Wolseley gave a picnic for ninety people at the Pyramids of Sakkara.[45] Five days later there was another military display to mark the beginning of the journey of the Sacred Carpet from Cairo to Mecca. The War Office questioned the wisdom of allowing British troops to participate but Wolseley replied that, in the absence of an Egyptian army or police force, the Khedive had requested a British presence to keep law and order. This amply demonstrated what the government at home were only just beginning to realise: that the Khedive's 'only authority rests upon our bayonets'.[46]

At the beginning of October Urabi was put on trial for mutiny. Wolseley was very keen to see Urabi and his leading supporters found guilty and sentenced to be hanged. He realised that many Liberals at home felt that Urabi was a nationalist and should not pay the ultimate price for his rebellion. Consequently, Wolseley hoped that the trial would be over before Parliament met on 24 October.[47] In the event Urabi was found guilty and was exiled to Ceylon. He returned to Egypt later as a private citizen.

Wolseley was rewarded generously for his management of the campaign. The Khedive decorated him with the Sultan's highest medal, the Grand Cross of the Osmanieh. Gladstone gave both Wolseley and Sir Beauchamp Seymour peerages. At first Gladstone had recommended that Wolseley should receive a viscountcy but, after being misinformed by Childers that it was usual only to grant a baronage, he was made Baron Wolseley of Cairo and of Wolseley and was promoted to the rank of Full General. He was delighted with the news, particularly as it would come accompanied by a grant which he would not have received had he been given a peerage as Gladstone originally intended a year earlier. He wrote to his wife: 'this augmentation to our income will prevent my "sniffling", as you always say I do, about the vastness of our fortune'. Negotiations on the size of the grant continued into the next year, and centred on the fact that a grant would normally cover the lifetime of the recipient and his son. Wolseley wrote to Gladstone that 'I have no sons to be provided for as a peer after my death, and I would therefore much prefer being given a sum of money to an annuity'. He also wanted a grant of £35,000 instead of the £25,000 originally offered. Eventually, Gladstone and the Cabinet agreed to give him £30,000 but, because of the difference in ages, only £25,000 to Sir Beauchamp Seymour, now Lord Alcaster.[48]

Elizabeth Butler, William's wife, was a noted painter of military subjects. She painted a picture of Wolseley and Adye, Buller and Butler called *After the Battle* which was accurate in every detail. Wolseley posed for the picture in London, but fidgeted a great deal despite his wife Louisa seating him on her knee. Highlanders patiently adopted the necessary poses for the soldiers. It was exhibited at the Royal Academy and engraved later. Wolseley wanted to own the painting but was too poor to purchase it himself. He wished that someone would buy it and give it to him as a present. Lady Butler's husband objected to her choice of subject since he sympathised with the Egyptians and, some time after 1896, ordered the picture to be cut up. Only a fragment, showing Wolseley, has survived.[49]

On 18 September the Queen wrote a letter to Wolseley which congratulated the troops under his command but said nothing about the personal abilities of the commander. He was greatly offended to find 'there is not one approving sentence in it'.[50] The Queen was intent on enhancing the reputation of her son, the Duke of Connaught, at his expense. She only changed

her mind when he wrote to her that 'Sir Garnet has been most kind to me
all the time I have been under his orders, and I don't wish to serve under
a pleasanter chief, or one in whom I feel greater confidence'.[51] Indeed,
controversy raged for some years after the campaign in Egypt over the
presence of the Duke of Connaught in Egypt. During the campaign Wolseley
had written home that Connaught was an extremely active brigadier but:

> I am distressed in my mind as to what to do, for I want to shove the Foot
> Guards into a hot corner, and they want this themselves, and they are the best
> troops I have, but I am so nervous that no injury should befall the favourite
> son of the Queen that I am loath to endanger his life.[52]

Edward Hamilton recorded after the battle that 'the Guards, according to
some accounts, are frantic with Wolseley for having kept them rather in
the background'. Whereas it was true that the brunt of the fighting fell to
the Highland Brigade, there is no evidence to suggest that the Foot Guards
were protected by anything other than the brevity of the battle. An article
in the *Manchester Guardian* in 1893 stated that Childers had ordered Wolseley
to protect the Duke of Connaught during Tel-el-Kebir. This suggestion was
hotly denied by both Childers and Wolseley.[53]

Another repercussion concerning personalities centred on the commander
of the 2nd Division, Sir Edward Hamley. He did not believe that his services
had been sufficiently recognised by Wolseley, nor had Wolseley accepted
the advice he had freely offered. Furthermore, in an article in the December
1882 issue of *Nineteenth Century*, Hamley argued that his division had been
denuded of troops before and during Tel-el-Kebir. Wolseley had unjustly
enhanced the reputation of the Highland Brigade and its commander,
Archibald Alison, at the expense of Hamley and his division.[54] These
allegations were largely ignored until 1895, when the biography of Hamley
by E. Shand was published. Reviewing it, the author of the official history
of the campaign, Frederick Maurice, sought to set out the true facts. Maurice
argued that Wolseley had discovered that:

> Sir Edward Hamley with all his theoretical knowledge of war, had completely
> lost touch of the practical working of large bodies of men, and that he was
> always so full of his own importance, that he could not be trusted to carry out
> orders that he received.

Indeed, he had been so disenchanted with Hamley's performance that he
had been tempted to leave him behind at Kassassin.[55]

The only blot on the Egyptian campaign was the medical services. Guy
Dawnay noted in his diary that the army medical department had completely
broken down. At Kassassin, after the battle on 28 August, there was no

brandy or chloroform at the hospital. The hospitals in Ismailia were no better, with no washing facilities, carbolic oil or antiseptic dressings. Diarrhoea medicine was in short supply and the patients were offered a diet of water melon and tough beef. The Queen asked Wolseley if the rumours were true when he visited her at Balmoral soon after his return. He was forced to admit that the hospitals had been very bad and that there had been a shortage of nurses. He promised that the War Office would do something to remedy the situation before Britain next embarked on a campaign abroad.[56]

The twin challenges facing the British government after the Khedive had been restored to his country were to withdraw the British garrison and re-establish an Egyptian government, police force, and army; and to restructure Egyptian finances on a secure footing. It soon became apparent that British assistance was required to a greater degree than anticipated. The Khedive had disbanded his police force and the elements of the army not defeated at Tel-el-Kebir had disappeared. British troops were necessary to maintain internal security, yet Britain needed her army back. The Queen was the first to grasp the new situation: 'short of annexation we must obtain a firm hold and power in Egypt for the future'. The leader of the Conservative party, the Marquess of Salisbury, pointed out the government's error in waiting until the Khedive had been overthrown before acting to save his position. Now the Khedive had been restored by foreign bayonets it was incumbent upon the British to help him settle his country.[57]

While Wolseley was absent in Egypt, Louisa and Frances went to Homburg to take the waters. The Prince of Wales was there and attempted to cultivate their friendship. With the Prince's reputation for womanising in mind, Louisa used her ten-year-old daughter as a chaperon and told Frances 'on no account to leave the room when the Prince came to call, even should he command it'. On their return to London, Frances went to her father's room at the War Office every day to follow the course of the campaign.[58]

At the beginning of October Wolseley, who had expected to leave Egypt soon after the Khedive's arrival, was ordered by the Duke of Cambridge to remain in Cairo because 'complications may yet arise, which it would be very important for an officer in your high and influential position to deal with'.[59] Only on 21 October 1882 did Wolseley and the majority of the British troops leave Egypt for home or India, leaving behind a garrison of approximately 12,000 British troops under the command of Major-General Alison. John Ardagh was given the task of restoring Alexandria after the bombardment.[60] After a short relaxing break in Paris, Wolseley resumed his duties as Adjutant General. In December 1882 Evelyn Wood was appointed Sirdar of the Egyptian army and the slow process of rebuilding the army under British officers began. Consequently the British government worked towards reducing the British garrison further and Alison was prepared to reduce the force to 8000 before the next summer and to 6000 by the autumn. In January and February Wolseley, whose advice was constantly sought by the new Secretary of State for War, Lord Hartington, recommended an immediate reduction of the garrison to 5000 men because 'there was no enemy to guard against, that the question was not military but political'. Indeed, he was against the retention of any force in Egypt at all. He viewed it as a source of weakness because the army was too small to keep such a large garrison outside Britain without a major increase to the establishment.[61]

Wolseley's opinion that Britain had no place in Egypt was echoed elsewhere. Lord Randolph Churchill told his audience in Edinburgh that the government had misled the public as to the value of Egypt and the Suez Canal: 'Egypt is not the high-road to India. The Suez Canal is a commercial route to India, and a good route, too, in time of peace: but it never was, and never could be, a military route for Great Britain in time of war'. The new British Consul in Cairo, Evelyn Baring, echoed these remarks, accepting that the occupation of Egypt meant that Britain had 'lost the advantage of our insular position'. Furthermore she had angered France by going into Egypt alone and 'until the formation of the Entente Cordiale of 1904, the most important claim was that England should fix a definite date for her evacuation'.[62]

The government was very keen to leave Egypt to the Egyptians as soon as possible. In October 1882 Lord Dufferin visited Egypt to report to the government on the future policy Britain should pursue. He was in favour of immediate evacuation, but a petition of 2600 Europeans in Alexandria asked Britain to remain in control. In January 1883 Dufferin issued a circular to the powers setting out the position of the British government:

> Although for the present a British force remains in Egypt for the preservation of public tranquillity, Her Majesty's Government are desirous of withdrawing it as soon as the state of the country and the organisation of proper means for the maintenance of the Khedive's authority will admit of it.[63]

It was not said who would decide when the Khedive was secure enough for a withdrawal. International assistance was vital for the restructuring of Egyptian finances once dual Anglo-French control ended in December 1882. International conferences on this subject began in June 1884, by which time Britain faced another serious problem arising from her continued presence in Egypt.

Egypt controlled the vast and poor province of the Sudan to the south of her frontier. In the summer of 1881 Mohammed Ahmed, an apprentice boatbuilder, declared himself the Mahdi or 'Chosen One', swore to regenerate Islam and march against all infidels, whether Christian or lapsed Moslems, to bring them to Allah's fold. His movement swept the Sudan, where the majority of the population lived in perpetual poverty, and threatened Egyptian control there. Gladstone made the position of his government clear in a statement to the House of Commons:

> It is no part of the duty incumbent upon us to restore order in that Province. It is politically connected with Egypt in consequence of its very recent conquest; but it has not been included within the sphere of our operations, and we are by no means disposed to admit without qualification that it is within the sphere of our responsibilities.[64]

Others, such as the Queen and some MPs, disagreed, believing that Britain had a moral duty to assist Egypt in the Sudan.[65]

It was unclear whether Egypt could defeat the Mahdi without British assistance. Granville reported to Gladstone on a conversation he had had with Wood. Wood 'has absolute confidence in that half of the Egyptian army which is officered by English officers. He has only negative confidence in the other purely Egyptian half. He does not rely upon them for action'. This was amply illustrated in November 1883 when an Egyptian army under a British officer, Colonel Hicks, was annihilated at El Obeid in the Sudan by the Mahdi's Dervishes. Further Egyptian defeats followed.

Debate then turned on how to persuade the Egyptian government to abandon the Sudan, what should be considered Egypt's southern frontier, and where the defence forces should be stationed. Wolseley argued that Egypt proper was in no danger of immediate invasion, since the Mahdi was still mainly operating in the south of the Sudan, but that certain strategic points, Khartoum, Berber and Suakin, should be reinforced, both to maintain Egyptian rule in the Sudan itself, and to reassure the population of Upper Egypt. He suggested that Egypt should be asked to give up all territory west of the White Nile with the exception of territory east of the great bend in the river just north of Khartoum. An Egyptian force under British officers should be stationed at Assuan in southern Egypt and that Wadi Halfa should be seen as the official frontier.[66] Hartington passed these recommendations on to Granville with his endorsement. Dufferin also signalled his approval of Wolseley's memorandum.[67] It was agreed that British troops should not withdraw from Cairo as planned. Baring, who had argued with the government for British assistance for Egypt in the Sudan, now changed his mind. As he wrote later: 'the abandonment of the Sudan, however undesirable, was imposed upon the Egyptian Government as an unpleasant but imperious necessity for the simple reason that, after the destruction of Colonel Hicks' army, they were unable to keep it'.[68] On 3 January 1884 Wolseley was asked to prepared a report on the garrisons in the Sudan and an estimate 'as to the possibility of all or any of them being withdrawn'. During discussions on how the garrisons should be withdrawn, the name that would haunt Gladstone's reputation forever afterwards was put forward – Charles Gordon.

13

Sudan

The decision to evacuate the Sudan left the Egyptian government with the task of withdrawing its garrisons from the region, and preventing the moral contagion of Mahdism spreading northwards into Egypt. The defeat of Colonel Hicks at El Obeid made it clear that the Egyptian army would be incapable of achieving these aims without British assistance. Britain had no wish to send her troops into the Sudan, in case this might suggest a permanent occupation. It was, however, willing to send a man whose reputation and status would ensure the loyalty of the tribes not yet suborned by the Mahdi. This would allow the evacuation to take place unhindered.

The name of Charles Gordon was first suggested to Sir Andrew Clarke, the Inspector General of Fortifications, who passed the letter to the Chancellor of the Exchequer, Hugh Childers, with the endorsement: 'If the Mahdi is a prophet, Gordon in the Sudan is greater'. Gordon had been Governor-General of the Sudan from 1877 to 1879. Childers consulted the Foreign Secretary, Lord Granville, who then asked Gladstone if he had any objection to using Gordon in the Sudan in some capacity. Gladstone wanted to know exactly how Gordon would prove useful.[1] The British Consul in Cairo, Evelyn Baring, was also consulted, and replied that he did not want Gordon.[2]

There the matter might have rested had it not been for the intervention of Wolseley. Gordon had just accepted a position in the Congo, at the request of King Leopold of Belgium, to crush the slave trade there. He wrote to Wolseley asking him to arrange his pension since he would soon be passing through London to resign his army commission. Wolseley was horrified that a man as great as Gordon was prepared to 'bury himself amongst niggers on the Equator'. He made an appointment to meet Gordon at the War Office on 15 January. Wolseley did not, at this stage, mention the possibility of Gordon going to the Sudan.[3]

During his visit to England Gordon was interviewed by the influential editor of the *Pall Mall Gazette*, W. T. Stead, who asked him for his views on British and Egyptian policy towards the Sudan. Gordon made it clear that he believed that the rise of the Mahdi was the fault of the government in Cairo. During his time in the Sudan, he had taught the people 'something of the meaning of liberty and justice, and accustomed them to a higher ideal of government than that with which they had previously been acquainted'. After he had left, the corruption of Egyptian officials had again descended on the poor. The Dervishes, 'the poor men', could be wooed from the Mahdi by negotiation.[4] Stead's headline article took London by storm. The call for Gordon to go to the Sudan was immediately taken up by the national press.

The name 'Chinese Gordon' was already well-known. Britain had been enthralled by the exploits of a British officer leading a few thousand Chinese irregulars, known as the 'Ever Victorious Army', to crush the Taiping rebellion and save the Chinese government in the 1860s. Gordon's efforts to stamp out the slave trade in the Sudan had met with the total approval of the anti-slavery societies. Wolseley, who had first met Gordon in the trenches of the Crimea, described him as a man who 'absolutely ignored self in all he did, and only took in hand what he conceived to be God's work'.[5] This was meant as praise, but it also suggested that Gordon was a loose cannon who could not be totally trusted to carry out the policy of a government if he did not agree with it. Baring was aware of this danger and was prepared to accept Gordon only on conditions: 'I would rather have him than anyone else, provided there is a clear understanding with him as to what his position is to be and what line of policy he is to carry out. Otherwise, not'.[6]

Gordon met Wolseley at the War Office and made it clear that he thought the policy of abandoning Khartoum and the eastern Sudan was mistaken. He agreed to go to Suakin, a Sudanese port on the Red Sea, to report on the situation if the British government requested him to do so. He made a brief trip to Brussels to ask Leopold's permission to delay his departure for the Congo. Gordon anticipated that the delay would be for no more than two months.[7] On his return, he met the four members of the Cabinet still in London, Lord Granville, Lord Hartington, Lord Northbrook and Sir Charles Dilke, in company with Wolseley. He agreed to go to the Sudan immediately. Colonel Stewart of the 11th Hussars, who had served in Egypt before, was selected to be Gordon's staff officer. The two men left from Charing Cross station on the evening of 18 January 1884, seen off by Granville, Hartington, the Duke of Cambridge and Wolseley. The latter gave Gordon £300 in cash he had raised by rushing round the London clubs when he realised that Gordon had no money on him.[8]

No records of the War Office meeting were kept, and it quickly became apparent that the participants held differing opinions on Gordon's mission. Gladstone had no opinion: he was absent at Hawarden at the time and did not even record Gordon's departure in his diary. Granville telegraphed the Queen that Gordon had been asked:

to report on the military situation in the Sudan, on measures for the security of Egyptian garrisons and of European population of Khartoum, on best mode of evacuating the interior and of securing safe and good administration of the sea coast by the Egyptian Government, also as to steps to counteract the slave trade.

Dilke thought Gordon was only going to Suakin to report, whereas Harting-ton thought that he was on a mission of peace to evacuate the garrisons. Wolseley had to send home for his notes of the conversation with Gordon.[9]

The confusion in London over Gordon's mission was then worsened by the actions of Baring in Cairo. Gordon and Stewart arrived at Port Said on 24 January, expecting to travel onward to Suakin immediately. Instead Baring asked them to Cairo for discussions. Baring changed the nature of Gordon's mission irrevocably. Instead of simply reporting on how to carry out an inglorious retreat and the abandonment of the Sudan to anarchy, Gordon was now to be Governor-General for the duration of the evacuation, and to establish a native administration capable of taking over from the departing Egyptian officials. This meant that Gordon needed an appointed successor.

Gordon wanted to be succeeded by Zobeir Pasha, whom he recognised as the most powerful man in the Sudan. Previously the two men had been in conflict, as Zobeir was the main slave trader. Furthermore, Zobeir's son, Suleiman, had rebelled against Gordon and been shot on Gordon's orders. A letter appeared to implicate Zobeir in the rebellion and his property had been confiscated and he had been placed under house arrest in Cairo. The two men met in Cairo, although it is not clear what transpired between them. Their relationship must have improved since Gordon repeatedly asked London and Cairo to confirm Zobeir as his successor.[10]

On his way down the Nile, Gordon stopped at Berber. There he issued the firman given to him by the Khedive announcing that the Sudan was to be independent and that the Egyptian garrisons were to be withdrawn. He hoped, by this action, to defuse the volatile situation and retain the loyalty of the northern tribes. He sent a letter to the Mahdi offering to have him confirmed as the governor of Kordofan but received no reply. Before Gordon even reached Khartoum, the situation in the Sudan had taken a dramatic turn for the worse. On 4 February a force of Egyptian gendarmerie under the command of the Englishman Valentine Baker was defeated at El Teb, near Suakin, by forces under the command of the Mahdi's ally, Uthman Diqna. The defeat showed that no reliance could be placed on the fighting abilities of the Egyptians and, should Gordon get into difficulties, British troops would need to be used in his rescue. The defeat also cut the fastest route for the evacuation of the Sudan garrisons, from Berber to Suakin. On 22 February, four days after Gordon's arrival in Khartoum, the evacuation of Egyptian families began by river. Some 2500 escaped before the Mahdi closed the river route. A few hundred escaped afterwards by various means.

Cairo and London repeatedly refused to allow Zobeir to be named as Gordon's successor. They feared the reaction of the anti-slavery societies, while Gordon realised that only Zobeir was strong enough to rule the country. In a series of telegrams Gordon told Baring that his mission no longer had any purpose. It was impossible to contact, let alone evacuate, all the isolated Egyptian garrisons. The Sudanese were unlikely to remain loyal to him for long since they knew that, as soon as he left, they would have to make their peace with the Mahdi. Gordon planned to leave Khartoum and hold the Equatorial Provinces for King Leopold but Baring refused him permission. On 11 March 1884 one of Gordon's last letters, to the ambassador at Constantinople, Lord Dufferin, made the seriousness of his situation clear: Khartoum was about to be besieged.[11] On the following day the telegraph to Khartoum was cut.

Gordon was not immediately alarmed because he still controlled a number of armed steamers on the Nile. He believed that Khartoum would soon be saved because he had heard that General Gerald Graham had defeated Uthman Diqna at El Teb on 29 February and on 13 March at Tamai. Graham was now in a position to advance across the desert to Berber to assist Gordon, but the government refused him permission. The force was withdrawn to Egypt, leaving behind only a small detachment to protect Suakin. This allowed the Dervishes to claim that they had defeated the British. On 4 April Gordon wrote in his journal: 'No human power can deliver us now, we are surrounded'.[12]

Gordon's situation was misunderstood in London. Although the telegraph had been cut, some messages were getting through: only a few from Gordon, but several despatches for *The Times* from its correspondent Frank Power. The sceptics in the Cabinet, led by Gladstone, believed that Gordon was deliberately disobeying orders sent to him by Baring, despite there being no evidence that Gordon was receiving them. When the Queen pressed the Cabinet to do something to save Gordon, Hartington replied that Khartoum was in no immediate danger, since it was well-stocked with provisions and military supplies, and in any case nothing could be done immediately because of the imminent hot weather and the risks of a military expedition were 'so great as to make the attempt an unjustifiable one'.[13] At least this demonstrated that Hartington accepted that some expedition might be necessary in the future. This was more than other members of the Cabinet: Granville refused to accept the idea of any expedition at all, while Gladstone

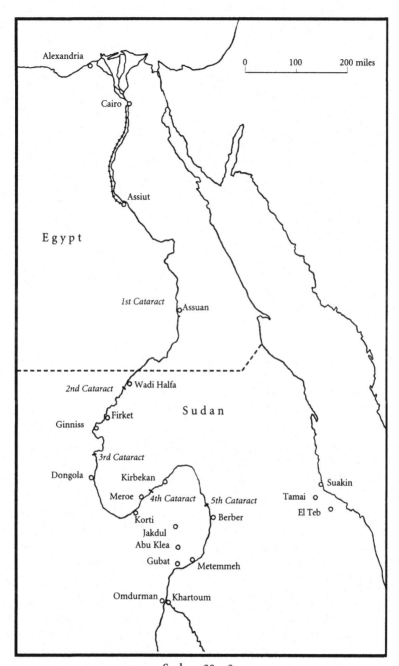

Sudan 1884–85

was so convinced that Gordon had disobeyed orders that he refused to accept that Gordon was besieged and in need of rescue.[14]

Hartington recognised that Gordon might be in some danger because Wolseley, painfully aware of his own contribution in sending Gordon to Khartoum, had written the first of many memoranda on the need for an expedition and how it should be carried out. As early as 8 February, after Baker's defeat at El Teb but before Gordon had reached Khartoum, Wolseley wrote a memorandum discussing the possible relief routes.

This was the opening shot in what became known as the 'Battle of the Routes'. Although the Intelligence Department considered as many as seven different routes, the choice appeared to be between the 245 miles from Suakin to Berber across the desert or the 666 miles along the Nile from Wadi Halfa to Berber.[15] Wolseley dismissed the Suakin-Berber route because 'about the last hundred miles of the route is almost destitute of water, and at other positions on the road water is so scarce that only detachments could move over it at one time'. These would be extremely vulnerable to attack. Therefore Wolseley was in favour of an advance along the Nile from Wadi Halfa. Supplies would be carried in the boats and a ready water supply would be available. Until he read the report of the authorities in Egypt, the Duke of Cambridge agreed with Wolseley's plan.[16]

The problem was that the Nile south of Wadi Halfa contained many cataracts, including the formidable Second Cataract at Wadi Halfa itself, which was four miles long and very steep. The Sirdar of the Egyptian Army, Evelyn Wood, and General Sir Frederick Stephenson, commanding the British army of occupation, began examining the possible routes at the end of March when they first suspected that Gordon was in difficulties. They were in favour of the adoption of the Suakin-Berber route, though Stephenson warned that any operations would be 'attended with much sickness and loss of life'. When Stephenson was as consulted by Hartington, he pointed out that only small and vulnerable cavalry detachments of between 300 and 400 men could advance across the desert at any one time because of the shortage of water and forage.[17] No expedition could be launched until the autumn and, in the meantime, a railway should be constructed along the route to carry supplies and water. The authorities in Egypt pointed out that the numerous cataracts on the Nile meant that steamers could not operate south of Wadi Halfa, and that the 180 miles between the Second Cataract and the Third at Hannek were practically unnavigable at any period. Their report was supported by Vice-Admiral Sir John Hay.[18]

Wolseley did not plan to use steamers as the authorities in Egypt thought. Instead, he planned to recreate the 1870 Red River Expedition on a far larger scale. The soldiers would be sen,t up the Nile in small boats which could be portaged over the cataracts as had been done in Canada. A committee of Red River hands, McNeill, Buller and Butler, reported that the project was feasible despite admitting to not having seen the Nile cataracts.

The choice of routes was ultimately determined by two factors: procrastination in London, and events in the Sudan. Sir Andrew Clarke had estimated the cost of the railway from Suakin to Berber at £1,500,000 and claimed that it could be built in three months. The government, still convinced that Gordon could extricate himself, was not prepared to sanction such great expenditure on a project which might never have to be put into use. On 19 May Berber fell to the Dervishes, ending the battle of the routes. As forces loyal to the Mahdi held both ends of the Suakin-Berber road, the Nile route was now the only one left.

Throughout April Wolseley pressed Hartington on the urgency of the need to make preparations for a relief expedition in the autumn. On 8 April he prepared a memorandum which provided the basic plan for an expedition using the Nile route. Hartington informed Gladstone of Wolseley's plan, to which Gladstone replied: 'I have never heard mention in Cabinet or otherwise of sending English troops to Khartoum, unless in the last and sad necessity of its being the only available means of rescuing him'.[19] Wolseley continued to badger Hartington with further long memoranda on 13 and 26 April and 9 May. On 15 May Hartington wrote a memorandum for the Cabinet in which he argued: 'Whether any expedition be ultimately despatched or not, I think it is clear that if we admit the possibility of having to send an expedition, no time should be lost in making some preparations, whatever the route which may be adopted'.[20] He met with no response.

The Cabinet was not prepared to discuss the issue since it had urgent political and diplomatic concerns. The proposal for a wide extension of the franchise was in danger of causing a crisis with the House of Lords. The long-awaited conference on Egyptian finance was soon to open in London and might cause a crisis in foreign policy. But the public was aware of Gordon's plight: a mass protest meeting in support of Gordon was held in Hyde Park in May and a public subscription to fund a relief expedition opened.[21]

Hartington was now totally convinced that Wolseley's alarm at the government's inaction was justified. On 1 July he asked Gladstone for a Cabinet specifically to consider the question of military preparations for the Sudan. On 15 July he despairingly reported to Granville that 'at the last Cabinet when it was mentioned, summoned as it was hoped to decide on it, I got five minutes at the fag end, and was as usual put off'.[22] It had not even been decided whether Gordon was to be rescued or abandoned. It was now impossible to build a railway from Suakin to Berber because of the hot weather and because the forces under Uthman Diqna were still too powerful. Therefore Hartington now put his weight behind Wolseley's proposal, made on 19 July, to concentrate six or seven thousand British soldiers at Wadi Halfa to set off for Khartoum on 1 October.[23] On 23 July Wolseley listed the preparations that needed to be made immediately. Steamers could only move supplies to Wadi Halfa during the period when the Nile was high, and this period would not wait on a decision from London. Rowing boats needed to be found, or built and shipped out, and a large number of camels purchased.[24]

Wolseley's memorandum coincided with the arrival in London of a message from Gordon, dated 22 June, which the Mudir of Dongola had received on 20 July. In it Gordon asked for the location and size of the relief expedition.[25] Hartington again pressed for troops to be sent as far south as Dongola to prepare the way for the expedition in the autumn. Gladstone replied that he could be no party to the despatch of a brigade: 'I do not think the evidence as to Gordon's position requires or justifies, in itself, the military preparations for the contingency of a military expedition'.[26]

Hartington now threatened to resign if preparations for a relief expedition were not ordered. He was in a strong position to make such a threat: as leader of the Whig faction in the Liberal Party his resignation could force the collapse of the government, in which case the important Franchise Bill would almost certainly be lost. On 25 July the majority of the Cabinet voted in favour of an expedition, with Gladstone in the minority. On 5 August Parliament granted a Vote of Credit of £300,000 to enable some preparations to be made if it proved necessary to send a relief expedition.

Wolseley immediately set in train the preparations he had already listed. The Duke of Cambridge cancelled his summer break, including missing the opening of the grouse season, so as to give him all the assistance he required. Colonel William Butler and Lieutenant-Colonel James Alleyne were asked to find 400 boats capable of carrying men and supplies for three and a half months to Dongola. On 15 August the destination was altered to Khartoum and twice as many boats were needed. The two men searched the naval and civil boatyards of southern England for suitable boats after the Admiralty reported that it would take between two and three months to build them. Orders were placed with forty-seven firms for boats thirty feet long and with a draught of two feet six inches to be fitted with twelve oars and a couple of masts. The first hundred boats were ready to leave England within a month. Three hundred Kroomen from West Africa were recruited to man the boats. The authorities in Canada were asked to provide 386 voyageurs, river boatmen, of the type used on Red River. Unfortunately, since 1870 the railway had taken over much of their work and made many of them redundant. Instead, the authorities sent the nearest equivalent in strength and endurance, lumberjacks who were used to driving timber along rivers. The voyageurs worked under a militia officer, Colonel Denison.[27]

Wood was asked to purchase 1200 camels to form a transport corps. Wolseley suggested purchasing camel equipment in India, but Wood and Stephenson were convinced of the quality of Egyptian saddles and failed to do so. This was just one of many errors which bedevilled the expedition. Another was that Wolseley assumed that camels would be widely available in Egypt and the Sudan. This was not the case and a British major, Major Herbert Kitchener, acting as an intelligence officer in the Sudan, reported this fact to the War Office. The knowledge that the British were preparing an expedition meant that the price of camels increased. Wood refused to pay the high prices demanded for the best camels and bought inferior animals.[28]

Back in June Wolseley had written to the Duke of Cambridge suggesting that a senior man should be appointed from among those in the British army in Egypt to supervise preparations. The Duke was in favour of either Major-General William Earle or Major-General Gerald Greaves. Both the Duke and Wolseley were surprised then Hartington proposed that Wolseley should take this command. As Hartington wrote to the Queen, on 23 August, Wolseley was to assume command of the troops in Egypt temporarily, 'not necessarily of an expedition if it should be despatched, but to direct and superintend the preparations and the organisation of the force'. In fact it was clear that he would command such an expedition since, as he explained to the Duke, Stephenson could not be given the appointment because 'no man can properly conduct or organise an operation in which he does not believe, in fact which he feels to be impracticable'.[29]

Wolseley's appointment was kept secret until the eve of his departure from England: the author Henry James dined with the Wolseleys just before the announcement but was not let in on the secret. Before leaving, Wolseley predicted to his wife that 'I ought to shake hands with Gordon near Khartoum, about 31st January next'. He was seen off by cheering crowds but had said a private farewell to Louisa at their home in Hill Street. If she had come to the station, 'I should have broken down altogether. I love you far more intensely now than I have ever done'.[30]

On 9 September Wolseley arrived in Cairo and took up residence in the Kassr-ed-Noussa Palace. He worked formidably hard organising the expedition and appointing his staff. The Duke of Cambridge had already had one attack of gout when hearing of Wolseley's appointment; he became virtually crippled at his plans and proposals. The first shock to the Duke was Wolseley's proposal to create a Camel Corps to form a desert column which would, in case of need, advance across the desert from Korti to Metemmeh thereby cutting the large eastward loop of the Nile. On 13 September he wrote to the Duke that he was concerned that 'the young soldiers under twenty-three years of age will not be able to stand the hard work which will fall upon all ranks after Wady Halfa is left behind'. Consequently he wanted a Camel Corps to be formed of picked men from the Guards and the Cavalry. The Duke was against the idea because it would mean taking the best men, making it impossible to send the Cavalry or the Guards in the future. However, when the Duke looked at the alternative, sending the Rifle Brigade or the Hussars, he realised neither were strong enough to supply Wolseley with the men he needed. Therefore he agreed reluctantly to the proposal. Wolseley was convinced that he was correct: 'These Camel Corps will really be worth any Brigade of troops I could collect here. In fact they will be, in reality, the very finest troops in the world'.[31]

Men from the 'Ring' featured prominently in the list of staff officers: Major-General Redvers Buller was appointed Chief of Staff; Evelyn Wood commanded the lines of communication; Major-General Herbert Stewart was given the command of the desert column; Lieutenant-Colonel Hugh McCalmont was made second-in-command of a brigade; and William Butler was asked to join the boat expedition. Wolseley was forced to make Major-General Earle, who was senior to his preferred choices, the commander of the river column, but made a member of the 'Ring', Colonel Henry Brackenbury, his second-in-command. On this occasion, however, the favourites did not always do great service to their chief. Wolseley complained to his wife:

> I have always gone on the principle of getting hold of all the really able men I can find, but the moment they feel they have an assured footing and can do really good Staff service, they torture themselves with jealousy one of the other, and sometimes even in their dealings with me are inclined to kick over the traces.[32]

Buller proved a great disappointment as Chief of Staff and was subject to frequent reprimands from Wolseley. Butler proved incapable of working in a team, and Wood was now so deaf that working with him was a strain on Wolseley's voice. Only Herbert Stewart earned his praise as 'the very best Staff Officer all round I have known since poor Colley's death'. Typically, the Duke of Cambridge objected to Wolseley's selections and argued that he was using too limited a pool of men and bringing on no new ones. Wolseley responded that his staff, at least the junior portion of it, was completely different from that of 1882, and that he did try and bring on every man who had passed the Staff College or who was highly recommended. Indeed he proposed to appoint Colonel Primrose to command the Guards Camel Corps as he was a Staff College man and had been highly recommended by Lord Rosebery.[33]

The prospect of fighting in the Sudan proved a powerful magnet to serving soldiers. Wolseley was inundated with requests from officers seeking employment, which he mostly turned down. One exception was Colonel Frederick Burnaby, who merely telegraphed news of his imminent arrival. Wolseley was willing to employ him because of his bravery, despite knowing that the Duke of Cambridge and government would not approve.[34] The Prince of Wales wanted to come but Wolseley refused him permission. The Prince then put forward the names of his friends. Wolseley accepted Lord Charles Beresford as his naval aide-de-camp and did not regret his decision.[35] He did later wish that he had turned down Colonel Stanley Clarke, who was made commander of the Light Camel Corps. He proved to be 'a charming man in society, but useless in the field in every way'. Both Wolseley and the Prince wanted Valentine Baker to be employed but the government refused to sanction his appointment as head of intelligence. The post went instead to Sir Charles Wilson, whom Hartington recommended.[36] Wolseley intended to use him to negotiate with the local tribes. Tragically, Wilson's role was later to change and lead to disaster.[37]

Troops were drawn from Britain, Gibraltar, Malta and from the British garrison in Bombay. A total of 11,000 men were to be used, including thirteen and a half infantry battalions. This was not an excessive figure because, apart from the garrisons of Alexandria and Cairo, detachments were to be allocated to Assuan, to be spread along the line of communications between Wadi Halfa and Hannek, and to hold strategic points like Dongola, Debbeh, Abu Hamed and Berber, as these places were reached. The fighting force was to be far smaller, consisting of 1050 Camel Corps, 400 mounted infantry, 100 Royal Marines forming the Naval Brigade, the 19th Hussars, and a selection of troops from the Royal Irish Regiment, the Royal Sussex, Black Watch, Berkshire Regiment, Royal West Kent, Essex Regiment and the Gordon Highlanders. Only this force of 2250 men would make the final advance on Khartoum.[38]

The troops on the river column were dressed in red and blue serge tunics, flannel shirts and serge trousers. The desert column was more colourful with grey serge tunics, ochre breeches, blue goggles and veils. Wolseley wore a khaki Norfolk jacket, khaki breeches, untanned boots and a solar topee and blue goggles.[39]

On 9 October Wolseley received his final orders from Hartington which had been approved by the Cabinet:

> The primary object of the expedition up the Nile is to bring away General Gordon and Colonel Stewart from Khartoum. When that object has been secured no further offensive operations of any kind are to be undertaken. Although you are not precluded from advancing as far as Khartoum, should you consider such a step essential to secure the safe retreat of General Gordon and Colonel Stewart, you will bear in mind that Her Majesty's Government is desirous to limit the sphere of your military operations as much as possible. They rely on you not to advance further southward than is absolutely necessary in order to attain the primary object of the expedition.[40]

By then preparations were well under way.

The official historian of the Sudan campaign, Colonel H. E. Colville, neatly summed up the challenge facing Wolseley:

> The Nile Expedition was a campaign less against man than against nature and against time. Had British soldiers and Egyptian camels been able to subsist on sand and occasional water, or had the desert produced beef and biscuit, the army might, in spite of its late start, have reached Khartoum in November.[41]

The accumulation of supplies at Wadi Halfa was the critical factor, since every 1000 men needed 4000 pounds of food for three months. The quantities required were vast: 1,608,500 tons of beef and 1,359,400 pounds of ships biscuits give an idea of the task. The supplies were transported to Wadi Halfa by steamers. Buller was responsible for drawing up the contract with the firm Thomas Cook for the supply of coal. He believed that the contract stipulated that coal would be delivered for as long as necessary. It was only after the steamers stopped running at the end of October, when the coal ran out, that Buller discovered that the contract was for a fixed period. A new agreement was quickly drawn up but ten days had been lost. Wolseley blamed himself for having trusted Buller too much.[42]

Wolseley's style of command was very personal in that he attempted to supervise every aspect of the expedition. When the steamers stopped running he had already gone forward to Dongola to begin negotiations with the Mudir there. He returned immediately to Wadi Halfa, however, to solve the coal question personally. At Wadi Halfa he made it clear that Buller was the chief of staff and that he did not see any point in having a dog if he had to bark himself. He then returned to Dongola so fast that the war illustrator Melton Prior thought it might be the fastest ride on record.[43]

By the end of October the whole of the Camel Corps had arrived at Wadi Halfa, where they met their camels for the first time. Training the men to ride camels proved highly entertaining. Wolseley was amused by the spectacle of a 'Life Guardsman clothed like a scarecrow and with blue goggles on, mounted on a camel, over which he has little control'. One member of the mounted infantry, Percy Marling, noted what happened on the first mounted parade: 'We had a mounted parade, first at the walk, and did fours, right and left and wheeling, and only about six men fell off. Then Curly Hutton sounded the trot, and in two minutes the air was thick with Tommies flying about at every angle'.[44] Their commander did not enjoy riding camels at all: he wrote to Frances that 'I never knew what the brute was going to do next, or whether it would lie down suddenly at any moment'.[45]

On the march from Wadi Halfa to Korti a routine was soon established: the troops would start at about five or six in the morning leading their camels until the sun got too hot, then would mount and ride for about eight or nine hours with a half hour break at noon. The camels proved one-paced, covering ground at a steady two and three-quarter miles an hour. The Egyptian saddles were of such poor quality that camels usually got sore backs after only four days. These sores were plugged with oakum in the same way that the holes in boats were repaired. This was not as cruel as it might sound because the tar acted as an antiseptic.[46]

Serious delays affected the start of the river column. Because the orders for the boats had been placed with so many yards, their equipment was not interchangeable. Despite the effort of the builders to pack the equipment with the boats, it became separated in transit and there was a delay at Wadi Halfa while the confusion was sorted out. The boats were then delayed for three days on the railway to Assiut because the Egyptian army commissariat blocked the line with 800 loads of food supplies. This meant that it was not until the end of September that the first steamer carrying the boats left for Assuan. Then at Wadi Halfa another ten days was lost when the whalers had to wait while sixty native craft were given right of way through the Second Cataract. Finally, on 1 November, the river column began to leave from Sarras. Butler realised that there was a serious problem: the boats were carrying 1000 pounds more than they had been designed for. He described this as 'the last straw that broke the camel's back'. It meant that the river column progressed up the Nile more slowly than planned until, on 25 December, the overload was reduced by half by transferring the remainder to camels, after which the speed of the boats increased to an average of ten miles a day.[47]

On 17 November Wolseley received his first direct message from Gordon, dated 4 November. Gordon gave him two pieces of important news. The first was that he could not read Wolseley's messages because his aide,

Colonel Stewart, had taken the cipher books with him when leaving Khartoum on 12 September. The murder of Stewart and Power by members of the Monassir tribe, after their steamer had run aground near Abu Hamed, meant that the Mahdi might have the British ciphers. Wolseley immediately gave instructions to Gordon on what keys to use for the two codes in *The Soldier's Pocket Book*.[48] The murders showed that the British advance be opposed, forcing him to advance in strength over each stage. The second piece of news was that Khartoum was in dire straits: the Mahdi had arrived at the Dervish camp near Omdurman, but Gordon felt that Khartoum could hold out for forty days with ease. This meant that Wolseley had to move faster. He offered a prize of £100 of his own money to the battalion that made the fastest run from Sarras to Korti. The Queen telegraphed her objection to this 'bribe', but Wolseley believed it effective. It was won by the 1st Battalion, the Royal Irish Regiment.[49]

Wolseley arrived at Korti on 16 December, where he hoped to be joined by the entire Camel Corps by Christmas Day. Conditions at Korti were uncomfortable and he was seriously bothered by sand getting into his eyes. He bathed them frequently with cold tea but was forced to retire early each evening because 'with eyes as bad as mine I cannot afford to weary them in this climate. It is the want of a good crop of eyelashes that makes you suffer in the desert'. He also wrote to Louisa that his bedstead made sleep difficult: its outside measurement was only two feet wide.[50]

At Dongola and Korti Wolseley entered into negotiations with the local rulers. He hoped to secure the loyalty of the Mudir of Dongola, Hussein Pasha Khalifa, by giving him the insignia of a Knight Commander of the Order of St Michael and St George. He also hoped to obtain camels from the local tribes. The knowledge, however, that the Sudan would soon be abandoned led to caution by the desert rulers. They made promises they had little intention of keeping. For example, Wolseley expected to find a column of camels at Korti, promised by the chief of the Kababish tribe, but none were waiting and it appeared that none were coming.

The lack of fresh camels seriously affected his plans. The river column was ordered to concentrate at Hamdah, above the Gerendid cataract, for an advance into the country of the Monassir tribe, to punish the murderers of Colonel Stewart and Power, and then to advance by Berber to Metemmeh to join the desert column for the final advance on Khartoum. Gordon's news made it imperative to save time by sending the desert column 176 miles across the desert to Metemmeh. But the shortage of camels meant that the advance would have to be made in two stages: first to the Jakdul Wells, one hundred miles from Korti, to establish a supply depot, then returning to Korti for more supplies. Only then would the column proceed to the wells at Abu Klea and set up another camp there, before again making a two-stage march on Metemmeh. From there Wilson and Beresford, in company with a detachment of infantry and the Naval Brigade, would take Gordon's steamers to Khartoum and confer with him. A few officers would be left with Gordon until the main force was in position to raise the siege.[51]

The plan was the only one that could have been adopted, given the pressure of time, but it was fraught with danger. When the expedition had been conceived it had been thought that there would be little or no fighting on the way to Khartoum. It had been assumed that the sight of British soldiers in the desert would persuade the Mahdi to raise the siege. It was also believed that the Dervishes were incapable of gathering intelligence as to the location and strength of the British columns. The need to make each advance in two stages seriously weakened the desert column, made it vulnerable to attack and gave the Dervishes warning of the approach. Wolseley himself acknowledged the danger: 'My thoughts bent on this desert march: it is a great leap in the dark'.[52] The telegraph extended only as far as Korti and Hartington refused Wolseley permission to advance with the desert column. While he trusted the abilities of its commander, Herbert Stewart, he itched to be at the front. He later told Buller: 'This is the first time in my life that I have been chained to the rear in a campaign, and I hope it may be the last'.[53]

On 30 December the desert column left Korti. Wolseley found the scene very moving, one 'the remembrance of which will be long impressed upon the memory'.[54] On the following day he received a messenger from Gordon that made him all the more aware of the vulnerability of his two columns. The written message, dated 14 December, read 'Khartoum, all right' but the oral message was serious. Gordon warned him not to leave Berber in his rear and to bring plenty of troops. This confused Wolseley who thought, wrongly as it turned out, that the oral message was more likely to reflect the truth. Gordon would have been aware of the chance that the messenger might be caught be the Dervishes and the written message found. Earle was ordered to concentrate at Abu Hamed and advance in strength on Berber. The desert progress continued its progress as planned. Yet Gordon needed the relief expedition to move faster. On the last page of his journal, written on the same day as the message, Gordon wrote 'Now MARK THIS, if the Expeditionary Force, and I ask for no more than two hundred men, does not come in ten days, the town may fall; and I have done my best for the honour of our country. Good-bye'.[55]

Stewart's column made its scheduled return from Jakdul to collect more supplies and then began the advance towards Abu Klea. On the evening of 16 January Stewart's force of 1500 men saw about 14,000 dervishes between them and the wells at Abu Klea. It was too late in the day for a battle, so defensive positions were built and the force settled for the night. Early on 17 January the desert column formed up in a square with the camels in the centre. Then 'with wild yells the Arabs moved across our left flank, in column of companies, and disappeared for a moment behind the rocks and grass in the wady. In half a minute they reappeared, close on the left rear, left wheeled into line, and charged'.[56] The skirmishers ran back to rejoin the square, temporarily blocking the line of fire from the square. This enabled the Dervishes to tear

> down upon us with a roar like the roar of the sea, an immense surging wave
> of white-slashed black forms brandishing bright spears and long flashing swords
> and the terrible rain of bullets poured into them by the Mounted Infantry and
> the guards stayed them not.[57]

The terrified camels in the centre began to struggle to be free, breaking the rear of the square, and enabling a few Dervishes to get inside before being killed. The Gardner machine gun fired about seventy rounds before jamming and the Naval Brigade struggled to unjam it. Its commander, Lieutenant Alfred Pigot, was killed, and all handling the Gardner except Beresford were killed. Finally the Dervishes retreated.

In all the British lost heavily for such a small force. Nine officers, including Colonel Burnaby, were killed along with sixty-five other ranks, and nine officers and eighty-five other ranks were wounded. Thirty-eight per cent of the Naval Brigade was either killed or wounded. The Dervishes also lost heavily: over 1100 bodies were found in the immediate proximity of the square. The battle of Abu Klea was immortalised in verse:

> The sand of the desert is sodden red,-
> Red with the wreck of a square that broke;-
> The Gatling's jammed and the Colonel is dead,
> And the regiment blind with dust and smoke.
> The river of death had brimmed his banks,
> And England's far, and Honour a name,
> But the voice of a schoolboy rallies the ranks:
> Play up! play up! and play the game![58]

The desert column did not stop to lick its wounds, but began the march on Metemmeh that afternoon and continued marching throughout the night.

On 19 January a gravel ridge was reached at Abu Kru and from it the Nile, Shendi and Metemmeh could be seen; so could a large force of Dervishes, ready to oppose the British force. A stray rifle shot wounded

Stewart in the groin and, after the deaths at Abu Klea of senior officers, Wilson was left in charge. The desert column was now reduced to 900 bayonets.[59]

Wolseley heard the news of the battle of Abu Klea on 21 January. He was impressed by Stewart's handling of the troops and was 'glad to learn that no Arab who ever got into the square, or very near it even, got away'. He confessed in this letter that he was extremely worried about Stewart, 'for his loss – even his being badly wounded – would really, at this moment, be a national calamity'. Unknown to him, Stewart had already been seriously wounded. On 28 January he learned of Stewart's wound and the activities of the desert column since it, and was furious with Wilson for making a 'foolish reconnaissance' of Metemmeh. Having given up smoking for a month earlier in the campaign, Wolseley now found that he was smoking as many as four cigars a day because of the strain.[60]

Wilson's command was disastrous: Marling noted that 'we are now run by a committee – Wilson, Boscawen, two Barrows, Charlie Beresford, and David Airlie'. The movement on Metemmeh after Abu Kru had really been an attempt to take it, only after its failure was it demoted to a reconnaissance.[61] All that had been achieved was to embolden the Dervishes by providing evidence of the weakness of the desert column, now heavily encumbered with wounded. Yet Wolseley was convinced that Wilson could have acted more forcefully. He wrote home that 'Sir C. Wilson, very useful for the political work, is no soldier: this is his first dose of fighting, and it has evidently hurt his nerves'. He sent a similar message to Hartington.[62]

On 24 January Wilson and a small detachment of the Royal Sussex Regiment and members of the Naval Brigade embarked on Gordon's steamers at Gubat. Beresford was unable to accompany them as planned because he was crippled by painful boils. The steamers made slow progress and suffered frequent breakdowns. On the afternoon of 27 January Arabs along the bank of the Nile called out that Khartoum had fallen and Gordon had been killed. Unable to believe the news, Wilson continued up river until, on the morning of 28 January, the town came into view. Although the Egyptian flag was still flying, 'Khartoum itself was firing on Sir C. Wilson's steamers'. No firing was heard inside Khartoum and Wilson could see that Government House and the surrounding buildings were completely wrecked. He assumed that the town had been taken and ordered the steamers to turn round. Messengers were left on a nearby island to gather information. They returned with the news that at dawn on 26 January 40,000 Dervishes had entered Khartoum at the point where its defences had been weakened by the falling Nile, and that Gordon had been killed. On 31 January the steamer carrying Wilson was wrecked and he and his troops landed on an island to await rescue. Lieutenant Stuart Wortley rowed back to Gubat for assistance and to bring the news of Gordon's death.[63]

Wolseley had been waiting at Korti for news from the desert with ever-increasing anxiety. He had sent Buller forward to take command as soon as he heard of Stewart's serious wound. Buller reached Jakdul on 2 February and was told that Khartoum had fallen and that Gordon was dead. At seven p.m. on 4 February Wolseley received the news. He was absolutely staggered by it and determined to avenge Gordon's death. He immediately ordered the military to take over control of the telegraph to Cairo so that the news would not leak out before he had sent a despatch to Hartington. He reported that Khartoum had fallen and that Wilson had been shipwrecked on his return but was quite safe. Nothing certain was known of Gordon's fate, other than the information given by the Sudanese near Khartoum, but Wolseley thought that he was probably a prisoner. He asked for instructions since 'the object of my mission to this country being no longer possible'. Telegrams were sent to Buller and Earle to halt where they were until further orders.[64]

The news descended on London like a thunderbolt on the morning of 5 February. Gladstone's private secretary, Edward Hamilton, described the situation as 'the blackest day since the horrible Phoenix Park murders'. The Queen was horrified, and 'telegraphed *en clair* to Mr Gladstone, Lord Granville, and Lord Hartington, expressing how dreadfully shocked I was at the news, all the more so when one felt it might have been prevented'. Gladstone was furious with the Queen for telegraphing *en clair*, especially because her message passed through the hands of several telegraphists as he made his way back to London from the country.[65] The press and public were angry and distraught: the initials G.O.M. used to describe Gladstone as a 'Grand Old Man' were reversed to M.O.G., 'Murderer of Gordon'. Gladstone obviously did not view the death of Gordon seriously: he earned opprobrium by attending a burlesque on the night the news broke. After swiftly growing public outrage, a day of national mourning was observed and a memorial service held at St Paul's Cathedral, attended by the Prince of Wales.

Wolseley was in urgent need of instructions because his orders had firmly limited him to operations to rescue Gordon. Although he had told Hartington that he could undertake operations against Khartoum soon, he confided to his wife that 'to begin a campaign at this season of the year with British troops on the Sudan would be simply madness'. On 6 February Hartington telegraphed him with surprising news:

In addition to the primary object of saving Gordon's life, if it be still possible, we desire to check the Mahdi's advance in the provinces of the Soudan which he has not yet conquered by any means in our power. It is even possible that a subsequent advance and recapture of Khartoum may be necessary.[66]

The government were prepared to send more troops to Suakin to operate against Uthman Diqna if that would help Wolseley, and he was free to take Berber if he thought it appropriate.

This was a complete reverse of policy by the same government that had so unwillingly despatched the expedition in the first place. As Wolseley pointed out to the Duke of Cambridge:

We cannot flatter ourselves that we are here to fight for an oppressed people, to help a population struggling to be free or to put down slavery. None of the spurious and clap trap pretexts under which we so often invade uncivilised countries will serve us here: we are now here to crush the Mahdi who unless crushed will crush Egypt and in doing so bring down the whole Turkish Empire about the Sultan's head.[67]

He appreciated the irony that a government that had been elected on high moral principles should now promote a campaign of pure conquest and revenge in defence of a territory, Egypt, which it had not intended to remain in for long.

His situation was more serious than he had at first thought. Now that Khartoum had fallen, the Mahdi had a large army at his disposal to oppose the British and had captured 15,000 rifles and fifteen camel guns with plenty of ammunition. On 7 February Wolseley informed Hartington that the Principal Medical Officer had warned that the force would lose 25 per cent of its strength during the summer due to sickness and invaliding, so that he would need four additional battalions. He concluded that:

To besiege Khartoum and take it next autumn will be a very interesting operation, but it will be one of some considerable magnitude. At present we must content ourselves with taking Abu Hammed and Berber, whilst the force you send to Suakin destroys Osman Digna's power.

The Suakin-Berber road could then be used to supply the force near Khartoum.[68]

While discussing future policy and operations with the government Wolseley was not aware of the state of his two columns. The truth was appalling. The river column was ordered to advance to Abu Hamed on 8 February, but on 9 February the destination was altered to Berber. However, on 10 February the river column encountered its first significant resistance and met with a serious reverse. At the battle of Kirbekan the commander, General Earle, was killed along with two colonels and nine other men, and forty-eight officers and men were wounded. The command was assumed by Brackenbury who began to doubt the ability of his force to reach Berber before mid March, whereas Wolseley expected the river column to arrive there by 28 February ready to join Buller's force to attack the town. The depth of the Nile was low and the cataracts ahead were unknown.[69]

The desert column was in an even worse state: 'There was hardly a pair of boots in the whole column. Some of the men cut up old rifle-buckets and tied the pieces with string to the soles of their feet'. The Naval Brigade marched barefoot. On 12 February Buller, now at Gubat, reported that Metemmeh could not be taken with the force in its present state because 'our camels are emaciated, and their carrying power small'. Both columns suffered from the poor quality of the packing cases used for food. Buller and Brackenbury found that much of the biscuit was unfit for human consumption and that the beef had rotted.[70] By 17 February Wolseley was fully apprised of the situation: Buller could not take Metemmeh or march to Berber. Therefore Brackenbury would be halted at Abu Hamed, to be joined there by Buller's column, in the hope that Berber could soon be taken by operations by both columns who would have been reinforced by supplies and men from the garrisons stretching down the Nile into Egypt. By 20 February Wolseley suspected that the columns would not even be able to achieve this goal and was forced to order Buller to return to Korti. Brackenbury was ordered to destroy everything in the neighbourhood of where Colonel Stewart and Power had been murdered and then withdraw to Abu Dom, near Merawi. Brackenbury began the retreat immediately, and 'descended in nine days what it had taken us thirty-one days to ascend'. He left Butler in command at Abu Dom with some troops and went to Korti with the remainder of the column where he handed over command to Wolseley. By 23 February Wolseley began sending men from both columns into summer quarters.[71]

Meanwhile the fate of Gordon had still to be determined. Officers from the Intelligence Department questioned the local population for information. It became clear that Gordon had been killed on 26 January when the Mahdi's troops had first broken in to Khartoum. No details emerged of exactly how Gordon had died. Some locals claimed that he had been shot while leading the troops in the defence of Khartoum, others said that he had waited calmly for death at the top of the steps of the Palace. The latter became the official version, being portrayed in the famous picture by G. W. Joy and added to the legend of Gordon as a Christian martyr.[72] However, some claimed that Gordon was still alive and had been taken to the Mahdi's camp. A report by Salome, an Egyptian professor employed by the War Office as a translator, revealed that his informant, Djamal-ed-din, said that Khartoum had fallen in the middle of December and that Gordon's letters, and presumably the last volume of his journal, had been forged. The Mahdists had reported the death of Gordon to prevent the British from continuing to campaign against them. These rumours were dismissed and it was finally accepted in mid March that Gordon had died on 26 January and that his severed head had been taken to the Mahdi.[73]

The failure to rescue Gordon weighed heavily on Wolseley's mind: 'My mind keeps thinking how near a brilliant success I was, and how narrowly I missed achieving it', and he regretted Gordon's death at the hands of a 'rabble'. He made a vow to give up smoking forever because 'it was the greatest of my creature comforts', and he wanted to punish himself for his failure. He never did smoke again. He read Gordon's journal, which further depressed him with its revelation of Gordon's belief that the arrival of a steamer with one hundred British soldiers would have caused the Mahdi to raise the siege. Wolseley recorded his sadness: 'if he had or could have only told me this I would have strained a point and risked the attempt'. Instead he had understood that Gordon had warned him to advance in strength.[74]

Wolseley put the blame for the failure squarely on the shoulders of two men: Gladstone and Sir Charles Wilson. He hoped that the news of the fall of Khartoum would kill Gladstone because 'it was owing to his influence, active measures for the relief of Gordon were not undertaken in time'.[75] His journal is filled with comments criticising Gladstone and other members of his government for their weakness and their failure to understand the military problems of the day. It is also rumoured that Wolseley taught his dog to growl at the word 'Gladstone'. In 1896 he greeted the news of Gladstone's retirement with relief: 'The arch traitor Mr Gladstone has reached the end of his ignoble career; an "extinct volcano" than can no longer vomit forth destruction to his country'. In 1898 he refused to attend Gladstone's funeral in Westminster Abbey. He wrote on the back of the invitation: 'Could not go to the funeral of a man who had all through his life preferred office to the honour and good of England'.[76]

At Korti he could hardly bear seeing Wilson because he could not help thinking 'that he might have been at Khartoum easily the day before the city was betrayed, and all might then have been well'. He repeated his criticisms of Wilson to Ponsonby when asked if Khartoum might have been saved. The emphasis was placed on the assertion that Wilson had lost his nerve, wasted nearly three days and then advanced too tentatively.[77]

An article in the June issue of *Blackwoods Magazine* tried to defend Wilson, arguing that the expedition had been sent out too late and that the delays near the start of the advance were more to blame than Wilson's actions or inaction. Wilson himself wrote a book in his own defence. He argued that the two advances needed to get the supplies to Jakdul had given the Dervishes time to concentrate their forces. Furthermore:

> It is evident, from the various accounts received, that the Mahdi had made up his mind to try and take Khartoum before the arrival of the English; and there is little doubt that if the steamers had left Gubat at an earlier date he would have attacked as soon as he heard they were on their way up, and the result would have been the same.[78]

Wilson did not receive any reward for his part in the campaign, but his career did not suffer: he continued to serve on border commissions as he had done before going to the Sudan.

Post-mortems on the expedition began while the force was still in the Sudan. The *Army and Navy Gazette* had lambasted the concept of using small boats on the Nile from the start. It suggested that they should be burnt for firewood or used for making matches; anything but sent up the Nile, which was a 'wicked waste of public money'.[79] Butler defended the use of the river column. Indeed he argued that the desert column had been unnecessary. He thought that, had the camels given to the Camel Corps been used in carrying supplies for the river column, the lighter boats would have made fast enough progress to make the trip across the desert from Korti to Metemmeh unnecessary.[80]

Others found fault with the desert column. Ian Hamilton, a participant on the river column, argued that it was 'a brain cell freak' of Wolseley's.[81] It was weak because it was composed of a 'heterogeneous crowd of samples from cracks Regiments'. Wilson agreed that this was a problem because: 'A cavalry man is taught never to be still, and that a square can be broken. How then can you expect him in a moment to forget all his training, stand like a rock, and believe no one can get inside a square?'.[82] However, Count Gleichen recorded that the desert column had spent five days being drilled to fight as infantry in early December. Wolseley admitted that 'it is a dangerous experiment, using cavalry as foot soldiers under such a trial', but argued that 'being picked men they ought to have done better'. He believed that his real mistake had been in not sending a sufficient number of able senior officers with experience of war with the column.[83] Yet, given Britain's record in small wars, the loss of senior officers at Abu Klea and Abu Kru was highly unusual and could not have been anticipated.

Recriminations continued while Wolseley was still in Egypt and when he returned home. The Duke of Cambridge criticised his selection for staff appointments for the autumn campaign, complaining that Wolseley never brought on new men but was wedded to the same members of his 'Ring'.

Wolseley replied that he had tried many new men in the Sudan and made caustic comments on many of them. Of the list of fifteen men given, Wolseley felt that of the eight tried under fire only five did either very well or fairly well; of the remaining seven, four were good but three were useless. Wilson lacked nerve; Colonel Boscawen was incapable of responsibility; Colonel White of the Essex Regiment was 'not fit to be a corporal'. Only Colonel Primrose, Brackenbury and Colonel Henderson of the King's Royal Rifles were worthy of further employment. Others who had done well had reached their ceiling for responsibility and should not be promoted further.[84] Wolseley was generous in his list of recommendations for honours and promotions; so generous, in fact, that the new Secretary of State, W. H. Smith, pointed out that such liberality diminished the value of the rewards. The Queen and the Prince of Wales were shocked at the omission of Stanley Clarke from the list and queried it as a possible accidental omission. Wolseley replied to Smith that it was no accident: Clarke deserved nothing and he regretted taking him to the Sudan, which he had done at the Prince of Wales's express wish.[85] Wolseley himself received the vacant ribbon of the Order of St Patrick and was elevated to a viscountcy. By special dispensation, it was agreed that the title would pass to Frances on his death.

During February and into March Wolseley was constantly concerned that the government did not realise the implications of its new policy in the Sudan. To take Khartoum in the autumn would mean the deployment of thousands of men. On 1 March he recorded in his journal that the English newspapers showed that the press were understating the complexities of the campaign: 'Men discuss the march of a force from Suakin to Berber as they would of marching from Aldershot to Plymouth. Camels are referred to as if they were as plentiful as rabbits are in Richmond Park, as if they required no food and never required rest and never died'. On 9 March he made the truth clear to Hartington: 'the campaign before us is the most serious affair we have had on land since 1815'. For this campaign he would require twelve extra infantry battalions, four squadrons of cavalry and two batteries of horse artillery. His advice was that Britain should get out of the Sudan and out of Egypt.[86]

The government had approved plans to reconquer the Sudan because of the public demand to avenge the murder of Gordon. Yet it was unclear exactly what the conquest of Khartoum would achieve in the long term. Wolseley requested permission to style himself Governor General of the Sudan in order to counter the Mahdi's growing power. The government refused him permission, despite the Queen being in favour. Gladstone and Hartington felt that such a title would 'commit ourselves too much to responsibility for government of Sudan, and you should restrict promises of protection to tribes and people within present sphere of operations, or to whom you have come under obligations'.[87] This suggested that the government had not completely reversed its policy of abandonment of the Sudan.

The future advance on Khartoum was partly dependent on the success of operations against Uthman Diqna near Suakin. These had begun under the command of Major-General Graham while Wolseley was still advancing up the Nile. Wolseley was in favour of these operations because, while the defeat of Uthman Diqna would not affect his own position immediately, the opening of the Suakin-Berber road would enable supplies to be pushed forward throughout the summer. To this end the government sanctioned expenditure on the construction of a railway along the route. He was, however, sceptical about the railway being ready in time. Its designer, Sir Andrew Clarke, had insisted on using the standard British gauge instead of a narrow gauge which could have been built faster.[88] Furthermore, Graham seemed incapable of forcing Uthman Diqna to battle. The construction of the railway was therefore constantly being hampered by minor skirmishes between the British troops and the Dervishes.

At the end of March Wolseley was asked by the government to go from Korti to Cairo to ease communications with Britain and to be ready to go to Suakin to report on the situation there if necessary. His wife and daughter joined him for a brief visit to Cairo and he enjoyed a few moments of much needed relaxation showing them the Bazaar and the Pyramids.[89]

This break came at a fortunate time for Wolseley because he was about to become involved in a dispute with the government over its policy towards the Sudan. On 1 March the Afghan village of Pendjeh was invaded by Russian troops seeking to influence the joint Anglo-Russian commission on the Afghan frontier. The government inflated this minor incursion, which did not seem to trouble the Amir of Afghanistan, into a full-blown dispute likely to lead to war between Britain and Russia. This provided the government with the excuse to end the plan for an autumn campaign in the Sudan. On 13 April Wolseley was warned by Hartington that, 'in the condition of Imperial affairs it is probable that the expedition to Khartoum may have to be abandoned', and that preparations should be made to withdraw the troops. He also received a private message from Hartington's private secretary, Reginald Brett, warning him that the country had turned against the Sudan war and was totally preoccupied with the prospect of war with Russia.[90] On 20 April the government announced that it had no plans for a future campaign in the Sudan; that all troops would be held in readiness for a war against Russia; and that the Army Reserve was to be called out.[91]

Devastated by the news, Wolseley threatened to resign. He accepted Hartington's argument that Russia might not believe the seriousness of Britain's sabre-rattling while a considerable portion of the British army was tied up in the Sudan, but he believed that it was important to inflict a defeat on the Dervishes to demonstrate British strength to the Muslims in India and the Ottoman Empire. Furthermore, the government had decided to keep the army in Egypt until the country was financially sound and while its southern frontier still needed to be protected against the Mahdi. Abandoning the Sudan now, before defeating the Mahdi, would lead to another campaign having to be launched in the future. Wilson, Buller and Kitchener all agreed with Wolseley but the government ignored their advice.[92]

Wolseley believed that the province of Dongola should be retained to keep the Dervishes out of the northern part of the Sudan and, should there be no war with Russia, to enable the autumn campaign to take place. The government refused: it wanted all of Wolseley's army out of the Sudan as soon as possible. The future of Graham's force at Suakin was less certain. At the end of April Hartington asked Wolseley to go to Suakin to report on the feasibility of holding the railway and of defeating Uthman Diqna. His departure was delayed by a severe attack of diarrhoea from which he was still weak when he reached Suakin.

There he discovered that Graham had been unable to defend the railway workers, that only twenty miles of the railway had been built, and that Graham had lost the confidence of his subordinates. Wolseley wrote that Graham appeared to be 'incorrigibly stupid' and incapable of taking advice. The weather was getting hotter and all military operations would have to be suspended during the summer months. Therefore, on 5 May, he telegraphed Hartington recommending the withdrawal of all the troops at Suakin and the abandonment of the railway. Hartington agreed to end military operations but wanted his estimate of the number of troops required to hold the existing railway through the summer. Wolseley was enraged by this telegram, writing to his wife that, because it had spent £750,000 on the railway, the government would 'prefer soldiers to perish here from climate than face the ridicule of having to remove the rails just put down'. On 14 May the government agreed to a total withdrawal from Suakin.[93] By the end of May Wolseley was back in Cairo, awaiting permission to return to England. He had little work to do and kept himself occupied working on a new edition of *The Soldier's Pocket Book* 'which always interests and amuses me'.[94]

At the beginning of June 1885 the Liberal government was unexpectedly defeated over the Budget. Gladstone tendered the resignation of his government and the Queen invited the Marquess of Salisbury and the Conservatives to form a new administration until a general election could be held. Wolseley was immediately concerned over who would be appointed Secretary of State for War. Michael Hicks-Beach's name was mooted. Wolseley had clashed with him when Hicks-Beach was Colonial Secretary and did not want to serve under him now. He was relieved but surprised by the choice of W. H. Smith, hoping that he would prove to be an army reformer: if not Smith would have to find a new Adjutant General.[95]

On 26 June the new government asked Wolseley to halt the withdrawal of troops from the Sudan while future policy towards the Sudan was discussed. He sent home a long telegram telling the government 'emphatically that the true policy is to carry out the Autumn Campaign as originally contemplated and approved of. The only other alternative being to pay the Turk well to come and take over the Soudan'. He was then asked for his assessment of the number of troops needed to hold Dongola even if there was to be no campaign against Khartoum. Wolseley set out the case for retention, despite being annoyed by a telegram from Buller pointing out the difficulties of supplying the force since the country was drained of all grain.[96] When the government had received all the information it came to its decision:

> Her Majesty's Government have decided that the retreat ordered by their predecessors is to be continued to a point which in your judgement provides for the security of Egypt; but they are not prepared to abandon the Railway, which should be completed.

The government was worried about the attitude of France towards Egypt. France was about to bring back about 20,000 men who had conquered Tonkin and held another 10,000 in camps near Marseilles. Smith therefore wanted to 'see half the Tonquin men well through the Suez Canal on their way home, and the 10,000 at Marseilles sent to their ordinary quarters, before we reduce our forces within reach of the Canal'.[97] Wolseley was allowed to leave for England, which he did on 7 July, reaching home on 13 July. He received the thanks of both Houses of Parliament on 12 August.

On 20 June, unknown to Wolseley, the Mahdi died of typhus and was succeeded by Khalifa Abdallahi. On 5 July the British evacuation of Dongola started and gradually all troops began to be withdrawn from the Sudan. On 30 December a mixed British and Egyptian force defeated the Dervishes at Ginnis, midway between Wadi Halfa and Dongola. This ended the immediate threat of a Dervish invasion of Egypt and by April 1886 British and Egyptian troops were concentrated at Wadi Halfa.[98]

14

Back at the War Office

The Gordon Relief campaign was the first failure in Wolseley's career as a commander. It would prove to be his last field command. It is therefore worthwhile to look at what kind of commander and man he was. His friend, William Butler, wrote an assessment of Wolseley's talents:

> Our chief was one of that rare make of men in whom the thing we call 'command' in the army is so much an essential item of their nature that one has no more thought of questioning it than one would think of asking a bird why he flew, or a river why it flowed. Wolseley was the only man I met in the army on whom command sat so easily and fitly that neither he nor the men he commanded had ever to think about it.[1]

Others agreed with this. For example, Evelyn Wood repeated what Sir Walter Scott had said of Napoleon by calling Wolseley 'a Sovereign among soldiers'. The Duke of Connaught praised Wolseley after the campaign in Egypt, forcing the Queen, normally one of Wolseley's detractors, to call him a *really* great General'. She added that she only wished that he would behave with tact and not make injudicious speeches.[2]

Wolseley was undoubtedly successful in the field, except for his last campaign, but was clearly not an easy man to work with. The Queen's private secretary, Sir Henry Ponsonby, wrote an analysis of Wolseley as a person: 'he does not inspire any love among those who serve under him though I think they have confidence in him. He thoroughly believes in himself and this makes others believe in him. He is hard and very likely unfeeling but this is useful if unpleasant in a general'.[3] Ian Hamilton who, having served under Wolseley on the Gordon Relief campaign before going to India and serving under Roberts, was ideally placed to contrast the two men. Hamilton emphasised that Roberts had the gift of making himself loved by those serving under him, which is why he was nicknamed 'Bobs'. Wolseley, and indeed Kitchener, did not set out to make themselves popular: their reputations were established by those who served under them because of their skills and efficiency as commanders. Hamilton concluded that 'Wolseley was the most impersonal commander I have ever met'. Yet he admitted that Wolseley was 'a soldier of quality' and, that had he gone to the Staff College instead of accepting the post of aide-de-camp to Roberts, he would have joined the Wolseley Ring.[4]

This suggests that Wolseley was highly capable of putting across his point of view and had such a clear vision of what needed to be done, both in the field and in the area of army reform, that his opinions could not be ignored. He was, in effect, a brilliant administrator who valued efficiency above all other attributes, both in himself and in those who served with or under him. Yet the man himself believed that his reputation as an army reformer depended greatly on his success in campaigns, because it kept the public aware of his name and therefore must have been damaged by his failure to rescue Gordon. He knew that he had many enemies and, while in the Sudan, had confided to Louisa that 'I believe there are many who would rejoice if this expedition failed, because its failure would be mine'. He even told his friend Evelyn Wood that 'the sun of my luck set when Stewart was wounded'.[5]

Later historians appear to have agreed with him: one claimed that his post-1885 career, 'in spite of the nominal importance of his successive appointments, was one steady process of disillusionment and decline, the long, slow denouement of his active career'. One biographer devoted only a few pages to Wolseley's career after 1885.[6] Yet the opposite is true: Wolseley returned from the Sudan chastened, but determined to devote his attention to turning the British army into a professional force capable of meeting and defeating any enemy, colonial or European, on the battlefield. The ingrained conservatism of the Duke of Cambridge meant that his efforts were frequently hampered, and in many areas he could do little more than prepare the ground for the time when, he hoped, he would succeed the Duke and create his model of a modern British army.

Wolseley was greatly assisted by a series of talented Secretaries of State for War. Indeed, his work was so appreciated by them that his term of office as Adjutant General, due to expire at the end of 1887, was extended for a further three years. This was a relief to him because he had been offered the governorship of Malta but was not keen to go: 'I don't care about the place, and I know my wife would hate it, but I cannot afford to be idle'.[7] The political turmoil of the period, caused by Gladstone's support for Home Rule for Ireland, meant that Wolseley served under three different Secretaries of State before his departure to take up the position of Commander-in-Chief in Ireland in 1890. W. H. Smith, who was the Conservative Secretary of State when Wolseley returned from the Sudan, remained in that office until January 1887, with an interlude when Henry Campbell-Bannerman took over during the short-lived Liberal government of 1886. Smith was then succeeded by Edward Stanhope, and it was during this period that some important reforms of the army were made.[8]

Wolseley was also active in his private life. He rose at six every morning, made himself a cup of cocoa, then wrote for three hours before beginning his official duties. He completed a new edition of *The Soldier's Pocket Book* in 1886, and also began his great opus, *The Life of Marlborough*. Louisa loyally supported her husband's activities, making helpful suggestions and correcting his appalling spelling.[9] The Wolseleys also entertained a wide circle of friends. Apart from military colleagues, they were friends with many of the literary figures of the time, including Henry James (who described Wolseley as 'a very handsome, well-mannered and fascinating little man with rosy dimples and an eye of steel, an excellent specimen of the *cultivated* British soldier'). Andrew Lang, Edmund Gosse and the Poet Laureate, Alfred Austin. Although Wolseley did not enjoy poetry and rarely read fiction, he was friends with the novelist Rhoda Broughton, whom he encouraged to insert more patriotism into her novels.[10]

In the late 1880s he instituted a Girls' Debating Society to prepare Frances and some of her friends for public speaking. Wolseley was not a feminist, in that he did not believe that women should be enfranchised or be independent, but did realise that society was changing. Women were now being better educated, more employment was open to them, and they could now sit on school boards and participate in local government.[11] Therefore Wolseley hoped to prepare Frances to take an active part in society when she was older.

In January 1886 he paid a short visit to Berlin to represent the Queen at the Jubilee of Kaiser Wilhelm I. He met General Helmuth von Moltke and Otto von Bismarck and was greatly impressed by both men. Back at the War Office, Wolseley waged a private war against the existing scheme for the manufacture and supply of equipment. The Khartoum expedition had revealed serious failures in the quality of the equipment given to the troops, such as defective cartridges, saddlery, swords, and bayonets. The Superintendent of the Royal Laboratory at Woolwich was forced to admit that the 2.5 inch shells were often faulty. Wolseley called for an inquiry to be made into the Woolwich system, claiming that the system had not improved since he had complained, back in 1870, of the use of perished wood in the manufacture of gun carriages. The Surveyor-General of Ordnance tried to calm him by suggesting that the faulty shells had been an isolated incident. Wolseley replied with other examples: the star shells for the seven pounder gun were larger than the calibre of the gun; many of the 2.5 inch shells were empty; a large number of cartridges jammed; and many bayonets and swords were made of such poor material that they twisted when first used. He also drew attention to the unwillingness of Woolwich to consider new equipment such as breech-loading artillery, machine guns and the Scott's sights for guns. The government became involved in the dispute and set up a Royal Commission on Warlike Stores under the presidency of Sir James Stephen.[12]

Towards the end of 1886 Wolseley began making preparations for 'a magnificent assemblage' of the army at Aldershot as part of the celebrations for Queen Victoria's Golden Jubilee in 1887. He and Louisa each received two tickets for the procession and the Thanksgiving Service in Westminster Abbey: one pair as peers of the realm, the other as military representatives. Louisa gave one of her tickets to Frederick Maurice's wife, and Wolseley gave one to his daughter's former governess, Miss Pannebakker. The two military reviews in mid July 1887, of the Volunteers in Hyde Park and the regulars at Aldershot, passed off very smoothly.

Despite the fact that Wolseley was often criticised for his use of publicity, he was asked to write an article on the army for a compilation of essays on every aspect of British life during the Queen's reign. He took this as an opportunity to reveal the extent to which the army had improved since the start of her reign in 1837 and to highlight those areas still in need of further and urgent improvement. In general, he covered the same ground as he had been over before: the lack of artillery in Britain; the need for better training for the men and more military education for officers; and increased pay. The Volunteers were praised for their patriotism, and an appeal made for compulsory physical education in schools. He criticised the government for its lack of policy and claimed that 'the party politician, with his dreams of universal peace, of general disarmament, and international courts of arbitration', was responsible for the ills of the army. By comparing the performance of the British army in the various wars of the reign, Wolseley showed how the Cardwell reforms had led to great improvements. On future policy, he repeated his appeal for the selection by merit of officers for higher commands, called for localisation to be extended to the cavalry, and wrote that the artillery should be divided into battalions and the field artillery entirely separated from the garrison.[13] In other words, he used this opportunity to publish his programme for further army reform, this time with the official sanction of the Duke of Cambridge.

One of the most important issues of the late 1880s was the vulnerability of Britain to invasion by France. This debate revealed the poor state of Britain's naval and military defences and had wider repercussions in that it also revealed the differences in opinion on how best to defend Britain between the War Office and the Admiralty. Wolseley was very closely involved in these arguments, exploiting the invasion scares in order to publicise the poor state of the British army.

Various events contributed to the home defence scare. As early as 1884

W. T. Stead had published an article in the *Pall Mall Gazette* drawing attention to the poor state of the navy, but the government had ignored it. In 1886 General Georges Boulanger became Minister for War in the French Cabinet and he, and his naval colleague, Admiral St Aube, made a number of bellicose statements on the strength of France. The head of the Intelligence Department, Henry Brackenbury, described Boulanger as 'a type of politico- military adventurer', whose actions might well prove unpredictable. Either Boulanger would direct his attention towards Germany and agitate for the return of Alsace and Lorraine, or he might seek popularity in France by turning on France's militarily weaker neighbour, Britain.[14] Then in January 1888 Lord Charles Beresford resigned from the Board of the Admiralty to stand as a Member of Parliament, specifically to draw public and government attention to the navy and its lack of plans for war. In April 1888 Wolseley gave a speech at a private dinner for the industrialist Sir John Pender to help Beresford's parliamentary campaign.

This speech was also a response to a speech by the Under-Secretary of State for War, St John Brodrick, at Guildford in which he had claimed that the responsibility for an efficient army rested firmly with the military authorities.[15] Not so, argued Wolseley:

> The answer to the question why the Army and Navy are not as strong as they ought to be is to be found in the system of our Government by party – that curse of modern England which is sapping and undermining the foundations of our country, which is depriving our statesmen of the manly honesty which was once their characteristic. What do we see when any new Administration comes into office? What directly takes place? It is the same with all Parties. The first thing is the endeavour made by the Minister in Office to obtain some clap-trap reputation by cutting down the expenses of the Army and Navy.[16]

The military authorities would not take responsibility for the state of the army so long as they were starved of men and money. Stanhope asked the Duke of Cambridge to reprimand Wolseley for his comments. The Duke did so but, in private, told him that he broadly agreed with his remarks.

The Prime Minister, the Marquess of Salisbury, made a strong attack on Wolseley for abusing his powers as Adjutant General to stir up trouble, ending his speech to the House of Lords, 'If he thinks his duty forces him to make such statements as these, let him come down here and make them, and we will answer them'. Wolseley wrote to Salisbury that he had been disturbed by the personal attack on him, and that 'had I known of your intention, I should not have failed to have been in my place in the House of Lords'.[17] On 14 May 1888 he made his maiden speech in the House of Lords. He argued that publicity was essential to gain the backing of the public for essential expenditure. Security would not be put at risk because 'there is no deficiency or weak point in our defences which is not well known to the military and naval Authorities of every great foreign nation as it is to ourselves'.[18]

Now apparently welcomed by Salisbury into the House of Lords, Wolseley soon allied himself with the Duke of Cambridge to take part in a debate on a motion proposed by the Earl of Wemyss on 29 June 1888 that the House welcomed the government's recent proposals to secure the defences of the country and of the Empire. Work had begun on improving the state of the defences but Wolseley and the Duke of Cambridge made it clear that there was a long way still to go before Britain would be secure. In his speech Wolseley repeated the often-quoted allegation of 'the possibility of 100,000 men being landed on our shores in a very short time from across the Channel for the purpose of capturing London'. He argued that ample shipping was always available in the French Channel ports, whereas the First Lord of the Admiralty, Lord George Hamilton, argued that ships would have to be moved from the Mediterranean ports, thereby giving Britain ample warning of French intentions and alerting the fleet. Much to the government's relief, after the public debate in the House of Lords, and Hamilton's statement in the House of Commons, the differences of opinion between the Admiralty and the War Office were thereafter voiced in private.[19]

Work had been under way to examine the state of Britain's defences over the past year. In June 1887 Lord Randolph Churchill had made a bombastic speech at Wolverhampton in which he argued that, despite the vast expenditure on the navy and army, neither force could guarantee Britain's security. The Cabinet demanded to know whether the situation was as bad as Churchill had portrayed. The Intelligence Department was forced to admit that the allegation that 'none of our fortresses are at present armed in accordance with the military requirements of the day' was accurate though being remedied slowly. London could not last long against a besieging force because there were only four weeks' supply of meat, thirteen weeks' of wheat, and four or five weeks' supply of coal within the capital. A consultative committee established by Stanhope at the War Office then highlighted the military importance of the ports of Portsmouth, Plymouth, London and Cork.[20]

Stanhope now asked the Intelligence Department to prepare a memorandum on the subject of a French invasion in order to clarify whether Wolseley's or Hamilton's figures for shipping were correct. This memorandum appeared to give more credence to Wolseley's figures rather than those supplied by the Admiralty. It was estimated that it would take France nine days to have five corps fully mobilised and concentrated on the north-west coast of France. However, it was also pointed out that, since the peace strength of the French army was about 480,000 men, 100,000 of them could be concentrated at the Channel ports without any general mobilisation having been declared. Brackenbury's tonnage figures showed that Wolseley was correct to suspect that France had sufficient shipping in the north for invasion. Brackenbury stated that the French army would probably land on the Sussex coast and noted that 'I am not aware that the Admiralty have undertaken the responsibility of watching the approach of an expedition'.[21]

The 1886 mobilisation plan allocated every battalion and unit of the regular army in the United Kingdom to two army corps and a cavalry brigade. A third army corps was to be composed of a mixture of regulars and auxiliaries. Wolseley, at the request of Salisbury and Stanhope, asked the Intelligence Department to prepare a series of memoranda on how the French army would prepare for invasion, the defence of London and mobilisation plans for the British army for home defence. These memoranda were extremely detailed. They included, for example, a proposal to raise more men by appealing for former regular and auxiliary soldiers to re-enlist, and a plan to seize and if necessary destroy the railways should the enemy gain a firm bridgehead. Their chief author, Colonel John Ardagh, argued that the construction of a ring of fixed defences round London would be cheaper than the alternatives of augmenting the navy or increasing the military forces in the area. Two rings of defences were planned: one to cover the outer approaches to London along the North Downs to the south and along the high ground north of London, and an inner line corresponding approximately with the present South and North Circular Roads. The estimated cost of these fortifications would be £480,000, which could be spread over a number of years.[22]

These memoranda met with a mixed response. The Admiralty and the navalists were totally hostile to the idea that the Royal Navy alone could not defend Britain against invasion. Wolseley, Buller and the Duke of Cambridge argued that, while they accepted that the navy should be the main bulwark against invasion, 'we believe that our naval supremacy may be paralysed if, on account of the insecurity of the capital, public opinion demands the retention of our fleets at home as our only security against invasion'. Therefore it was essential that 'London must be defended by an active army in the first line, and a second line in strong position'. Furthermore the plans must be drawn up quickly since 'already villas and villages have occupied some of the best points for defence on the great chalk ridge', and this problem was only likely to get worse as London's suburbs grew.[23] The navy ultimately won the day. Although Stanhope was given £600,000 for fixed defences around London, and the whole line of fortifications was surveyed and plans drawn up for the defence works, few were ever built. Those that were built were usually little more than extensions to existing military buildings, for example, Tilbury Fort and Warley. However, sixty 'Stanhope storehouses' were built and were of great use during the mobilisation for the Boer War. The navy received £21,500,000 for the construction of new ships under the 1889 Naval Defence Act, and a further £30,250,000 in the 1894 Spencer programme.[24]

One feature of the debates over Britain's vulnerability to invasion was the revelation of the apparently irreconcilable differences between the Admiralty and the War Office. As Wolseley pointed out to the members of a Royal Commission under the presidency of Lord Hartington in 1889: 'The Admiralty, to my recollection since I have had anything to do with the War Office, have never conceded anything, no matter how small, to us'.[25] The government attempted to rectify the situation by setting up a number of inter-departmental committees, but these achieved little. For example, the Landing Places Committee met eleven times between 1891 and 1894 and served only to exacerbate the differences between the Admiralty and the War Office. In 1894 its report concluded that there was no need for such a committee to exist since an enemy could not get past the navy to land on Britain's shores.[26] The Joint Naval and Military Committee set up in 1891 only dealt with the defences of military and mercantile harbours, differentiating between the responsibilities of the naval and military commanders of the ports and harbours.

The invasion debates also had another unforeseen consequence: the navy fought back and created its own doctrine of home and imperial defence. Four days after Wolseley's speech on invasion in the House of Lords, Vice-Admiral Philip Colomb presented a paper at the Royal United Service Institute. He argued that all that was necessary for Britain to be secure from invasion was an enlarged navy. With more ships, the fleet would be able to achieve the multitude of tasks it would face in time of war, as well as defend Britain against invasion. In his opinion, the role of the army was to undertake limited operations in naval interests such as the defence of coaling stations abroad. This lecture has been viewed by some commentators as the launching point of the Blue Water school of thought.[27] This school called for large battle fleets and a large number of smaller ships to maintain a close blockade of the enemy coast. In 1890 A. T. Mahan published *The Influence of Sea Power on History* and in 1892 *The Influence of Sea Power upon the French Revolution and the Empire*. Both books were well received within naval circles. While Wolseley disputed Colomb's theories, he believed that 'Mahan's books have done the country, and the Navy for that matter too, a world of good'. But he remained wedded to his idea that the army had a greater role to play than that assigned to it by the navy.[28]

Britain was not seriously threatened with invasion during this period. Despite Boulanger's bellicose statements there appears to be no evidence that France ever produced any plans for an offensive against Britain in the 1880s. Wolseley found no hatred of Britain when he visited the battlefields of the Franco-Prussian War in France in August 1889. However, the invasion scares served several purposes both positive and negative. For example, Salisbury warned Evelyn Baring to be cautious in Egyptian financial affairs because the French

> already, I am told, look upon a war with England as the cheapest of the three alternatives open to them. They are so unreasonable, and have so much incurable hatred of England, that I should dread any very glaring exhibition of our sovereignty in Egypt at this moment.[29]

In February 1889 Wolseley endorsed this sentiment, fearing war with France over Egypt because Boulanger now headed the new French government.[30] The positive outcome of the debates was that he had successfully drawn public and parliamentary attention to the poor state of the British army and was now in a stronger position vis à vis the Duke of Cambridge to gain political support for further reforms.

The home defence debates showed that Wolseley and the Duke of Cambridge could cooperate when necessary. The Duke had readily agreed to the extension to Wolseley's term of office but soon had reason to regret his decision. A series of articles by Wolseley in the *Fortnightly Review* in 1888 and 1889 caused little controversy apart from annoying the Duke of Cambridge by appealing for 'battle training' rather than mindless drill. But in 1890 he wrote a series of articles on the British army for the American journal, *Harper's Magazine*. Again he covered the same ground as in earlier articles, appealing for better pay, more practical uniforms and the need for a Secretary of State who knew something about the army, etc. The very fact that these articles were appearing in the United States aroused the Duke's fury because he believed that the Americans might take them as a statement of future reforms which would shortly take place within the British army. He complained to the Queen's private secretary, Sir Henry Ponsonby, about one article in particular, because it 'contains doctrines and views I deeply regret and highly reprobate'. The Duke requested Ponsonby to ask the Queen to write a letter of reprimand to Wolseley, to be sent either through Stanhope or the Duke. Ponsonby's reply was that the Queen would write the letter if the Duke told her what to say. The

Duke wanted the Queen to tell Wolseley 'not to publish anything or even to speak as seldom as possible on Army matters'.[31] The Queen duly wrote to Wolseley, who thereafter wrote only for the less public military journals.

In 1887 Charles Dilke wrote to Wolseley asking 'if there is any speech or anything published of yours in which you have [given] "counsels of perfection", i.e. things that might be done if the public was willing to spend the money that really might be spent'.[32] The result of their correspondence was that Dilke quoted him in *The British Army* as saying that he:

Thinks that our army is clumsily and badly organised, drilled on an obsolete system, and dressed in ridiculous and theatrical costumes, that its tactical instruction is far below what it should be, and that a large proportion of the superior officers are not fully competent to command in modern war.[33]

The army was also desperately short of men and unprepared for war.

The manpower crisis showed little sign of easing during the 1880s, indeed it was worsening as the traditional reservoir from which the rank and file were recruited, the agricultural labourers, shrank as over four million had left the countryside for towns since 1840. In 1883 Wolseley had made the situation clear:

We have cut our army coat in accordance with the amount of money which we have fixed arbitrarily as to what its cost should be, in utter disregard of the size of our body, the proportions of our limbs, or the objects for which any coat at all is required.[34]

An addition of 18,000 men to the army had been made in response to the 1885 crisis in India, but most of these men went to increase the British establishment there. The occupation of Egypt by eleven and a half infantry battalions was not taken into account, and in 1885 Wolseley argued 'if in some ten or more years hence we find ourselves in a position to withdraw from Egypt, it will be easy to adapt the army organisation, which had been framed to meet the greater difficulty, to circumstances that have changed for the good in our favour'. Once the Sultan of Turkey had refused to sign the Drummond Wolff Convention in 1887, there seemed little likelihood of Britain being able to withdraw from Egypt in the near future. Wolseley had some political support: Campbell-Bannerman also felt that the establishment should be increased.[35] Yet the governments were unwilling to do anything which cost money, particularly after the Chancellor of the Exchequer, Randolph Churchill, began a campaign both inside and outside Parliament to reduce naval and military expenditure, which led to his resignation in December 1886.

Wolseley viewed India as a bottomless pit forever demanding more British troops while pursuing a plan of defence he thought was faulty. His basic premises were that the Second Afghan War had shown that Afghanistan was not the most suitable battleground for a major war with Russia, and that Britain was too weak to be able to provide the Indian military authorities with the number of soldiers they were demanding. He argued that other areas should be selected for war against Russia, alliances should be made with powers also opposed to Russian aggrandisement, and India should be told firmly to rely on her own military resources.[36]

He also still believed that Britain should make an alliance with Turkey and strike at the periphery of Russia, for example, from the Black Sea towards the Trans-Caspian railway, from the Persian Gulf with the same aim, from the Baltic against the Russian capital St Petersburg, or from Vladivostock on the Pacific seaboard. His opinions were supported at the War Office by Brackenbury but viewed with horror by Roberts who wrote of them:

> They know nothing about India, and they care nothing. Their object is to have everything in their own hands, and if they are able to guide the nation when war breaks out with Russia, they will embark on some wild scheme of operations in the neighbourhood of the Black Sea, and when they are hopelessly involved they will cripple India by indenting upon us for troops and transport.

Roberts suspected that the War Office was about to tell him the future plan would be to keep India on the defensive while offensive operations were confined to the Caucasus.[37]

In fact the War Office was fast concluding that India was not as vulnerable to invasion as it thought and could not actually be defended against Russia in any case. A colonel in the Indian army, H. B. Hanna, later wrote three very detailed books which outlined the enormous difficulties Russia would face during an advance through Afghanistan, and it was clear that Indian difficulties would be no less extreme.[38] The Sultan of Turkey had been obstructive over Egypt and seemed unlikely to be a reliable ally, and Britain had allowed Russia to gain a foothold in Persia, so an alliance with the Shah was improbable. The Amir of Afghanistan remained as independent as ever. Charles Dilke and Spenser Wilkinson made a clear analysis of the problems of Indian defence in their book *Imperial Defence*. They concluded that neither the War Office nor the Indian military authorities' plans could guarantee success against the vast armed resources of Russia. From April 1887 onwards Stanhope warned India not to depend on more battalions being sent from Britain, but the Indian military authorities continued to include massive reinforcements from Britain in their mobilisation plans. It was not until 1892 that India was finally informed of the need to rely on her own resources only.[39]

From the first article Wolseley had written on army reform in 1871, he had persistently appealed for a statement to be made on the purposes for which the army existed. Without this statement, he argued, it was impossible for the War Office to estimate the size of the establishments required. Successive governments had resisted his appeals, fearing that such a statement might work against a democratic system by forcing a later government to accept another party's policies. In 1888 Wolseley tried again and at last met with some success. On 8 December 1888 Stanhope wrote a memorandum, which bore his name, on the purposes of the army. It was circulated only to the Cabinet and reissued in June 1891, but still not made public.

A comparison of the provisions demonstrates the debt Stanhope owed to Wolseley's memorandum of 8 June 1888. In both, aid to the civil power was made the first priority. On the second requirement of the army, Stanhope contented himself with the vague phrase 'to find the number of men for India which has been fixed by arrangement with the Government of India'. Wolseley, on the other hand, went further in calling for a fixed establishment of British troops in India and the coaling stations of '19,000 effective and well-trained young soldiers'. Stanhope placed the provision of men for fortresses and coaling stations under another heading, pledging to keep the garrisons at the 'scale now laid down'.

The fundamental differences between Wolseley's interpretation of military requirements and the opinions held by Stanhope appears in the last two headings. Wolseley argued the need to provide, exclusive of troops abroad, 'three complete Army Corps and six brigades of Cavalry, all being of Regular troops. This field army to be in addition to a large force of Auxiliary troops'. This was to provide for home defence against invasion. In contrast, Stanhope stipulated the ability to mobilise two army corps of regulars and one of a combination of regular and Militia troops. Lastly, Wolseley proposed the additional provision of two army corps and one cavalry division, and the necessary troops for protection of the base and line of communications for action abroad, without specifying where this force was likely to be deployed. In contrast, Stanhope added:

> But it will be distinctly understood that the probability of the employment of the Army Corps in the field in any European war is sufficiently improbable to make it the primary duty of the military authorities to organise our forces efficiently for the defence of the country.

This reflects the attitude of governments following the omission in 1868 from the preamble to the Mutiny Act, which defined the purpose of the army, of the phrase 'the preservation of the balance of power in Europe'.[40]

Wolseley was not satisfied with the Stanhope Memorandum, primarily because he had not achieved his aim of increasing the size of the army. He wrote in a memorandum in December 1888 that, 'the mobilisation scheme of 1886 has so misled the Secretary of State, and it is feared the Government also, that it is very much to be regretted we did not in the first instance pay over excessive attention to the mobilisation of a manoeuvring army for the defence of England against invasion'. He argued that the recent plans for home defence were based on what was possible, not on what was necessary. The government had not questioned the numbers and had ignored Wolseley's demands for greater resources for home defence. Therefore he concluded his critique of the Stanhope Memorandum by stating that:

> the responsibility for that decision is theirs [the politicians'] exclusively. It is not based in any degree on the opinions of the military authorities who wish to place on record their unanimous opinion that this country cannot be rendered safe from invasion with a smaller mobile force of regular troops than three complete army corps and a cavalry division assisted by the auxiliary forces of the Crown.[41]

The army continued to be short of men and money and Wolseley noted that 'whenever I ask for anything I always feel like a poor relation when he asks his rich friend to help him'.[42]

This quotation is particularly apt given his own financial situation at the time. An unwise investment had swallowed up most of the grant of £30,000 he had received on becoming a baron. Wolseley had purchased a house in Hill Street, Mayfair. It was rather cramped and noisy, although he made improvements to it by, for example, installing a back staircase. By 1886 he was finding the upkeep of the house hard to afford. Property prices were depressed in London and, whereas a few years previously, the house had been valued at £15,000, now it was only worth £10,000. He explored the possibility of letting it and hoped to get £600 a year rent but an agent thought £550 more likely.[43] The Queen, who was discreetly made aware of the situation, helped Wolseley in 1888 by offering him a grace and favour building, Ranger's Lodge in Greenwich.[44] The family moved there and had far more space for entertaining. Hill Street was rented out until property prices recovered and it could be sold.

Since the government had no intention of increasing the size of the army or the forces for home defence, Wolseley turned his attention to ensuring that these defensive forces were as efficient as possible. He was particularly concerned to make the Volunteers, Britain's third line of defence after the navy and the regular army, as effective as possible. He acknowledged that the Volunteers were well drilled, but wanted them to learn the higher duties of soldiering, such as the use of bivouacs and outposts, and to establish corps of signalling and a medical corps so as to take over some duties from the hard-pressed regular army. He also emphasised that the Volunteers should learn to shoot better. The public often gained the wrong impression that the Volunteers shot very well because they looked only at the results of a few first-class shots at the annual meeting at Wimbledon, whereas 'military efficiency lay in having a large proportion of average shots in a regiment'.[45]

Since it seemed that not enough money could be found to pay the regulars a decent wage and encourage the recruitment of educated men, the Volunteer movement was also seen by Wolseley to have a role to play in encouraging educated men to undertake some form of military training. The Master of Balliol College, Oxford, Benjamin Jowett, agreed with this sentiment and invited him to speak to the undergraduates at the Sheldonian Theatre on the subject of military service, on the grounds that the 'army is unpopular because it represents a set of influences opposed to popular government. It would be otherwise if the army and navy would be regarded as the two great public schools of England'.[46] Wolseley took up this challenge, demonstrating that because of the large number of annual recruits to the regulars and the auxiliaries:

> That was their great military school, which contained about 617,000 pupils ...
> As regarded numbers, it must, therefore, be allowed that theirs was indeed the greatest of the national schools, and when they came to consider what it was they taught their pupils, he believed its importance as an educational factor would be still more fully acknowledged.

According to the report of the speech in *The Times*, he was well-received until he chided his audience by asking them, 'was it creditable to that great and ancient University, once the Head Quarters of the Royal Army of England, that men enough to maintain even one small battalion of Volunteers could not be found there?' The audience was notably silent on this point. In fact, Wolseley's speech caused an uproar in the university and Jowett wrote to him to apologise. He also suggested the names of two tutors for Wolseley's daughter Frances.[47]

Wolseley was convinced that 'our military training is too much sacrificed to show parade movements, and that the soldier can be better disciplined, both in body and in mind, by being taught the duties and evolutions he *must* practice before an enemy, than by parade movements only possible in peace'.[48] The Duke of Cambridge enjoyed these public parades and was not convinced of the need for a new drill book. In 1887 he turned down Wolseley's proposal for a committee of men with recent experience of war, with Wolseley as chairman, to compare the British drill book with those of the French and German armies. But in 1889 a new drill book was produced. In a speech reported in *The Times* in February 1889 Wolseley said of it that, 'if it were read carefully and between the lines, it must be admitted that troops trained in accordance with the rules and regulations there laid down would be fit to meet the troops of any country in the world'. Nevertheless in private he complained to the Duke of Connaught that 'there can be no doubt that the new Drill Book is somewhat too minute' and that it still contained antiquities.[49]

Wolseley stated that 'my notion of a good Battalion is one that can shoot well, so that it may be able to kill its enemies: that is thoroughly practised in outpost duties, night marches and in the tactical combinations of modern battles'.[50] There were many obstructions to the fruition of this aim. For example, the Duke of Cambridge allegedly objected to the practising of night marches on the grounds that it would tire out the cavalry horses. The organisation of the army also made training difficult: the army was not only spread across the empire but was also fragmented into small detachments within the United Kingdom. Work was under way to concentrate the army into larger garrisons, but the work was hampered by the concern of the Home Secretary that the army might be less available for the enforcement of law and order if concentrated into garrisons. With Wolseley encouraging his fellow reformers to improve the system of training, Evelyn Wood achieved notable successes, first at the Eastern Command based at Colchester and then at Aldershot.[51]

Wolseley wanted to provide the British army with the best firepower possible. During the 1880s the Lee-Metford magazine rifle was introduced which increased the rate of fire and accuracy of the infantry. He pressed an unwilling Stanhope to spend money by calling out the Army Reserve for training with the new rifle.[52] Stanhope agreed, and from 1890 to 1892 all the Reserve was called up for musketry drill although, rather oddly, no target practice was included in the training.

The possession of machine guns has commonly been seen as the reason why the British army conquered vast areas of Africa so easily. For example, Hilaire Belloc wrote:

> Whatever happens, we have got
> The Maxim Gun, and they have not.[53]

Yet Wolseley was aware that machine guns were not yet totally reliable. Two Gatlings had been used at Ulundi in 1879, but it was only in 1881 that the Ordnance Department conducted trials to compare the Gatling, Nordenfelt and Gardner guns. Wolseley was supplied with Gardner guns on the Khartoum expedition, and the army borrowed six Gardners from the navy for the 1885 Suakin expedition. He was not favourably impressed by their reliability, writing to the Surveyor General of Ordnance in August 1885, that the Gardner had jammed at a critical moment during the battle of Abu Klea and, that 'unless a better machine gun is to be had, I could not recommend any large expenditure at present upon such an arm'.[54]

Wolseley saw the machine gun as the weapon of the future once its technical shortcomings had been overcome. In 1887 the Maxim gun was manufactured. Much lighter than its predecessors, at thirty pounds, it could be handled by an infantry machine gun team in battle, although its manoeuvrability was still limited because of being fixed to a four hundred-weight carriage. The Maxim was also superior in its range and rapidity of fire and less prone to jamming. Wolseley therefore pressed for the introduction of at least two machine guns into every cavalry and infantry brigade, giving a total of fourteen guns per army corps. Progress was slow: the machine gun was accepted as an infantry weapon not an artillery gun as the French had mistakenly thought in 1870, but the cost of the Maxims meant that, although each battalion was supposed to have access to one gun for instructional purposes by 1890, even in 1894 most soldiers were being trained on the outdated Nordenfelt and Gardner guns.[55]

The poor performance of many senior regimental officers on the Gordon Relief expedition led Wolseley to renew his battle with the Duke of Cambridge for the introduction of some form of selection for the higher ranks of the army. The Duke remained firmly wedded to the idea of promotion by seniority. Wolseley wrote to his brother Richard that 'we live in an era of selection', since examinations now ensured a fair system of entry to the Civil Service and many professions, such as lawyers and engineers, were introducing examinations to ensure standards. Indeed, when his brother George was not promoted to the command of a brigade in 1886, Wolseley fully supported Roberts's decision because he believed that George was not ready for such a promotion.[56] But there was the problem of how to ensure an impartial system in the army which could compare the performance of officers serving in Britain with those stationed abroad, especially in India. Furthermore, since only a limited number of officers had any experience of war, there was apparently no way, in the absence of annual large-scale manoeuvres, to compare officers in peacetime.

The establishment in 1890 of a Promotion Board went some way to achieve a solution. The Parliamentary Under Secretary, Ralph Thompson, described it as 'a sort of advisory Board to HRH to enable him to select the proper officers to recommend for promotion'.[57] The Duke of Cambridge naturally assumed that the establishment of the Board was a criticism of his choices, and strongly remonstrated with Stanhope for insisting that Wolseley should be a member of the Board. Stanhope replied that he believed Wolseley's opinions essential to the Promotion Board, not only because Stanhope himself generally held a high regard for his opinions on many issues, but also because he had campaigned for so long for improvement in the promotion process that it was inconceivable to omit him as a member of such a Board.[58]

Another victory was achieved by proposing that a substantial saving could be achieved by reducing the size of the General Officers' List. Both Childers and Smith had achieved some reductions in the size of the list but in August 1887 Wolseley wrote in a memorandum for Stanhope that a further reduction could be made. He favoured culling the General Officers' List to sixty-three, the number employed at the time, with a reserve in case of ill-health or incompetence. Stanhope responded favourably to his ideas and outlined the advantages of the scheme for the Queen:

> Selection will be introduced, not in the difficult form of choosing individuals out of a large number for merit, but in the simpler form of asking, when a Major-General's command becomes vacant, who is the best qualified to fill it? The result of this scheme will be that all general officers will have been selected on the ground of their fitness to hold a General Officer's appointment, which has not hitherto been the case, and the General Officers' list will contain a number of men specially qualified for employment in time of emergency.

The number of general officers was reduced to one hundred, and the scheme came into effect on 31 December 1890.[59]

One vital function of the War Office was to prepare the army for war, and it was in this area that Britain lagged behind the armies on the Continent. The situation was, however, improving. The construction of storehouses around London, and between Aldershot and Southampton, to speed the despatch of the First Amy Corps were improvements, but the decentralisation process was very slow. Even in 1897, when Lieutenant-General Lord Methuen tried to mobilise one brigade at short notice, he was appalled to be informed by Woolwich that the depot would be closed for the next four days.[60] Although the mobilisation plan stipulated what units belonged to each brigade and the staff requirements, the staff was not fixed. The appointment to command a division was no guarantee that the commander would retain that position should the division be sent abroad. For example, the Queen approved the appointment of Evelyn Wood over her son the Duke of Connaught to Aldershot in 1888 only on the understanding that 'she was not pledged to approving his selection for the command of the first expedition that may be sent abroad'.[61] Wolseley pressed so hard for selection partly because he believed strongly that the command in peace time should be appropriate for war.

The main difference between the military systems of Britain and the Continent was the lack of a British Chief of Staff's department to coordinate plans for war. The Hartington Commission examined the whole framework of military and naval planning and concentrated on this issue. In his evidence to the Commission, Wolseley began by stating that Britain needed such a department:

> more than any nation abroad for many reasons, particularly on account of the peculiar constitution of our army, and the fact of its being scattered all over the world, and of the numerous responsibilities which devolve upon it, and consequently the numerous phases of war for which it should be always prepared.[62]

The sheer volume of work created by the need to prepare the intelligence and the plans of war for the many possible enemies or combination of enemies Britain could face made a Chief of Staff necessary.

Wolseley was prepared to provide details on the functions of the Chief of Staff. These would correspond closely with the existing functions of the Adjutant General: responsibility for discipline would be removed, but responsibility for training, at present the task of the Commander-in-Chief, would be added. This would free the Chief of Staff to be 'the recognised adviser of the Commander-in-Chief, and one of the advisers of the Secretary of State, his great function would be the preparation of the army for war'.[63]

Wolseley's description of the position and functions of the Chief of Staff happened to coincide with the position he himself would like to occupy. By removing authority over the discipline of the army from his department, he would rid himself of a great mass of petty administrative work, leaving himself free to concentrate on the areas of military affairs of most interest to him. By removing the supervision of training from the Duke of Cambridge, he would be in a position to institute a more modern and relevant system of training for war in the British army. Wolseley's desire to allow the Chief of Staff direct access as an independent adviser to the Secretary of State stemmed from his wish to promote his reform proposals without the dampening interference of the Duke of Cambridge. He wanted this independence for himself but not necessarily for others. This becomes clearer later when looking at his reaction to the terms of the Order in Council, which redefined the relationship between the Secretary of State for War and his military advisers, when he became Commander-in-Chief.

The Hartington Commission made a number of important recommendations. A defence committee of cabinet ministers, soldiers and sailors should be established to examine the Estimates and determine the needs of both the army and navy from a plan of imperial defence. It recommended the abolition of the post of the Commander-in-Chief and its replacement by a War Office Council. The most important recommendation concerned the establishment of a department of the Chief of Staff. This would include the intelligence division and mobilisation division presently under the aegis of the Adjutant General. The Chief of Staff would directly advise the Secretary of State on all matters of general military policy, including the strength, distribution and mobilisation of the army. The department would collect military information, prepare defence schemes for the Empire, prepare plans for war, liaise with the Admiralty and generals in command in foreign stations, and report annually to the Secretary of State on the military requirements of the Empire.[64]

Two members of the commission dissented from the report. Randolph Churchill accepted Wolseley's arguments for the abolition of the War Office and Admiralty and its replacement by a Ministry of Defence, to be presided over by a single minister. Campbell-Bannerman wrote a long dissent to the report arguing against the creation of a Chief of Staff on the grounds that it was 'likely to reintroduce, perhaps in a worse form, some of the very evils which the organisation of a Council of General Officers would be designed to remove'. He wrote to Hartington that 'what I fear is that your new Chief of Staff will be virtually a new Pope; and therefore I am against him'. Campbell-Bannerman also believed that Britain did not need to adopt the continental practice of a General Staff. Britain had no aggressive intentions towards her neighbours and, if the General Staff lacked a clear role, the danger existed that it might create one for itself and draw Britain into wars.[65]

The Cabinet ruled against the abolition of the post of Commander-in-Chief while accepting the desirability of a Chief of Staff. At first, Wolseley was in favour of the abolition of the post of Commander-in-Chief. He wanted the Chief of Staff to be even more powerful than the Commission envisaged; the Chief of Staff 'should in fact be the Secretary of State's Military Critic as the Financial Secretary is his financial critic'. Given that the Cabinet refused to abolish the post of Commander-in-Chief, Wolseley changed his mind. Indeed he went further and denied he had ever been in favour of the abolition of the post, telling Ponsonby that:

> The Duke will not accept the position of Chief of the Staff. Indeed, after being so long Commander-in-Chief it would be impossible for him to do so. I still hope the office of Commander-in-Chief may not be done away with. You know I am not one who would oppose any reform than means progress or the adoption of new ideas. But this proposal is to go a step backward. We sorely want a doctor, I admit, but Brackenbury and Co. have sent us an executioner.[66]

He suspected that Brackenbury had framed the responsibilities of the Chief of Staff in the hope that he would himself be appointed to the new post. Wolseley's greatest alarm was caused by the Hartington Commission's recommendation for the establishment of a new Army Board on which all members would have equal access to the Secretary of State. He believed that this system would be unworkable in practice, and would remove all authority from the head of the army, whether he be termed Commander-in-Chief or Chief of the Staff.

The debate assumed some urgency towards the end of 1890 because Wolseley's term of office as Adjutant General, already extended once, was about to end. It was necessary to decide whether the new Adjutant General should retain the same title, or whether Wolseley's proposal, made to the Hartington Commission, that the Adjutant General should be the Chief of Staff, should be adopted. In April Stanhope had told the Duke of Cambridge that the Cabinet had decided that the post of Adjutant General should be filled up without 'the intervention of a Chief of the Staff in any form', in other words an additional post was not to be created. The Duke replied that he accepted that the Chief of Staff should not be separate from the Adjutant General, but suggested that the new officer should be termed 'Chief of the Staff and Adjutant General' and should exercise the Chief of Staff's duties to the Commander-in-Chief. Stanhope responded that the Cabinet would not agree to this proposal.[67] In September Buller wrote to the Duke that he had been gazetted as 'Adjutant General to the Forces', the old title, whereas he had thought that he would be gazetted 'Adjutant General and Chief Staff Officer of the Forces', the title which he preferred.[68] Buller failed to get his title changed. The position of Chief of the Staff was not created permanently in peace in the British army until 1904.

By 1890 Wolseley had laid out the framework of a modern professional British army in a series of memoranda. There had been occasional notable successes, some improvements and a few failures. The purposes for which the army existed had been defined, but not wholly to his satisfaction. The home establishment of the army was still too small but the public had been made aware of this through the invasion scares. A sign of improvement for the future appeared to be the Cabinet's reluctance to send further British battalions to India for its defence. Britain was now better prepared for war, with a workable mobilisation plan and home defence structure. There was the hope that the quality of senior officers would improve with the establishment of the Promotion Board. But the real failure lay in the efficiency of the army. Wolseley had not succeeded in getting a modern drill book produced nor regular large-scale manoeuvres introduced. Lack of expenditure continued to affect the purchase of modern armaments, particularly artillery. The blame for many of these failures could be placed with the Duke of Cambridge, but it remained to be seen whether, in the future, Wolseley would achieve more success in the battle for funds with the politicians.

Both Stanhope and the Duke of Cambridge wrote letters to Wolseley as he was about to leave the War Office praising him for his work. The Duke acknowledged their differences of opinion, but wrote:

> I must tell you how much I have at all times appreciated the assistance I have derived from you as Adjutant General of the Army. The changes that have so constantly taken place – and alas, we live in an age of perpetual change – have rendered the duties of your office especially arduous, and I have always admired the characteristic vigour and energy you have thrown into them.[69]

Financial problems still worried him since the house at Hill Street remained unsold. As Adjutant General Wolseley was expected to maintain high standards which necessitated the purchase and maintenance of a stable of riding and carriage horses. His army salary barely covered his daily expenses and investments provided the bulk of his income. In addition, he was responsible for his siblings: both George nor Frederick were profilgate and Wolseley often lent them money to save the family name. He willingly supported his unmarried sister, Caroline, and was distressed to learn in 1890 that she was seriously ill with 'some long named disease of the stomach which is very dangerous'.

Wolseley was exhausted at the end of his term of office as Adjutant General. He had achieved much, but felt that he could have done more had it not been for the Duke. Financial problems still worried him since Hill Street was unsold. Personal problems also intruded: his favourite brother Dick had died in 1887 and, now in 1890, his sister Caroline was seriously ill with 'some long named disease of the stomach which is very dangerous'.[70] He needed a rest and hoped that Ireland would provide it.

15

Ireland

In 1890 the Duke of Cambridge showed no sign of retiring now that the government had turned down the recommendation of the Hartington Commission for the establishment of a Chief of Staff. But the Duke was getting old and would be unable to continue in office for much longer.[1] Although Wolseley had set his sights on succeeding him as Commander-in-Chief, now he was leaving the War Office having been Adjutant General for seven years. He needed to find a new appointment which would keep him in the running until the Duke retired. This meant staying in close contact with the War Office and keeping a watchful eye on developments: he had already refused an offer of the Governor Generalship of Victoria, Australia, because it was too far away from the centre of power. In April 1890 he was offered the post of Commander-in-Chief of India. In the early 1880s this post had seemed very attractive to Wolseley, offering the freedom to reform the army along his own lines and the opportunity for further command in the field, but since the Pendjeh crisis had been resolved, war between Russia and Britain over India appeared only a remote possibility. Furthermore, he had by now established himself as an army reformer in Britain and had achieved some successes in this area. Accordingly Wolseley wrote to Stanhope declining the post on the grounds that if 'profound peace reigns in India to go there would be to me professional suicide'.[2]

The question of his future was complicated by the fact that the Queen was seeking a senior position for her son, the Duke of Connaught, in order to set him up to succeed the Duke of Cambridge. Various appointments were suggested by the Queen such as the Aldershot command or that of Quartermaster General. The Queen had been anxious to secure the Aldershot command for her son in 1888 when it had been vacant, but the government had turned down her request on the grounds that the Duke of Connaught was too inexperienced. Instead it had given the appointment to Evelyn Wood.[3] In 1890 the Queen hoped that Wood might be persuaded to step down, but there is no evidence to suggest that Stanhope ever took this possibility seriously. Buller had been promoted to Adjutant General on Wolseley's departure, which left the Quartermaster Generalship vacant. The Queen pressed the government to consider her son for this post, which would give him vital experience of War Office administration. The government declined, ostensibly because it was considered that the post of Quartermaster General would be a come-down after the Bombay command, but really because it did not want another member of the royal family in a senior position at Horse Guards.[4]

Wolseley was aware of the Queen's desire for an important appointment for her son and made it clear that he was willing to accept whichever post the Duke of Connaught declined. Wolseley erroneously thought that the choice lay between Ireland and Aldershot. In fact the choice lay between Portsmouth and Ireland. Wolseley was offered the more senior position of Commander-in-Chief in Ireland, in succession to Prince Edward of Saxe-Weimar, and the Duke of Connaught accepted the Portsmouth command.

Wolseley immediately began making arrangements for accommodation for his family in Dublin. Their friend Henry Campbell-Bannerman, a former Irish Chief Secretary, was consulted and advised them not to accept the Secretary's Lodge. The back rooms were uninhabitable, and it was very damp with defective drainage and a poor water supply. With great amusement Louisa reported to her husband that a Board of Works report on the building had pronounced the source of its water safe but had added the recommendation that 'the pump handle should be removed'.[5] Wolseley decided to live at the headquarters of the military administration in Ireland, the Royal Hospital, Kilmainham, which was in a state of considerable disrepair. He consulted Louisa from Dublin, she having remained at Ranger's Lodge, on every aspect of the rebuilding and redecoration. He risked the wrath of the Duke of Cambridge by seeking leave to spend Christmas 1890 in Greenwich, justifying the abandonment of his military and linked social duties over the festive season on the grounds that the Royal Hospital still lacked a roof. The building was finally ready for human habitation in the late summer of 1891. Louisa and Frances came to Dublin then, after Frances had enjoyed her first Season in London, where she had proved popular and had been widely admired for her dress sense.

The administration of Ireland was divided between the civil side, with the Chief Secretary acting as the link between Dublin and Westminster, and the military side presided over by the Commander-in-Chief. Two infantry divisions and a cavalry brigade – a total force of 25–30,000 troops – were permanently stationed in Ireland. These were nominally divided between two commands based at the Curragh, near Dublin, and at Cork, but in actual fact the army was dispersed in small outposts scattered throughout the country. Wolseley felt that this was inefficient for training purposes and urged a concentration of the army in Ireland on the lines earlier followed

on the mainland. His appeal was turned down on the grounds of the cost
of building barracks. Aid to the civil power was the principal requirement
of the British army as laid down in the Mutiny Act and repeated in the
Stanhope Memorandum. Troops were called out for this purpose in England
during this period, for example to counter strike action at Ackton Hall
Colliery, Featherstone, in September 1893, but in Ireland the power was
used with care.[6] The army was only to be used to assist the police in cases
of extreme emergency. There were strict regulations governing what the
army could be called upon to do and any action had to be fully reported
in writing to the Royal Hospital.[7]

Ireland was an extremely important source of recruitment to the British
army. It provided a disproportionate number of men; it has been established
that in 1871 4.38 per cent of all eligible Irishman joined the army in contrast
to only 2.09 per cent of all eligible Englishmen. The level of Irish recruitment
was affected by local factors: high levels of emigration in the 1850s had led
to a fall in enlistments but a slump in emigration between 1875 and 1880
had brought about a surge. The hope of Home Rule dampened recruitment
again, and in 1893 the Chief Secretary, John Morley, drew Wolseley's attention to the fact that 'the number of Irish NCOs and men has gone down
from 237/1000 twenty years ago to 135/1000 today'.[8] Wolseley could only
hope to reverse the trend by emphasising the importance of good treatment
of Irish soldiers while in the colours and in the Army Reserve.[9] He drew
Buller's attention to the case of one former soldier he had read about in
an Irish newspaper who had encountered great difficulties when wanting
to re-enlist. He pointed out that such adverse publicity would damage
recruitment.[10] There is little evidence to suggest that Irish soldiers were
disloyal to Britain, but Wolseley was aware of the incipient danger of
releasing large numbers of men trained in the use of weapons back into
civilian life. If these men were not treated well when in the army then, if
political tensions reached breaking point, their military training might be
turned against their masters in Ireland.

Wolseley was proud to be a member of the Anglo-Irish Protestant
ascendancy. He despised the Irish for their poverty and their 'Popish
superstition', and believed that they deserved to be ruled by the Protestant
minority. In an early letter home, he wrote on the Irish that 'they are a
strange, illogical, inaccurate race, with the most amiable qualities, garnished
with the dirt and squalor which they seem to love as dearly as their religion'.[11]
When he arrived in Ireland the Chief Secretary was a staunch Unionist,
Arthur Balfour, the Marquess of Salisbury's nephew. He was succeeded,
when the Liberal government came to office in 1892, by John Morley, who
'dislikes Ireland and the Irish very much'.[12] The fact that the men holding

the two most important offices in Ireland, those of the Chief Secretary and
the Commander-in-Chief, disliked the majority of the population could
have been inflammatory had it not been that, after the turmoil of the 1880s,
Ireland was entering a period of relative tranquillity. The number of agrarian
outrages was falling and political activity had quietened since the defeat of
the first Home Rule Bill. Indeed, in January 1893, Wolseley felt able to
report that Home Rule 'as it was understood for the last five or six years
is little thought of now'.[13] This state of affairs had arisen largely because
of the coincidence of a Unionist government and the disarray of the Irish
political party which had split over the O'Shea divorce case, in which its
leader Charles Stewart Parnell was cited as co-respondent.[14] When Parnell
died in October 1891 the Irish lacked a leader strong enough to have a
major effect on British politics, a state of affairs that continued into the
early years of the next century.

Gladstone was determined to establish Home Rule in Ireland: indeed,
after the 1892 General Election, he was dependent on the Irish MPs to
remain in office. In 1893 he introduced a new Home Rule Bill.[15] Unlike its
predecessors it passed the House of Commons, but it was thought likely
that the Lords would reject it. Wolseley did not vote on either Home Rule
Bill but there can be no doubt that he was hostile to the concept, declaring
it 'the silliest and most villainous proposal ever before put before the English
people in a cloud of lies'.[16]   •

Home Rule inflamed political opinion in Ireland. In April 1893 Balfour
warned the Protestants of Ulster of the threat to their future. Home Rule

> means that the whole patronage of Ulster is to be handed over to a hostile
> majority in Dublin. You, the wealthy and orderly, the industrious, the enterprising
> portion of Ireland are to supply the money for that part of Ireland which is less
> orderly, less industrious, less enterprising and less law-abiding.[17]

Riots seemed imminent in Belfast and troops were despatched to reinforce
the garrison there. By the end of April Wolseley was relieved to report that
law and order had been restored with little damage to life or property. He
added the warning that 'Ulster is determined to resist, and *will fight à
outrance* if at any future time she be cut off from England'. Privately he
told his friend Frederick Maurice that he would be glad to lead the Ulstermen
in their fight. He also wrote to Ponsonby intimating 'indirectly that I could
not stay here if Civil War took place'.[18] The Lords, as expected, rejected
the Home Rule Bill and Ireland settled back into an uneasy peace; but
opinions had become polarised. In Ulster Protestants set up defensive
organisations and in the south the Gaelic League was founded to educate
Catholics in their past.

On one occasion when the Duke of Cambridge reprimanded Wolseley for not writing regular reports on Irish military affairs, Wolseley replied that, apart from routine matters, 'I have little military work to do and still less to write about'.[19] He created work for himself, since long periods of inactivity were an anathema to him, and made numerous extensive tours of Ireland. Stanhope was impressed by this display of energy but worried about what Wolseley would find to do when he had been all over Ireland several times.[20] He need not have been concerned: Wolseley had a number of comments to make on Irish military affairs.

The first was that he discovered that the Irish staff establishment was grossly inflated. Since many of his proposals on reform had previously been rejected on the grounds of cost, Wolseley felt sure that his recommendations on the Irish staff would be accepted since they would lead to a saving of £3600 a year. This was not to be the case: the Duke of Cambridge replied that he was dismayed by his suggestions, since it was his belief that the army needed a rest from the changes of recent years. When Wolseley heard that a new General Officer Commanding Artillery in Ireland was to be appointed, a post he felt superfluous, he suspected that his letter had not been passed to Stanhope. He wrote to the private secretary at the War Office, Fleetwood Wilson, on the subject of the Irish staff. Wilson replied that Stanhope had no plans to take any action. Wolseley's response was that 'I have nothing more to say, except that as a taxpayer I feel that my money is shamefully squandered'.[21]

While Adjutant General, he had attempted to improve training and military education in the army but had been thwarted by the Duke of Cambridge. In Ireland Wolseley was freer to take steps in this direction. He revived the Military Society of Ireland and invited talented speakers to address it. He also inaugurated a system of training which would begin at company level in March and gradually increase in size, culminating in the annual manoeuvres in the autumn. He was disappointed by what the manoeuvres revealed: the 1892 manoeuvres demonstrated 'a sad want of tactical knowledge and military instinct on the part of all the Commanding Officers of Battalions and the Majors of Artillery'. The cavalry command broke up over distances; the artillery generally lost 'many guns during the action from want of tactical handling'; and the infantry attacks were 'absurd in conception and futile in execution'. He was considerably more heartened by the successful manoeuvres held in Cork in the same month, though he still felt that the commanding officers were weak in tactical knowledge.[22] Reports of other exercises, for example the manoeuvres of all arms held in Hampshire in 1891, tended to agree with Wolseley's assessment of the tactical abilities of the British army. It was clear that there was a need for regular large-scale manoeuvres of the size not seen since 1872.

Wolseley remained in touch with War Office matters during his regular visits to London to sit on the recently-established Promotion Board. This was not working as well as anticipated: there was plenty of evidence that the Duke of Cambridge's selections were being approved without serious consideration of alternative candidates. Wolseley urged Campbell-Bannerman to watch the Duke more closely. For example, in 1894 the Board recommended that the next colonels of artillery should be John Alleyne and Frederick Maurice, but Wolseley heard privately that the Duke had said that he did 'not care a damn for the Promotion Board and that Colonel Hamers shall certainly be promoted'. A year later there was another crisis to which Wolseley contributed. The Promotion Board recommended Colonel Frederick Carrington for the Shorncliffe command but Wolseley persuaded Campbell-Bannerman to appoint Evelyn Wood instead. Buller was so outraged that he actually threatened to resign over the matter.[23]

In 1891 it was generally accepted by many in the War Office that the short service system had received a fair trial and must be re-examined and subjected to improvements where necessary. Stanhope therefore set up the Wantage Committee to undertake a thorough examination of the terms and conditions of service in the army. Wolseley was not convinced that the committee was necessary at all. He argued that the Cardwell system had not broken down, 'but that all our present difficulties and misfortunes have arisen and are at present directly attributable to the fact that his system has been glaringly and most injudiciously departed from'. He highlighted the fact that the balance between battalions at home and abroad had not been maintained which was '*the* principle upon which Mr Cardwell organised the army'.[24]

The news of the new committee bolstered the hopes of the opponents of short service: for example, in a flurry of letters from India, Roberts tried to drum up support for an extension of the terms of service. He wrote to the Assistant Military Secretary at the War Office, Lieutenant-General J. H. Gordon, that 'there can be no manner of doubt that the root of the whole question of recruiting for the British Army lies in India'.[25] Unfortunately for Roberts, there was considerable doubt. Both Buller and Henry Brackenbury wrote to him arguing that, however desirable it might be to extend the length of service in the colours and to increase the average age of soldiers, the recruitment climate dictated against this. The Wantage Committee provided a severe put-down for Roberts, declining even to consider the efficiency of the army in India. The dismissal of his opinions left the way open for Wolseley to conduct a review of the short service system and the efficiency of the home battalions on his own terms. Indeed in his review of the evidence presented to the committee, Roberts quite rightly pointed out that Wolseley and Buller had presented their evidence with the determination to defend the cause of the existing system and to allow only minor revisions to it.[26]

The main concern of the Wantage Committee was to form an opinion on the efficiency of the home battalions. In this it was hampered by the lack of statistical evidence from those who claimed that the battalions were inefficient. Wolseley was singled out for praise in this respect in the summary of the committee's report for having at least presented 'a tolerably consecutive story', to illustrate his statements.[27] He agreed with other witnesses on the overall inefficiency of the home battalions but approached the issue from a different angle. When he said that 'I do not know a single battalion outside the Guards fit to go into the field and fight against any European nation', he was not admitting the system was a failure but applauding it as a success. For Wolseley the 'home Army ought always to be the nursery for the Army abroad', and little more than large depots 'provided a thoroughly efficient Reserve of about 80,000 men is maintained'.[28] Wolseley, his colleagues and the members of the committee were unanimous in saying that the home battalions were inefficient because of the task of providing drafts for their foreign battalions. He perceived this as a very serious problem and argued that 'if these drafts are maintained for the battalions abroad, the battalions at home will be like a lemon when all the juice is squeezed out of it, they will be of little fighting use'.[29]

Wolseley believed that there were three possible solutions to this difficulty. The first, which had been tried before, was to withdraw battalions from foreign stations. The second was that the army should be increased in size by twelve battalions, which would be expensive. The third was that a system should be established whereby battalions in danger of having to send a large number of drafts abroad in the near future should be allowed to recruit over establishment in order to maintain at least the numerical efficiency of the battalion.[30]

Many regimental officers voiced their concern over the poor physical quality of the recruits. Wolseley argued that a few years' training was sufficient to build up the physique of even the special enlistments, so their condition on arrival at the battalion was irrelevant.[31] He was far more anxious about their intelligence, since he believed that the modern battlefield required educated men capable of acting on their own initiative. Therefore he pressed for an increase in pay to encourage better men to join the army. He suggested that 'a small increase of 1d. or 2d. a day would not do; the day for tinkering at this question is past and gone, you must substantially add to the pay of the soldier if you wish to have an efficient Army on a voluntary principle'. Unlike other witnesses, he did not propose a further reduction in stoppages: far from it, Wolseley wanted an overall increase of pay of 6d. for the home army and of 1s. to those serving abroad, out of which the soldier would pay for everything except his outer clothing.[32] This would still mean that the British army was cheap: in 1891 Britain spent £85 12s. 8½d. per man, whereas the only other country, the United States, whose army was recruited on a voluntary basis cost £238 per man.[33]

Wolseley was a strong proponent of the Army Reserve. By the time the Wantage Committee began its proceedings it had reached a significant size and should have been capable of fulfilling all its roles. In 1891 the total home establishment of all arms was 104,591 men and the total Army Reserve was 59,216. Of the home establishment 79,639 men were deemed effective, in other words aged twenty or over and trained for at least a year. Therefore a total of 24,952 soldiers or 23.8 per cent of the home establishment would have to be replaced by men from the Army Reserve, leaving a total of 34,264 soldiers to act as a reserve to replace the casualties of war.[34] This seemed to be an improvement on the situation during the Crimean War, but it must be remembered that these figures assume an even number of effectives in each battalion, that no drafts would be sent to any battalions abroad other than to those at the front, and that the war would be of short duration so that the Reserve would not be used up replacing casualties or acting as a reserve and reinforcement to the battalions at war before an equivalent number of men had reached the age and standard of efficiency to be sent abroad. These were dangerous assumptions to make given the decreasing quality of recruits.

The report of the Wantage Committee demonstrated that it had accepted Wolseley's arguments, made since 1871, on the role of the Army Reserve. It defined the purposes of the Army Reserve as: first, to raise units from peace establishment to war establishment; secondly, to take the place of soldiers who were too young to be sent abroad or were still recruits; thirdly, to replace the medically unfit; and lastly, to 'retain sufficient men in reserve in the second line to fill up the casualties occurring at the front, until such time as the men left behind as recruits, or as immature, have become sufficiently trained or physically developed to take their place in the fighting line'.[35] The evidence given to the Wantage Committee by the senior military men shows that they were unanimous in their desire that the Reserve should be trained. The Duke of Cambridge said 'I think the Reserve are a very fine body of men, but as we never see them, we do not know whether they are qualified to take their places in the ranks'. Buller argued that the Reserve should be permitted to train with the Militia, the Volunteers, or with their own regiments. Whereas Buller would have been satisfied if the men in the Reserve trained for six days per annum, Wolseley was adamant that the period should remain the same as in the existing regulations – twelve days. He wanted this period to be consecutive, as he had recommended before, either with the auxiliary forces or with the regulars. The Wantage Committee reported in favour of periodical training of the Army Reserve 'without which no Reserve can fairly be said to be efficient'.[36]

The value of the infantry and artillery reserve was accepted by the Wantage Committee but the members did question the usefulness of the cavalry reserve. Wolseley himself had no doubts on its value. The cavalry had always resisted sending men to the Army Reserve, although Wolseley argued in favour of it, pointing out that the troopers in the much-admired German and Austrian cavalry regiments received only three years' training before joining the reserve. He was convinced that after ten years a cavalry soldier was of little value because he had lost his nerve. He never went into details about why this should have been the case; it might have been that when a man married and had a family to care for he might be less willing to risk his life in a cavalry charge. He also pointed out that figures showed that most cavalry reservists were employed in looking after horses and on recall to the colours, although their knowledge of cavalry drill might be rusty, they could still release other men, such as grooms or drivers, from their jobs without any retraining.[37]

The Wantage Committee was not totally convinced by Wolseley's arguments. It reported that:

> Important evidence has been given before the Committee, tending to show that the Cavalry soldier transferred to the Reserve deteriorates rapidly in knowledge of his Cavalry duties, and that, after a comparatively short time, he becomes unfit to resume his place in the ranks without some preliminary training, though he may still remain fit for duties in the Transport service.

The committee also pointed out that there was a limit to the numbers required for transport and therefore recommended the extension of service in the cavalry to nine years with the colours and three in the Reserve.[38]

The Wantage Committee heard evidence on the question of using the Reserve for small wars. The Duke of Cambridge outlined the reasons why the question was under discussion: 'it was the intention that the battalions on the higher strength should be ready to take the field for small wars without calling on the Reservist, but by building up the higher establishments so rapidly we have filled them completely with boys as a rule'. Wolseley claimed that the 'eight battalions of the First Army Corps are not supposed to be independent of being strengthened by the Reserve'. He spoke in favour of giving the government the power to call out at least 10,000 to 20,000 men from the Reserve 'although the reason for doing so might not amount to a "great national emergency" '. In other words these men should be available for small wars. The committee admitted that it could not suggest any method by which the Army Reserve could be used for small wars. It shied away from recommending that the men in the Reserve should be liable for service during the first period of Reserve service, but did suggest that a list should be drawn up of men willing to volunteer to return to the colours in the case of a small war.[39]

The evidence the Wantage Committee heard painted an alarming picture of the state of the home army, but the committee was apparently incapable of suggesting any radical reworking of the short service system that might remedy the defects. Instead the report of the committee proved disappointing: instead of the far-reaching revision of the Cardwell system hoped for by many military men, it merely proposed minor alterations. Deferred pay was to be replaced by a gratuity of £1 for each year of service. In the meetings of the War Office Council to discuss the report, senior officers like Buller and Wood, who had given evidence against deferred pay, were forced under pressure from Stanhope to retract their statements. As a result deferred pay was not abolished till 1898. Against Wolseley's wishes, a recommendation was made for the abolition of all stoppages and for the modification of the clothing regulations. The committee did support him, however, in calling for an increase in pay up to the market rate for unskilled labour. The War Office Council, though, argued that 'it is considered that an increase of battalions is more important than an increase to soldiers' pay. It was not considered that an increase would get either more, or a different class of men'.[40]

The report of the Wantage Committee may have been disappointing in its failure to make concrete suggestions on how to improve the state of the home army but it marked a significant victory for Wolseley: the short service system would not be called into question again, no consideration of a separate long service army for India had been made, and the principle of the Army Reserve had been upheld. The most pressing issue ignored in the committee report was the size of the home army. The battle for a substantial increase would have to be fought with the government by a new Commander-in-Chief, once the Duke of Cambridge finally retired.

With the short service system secure and so little military work in Ireland, Wolseley felt free to turn his attention to literary activities. He produced several articles on important military figures, such as General Sherman, for the *United Service Magazine*. He was well paid for all these articles which helped his finances. He also began work on a biography of the Duke of

Marlborough and completed two volumes. He soon found that writing a biography was a far greater challenge than writing articles. The result was a turgid manuscript littered with repetitions and errors. His editor at Constable and Co., Mr Bentley, wrote to him with a great number of criticisms. Wolseley was deeply wounded and wrote to Louisa: 'I have no intention to rewrite the work, and I will not do so, nor could I write it better'. He did, however, begin revising the proofs which necessitated a great deal of correction despite the fact that the 'horrid letter from Bentley has taken away most of my interest in the work'.[41] The volumes on Marlborough were published in 1894 to mediocre reviews. Wolseley sent a copy to the Queen with the inscription: 'I hope the Queen and Empress will deign to accept this story of a great Englishman from the Author who is Her Majesty's devoted subject and faithful soldier'.[42] His realisation that he was not a great biographer did not stop him from also writing a biography of Napoleon, published in 1895.

Wolseley also had the leisure to worry about his family and the state of his finances. The house in Hill Street had been rented out when the Wolseleys moved to Ranger's Lodge rather than sold, because the London property market was depressed. Now in Ireland, Wolseley had no excuse to hold on to the house and put it up to auction in May 1891 with a reserve price of £13,000. It did not reach its reserve and he withdrew it from the market. A year later it appeared that the property market was improving and Wolseley hoped to raise £14–15,000 from the sale. Even this sum would leave him little profit since he had made extensive improvements to the property, but the additional £700 a year it would allow him for expenditure would be very welcome.[43] It is not clear when exactly the house was sold, or for how much, but it seems likely that it was only shortly before he returned to London.

Wolseley's confidant, his brother Dick, had died in 1887 and his main correspondent was now another brother George. George had little money sense and frequently pressed Garnet for loans. In March 1892 Garnet finally lost patience with him and told him to pay his own bills as he could barely afford his own. George's son, Garnet, stayed with his uncle for a time in Ireland and showed every sign of having inherited his father's profligacy. George served in India but was unhappy there and in September 1892 wanted to return to England. His uncle advised against this because he could not afford to do so 'with a sick wife and spendthrift son'.[44] In April 1892 Garnet's unmarried sister, Caroline, died quietly in London: this deeply upset him. Her death did at least relieve him from having to pay for her upkeep but another family financial responsibility soon took its place. Fred had gone to Australia to be an inventor and to make his fortune. His inventions had mostly failed and Garnet sent him thousands of pounds to keep him from bankruptcy, not wanting Fred to blacken the Wolseley name. Just as it seemed that Fred was on the brink of success, with the invention of a sheep-shearing machine, tragedy struck and he was diagnosed with cancer. Garnet was forced to send him money for his own and his wife's support. Fred eventually returned to England in 1898 and died in January 1899, whereupon Garnet made financial provisions for his widow.[45]

Pressing family concerns also affected Wolseley nearer home. Frances was now of an age to seek a husband. In April 1894 Frances was very close to Lord Castlemaine and it seemed likely that they would marry. Louisa was extraordinarily hostile to the friendship, feeling herself excluded from her daughter's life. Frances complained to her father of the way in which her mother constantly criticised Lord Castlemaine for his lack of wit and on personal appearance. Wolseley replied that Louisa was very sensitive but loved her very much: 'I have often been jealous of you because I felt she loved you more and thought more of you than me'.[46] Wolseley did some research on Castlemaine's financial means and found that he owned 11,444 acres in West Meath from which he gained an annual rental income of £7000. This should be quite enough to keep Frances in considerable comfort and her parents were in favour of the match. However, in May Frances refused his hand because she felt she did not love him sufficiently. Her father was worried by this, not so much because Frances had refused him, since Wolseley accepted that she was not in love, but more so because Frances appeared rather frigid and cold and unlikely to win many 'admirers from the vulgar herd, and it is with them we all have to deal in life'.[47]

Both Wolseley's and Louisa's health suffered while they were in Ireland. Louisa was plagued by insomnia, a complaint from which she had never previously suffered. She spent much of each summer staying with friends in England or visiting the Wolseley family, cousins of her husband, in Staffordshire. She also participated in the Victorian habit of taking a cure at one of the European spas each year, most frequently Marienbad or Homburg. Wolseley suffered greatly from indigestion. In 1892 he wrote to Louisa that:

This continued indigestion is useful in one way; it makes me remember that I am in my sixtieth year. This is very necessary, for I feel so well and young otherwise. I have played my part on the stage of life and have been much blessed by God. But I have not risen to what I had hoped and have had no opportunity afforded me to test any higher qualities there may be in me.[48]

He sought relief from indigestion by spending much of the summer out of Ireland on cruises. Sir John Pender, the industrialist, invited him for several, including one to visit Constantinople and the Crimea in 1894. Later he also cruised with Sir Donald Currie, the owner of the White Star shipping line. Louisa did not accompany her husband on these cruises because she was a very poor sailor.

Wolseley was depressed by the state of his career, convincing himself that he was a failure. He had always hoped to command in a major war against a European power which would bring him lasting fame. On many occasions he wrote of his preference to die gloriously in action than in bed.[49] He was alarmed that he was being overlooked by the War Office when there was some doubt in 1894 whether he would be made a Field Marshal, but he received his Field Marshal's baton on the Queen's Birthday.[50] He was also disturbed by the state of society in Britain and the rise of socialism. Archibald Forbes described the period as 'an era of agitation, upheaval, restlessness, strikes, caprice', when the 'whole community of labour is a-quivering with St Vitus's dance'.[51] Strikes were becoming commonplace and more serious; indeed, in 1891 the Metropolitan Police went on strike for more pay. Wolseley was appalled by the growing examples of socialism and predicted that if the politicians did not act, 'in the end the man of talk will give way to the man of action. A new Cromwell will clear the country of frothy talkers'. He wished that he was young enough to be that Cromwell.[52]

The European situation was also alarming now that France and Russia had concluded an alliance. Both countries were potential threats to Britain and her empire and could combine in their destruction by threatening the freedom of the Suez Canal and, thereby, cut Britain's lifeline to India and the Far East empire. The immediate effect was on Britain's position in the Mediterranean. Even before the alliance had been signed, military and naval authorities cast doubts on Britain's ability to uphold its policy of supporting Turkey against Russian aggrandisement. In March 1892 a joint report by the Intelligence Departments of the War Office and Admiralty concluded that: 'unless we are acting in concert with France, the road to Constantinople for a British fleet bent on a belligerent operation, lies across the ruins of the French fleet'. Their worst fears were soon to be realised, when that year a Russian squadron sailed through the Dardanelles to join the French Mediterranean fleet at Toulon. Russia now had access to a warm water port and the Admiralty was reluctantly forced to admit that the Royal Navy had ceased to control the Mediterranean. The consequence for Britain was that the axis for its policy in the Eastern Mediterranean began to turn from Constantinople to Alexandria.[53]

By 1895 it was clear that the Duke of Cambridge's health was failing, his ability to remain in office fading, and that Buller was doing most of the work. Throughout May and June pressure was put on the Duke to retire from office. He fought a long and hard battle against it, using his family connections with the Queen to retain his position. In the event, it was the Queen herself, realising that there was no political support for the Duke, who persuaded him to retire.[54]

The question of who should be the Duke's successor at first seemed to be a simple one: Campbell-Bannerman wanted Buller. Roberts was easily dismissed as a candidate because of his lack of knowledge of British military affairs. The Duke of Connaught, who the Queen expected to be appointed, was deemed too inexperienced and, given the Duke of Cambridge's abuse of his royal connections while in office, there was a general unwillingness in political circles for another royal appointment. Wolseley was left out of the calculations. He had not been active in War Office affairs since the Wantage Committee and Campbell-Bannerman probably genuinely thought him no longer interested in the post. Unknown to either man, it is likely that Buller withheld Wolseley's proposals for reform from Campbell-Bannerman in order to strengthen his own position. On 16 June 1895 the Queen telegraphed her private secretary, Sir Arthur Bigge, that she approved of Buller's appointment.[55] Shortly afterwards, and before the appointment was made public, the Liberal government fell from office and the whole question of who should be the next Commander-in-Chief was reopened.

16

Commander-in-Chief

Wolseley had wrongly assumed that the retirement of the Duke of Cambridge would lead to the appointment of the Duke of Connaught as the Duke's successor. He considered that he had a right to be appointed Commander-in-Chief but was prepared to stand aside in favour of the Queen's son. On these grounds, he accepted the offer of the post of Ambassador to Germany. The news of the appointment of Redvers Buller came as a great shock. He wrote to his friend John Ardagh on 12 July 1895: 'The blow nearly stunned me, for to be sent about one's business five years earlier than even the ordinary general is retired at, and to be superseded by one of the lieutenants whom I myself created, is treatment I never contemplated possible. There has been some intrigue at work that I cannot fathom'.[1] A few days later he wrote to Evelyn Wood on similar lines:

> I don't envy the feelings or conscience of the junior comrade who consents at this juncture to be put over my head. But then all men do not look at such points of honour in the old fashioned fashion that I have always felt for the few men who in my early life helped me up some of the difficult rungs of life's ladder.[2]

Buller himself was aware of Wolseley's feelings and had written to Campbell-Bannerman in June that, 'I feel my appointment to such a post would possibly pain Lord Wolseley'.[3]

The new Unionist government faced the task of appointing a Commander-in-Chief. The Queen again pressed the claim of her son. However, the government had no intention of making the Duke of Connaught the new Commander-in-Chief, as on 4 August 1895 the new Secretary of State for War, Lord Lansdowne, made this clear in a letter to Salisbury. The Duke of Connaught's candidature was not being considered seriously.[4] On 6 August Sir John Ardagh wrote a memorandum outlining the relative merits of the candidates. He argued that the Duke of Cambridge had favoured Buller because he had less talent than Wolseley:

> He would like to have Buller too because he believes he would not go too fast, and would have things as they are, until the Duke of Connaught is ripe to step

into his shoes: whereas he apprehends that Wolseley would make it evident that the army could be successfully commanded, and greatly improved without a Royalty at its head.

Wolseley would have agreed with this assessment had he known of it: a day later he wrote to his brother George that Buller was considered a safe pair of hands because he would just let the army mark time, whereas Wolseley would continue the reforming process.[5]

On 7 August 1895 Lansdowne wrote to the Queen formally recommending Wolseley for the post of Commander-in-Chief. He ignored the Queen's objections that Wolseley had promised to go to Berlin, and stated categorically that political and military opinion was adamant that the Duke of Connaught was too inexperienced for the post. The Queen was hostile to the idea of Wolseley as Commander-in-Chief 'as he is very imprudent, full of new fancies, and has a clique of his own'. Telegrams continued to pass between the government, the Queen and the Kaiser on the subject until finally, on 17 August, the Queen telegraphed Lansdowne, 'I sanction Wolseley's appointment, but I do not think it a good one'.[6] The appointment was made public on 19 August.

Wolseley had attempted to conceal his anxiety over his future by going on a cruise in the North Sea, leaving Sir John Ardagh to fight his case in London. He had already confided his fears to Ardagh over his future financial position: if he was not to be Commander-in-Chief, he would have to discharge servants and sell his horses and carriages because he was very poor.[7] Above all he could not understand the slur on his career that the appointment of Buller suggested. Even when securely in office, Wolseley never forgave Buller, who remained Adjutant General, for what he perceived to be his disloyalty. In order to try and improve their relations, Buller wrote to Campbell-Bannerman asking for a copy of the letter in which he had said that he did not want to offend Wolseley by accepting the Commander-in-Chiefship because Wolseley 'has got it into his head that I had plotted against him behind his back, and had tried to supplant him in what he held to be his birth right'. Unfortunately for Buller he got the date wrong, asking Campbell-Bannerman for a letter written in June 1897 instead of 1895, with the result that Campbell-Bannerman could not find the letter and Buller could not placate Wolseley.[8]

Poor relations between Wolseley and Buller were not the only thing that soured Wolseley's term of office: he also had professional and personal disagreements with Lansdowne. The professional disagreements stemmed from the Order in Council Campbell-Bannerman had made public in a speech to the House of Commons on 21 June, which Lansdowne planned to implement without amendment. The principal reason behind the recommendation of the Hartington Commission for the abolition of the office of the Commander-in-Chief was that it was felt that too much power was concentrated in his hands. He was so overloaded with work that important areas, such as the preparation of plans of war and of defence, were often overlooked. The Order in Council reorganised the internal departments of the War Office. Under the new rules, the Commander-in-Chief's functions would be greatly modified. He was to be the 'principal adviser of the Secretary of State', but associated with him were to be four other military heads of department, each 'directly responsible to the Secretary of State'.[9] The Military Secretary and the Director of Intelligence would report to the Commander-in-Chief. Responsibility for the discipline of the army was to be given to the Adjutant General. All heads of department would meet in a new Army Board, under the presidency of the Commander-in-Chief, to discuss questions raised either by one of the members or by the Secretary of State. Lansdowne announced the arrangement to the House of Lords on 26 August.[10]

Wolseley was horrified by the proposals put forward by Lansdowne. He had accepted the appointment 'assuming there will be no material alteration in position of Commander-in-Chief'.[11] In a series of letters he made clear his opinion that the public would hold him, as Commander-in-Chief, responsible for the efficiency of the army, not realising that this responsibility had been devolved to the Army Board. In August Wolseley suggested a few vital 'emendations', such as inserting into the list of the duties of the Commander-in-Chief the phrase, 'and shall be responsible for their fighting efficiency'. He also wanted the old phrasing of the Adjutant General's role in the discipline of the army restored: instead of the new phrase 'responsible for', he wanted the Adjutant General to be 'charged with' the discipline of the army. This would leave the Commander-in-Chief ultimately in charge, a fact that he considered important since during the New Forest manoeuvres that year two battalions had shown a distinct unwillingness to march and the public held the Commander-in-Chief responsible. In views of the financial battles that had previously so often emasculated his reforms, Wolseley suggested that the Accountant General should be made a member of the Army Board.[12]

In October Wolseley made another attempt to influence Lansdowne: he produced his own draft Order in Council 'as a sort of compromise between the extremely civilian views embodied in the Hartington Commission Report, and the purely military view of the armymen who have experience in army administration'. He remained firm on the idea that the Commander-in-Chief should be responsible for the discipline of the army and, if he were not, then 'it is impossible he could be in any way responsible for that fighting efficiency'. He suggested that the duties of the Commander-in-Chief could be safely reduced by removing from him responsibility for all the departments dealing with manufacture, stores, and armaments, while leaving personnel within his gamut.[13] Despite his appeals for greater powers, Lansdowne refused to amend the Order in Council immediately, preferring to wait and see how it operated in practice.

Wolseley had some allies in his battle with Lansdowne. In September 1895 he wrote to Wood seeking his support: 'It would be a matter of the first consequence to the army that we soldiers should hold together to try to guide the new Order in Council to run in military grooves'. He reminded Wood that it was in his and Buller's own interests to support their chief in his struggle to amend the Order in Council because one of them might succeed him as Commander-in-Chief after Wolseley's term had been completed.[14] He also had support from outside the War Office: in January 1897 Spenser Wilkinson wrote an article in the *National Review* arguing that the politicians had put Wolseley 'in a strait-waistcoat of a civilian war-office and of a council of his own subordinates. Such conditions would paralyse a Napoleon'.[15] In contrast Ardagh, who had done so much to secure Wolseley his new appointment, was in favour of a reduction in the powers of the Commander-in-Chief and, in a memorandum to Lansdowne, supported the idea that 'the Head Quarter Staff collectively under the Adjutant General should be empowered to press their views and practically overrule the Commander-in-Chief in the War Office Council'.[16]

Wolseley had no intention of allowing this to happen, and one historian has correctly interpreted the key to the poor relations between Lansdowne and Wolseley as the dispute over the meaning of the terms 'limited responsibility' and 'general supervision'.[17] Wolseley was adamant that his heads of department should not have direct access to the Secretary of State, because this implied 'limited responsibility'. Nor did he feel that he could carry out 'general supervision' if he did not always know what his heads of department were doing. The drive towards the reform of the army needed a leader, but subjecting the actions of individual heads of department to the 'general supervision' of the Commander-in-Chief, when presiding over meetings of the Army Board, put him in the position of a commentator or a referee and not a leader. There was the danger that, by the time issues were raised at the Army Board, one or more heads of department might have already gone too far in a direction which suited their purposes but which Wolseley could not view as in the best interests of the efficiency of the army as a whole.

He did his best to circumvent the regulations, ensuring that the heads of department knew of his dissatisfaction with the regulations, and trying to institute a new procedure whereby he would be consulted on the actions of the heads of department before any proposals were presented directly by them to the Secretary of State. For example, Wood recalled that Wolseley ordered him to address him on any matters he wished to put to the Secretary of State. The result was that Lansdowne minuted papers to Wood, but received them back through Wolseley.[18] Lansdowne detested this practice but Wolseley continued, not only because it strengthened his own position, but because he felt that Lansdowne was incapable of understanding the complexities of military affairs.[19] The Permanent Under Secretary, R. H. Knox, sought Campbell-Bannerman's advice on how to implement this part of the Order in Council. Campbell-Bannerman replied that he felt that 'the real difficulty is to combine independence with co-operation'. The Army Board was the best solution but, 'I suspect the Viscount and the two VCs are rather too many lions in one cage'.[20] He was right: personal relations were the key to the whole question. The members of the Army Board were at, or near, the peak of their careers, had known each other for a number of years, and consequently battled for supremacy, scoring against each other rather than pulling together to produce an efficient army.

It was ironic that the first war of Wolseley's term of office was against an enemy he himself had defeated twenty years earlier. The Asante king, Prempeh, had angered the authorities at Cape Coast Castle by refusing to pay the remainder of the indemnity imposed on his predecessor, Kofi, after Wolseley had defeated the Asante in battle and burned their capital Kumasi. Furthermore, Prempeh encouraged the slave trade, a source of wealth for his people, and renewed the practice of human sacrifice. The Colonial Office appealed to the War Office to lend British troops for an expedition under Sir Francis Scott, to crush the Asante permanently. As with Wolseley's expedition, it was planned to use native troops both as carriers and to undertake much of the fighting. However, in November 1895, the War Office was informed that Scott was unlikely to raise the number of Hausa originally estimated and would need more British troops. Wolseley proposed adding fifty men to the half battalion being sent from England under Colonel Frederick Stopford and increasing the number taken from the West India Regiment at Sierra Leone. The campaign progressed smoothly, marred only by the death of Prince Henry of Battenburg, a special service officer, from fever. It brought Robert Baden-Powell to Wolseley's attention, which later secured him an important role in the South African War.[21] The threat of the Asante was ended forever by the annexation of their country.

The manpower crisis was the most serious challenge facing Wolseley on his return to the War Office. While the Wantage Committee had upheld the principle of short service, it had done nothing to remedy the discrepancy between the number of battalions abroad and at home. In June 1888 he had set out a case for increasing the army by eleven infantry battalions and seven batteries of artillery, which, together with other miscellaneous increases, would have added 23,000 men to the army.[22] Stanhope had declined to take action.

In 1896, spurred on by an able and detailed memorandum by the Director of Military Intelligence, Major-General Edward Chapman, Wolseley wrote a very comprehensive survey of the military requirements of the Empire. This aimed to set down 'a full view of the extent to which the Regular Army can, and of the extent to which it cannot, perform what have been laid down as its duties'. He summarised the requirements for garrisons in India and the colonies including Egypt, concluding that a total of 102,680 men had to be maintained abroad. The home army was manifestly incapable of meeting the demand for trained drafts, and had only been able to do so by 'a perpetual series of makeshifts, by transfers, by enlarged depots, by bounties, by robbing Peter to pay Paul, by the denudation of the home cadres, by a succession of struggles and expedients which combine to keep it in a weak and exhausted condition'. The garrison artillery had only thirty-six companies at home to feed sixty-seven abroad; there were seventy-six infantry battalions abroad fed by sixty-five at home; and only the Cavalry and the Engineers were able to cope with the demand for drafts. He argued that the home army would be fit for home defence when the number of soldiers would be increased by the mobilisation of the Volunteers, Militia and Yeomanry, but even then the artillery needed ten more batteries. Wolseley concluded that eleven new infantry battalions were required to balance the system; fifteen, if two more battalions were sent to the Cape, as he recommended.[23]

Lansdowne proved surprisingly responsive to Wolseley's memorandum. He asked the actuaries to assess the cost; the reply was £2,000,000. Lansdowne then asked Wolseley to reconsider his proposals and to investigate whether savings could be made in other branches of the army. Wolseley argued that the increase of thirteen infantry battalions and at least five batteries of field artillery was essential, but that two cavalry regiments could be reduced and the horse artillery reorganised. He also raised the controversial question of stationing some Guards battalions abroad.[24] His memorandum was then referred to the Army Board in December, where it had a mixed reception.

At this meeting of the Army Board, the first of any major consequence, its members showed the independence of thought hoped for by Campbell-Bannerman and Lansdowne when reorganising the War Office. The board agreed to reduce one rather than two cavalry regiments, but it supported Wolseley's proposals on the garrison artillery, and agreed with his argument that a total of seventy-seven battalions was needed at home to feed seventy-seven abroad. It then dismissed his appeal for an increase to the horse artillery and reduced his request for more field artillery to one battery. The Board recommended that one regiment of the Household Cavalry should be reduced and ignored Wolseley's opposition to this proposal. It watered down his demand for thirteen new infantry battalions by arguing that, if two new Guards battalions were raised and three sent abroad, the balance of infantry of the line at home and abroad would be reduced to seventy-four. Consequently only seven new infantry battalions would be needed.[25]

The production of concrete proposals by a board rather than an individual strengthened Lansdowne's hand when approaching the Cabinet with proposals for such a dramatic increase in the army. Lansdowne, however, though an able man, was a weak member of the Cabinet and only managed to obtain an increase of £120,000 to the 1897 Estimates. This was a long way from the £2,000,000 needed to carry out the planned increases in their entirety, yet it was a small step towards it. The Army Board was disquieted by the information that it would not be allowed to order new 10 inch and 9.2 inch guns to modernise the artillery. No new orders were to be placed, though existing orders would be completed.[26] This decision by the Cabinet was to have serious repercussions three years later in South Africa.

By the end of 1896 both Lansdowne and most of the Cabinet were convinced that substantial increases were needed to the army: the question remained of what, when and how much. The onus was therefore on the War Office to maintain the impetus. However, in January 1897 Wolseley became seriously ill and was forced to take a long absence from the War Office. He first contracted a throat infection which refused to heal and which was complicated by an attack of jaundice. In July he had some glands in his neck removed. He spent much of his sick leave in Brighton hoping that the sea air might cure him. Frances was shocked by his appearance when she visited him, recording in her diary that her father was 'much changed, shrunk and weak'. To convalesce Wolseley took a cruise in the Mediterranean.[27] He finally felt fit enough to resume work in September 1897. Yet he was not really well: thereafter colleagues noticed a change. Buller noted that 'the old Duke seems to have outstayed Lord Wolseley, who has either got office where he is when he is no longer the man he was, or else he was never the man I thought him'. Neville Lyttelton echoed these remarks. Edmund Gosse noticed that Wolseley's memory was failing: he would greet the same person twice within a short period, always expressing amazement that he had not known of that person's arrival. He sometimes failed to recognise his own secretary and often denied having written memoranda and minutes.[28]

In September Wolseley reported to Lansdowne that he was fully fit and had almost got too fat to fit into his uniform. He embarked on a tour of Scotland, receiving honorary degrees from the universities of Edinburgh and Glasgow, and making inflammatory public speeches on the state of the army. The strongest of these was at Glasgow where he declared:

> Our Army machinery is overstrained and is out of gear. I speak in the presence of many whose technical knowledge will enable them to contradict me if I am wrong, when I say that, if a machine which is calculated to manufacture a certain amount of stuff annually has some 20 per cent extra work forced upon it, the machine will, sooner or later, certainly break down. Yet that is what we are risking with our Army. Our Army machinery is no longer able to meet effectively the demands now made upon it.[29]

Hugh Arnold-Forster recalled the outrage of the politicians when reading of this statement, and recorded his amazement that the Under Secretary for War, St John Brodrick, should have signalled his agreement with Wolseley's arguments.[30]

In November 1897 Wolseley produced another memorandum on the size of the army. In it he proposed an increase of twelve infantry battalions, arguing that neither home defence nor the requirements of colonial defence had been covered adequately in his previous memoranda. In the event of a war with France, the two battalions stationed in the Channel Islands would be incapable of forming part of the home establishment; six extra battalions were needed to defend London, the south coast and Dublin. This brought the total to eighty-three battalions at home. Since the increase to the Guards had been sanctioned, seventy-seven of these eighty-three battalions would be of the line. But the Colonial Defence Committee had asked for an extra battalion for Mauritius and another at Bermuda, which meant that eighty-one battalions would be abroad (one was temporarily stationed on Crete to serve during an emergency there). Three of the eighty battalions permanently abroad would come from the Guards, leaving seventy-seven to come from the line. The grand total of battalions needed at home and abroad was 154, whereas the establishment was only 142: consequently, Wolseley pressed for twelve new infantry battalions of the line.

In this memorandum he also proposed a revision of the Cardwell and Childers system of the organisation of regiments. He argued that the addition of twelve new battalions would balance the existing system and 'will give an opportunity for largely extending the four battalion system which already exists in the Rifle Corps and Rifle Brigade. Every additional four battalion regiment increases our elasticity and our power of having more battalions abroad than at home'. It would also increase Britain's ability to send a small expeditionary force abroad without calling out the Reserves.[31] Lansdowne replied that a Bill was under preparation to add a requirement for some reservists to serve abroad in small wars and that he did not therefore consider that part of Wolseley's arguments valid. Lansdowne did, however, give his tentative approval to the most radical proposal, the extension of four battalion regiments. He set up a committee of Ralph Knox, Frederick Stopford and Evelyn Wood to examine the question. The Army Board met on 2 December 1897 to consider the matter and, while it was in favour of four battalion regiments, it urged caution, remembering the outcry over the establishment of linked battalions almost twenty years earlier.[32]

At the end of 1897 success was in sight. On 2 December Lansdowne outlined his proposals for the Cabinet: ten new battalions were to be created and the establishment of home battalions increased by eighty men.[33] The Cabinet assented to these proposals and, in addition, approved the abolition of the stoppage for groceries, the abolition of deferred pay and its replacement by a messing allowance and a gratuity of £1 per year of service, and the intro-duction of a facility to allow discharged soldiers to re-engage without refunding their deferred pay. As Salisbury informed the Queen: 'The Army will be larger and better paid, and the Cardwell system will be rendered rather more elastic. But the Cardwell system remains still there'. Wolseley opposed the replacement of deferred pay by a gratuity and messing allowance: 'you want to add half an inch to the height of a man's collar, and you recoup yourself by cutting the same amount from the tail of his coat'.[34]

Inevitably, perhaps, the Treasury fought back against the proposed increase of 9000 men to the army. Lansdowne and the Chancellor of the Exchequer, Sir Michael Hicks Beach, fought a protracted battle in the Cabinet and, to Wolseley's dismay, the Treasury succeeded in gaining some of its points. On 3 February 1898 Lansdowne informed the Army Board that recruiting could be opened for six new battalions: the decision on which regiments could raise new battalions was to be left to the discretion of the Army Board.[35] The establishment of home battalions was to be raised to 800 men. Wolseley had only succeeded in gaining half what he had asked for but it was, nevertheless, a significant increase to the army. He had also demonstrated that he could work well with Lansdowne when the arguments were clear. Indeed Lansdowne had been prepared to support him to the extent of tendering his resignation to Salisbury in February 1898 if his Cabinet colleagues would not support Wolseley and himself against the Treasury.[36]

Wolseley deplored the demands India made on the home army: the increases he fought so hard for would not be necessary if his concept of Indian defence was adopted. In 1896 he was given the opportunity to state his views on the effect India had on the military requirements of the Empire when he was invited to give evidence to the Royal Commission on the Military and Civil Expenditure of India. He argued that the need to send so many drafts to India annually was 'a serious inconvenience to our military organisation' and affected recruitment adversely. He made the dramatic statement that since 'our Army was really a great reserve for the Army in India', India should therefore pay for 'everything connected with the Army'. A survey should be undertaken to estimate how many troops were maintained solely for Indian purposes. This would include the garrisons of colonies such as Mauritius and Aden, which were staging posts on the sea route to India and of little value otherwise to the empire, and the training and pay of men raised to supply drafts to, and the establishment of the British army in India. This proposal was so politically unacceptable that little comment was made on it.

More controversially Wolseley went on to make criticisms of the performance of sepoys in India, which he based on his experiences during the Mutiny. His comment, 'We should not like to put out Indian troops in front of European soldiers. I should not like to fight France or Germany or any other army with Indian troops', aroused outrage both in Britain and in India.[37] The Times reprinted extracts from an Indian newspaper, the Pioneer, which were highly critical of Wolseley. The Queen was also furious with his criticism of her Indian troops. Wolseley replied, defending his evidence: 'He would never flatter the native soldier by allowing himself to think himself the equal of the British soldier as a fighting man. Lord Wolseley thinks it would be extremely dangerous to the Empire to do so'.[38] The Queen recognised that British rule in India rested on the foundation that the Indian was inferior to the British and therefore did not press her case; nor did she ask for a public apology from him.

Recruitment was the next urgent problem facing Wolseley. His argument was 'that if you want an article you have to pay for it. With regard to the inducements that ought to be held out, I think, to a man to enlist, those inducements can be either in the shape of money, or they might be in the shape of employment when he leaves the army'. Lansdowne dismissed Wolseley's appeal to increase the basic pay of the soldier. He argued that if the pay of the home army was increased, then pressure would mount to increase the pay of the soldier in India. This would further overstrain the already stretched purse of the Indian taxpayer and be politically dangerous.[39]

In January 1898 Lansdowne suggested that an increase in the number of three-year enlistments might provide a temporary solution to the recruiting crisis, as it had done in the Foot Guards in the 1880s. The Army Board replied that, since these men would be ineligible for foreign service, they should be considered supernumerary to the establishment.[40] It was apparent that, for political reasons, Lansdowne was seeking a temporary solution to a fundamental problem. Having secured a major increase to the army, he needed to be able to announce in Parliament that the men had been found. He appeared less concerned with the efficiency or usefulness of these men: it was numbers that counted. In contrast, Wolseley and the Army Board could see little point in a large number of three-year enlistments of men who could never serve abroad.

It was soon apparent that the increase of six battalions had worsened the situation with regard to the quality of recruits. At the end of 1898 Lansdowne reported to the Cabinet that three new battalions had been raised and three more were being recruited. He admitted that although many 'specials' – men under the minimum physical requirements – had been enlisted, most reached the standard within a few months. Nevertheless he felt 'it cannot, however, be pretended that the present rate of progress is such to relieve us of anxiety as to the possibility of filling the enlarged cadres of the Army on the terms we now offer'.[41] Wolseley felt more anxiety than Lansdowne. He wrote to Butler that recruitment was in an appalling state: '*over* one third are below even the low physical standard laid down for recruits. In fact at this moment *over* one half of the *Home* army are unfit to carry a pack or do a week's – I might perhaps say a day's – hard work in the field'.[42] He could see no solution to this critical situation other than a substantial increase in pay. He was supported in this opinion by the Army Board.

The utilisation of the Guards eased the problem of finding enough troops to serve abroad. The proposal to send the Guards abroad had first been proposed by Stanhope in July 1891 and was continued by his successor Campbell-Bannerman. Under the plan, the Brigade of Guards would be increased by adding a battalion to the Coldstream Guards and merging the single-battalion Cameron Highlanders with the Scots Guards, giving the latter a third battalion. The Guards would then be composed of nine battalions, three of which would serve on the Mediterranean stations and be relieved every three years. There was vociferous opposition to the plan from former Guardsmen, including the Duke of Cambridge, and the Queen. The Prime Minister, Lord Rosebery, forced Campbell-Bannerman to abandon the plan because 'Europe might think we were coming to our last gasp when we send the Guards out of England'.[43] In 1896 Wolseley realised that the War Office really was at the 'last gasp' when it came to finding efficient soldiers for service abroad and revived the scheme. Somewhat surprisingly, given the strength of his opposition to the scheme when proposed before, the Duke of Cambridge wrote to him that the Guards must be prepared 'to make this slight sacrifice to their individual comforts and convenience in order to benefit the efficiency of the army in general'.[44] With the support of the Duke of Cambridge, royal and political opposition fell away, the opinions of Guards officers were ignored, and the Guards were sent to Gibraltar.

Buller wrote in June 1895 that 'the main blot on our military system is the failure of the Reserve to support our forces on the outbreak of a small war'. He argued for an alteration in the terms of enlistment so that all soldiers would be liable to be recalled to the colours during the first nine months of their service in the Army Reserve. This, he claimed, would provide 16,000 trained men immediately.[45] The subject of giving the government the power to recall men to the colours for small wars was discussed at a meeting of the Army Board, which Wolseley attended, in February 1896. The Board favoured the suggestion and only Brodrick aired doubts as to the wisdom of offending employers.[46] A Bill to make this change was presented to Parliament in the 1896 session but was rejected.

Given Wolseley's active participation in these measures, what followed seems extraordinary. In his November 1897 memorandum calling for an increase to the establishment of the army Wolseley had justified his arguments by stating that 'if given, it will enable us to meet the third demand on our Army, that namely, of being able to send a small force abroad without the help of the Reserve'. Lansdowne replied that he had thought the whole point of the Reserve Forces Bill was to make reservists liable for service during their first year in the reserve, and therefore there was no question of sending home battalions abroad to fight a war without them being strengthened by the addition of some reservists. Wolseley's reply stunned Lansdowne:

> The proposal to bring a Bill last Session of Parliament to make the Army Reserve in their first year of service liable to be recalled to the Colours for service for which they were not originally intended, was not proposed by any military adviser of the Secretary of State. When the proposal was discussed by the Army Board, it was felt that the men to be made liable during the first year of their Reserve service for further service in the Ranks, should be only liable to such recall, in the event of war or of imminent war.

This may be seen as evidence that his memory was failing. He had attended the relative Army Board meeting and the draft Bill had only been subject to minor alterations during his illness. The amended Reserve Forces Act, containing a liability for foreign service, was passed in 1898. Under the terms of the Act, 5000 reservists were offered additional pay if they volunteered to be liable for recall to the colours in the event of a small war.[47]

One other point of importance with regard to the Army Reserve was that the adding of battalions to the army actually decreased the size of the Reserve. The influx of young untrained men into the ranks necessitated the retention of experienced soldiers to train them and provide a solid backbone to the new battalions. The military authorities then went even further and controversially recalled some men from the Reserve to add support. The crucial discussion took place in a meeting of the Army Board in January 1898. Lansdowne took the lead, suggesting that men would be needed from the Reserve during the next two or three years to lessen the strain of the overall increase in the size of the army. Wolseley put forward a proposal to invite infantry reservists who had at least two years' Reserve service remaining to rejoin the colours for service in the regiments to be strengthened. He was not at all happy about this proposal, particularly if the numbers to be invited and the period of their extended service were to be unlimited. He believed that a sufficient number of recruits would be forthcoming so as to make the recall of reservists unnecessary, but was prepared to accept the arguments of his colleagues that the immediate requirement was for trained men and not a large number of raw recruits. He gave his assent to the proposal to use the Reserve for this purpose only when Lansdowne convinced him that 'this recall of men from the Reserve must be regarded as a purely temporary expedient to meet a temporary demand'.[48] The result was that the size of the First Class Army Reserve fell from nearly 71,000 in 1897 to just over 62,000 in 1899.

This fall in the size of the Army Reserve meant that the army would encounter great difficulties in conducting a war of any length or complication. Wolseley outlined the seriousness of the situation in a memorandum to Lansdowne in January 1899. He produced a series of statistics to show that if two army corps were mobilised for service abroad then only twenty-two of the fifty-four in the two army corps could be completed using their own reservists, the others would have to borrow men from the rest of the Reserve. Furthermore, the process of mobilisation would leave only 12,330 line reservists at home to act as reinforcements and to replace casualties. This was not enough and, after a period of four months, the Militia would have to be embodied to release more regulars. Lansdowne was not convinced that the situation was so serious and replied that there was a 'liberal surplus' of reserves for drafts.[49] Wolseley's fears were to be justified by the end of the year when most of the home establishment was sent to South Africa.

As Commander-in-Chief, Wolseley continued his struggle to ensure that only the best men were selected for the higher ranks of the army and for staff appointments. In January 1896 he wrote to the Permanent Under Secretary that he had decided to 'refuse to recommend any colonel for promotion whom I do not believe to be fit to command troops in the field as a Major-General. This disposes of the question of "seniority versus efficiency"'. He outlined his plans to reduce the size of the General Officers' List by writing to eight of the worst officers to inform them that they had no chance of further employment and should retire from the army. He wrote to the Commander-in-Chief in India, General George White, asking for his recommendations of suitable men for rapid advancement so that officers serving in India would have the same chance of promotion as those officers serving at home.[50] His plan met with the approval of Lansdowne, who wrote to Salisbury that Wolseley was determined to get rid of incompetent senior officers, and 'we are now very particular not only as to the colonels, but as to the seconds in command of regiments. I fancy that in many quarters he is already attacked as "ruthless"'.[51] Ruthless or not, Wolseley was adamant that this process was essential for the good of the army, despite the opposition he met from within the War Office. The opposition of officers hoping for or expecting promotion ensured that the War Office had to move more cautiously in the direction of pure selection than Wolseley wanted. At the end of 1897 a War Office committee on selection recommended that in 1898 one quarter of the promotions to the rank of Major-General should be made by seniority, in 1899 one fifth, and from 1900 all promotions to be made by selection only.[52]

Wolseley could be just as ruthless with appointments at the War Office itself. At the end of 1897 he bid farewell to Buller as his Adjutant General with no regret, since he had no longer trusted Buller after the struggle to become Commander-in-Chief. Buller took up the Aldershot command. His replacement was Evelyn Wood, who still maintained good relations with Wolseley: the two men had corresponded on training methods when Wolseley was in Ireland. A further change was made abruptly with the connivance of Lansdowne. The Inspector General of Ordnance, General Edwin Markham, was a weak man. Rather than assist Wolseley in his attempt to modernise the artillery through the purchase of the new quick-firing guns, Markham set up experiments to show that existing artillery could be converted. Wolseley decided to get rid of him by offering him a five-year term at Sandhurst, which would keep him employed for three more years than would have been the case had he remained Inspector General of Ordnance. His replacement was Henry Brackenbury, who Lansdowne described as being 'head and shoulders above all competitors'.[53] Wolseley was content with this appointment because he thought very highly of

Brackenbury's abilities. At one stage he had considered Brackenbury a member of his 'Ring' until, while serving in India, he had supported Roberts's views on Indian defence and then had earned his contempt by being a member of the Hartington Commission. Nevertheless, the two men worked very well together.

Brackenbury's appointment coincided with the decision of the government to place the ordnance factories under military control. This necessitated an amendment of the 1895 Order in Council. The Queen seized the opportunity to suggest to Salisbury that the Order in Council ought also to be changed 'with a view of re-establishing the position of the Commander-in-Chief, especially with regard to the discipline of the Army. He ought not to be a head of department, but the Supreme Military Chief responsible to the Sovereign (the head of the Army) for its *military*, as opposed to its *civil*, administration'. At the Queen's request Wolseley visited Salisbury to argue his case. Salisbury reported that Lansdowne, in refusing to permit any alteration to the Order in Council, considered the matter serious enough to threaten resignation. He wanted to avoid this, since there was the danger that Lansdowne's resignation would lead to the departure of other Liberal Unionists and to a political crisis. In May 1899 the Queen abandoned her campaign, but she wrote a memorandum to Lansdowne: 'The Queen has been unable to modify her views upon this important subject. Her Majesty will, however, no longer press these, but desires that this memorandum may be officially recorded at the War Office'.[54] This was a victory of sorts for Wolseley. It meant that during the in-fighting at the War Office after the disasters of the South African War he knew he could depend on royal support on the subject of the responsibilities of the Commander-in-Chief.

Determined to improve the training of the British army, in November 1895 Wolseley pressed Lansdowne for permission to use Richmond Park as a training ground (Wimbledon Common being far too like a parade ground and unsuitable for practising outpost duties). He pointed out that he had tried to get the Duke of Cambridge's assent for the manoeuvres previously (necessary since the Duke was the ranger) but had always been turned down on the grounds that the Duke raised pheasants in Richmond Park.[55] In 1898 the government purchased a large area of Salisbury Plain for manoeuvres but would only provide the finance for large-scale manoeuvres in 1899. Wolseley brought forward evidence to show the urgency of these manoeuvres. He cited his visit to the Aldershot manoeuvres of 1896 where he had been shown a good standard of training. In contrast, an unexpected visit to the exercises held by the South Eastern Command at Dover showed the 'want of tactical training in many squadrons and companies'.[56] He won the argument. In August and September 1898 the cavalry exercised; the last fortnight of August was devoted to various drills of all arms; and in the first week of September large-scale manoeuvres were held between an army corps commanded by the Duke of Connaught and another led by Buller.

Wolseley wrote a very detailed memorandum on the Salisbury manoeuvres for Lansdowne. He stated that the organisation of the manoeuvres meant that 'it would optimistic to say that the fullest tactical value was obtained from each day's operation'. The shortage of water on Salisbury Plain, and the difficulties encountered in obtaining and utilising large amounts of civilian transport to augment that provided by regiments and the Army Service Corps, meant that at the end of each day the men were marched off to pre-prepared camps. He made many other important points; 'the extent of front covered by each force was on occasions remarkable, and at times excessive'. This would not have mattered of the staff had been better at their jobs, but Wolseley noted that there was a tendency to deploy troops too soon, and that 'full advantage was seldom taken of the conformation of the ground to conceal the advance of attacking columns'. Therefore the intentions of each force should have been obvious to its opponents long before action was resumed; except that he also noted that scouting and reconnaissances were poorly undertaken. This was a particular weakness of the cavalry and he made many suggestions on how the cavalry could balance its twin duties of reconnaissance for the whole force, and concentration for its own fighting requirements. The performance of the artillery and engineers met with general approval.

Although he was impressed by the performance of the infantry soldiers despite their youth, Wolseley was rather less pleased with their commanding officers. He noted that the formations had frequently been faulty: men were being exposed to artillery fire; open order was often adopted too early or too late when attacking; and the use of the ground was poor. He was disappointed by the use of machine guns, noting that 'to collect machine guns together and employ them as batteries is a mistaken use of the weapon'. Furthermore, the machine gun was viewed by him as primarily a weapon of defence: commanders had been too willing to bring machine guns into action regardless of whether the circumstances demanded their use. Despite his criticisms, he was generally satisfied with the state of the army as revealed by the manoeuvres but stressed that improvements still needed to be made.[57] Yet a year later in South Africa the senior regimental officers would repeat the errors Wolseley had drawn their attention to, with disastrous consequences for the men they commanded.

During the manoeuvres the news that Khartoum had been retaken by an Anglo-Egyptian army reached Britain and Wolseley had a royal salute fired in celebration.[58] This was the culmination of the long and slow campaign to reconquer the Sudan begun in 1896. Britain's position in Egypt had assumed a greater importance because of the Franco-Russian alliance. Now the authorities in London and Cairo viewed any interest taken by a foreign power in the region of the Upper Nile as a direct threat to Britain's hold on Egypt. There was the rather far-fetched fear that a foreign power might dam the Nile causing the collapse of agriculture in southern Egypt. Italy was not seen as a serious threat: its presence in Abyssinia had been viewed as barrier to Dervish expansion from the Sudan until they withdrew after being defeated by the forces of Emperor Menelek at Adowa in 1896. French activities were viewed more seriously. France had never forgiven Britain for taking advantage of a moment of political weakness to enter and hold Egypt alone. France was active in the Sahara and it seemed likely that a move would soon be made towards the region of the Upper Nile.

The British and Egyptian governments decided that the best way to prevent French encroachments into the region was to reconquer the Sudan. Wolseley was consulted on 12 March 1896, when the Cabinet were deciding future policy towards the Sudan, and recommended caution. He was alarmed later that month to hear that Kitchener, the Sirdar of the Egyptian army, and Lord Cromer (formerly Evelyn Baring), the British Consul, were purchasing boats and camels for a major expedition to Berber. He did not immediately realise that on 15 March the Cabinet had given the two men the total authority to accept orders only from the Foreign Office, under whose auspices Egypt lay. The campaign was to be, as Cromer termed later, 'a Foreign Office War'. Cromer announced his intention to treat War Office directives 'not as instructions, but simply as the views of Her Majesty's Government's military advisers, for careful consideration'.[59] Wolseley attempted in vain to force a War Office liaison officer upon Kitchener.[60]

Wolseley naturally resented the isolation of the War Office from an expedition in an area of which he had much personal knowledge. In May 1896 he wrote to Lansdowne that, 'unless you desire it, or in the case of some evident necessity for doing so, I do not propose, in the future, to criticise Sir Herbert Kitchener's arrangements, not to call attention to any measures which may appear to me to entail avoidable risk'. Lansdowne felt this statement was going too far in the direction of abandoning all responsibility for the campaign. He told the Cabinet that, while he supported Wolseley's argument that the War Office should not be held responsible for any mistakes made in the Sudan, he had told him that he must keep abreast of events because, should a disaster occur, the British army would inevitably be called upon to rescue the Egyptian army.[61]

By October 1897 an element of involvement by the British army was becoming more likely. A French force of 163 officers and askaris, under Captain Jean Marchand, began a march across Africa from Gabon to establish a French position on the Upper Nile. Kitchener's force also suffered a minor set-back at Berber. Therefore Lansdowne wrote to Salisbury that 'Lord Wolseley, assures me that in spite of our "overdrawn account" of battalions abroad, we could, for such an enterprise as this, lay our hands on the eight battalions which would be wanted. The assumption of course is that we should get them back in a very short time'.[62] Cromer resisted this proposal until Kitchener requested more troops on 31 December 1897 after hearing rumours that the Khalifa was massing a huge army at Omdurman. Control of the campaign was retained by Kitchener, although Wolseley sent Lieutenant-General Francis Grenfell to take command of the British army in Egypt precisely because Grenfell had experience of campaigning in Egypt. After protracted negotiations over the size and composition of the British force, eight British battalions and a regiment of cavalry took part in the Battle of Omdurman on 2 September 1898.[63] The battle was totally one-sided: Sudanese casualties have been estimated at between ten and twelve thousand whereas the Anglo-Egyptian force lost only 482 dead and wounded.[64] The superiority of modern weaponry was amply illustrated against a weaker-armed enemy: Wolseley proudly told an audience of Volunteers that no Dervish got within 1000 yards of the British line.[65] This battle gave the British army a false sense of confidence and superiority. A year later the Boers would teach it what marksmanship really meant.

After the battle of Omdurman, Kitchener was ordered south to Fashoda where Marchand had raised the French flag. His orders were to evict Marchand but not to use force unless fired upon. Kitchener tactfully advanced under the Egyptian not British flag, signalling that the Sudan was a province of Egypt rather than a British conquest. The two men met at Fashoda and waited civilly together while telegrams flurried between London, Paris and Cairo. At one time it seemed that war was imminent between Britain and France and in London the Admiralty drafted war orders for the Home, Mediterranean and Channel fleets. Common sense prevailed: the French government, distracted by the Dreyfus affair, ordered Marchand to withdraw from Fashoda.[66] The Sudan was now to be governed jointly by Britain and Egypt.

At the beginning of 1899 Wolseley and his wife at last realised their dream of owning a property in the country by purchasing a farm house in Glynde, Sussex. It was a substantial building with thirty-six rooms; surrounded by a large garden in which Frances could indulge her passion for gardening. The women moved to Glynde in April but Wolseley retained rooms in town, visiting Glynde at weekends or when he was ill. In May 1899 the

Queen granted him a grace and favour apartment in Hampton Court Palace at a low annual rent of £25, to include the cost of redecoration. Louisa exercised her talent for setting up home and Wolseley's original biographers, Frederick Maurice and George Arthur, commented on how attractive she had made it.[67] Wolseley split his time between his rooms in town and the two properties. He needed the relaxation afforded by Glynde because the last eighteen months of his term of office as Commander-in-Chief proved very stressful. Britain went to war in South Africa.

17

The South African War

In 1879 Wolseley had predicted that the Transvaal contained a vast quantity of unexploited mineral wealth.[1] In 1886 huge gold reserves were discovered in the Witwatersrand. The impact on the economy of the Transvaal was staggering: whereas in 1886 the total revenue was £196,000, by 1896 it had risen to nearly £4,000,000. By 1899 two-thirds of the Rand mines were owned by British stockholders and British investment in the country totalled around £350,000,000. Most of the mining was done by the British too: a census in Johannesburg in 1896 revealed that there were 16,000 British settlers against only 6,205 Boers.[2]

The British and other foreign settlers became known as the *Uitlanders*, or foreigners. In the 1890s they began agitating for the franchise but the Transvaal government was not prepared to extend the franchise to all the *Uitlanders* and imposed strict residency terms to limit their numbers. Since 1881 the Transvaal had become virtually encircled by British colonies or spheres of interest. To the north, the British South Africa Company of Cecil Rhodes controlled the territory now named Rhodesia.[3] The only territories in the region not loyal to British interests were South West Africa, ruled by Germany, and Mozambique, under Portugal.

In 1895 the new Unionist government soon demonstrated that it had little patience with the attempts of Paul Kruger's government to promote the total independence of the Transvaal.[4] Salisbury threatened the use of force if Kruger did not reopen the drifts across the Vaal river, closed by a tariff dispute. Relations between Britain and the Transvaal worsened considerably at the end of 1895 when a confederate of Rhodes, Dr Leander Starr Jameson, led a band of colonists into the Transvaal, hoping, with the support of an uprising in Johannesburg, to force the Transvaal to its knees and provoke a British annexation of the country. The *Uitlanders* in Johannesburg failed to rise and Jameson and his men were captured by the Boers. The complicity in the raid of Rhodes, the Prime Minister of the Cape, was undeniable and he was forced to resign his office. The Colonial Secretary in London, Joseph Chamberlain, covered his tracks better and saved his career.[5]

Wolseley had no doubt that the Transvaal ought to be a British province. He despised the Boers and thought them 'in some respects far inferior to the Zulu, and the most ignorant and bigotted [sic] and small-minded of white men'. He regretted the failure of the Jameson raid since he was convinced that its success would have turned the Transvaal into an English province.[6] Chamberlain was prepared to continue applying pressure for the Transvaal to extend its franchise, even to the extent of threatening the use of force. He began to view South Africa as the region where British imperial interests must be upheld. Not only was the Cape an even more vital trading route to the east than the Suez Canal, but the telegram from Kaiser Wilhelm II to Kruger, congratulating him on suppressing the Jameson Raid, seemed to Chamberlain to show the danger of European interests in the region against Britain. In 1897 Sir Alfred Milner was appointed High Commissioner in South Africa. He was a high imperialist, unwilling to tolerate any threat to British interests.[7] The coincidence of ambitious imperialists in London and Cape Town, with a Commander-in-Chief who wanted to avenge the shame of Majuba, led to a potentially explosive situation. It made it more likely that force would be resorted to in order to settle diplomatic issues.

There can be little doubt that Chamberlain, Milner and many in the government thought that a war with the Transvaal would be an easy undertaking, and that this led them to pursue an aggressive policy towards the Boers. After the war the government denied that the War Office had ever informed it that war with the Transvaal would be complicated and difficult, and expressly blamed Wolseley for this state. The arguments were examined at length by the Royal Commission on the Preparations for the War in South Africa, known as the Elgin Commission.[8] It is clear, however, that the War Office did inform the government that waging a war so far from Britain would be a severe challenge on military resources, but that the government did not always take on board the advice supplied by the military authorities. The key to this apparent lack of communication lay in the relations between Wolseley and Lansdowne. Wolseley complained privately that, 'I have to deal in Lansdowne with a man of the smallest mind and who is surprisingly ignorant on every point connected with soldiers and with war'.[9] There is ample evidence to demonstrate that Lansdowne did not keep him informed on vital points of diplomatic negotiation and that all military planning consequently had to take place in a vacuum.

Part of the reason why the government did not keep the military fully informed may lie in a memorandum Wolseley asked the Director of Military Intelligence, Sir John Ardagh, to prepare in 1896. Wolseley was aware that, following the Jameson Raid, the Boers had begun to order vast stocks of rifles and ammunition, including the most modern artillery guns from Krupps and Creuzot. Ardagh's memorandum, issued as *Military Notes on the Dutch Republics*, carefully analysed the latest almanac of the Transvaal

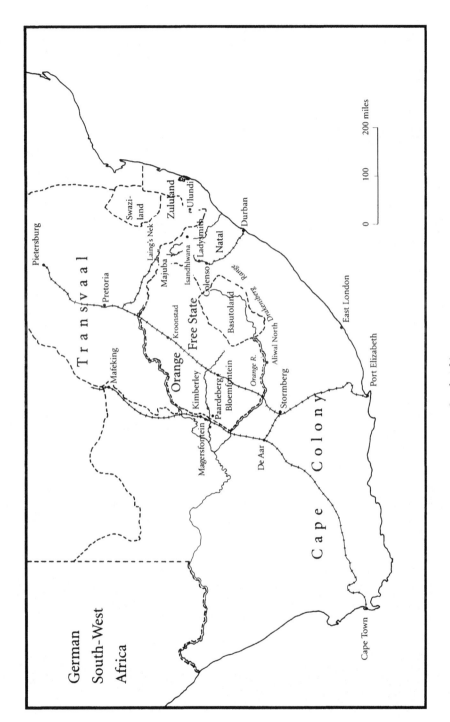

South Africa

to establish the number of burghers liable for military duty. He gave a total of 25,457 men for the Transvaal and, because he was convinced that the Boers of the Orange Free State would join their northern brethren, added their numbers too. To these men he included the former artillery men from Germany, who were being encouraged to settle in the Transvaal, and an estimate of foreign sympathisers: the total force Britain might have to face was 48,000. Ardagh also commented on strategy, arguing that the occupation of the main towns, Johannesburg and Pretoria, would deliver the country to British control. He noted that since the number of mules that would be required to transport British forces exceeded the supply, an advance along the Cape-Transvaal railway was the most suitable strategy to be adopted. This assumed that the Orange Free State would be hostile.[10]

Wolseley passed this memorandum to Lansdowne who showed it to Salisbury. Salisbury confessed to Lansdowne on 21 April 1897 that 'I am astonished at reading the recommendations of Sir J. Ardagh'.[11] He felt that Wolseley and Ardagh were trespassing into areas of government policy: it was not their place to argue that adequate preparations for defence or offence could not be prepared until a decision on the attitude of the Orange Free State was taken. Most of all Salisbury strongly objected to Wolseley's and Ardagh's request that a decision be taken on the possibility of blockading the Portuguese port of Lourenço Marques, through which most of the Boer imports of armaments were made. Both military men were prepared to risk a war with Portugal, which had negligible military resources, in order to stop the imports. The indignation expressed by Salisbury and Lansdowne in 1897 may go some way to explaining why in 1899 Wolseley and the War Office were left so much in the dark about the state of diplomacy.

The report of the Elgin Commission stated that 'the general impression to be derived from the whole circumstances [of the war] must be that the special function of the Commander-in-Chief, under the Order in Council of 1895, viz.: "the preparation of schemes of offensive and defensive operations", was not exercised on this occasion in any systematic fashion'.[12] Lansdowne had told the commissioners that 'I cannot call to mind any proposal on the part of the Commander-in-Chief for a large strengthening of our position in South Africa as an antidote to the Boer preparations'. He claimed that Wolseley had been silent on the subject of South Africa between 1896, when he had proposed to send two additional battalions there, and June 1899.[13] This is untrue. Wolseley had been active throughout this period in responding to appeals for more men from Milner and in seeking defensive plans from the officers in command in Natal and in Cape Colony. Lansdowne would have been made aware of Wolseley's memorandum to the Permanent Under Secretary on 20 April 1898 drawing his

attention to recent communications from Milner on the danger posed by
the Boer preparations. Wolseley had asked for reinforcements on that
occasion 'to make the force there complete in all arms'.[14] Beyond this
memorandum he had no need to request the despatch of more men to
South Africa since the diplomatic situation appeared reasonably quiet and
war likely only in the long term. Furthermore he knew that reinforcing the
South African garrisons would be difficult: British troops were active on
the North-West Frontier of India and forming a garrison in Crete, apart
from being on standby to reinforce the Egyptian force reconquering the
Sudan if necessary.[15] The home army was also undergoing a period of rapid
expansion at this time which detrimentally affected its efficiency.

Wolseley did encourage the military authorities in South Africa to draw
up defence plans. This was in accordance with common practice: the War
Office accepted that the man on the spot was best able to make detailed
plans which would then be forwarded for War Office approval. In 1896 the
General Officer Commanding in South Africa, Lieutenant-General Sir William Goodenough, had sent plans to the War Office. In his memorandum
he expressed most concern about the lines of communication and made
suggestions on the numbers of men required to defend the vital road bridges
over the Orange River and the railway junctions in the northern Cape
Colony. His plan of defence for Natal also emphasised the protection of
the lines of communication, particularly guarding Van Renen's Pass through
the Biggarsburg from the Orange Free State into Natal.[16] Goodenough's
plans were approved by Lansdowne in September 1897.

At the end of 1898 Wolseley was sufficiently concerned by the growth of
Boer armaments to set up a committee at the War Office to draw up a list
of questions on South African defence to be answered by the new General
Officer Commanding, Wolseley's friend, William Butler.[17] Butler was
undoubtedly not the man for the job; he was known in public to sympathise
with the underdog, whether it was the Irish against their English overlords,
the Egyptian fighting to retain their independence from European financial
interests, or the Boers seeking to retain their independence from the British
yoke. Given Butler's attitude, there was little chance that he would respond
favourably to the letter from the War Office. He wrote in his autobiography
of his opinion at the time: 'I have full reason to think now that even at that
time a section of people, including several prominent persons in the War
Office, were at work to bring that war about at an early date'.[18] After much
prodding, Butler sent a defence plan to the War Office in June 1899. This
stressed that, in the event of war, the northern triangle of Natal could not
be held against Boer forces. The main thrust of Butler's argument was that
the authorities in Britain were underestimating the probable consequences

of a war with the Transvaal. He believed that the Orange Free State would be drawn into the fight, and that British lines of communication would be threatened in the rear by a rising of the Cape Boers and the native tribes in Basutoland, Pondoland and the Transkei. Butler was unhappy in his position in South Africa, and the War Office was none too pleased by his dilatoriness in sending a reply to its letter. On 4 July he resigned his post and was replaced by Major-General Penn Symons.[19]

On 31 May 1899 the Bloemfontein Conference opened to discuss the franchise question. The Under Secretary for the Colonies, Lord Selbourne, gave a clear idea of the British position: 'We take our stand on the duty and right of every civilised government to protect its subjects resident in foreign countries when they are oppressed and our own especial interest in everything South African as the Paramount power there'.[20] Milner was not hopeful of a satisfactory solution and requested British reinforcements of between ten and thirty thousand men to defend Natal. The government ignored his plea, since it felt that the despatch of reinforcements might precipitate a conflict and it was aware of a lack of support for war in Britain. Lansdowne's attitude was 'I have never heard of sending out reinforcements to a country which might become a theatre of war merely in order that the reinforcements might successfully defend themselves against attack'.[21] He did not confide in Wolseley on the state of diplomacy and most of Wolseley's information on the progress of the Bloemfontein Conference came from Chamberlain.

No detailed plans of defence or offence could be prepared until the government made a decision on the likely attitude of the Orange Free State. Troops could not be switched between the Cape and Natal at short notice; no railway existed running through British territory linking the two colonies; and sea conditions at the port of Durban were often such as to delay considerably any embarkation or disembarkation of men and supplies. The Orange Free State had remained neutral in the First South African War but was also purchasing war matériel. Therefore, despite the apparent show of neutrality by hosting the conference at Bloemfontein, it seemed likely that the Orange Free State would be hostile in a a future conflict between Britain and the Transvaal.

The importance of a decision on this issue cannot be overstated. If the Orange Free State were to remain neutral then forces would still have to be stationed on the northern frontiers of the Cape to guard against any sabotage of the road bridges over the Orange River and the major railway junctions in the Cape by sympathisers with the Transvaal. The bulk of British forces would be despatched to Natal and use the passes through the Drakensburg range to enter the Transvaal. The problems faced by crossing mountainous terrain would be different from those faced by the open country of the Orange Free State, and the force would have to be composed with this in mind. If the Orange Free State were to join the Transvaal, then the British faced the option of either advancing from Natal or from the Cape. With the Orange Free State hostile, it would seem likely that the main force would advance from the Cape, but a substantial force would be required to hold the passes into Natal against large Boer raiding parties. In his first major memorandum on the immediate preparations for war on 8 June 1899, Wolseley assumed that the Orange Free State would remain neutral and correspondingly urged the collection of supplies at the Cape and at Pietermaritzburg in Natal. By the end of September, Lansdowne had still not given him a definite answer on the likely attitude of the Orange Free State. Wolseley suggested forcing the issue by demanding guarantees of neutrality from the Orange Free State, including British occupation of the main railway bridges and passes.[22]

On 5 June the Bloemfontein Conference broke up without reaching any agreement. Wolseley prepared a memorandum on the military strength of South Africa. He anticipated that, in the case of war, Britain would have to send the entire First Army Corps, one cavalry division, one battalion of mounted infantry and four infantry battalions for the lines of communication. He proposed the immediate mobilisation of the First Army Corps on Salisbury Plain, without calling out the Army Reserve because 'it might probably wake up the Transvaal to the fact that England was at last serious, and by doing so prevent war altogether'. Wolseley did not believe this mobilisation would precipitate a war since neither the Boers nor the British could take the field until October, when there would be sufficient grazing for animals. In addition he urged other measures which could be done more or less in secret, without damaging diplomatic negotiations, such as the despatch of three companies of the Army Service Corps, and three field companies of Royal Engineers to strengthen the weak areas in the South African establishment. He also argued that the purchase and collection of large quantities of supplies and mules should be sanctioned immediately.[23] The Cabinet was shown Wolseley's memorandum, and on 20 June Salisbury reported to the Queen that the Cabinet had 'resolved that the moment had not come for sending reinforcements; but that for the present quieter preparations should be pushed forward'. In July the War Office sent more artillery, engineers and departmental corps to South Africa; Butler was authorised to purchase mules for transport, and special service officers were sent out to raise companies of men in South Africa to defend specific locations. On 7 July Wolseley again repeated his proposal for the mobilisation of the army corps on Salisbury Plain and requested a vote of credit for the purchase of supplies but he failed to achieve either of these things.[24]

Despite the Cabinet's unwillingness to spend money on preparations for a war in South Africa, Wolseley and Lansdowne were able to settle the question of the command of the First Army Corps. In June Buller was offered the command and unwillingly accepted it. Neville Lyttelton was present at the meeting between Buller and Lansdowne, and recorded that Buller had 'expressed very strong objections to accepting the command, said he was sick of South Africa, and if he was forced to go out would come away as soon as he could'.[25] Buller was reluctant for two reasons. He was unsure of his ability to be in command: for example, when he had been offered the post of Commander-in-Chief in 1895 he reminded Campbell-Bannerman that 'I have never really been tried as a head man – personally I am always inclined to think of myself a better second fiddle than a leader'.[26] He was also worried about the government's lack of plans: he later told the Elgin Commission 'there were no instructions, and I went out with a force based on the understanding that I was going to do a definite thing'.[27] He favoured the railway route through the Orange Free State but Lansdowne refused to agree to this until the Orange Free State had made its position clear. At a second meeting between Buller and Lansdowne, on 6 July, Buller again urged the necessity of a decision. Wolseley was no more successful.[28] But he did succeed in persuading Buller to accept the command of the First Army Corps, calling him the 'luckiest man alive'. He assumed that Buller was as keen for a fighting command as he himself was: Wolseley was disappointed to be told in September that he was too old to command troops in the field.[29]

On 13 July the Commander-in-Chief's committee to consider questions relating to operations in South Africa began its meetings.[30] This committee served two basic functions: first, it facilitated communications between the departments in the War Office to a greater extent than Wolseley felt could be achieved by the Army Board (though the membership of the committee was similar); and secondly, Wolseley could use the committee to present Lansdowne with definite proposals which, by demonstrating that they had the support of the whole military side of the War Office, would carry more strength than proposals made by him alone. The principal issue facing the committee was how to get as many men as possible into South Africa in the period before the government would accept the need for the mobilisation and despatch of the First Army Corps.

On 18 July the committee met to examine Lansdowne's proposal to reinforce South Africa immediately by taking a brigade from India. The committee reported that it was 'unanimously of opinion that the whole force should be sent from home'. Wolseley explained that 'it would be much better for our position in the world if it were clearly shown that we could send an Army Corps abroad without in any way drawing from our foreign garrisons'.[31] Lansdowne admitted the strength of the committee's arguments but stressed that the force from India could reach Natal faster than one from Britain. He ignored Wolseley's other objection to the employment of Indian troops: that they would come from India 'sodden with drink, fever, and venereal'. Lansdowne, a former Viceroy, had more recent experience of India than Wolseley, and knew that the British army in India had been thoroughly reformed by Roberts.[32] In August the committee added another objection to the use of Indian troops – India could not spare them. Wolseley was on solid ground with this argument: throughout the 1880s India had increased its demand for British battalions and drafts, usually to the detriment of the efficiency of the home army, but now suddenly it was being claimed that India had troops to spare. The committee argued that the Viceroy had only offered the service of a brigade until the end of the year. Once time spent at sea was deducted, the troops would spend only two and a half months in South Africa and this length of service was insufficient to weigh against the cost of transportation. The decision on whether to accept the Viceroy's offer was postponed.

Wolseley was still having to plan for war in a vacuum. On 17 August he wrote to Lansdowne complaining that: 'I do not see all the telegrams that pass between the Colonial Office and Sir A. Milner, but from those I have read I gather he is anxious about the weakness of the military force we now have in South Africa'. Wolseley shared Milner's fear about the possibility of a Dutch rising in the Cape and urged the immediate despatch of an infantry division, a cavalry regiment, and two brigade divisions of artillery, totalling 10,000 to South Africa. From what he did know of the state of diplomacy, he formed the opinion that the Natal route into the Transvaal would be used and that 10,000 men were required urgently in Natal to prevent the Boers from taking the initiative and capturing Ladysmith, an important railway junction, and the northern industrial triangle of Natal.[33]

Lansdowne replied that Chamberlain believed that the political position in South Africa was improving and that the immediate necessity for reinforcements had passed. Nevertheless Lansdowne accepted the figure of 10,000 men as necessary for Natal's defence. He repeated his proposal that these should come from India because then, if the Orange Free State should prove hostile, the entire army corps could advance from the Cape along the railway secure in the knowledge that a division from outside the army corps was defending Natal, so that the corps itself would not need to be split. Wolseley's reply referred to his continuing ignorance of the state of diplomacy:

Your note of the 20th is written in so hopeful a spirit of peace in South Africa
that I assume the Cabinet has information on the subject not known to the
press. To judge of the matters there from the daily papers, it would seem that
every preparation is being made by Mr Kruger for war, and that he is striving
to force a war policy upon the Orange Free State also. At this moment we are
not locally prepared for war in South Africa, so that if it comes upon us under
present circumstances we shall surrender the initiative to Kruger.[34]

He had informed Lansdowne that there would be a gap of three or four
months between the date when the army corps was mobilised and when it
could start its campaign in South Africa. The Cabinet had been informed of
this fact in early August but appeared to disregard its possible consequences.

A communication from Bloemfontein on 28 August suggested that the
Orange Free State would remain neutral in any war between Britain and
the Transvaal. Wolseley was still under orders from Lansdowne, repeated
the day before this communication reached London, 'to be *in utrumque
paratus*', with a plan for each contingency.[35] Neither he nor Buller were
satisfied with this complete disregard for the demands of offensive and
defensive planning. On 5 September, with Wolseley's support, Buller wrote
a clearly worded memorandum to Salisbury. He argued that 'there must
be some period at which the military and the diplomatic or political forces
are brought into line, and in my view, this ought to be before action is
determined on – or in other words, before the diplomat proceeds to an
ultimatum the military should be in a position to enforce it'. The military
could not be ready because 'I have never had the route fixed'. On the same
day Wolseley voiced similar concerns to Lansdowne:

> The Government are acting without complete knowledge of what the military
> can do, while the military authorities on their side are equally without full
> knowledge of what the Government expects them to do; nor are they given
> authority to make such antecedent preparations as will enable them to act with
> the least possible delay.[36]

Vital time had been lost, and Wolseley urged a delay in the break of relations
between the Transvaal and Britain for at least five or six weeks to collect
a substantial force in Natal.

The government were at last prepared to take some action. On 5 September
the Transvaal government withdrew its proposal of 22 August to offer a
five-year franchise conditionally. The Cabinet Council met on 8 September
and sent its refusal to accept this to the Transvaal on the same day. It also
ordered the Viceroy to despatch troops to South Africa. Wolseley's opinion
was sought and he recommended that Lieutenant-General George White,
who would command the Indian brigade, should be under Buller when the

First Army Corps was eventually sent.[37] Wolseley was alarmed that suddenly the politicians in London were increasing the likelihood of war while the military were still not allowed to prepare. He was so alarmed that, on 8 and 28 September, he urged Lansdowne to 'postpone by diplomacy for one month at least any overt act of hostility on the part of the Transvaal'. He informed the government in no uncertain terms that 'we have lost time'. He and his colleagues had plans for the purchase of stores and pack animals, and the commanders of the divisions and brigades within the First Army Corps had been decided. All that remained was for the government to sanction the necessary expenditure to put the plans into practice. Last but not least, he needed a definite opinion of the future conduct of the Orange Free State.[38]

Wolseley's memorandum made some impact but it was far too late. The Cabinet now gave him permission to spend £64,000 on specified items. A major problem was the shortage of mules: without adequate numbers the division from India being sent to Natal would be immobile. Wolseley had had men ready to buy them for some weeks but they now had to compete with the Boers for their purchase and there was not a sufficient supply for both forces. Lansdowne bitterly complained to Salisbury 'will no one invent the "motor mule"?'[39] Finally all Wolseley's appeals for a decision to be made on the attitude of the Orange Free State were recognised: on 25 September Lansdowne urged a decision on the Cabinet. He argued that the recent pronouncements of the President of the Orange Free State, Marthinus Steyn, suggested that it would be hostile.[40] Two days later the Orange Free State concluded an alliance with the Transvaal: London remained ignorant of this for some time.

Events in South Africa now assumed a momentum of their own. On 27 September the Transvaal forces were called out, but it was not until 7 October that the First Army Corps was mobilised and the Army Reserve called out. On 9 October Kruger issued an ultimatum demanding the withdrawal of British reinforcements sent to South Africa and the recall of those still on the high seas. Two days later this ultimatum ran out and the Boers crossed into Natal heading for Ladysmith, Pietermaritzburg and the coast. Buller and the First Army Corps did not reach the Cape until the end of the month.

The British government entered the Second South African War on the assumption that it would be as quick and cheap as other colonial conflicts. Newspapers such as *The Times*, the *Morning Post* and the *Daily News* were particularly jingoistic.[41] Joseph Chamberlain had warned the House of Commons in 1896 that 'A war in South Africa would be one of the most serious wars that could possibly be waged. It would be in the nature of a

Civil War. It would be a long war, a bitter war, and a costly war'.[42] Yet
his own diplomacy had brought about that war. The general attitude of
the public and the government was that the British army was capable
of defeating the Boers with ease and that the Boers would not put up
much of a fight. The despatch of the First Army Corps was seen as an
opportunity to avenge the defeat and ignominy of Majuba. Some military
commentators shared this optimism. An article in the August 1899 issue
of *Blackwood's* illustrates this:

> The idea is very prevalent in this country that war with the Transvaal means
> a terrible and bloody struggle – that such a conflict would severely tax British
> military resources, that it could not be concluded without a vast expenditure
> of money, and that it must necessarily demand consummate leadership to
> bring to a successful issue. For this view there appears to be no adequate
> justification.[43]

Wolseley did not share this optimism: on 12 September he had written to
the Duke of Cambridge that 'if this war ever comes off it will be the most
serious war England has *ever* had, when the size of our Army to be engaged
and the distance of the seat of the war from England are taken into
consideration'.[44]

Until the First Army Corps arrived in South Africa British forces in the
region were outnumbered by the Boers by four to one. This disparity
affected the entire strategy of the war. In *The Times History of the War*,
L. S. Amery suggested that 'the keystone to the whole scheme was the
assumption that Sir G. White could hold his own in Natal for a indefinite
length of time. That assumption gave way at the very outset and the great
army corps had to be broken up to stop the gap which the scheme overlooked'.[45] The Boers besieged the Indian brigade in Ladysmith and mounted
sieges of Mafeking in Bechuanaland and Kimberley in Cape Colony. Amery
blamed Wolseley for siege of Ladysmith, yet as Wolseley told the Elgin
Commission: 'no one thought that the [British] troops would occupy
Ladysmith. The district in front of Ladysmith is called Biggarsburg, a very
strong position'. If this could not be held the troops should have fallen
back behind the Tugela rather than remain in Ladysmith which, being
situated in a hollow, was unsuitable for a sustained defence.[46] The Governor
of Natal, Sir William Hely-Hutchinson, was adamant that the whole of
Natal should be defended, and refused to consider the question of a strategic
withdrawal. Butler's plan for the defence of Natal had foreseen the need
for a retreat but his successor, Major-General Symons, accepted Hely-
Hutchinson's arguments and left garrisons in northern Natal and later
concentrated them in Ladysmith.

Symons was killed at the battle of Talana on 20 October and White took over the command. White told the Elgin Commission that he had not withdrawn the troops to behind the Tugela because he had not known if any defensive positions had been prepared there. Wolseley was furious with White 'who has played the Devil with all the schemes by his ignorance of strategy'.[47] Buller was forced to split the army corps: he himself took command of the force to relieve Ladysmith, sending Lieutenant-General Lord Methuen and Lieutenant-General William Gatacre to relieve Kimberley and Mafeking.[48] British strategy had been ruined at the outset by the Boers' rapid advance. Now, instead of advancing into Boer territory, the British were forced to repair the damage caused by the tardy despatch of the First Army Corps and White's error.

The War Office traditionally delegated all military decisions on strategy and tactics to the commanders on the spot and Wolseley could only watch with frustration as serious military errors were made. He and the entire British public were horrified by the events between 10 and 15 December 1899 which came to be known as 'Black Week'. All three British columns met with disaster as they repeated the basic errors Wolseley had highlighted after the Salisbury manoeuvres the previous year. At Stormberg British companies became separated from the main column and 561 were taken prisoner. The British army had not suffered from prisoners of war since Napoleonic times. At Magersfontein the British deployment was so bad that the Highlanders were fired upon by the Boers before they were in a position to return fire. At Colenso in Natal Buller sent troops forward in a frontal assault across exposed terrain in broad daylight. His error was compounded by the conduct of the artillery commander, Colonel Charles Long, who advanced his guns too far forward, losing much of his force to Boer rifle fire. The remnants retreated, leaving behind ten guns. The Boers were teaching the British an unforgettable lesson on warfare when both sides had modern weaponry.[49]

After Colenso Buller was extremely despondent and heliographed White in Ladysmith and the government at home recommending the surrender of the town. Unknown to Wolseley, Field Marshal Frederick Roberts, then commanding in Ireland, had been scheming with Lansdowne to gain the South African command. When on 16 December the Cabinet decided to appoint Roberts over Buller, Wolseley was only informed on the next day. He wrote a letter of complaint to Lansdowne over the lack of consultation but promised that his offence concerning the oversight would not affect his conduct as Commander-in-Chief.[50] The Queen also objected on her own and Wolseley's behalf, but Arthur Balfour told her private secretary, Sir Arthur Bigge, that 'it was impossible to consult the Commander-in-Chief upon such an appointment, as his well-known jealousy of Roberts made his advice on such a subject perfectly worthless'.[51] Wolseley wrote to his wife that he expected Buller would resign. Buller did not: he knew his limitations and was probably secretly relieved to be reduced to command only in Natal. Soon after this Wolseley accepted that Buller had 'lost his reputation as a skilful leader'.[52] Buller showed this without doubt at the battle of Spion Kop in January 1900 when the British took the position and then withdrew through lack of reinforcements, leaving the Boers to regain the high ground. For the first time ever photographs of the British dead were published in the press.

Although the government was at fault for its strategic errors, which were then compounded by tactical errors by the military in South Africa, Wolseley cannot escape all censure. The staff appointed to the expeditionary force proved a major disappointment and he was personally responsible for many of the selections. For example, he wrote to Buller in September strongly recommending the services of Sir George White as Buller's second in command. Later he was so angry with White for 'allowing himself to be cut off' in Ladysmith that he recommended to Lansdowne that White should be removed from his command. Lansdowne declined to do this.[53] Once Buller was forced to go to White's rescue in Natal, Methuen was left in charge of the advance on Kimberley. Neither Wolseley nor Lansdowne thought Methuen capable of 'an almost independent command', and Wolseley advocated sending Grenfell from his command in Malta to South Africa. Lansdowne favoured General Lord Kitchener, but noted in a letter to Salisbury that Wolseley 'doubted South Africa being big enough for Buller and Kitchener, both being "masterful men"'.[54] When Lyttelton drew up the list of the staff, he excluded Gatacre, whose performance in the Sudan had not been impressive: Wolseley restored Gatacre's name to the list. Gatacre was sacked and sent home by Roberts after Reddesburg for his failures in command.[55]

Major Cairnes, who served under Buller, argued later that: 'One after another have the pets of the War Office, the men so arrogantly styling themselves "of the modern school", proved their hopeless incapacity for the leadership of troops in the field'. Indeed Roberts sacked five generals, six cavalry brigadiers, one infantry brigadier, five commanding officers of cavalry regiments and four commanding officers of infantry battalions.[56] Not all these men had been selected by Wolseley and he agreed with Amery's comment that:

The course of the war showed that among our generals were to be found a few leaders of boldness, tactical insight and organising power, and it had brought to the front many more who at its outbreak were unknown junior officers. But it also revealed the fact that many of our generals, who had risen simply by seniority, were nothing more than rather aged regimental officers.[57]

Wolseley had noted when observing manoeuvres that the junior officers were often keener on their job and had a more professional outlook than their seniors. He was not therefore surprised that relatively junior officers like Major-General John French and Major Douglas Haig, later to command the British army in France during the First World War, rose to prominence.

Hugh Arnold-Forster commented that 'much would have been gained if the higher commands were assigned in peace to those likely to exercise them in war'.[58] This was clearly not the case, and Wolseley must bear much of the blame. It was discovered that the staffs of many formations, like the medical corps and mounted infantry, existed only on paper. Staff officers were borrowed from units it was wrongly thought would not be required. When these units were mobilised, further chaos reigned. Because of the constant updating of mobilisation arrangements, lists of staff for the First Army Corps were in existence at the War Office. The officers concerned mostly held the positions in peace that they were intended to occupy in war but, as Lyttelton noted, 'Wolseley had a liking for what may be called "fancy" brigades, Scotch, Irish and Light Infantry, consequently few brigades went out as they stood'.[59] The consequences were predictably disastrous; much delay in the progress of the field force must have been caused by the time needed for the new staff organisation to learn to work together. In his evidence to the Elgin Commission, Major-General Henry Hildyard said that 'he believed that the brigade which he commanded [the 2nd] was the only one which went out as a brigade and had been trained as a brigade at Aldershot under its old commander before its embarkation, and said that much advantage was derived from this fact'.[60] There was no justification for Wolseley's interference in previously made arrangements other than his arrogant belief that he knew the best structure for the British army and its best senior officers.

Wolseley viewed the composition of the army despatched to South Africa as a vindication of the army system he had persistently advocated over the past thirty years. In a memorandum in January 1900 he wrote:

I have no hesitation in saying that no army has ever left our shores composed of finer soldiers than those of which our army now in South Africa consists. All are seasoned men. There are no recruits or youths under twenty years of age among them. Had we not possessed the Army Reserve it would have been impossible to have sent to South Africa the Regular Army now serving there. Some weak points have been discovered and they will be at once rectified; but although this is the first time we have ever called out our whole Army Reserve we have every reason to be satisfied with the rapidity and ease with which this mobilisation of our army was effected.[61]

The weak points were that there were not enough khaki uniforms to give each soldier a spare set, since a decision had been made in August, on the advice of the medical officers, that serge should be used instead of drill. Furthermore, it was discovered late that the rifles issued to the Army Reservists were incorrectly sighted. Beyond that the mobilisation of the First Army Corps had been almost perfect and, despite Wolseley's preference for the mobilisation of the entire Second Army Corps in November, mobilisation of individual divisions progressed smoothly during November and December.[62]

As early as 30 September, before the First Army Corps had even left Britain, Wolseley warned Lansdowne that once this corps had gone, there would be only thirty-eight and a half battalions of Foot Guards and infantry of the line and thirty-six batteries of artillery left in Britain. He urged that immediate steps be taken to strengthen the home army and pointed out that 'our Army organisation provides for the contingency now before us': thirty-seven Militia battalions should be called out, the remaining cavalry regiments and artillery batteries raised to their war establishment, and no drafts other than to South Africa should be sent to battalions serving abroad. Lansdowne agreed with these proposals, although there was some dispute as to how many Militia battalions should be called out and whether the Irish battalions should be allowed to serve in Ireland.[63]

By the end of 1899 Britain was running out of troops while the demand for men for South Africa showed no sign of diminishing. There was also the danger that either France or Russia, or both since they were allies, might take advantage of Britain's weakness. In 1899 the French Foreign Minister, Théophile Delcassé, visited St Petersburg and in 1900 the French and Russian chiefs of staff met and agreed that in certain eventualities Russia would support France in the event of a war with Britain. Secret service operations were stepped up in India and Afghanistan to monitor Russian intentions but since only one division from India had gone to South Africa, there was no great concern over the security of the region.[64] The threat from France was seen as far more serious: the two countries had come close to war over the Fashoda Incident in 1898. Both the military attaché in Paris, Colonel Dawson, and the ambassador, Sir Edward Monson, warned that 'the idea of war with England would be popular with the army and with many influential classes'.[65] In December Salisbury asked the president of the Defence Committee of the Cabinet, the Duke of Devonshire, to set up an interdepartmental committee to report 'on the hypothesis that we are to have a French war next October'.[66]

Wolseley's immediate concern was to raise more men, both for the home army and for South Africa. In a series of similar memoranda he reminded the Cabinet that in 1888 it had been decided that the minimum force for home defence should be two army corps of regulars and a third composed of the Militia. Therefore, in addition to the force in South Africa, Britain needed 42,500 men and 1270 officers. Since these obviously could not be found overnight Wolseley proposed to bring back battalions from Hong Kong, Singapore, Ceylon and Halifax, raise more recruits and encourage former soldiers to re-enlist. He noted that, according to the March 1896 estimate of the number of discharged soldiers in the United Kingdom, there were 287,000 men under the age of forty-four of whom Wolseley thought 170,000 would be of fighting age.[67]

These proposals were of such a serious nature that Lansdowne thought that it was essential to explore their practicability before presenting them to the Cabinet. He believed that the proposals needed to be considered under two headings: what should be the permanent increase to the size of the army; and what immediate steps were necessary for the war in South Africa.[68] The Military Secretary, Major-General Coleridge Grove, thought that the main problem would be to find a sufficient number of officers, and that the solution might be to offer a number of one year commissions and to take Marine officers into the army. The Adjutant General, General Evelyn Wood, thought that a large bounty would need to be offered to obtain the men. He was convinced that the Militia would be sufficiently trained to repel invasion in October, which was generally accepted as the most likely time for such an enterprise to be launched by France. The Quartermaster General, Lieutenant- General Charles Mansfield Clarke, reported that housing such a vast number of men would be virtually impossible. The Director General of Ordnance, Henry Brackenbury, commented in detail on the stores of equipment and clothing and pointed out that ordnance would be a major problem unless orders were placed immediately.[69]

Having received these responses, Lansdowne replied to Wolseley's memorandum on 17 January. He suggested that Wolseley was over-optimistic on the numbers of old soldiers who would come forward, and argued that 'the difficulty of getting officers for thirty-two new battalions would, I believe, be prohibitory'. Therefore existing resources must be depended on for the present war. He accepted the need to increase the size of the army permanently by twelve battalions, and proposed raising them by a combination of raw recruits and veterans. However, Wolseley's recommendations for urgent increases in the cavalry, engineers and departmental troops would be put into practice immediately. The Defence Committee of the Cabinet approved Lansdowne's proposals on 20 January.[70]

Wolseley was unhappy at the way the Cabinet had treated his recommendations. He pointed out that, once the 7th Division had left, only twenty-three battalions would remain; this figure plus the twelve battalions to be raised and the three already sanctioned gave a total of thirty-eight; 'I take it therefore that I am justified in assuming that this number represents what the Defence Committee consider necessary for safety'.[71] He wanted to ensure that, should France successfully invade Britain, he had written confirmation that the Cabinet had considered that Britain was adequately defended, against the contrary opinion of the Commander-in-Chief. On 27 January Lansdowne informed Wolseley again that the Cabinet refused to sanction the raising of the twenty-one new battalions he wanted, but was prepared to raise more veterans for one year's service for home defence. These were called the Royal Reserve Battalions and approved by the Queen in February. Wolseley threatened to resign over the question of the number of battalions to be raised but was persuaded not to by his colleagues and Lansdowne.[72]

These measures strengthened the home army but did nothing towards providing more men for South Africa. One further source of men was the Volunteers. The terms governing the Volunteer movement subjected them to service only at home, but the patriotism of some commanding officers, notably Colonel E. Balfour of the London Scottish and Colonel H. Vincent of the Queen's Westminsters, led them to offer the War Office their regiments for service abroad. Wolseley was keen to use these men abroad but, until the disasters of Black Week, the Inspector General of the Auxiliary Forces, Major-General Thomas Kelly-Kenny, and the Adjutant General were opposed.

On 15 December the Lord Mayor of London, Sir Alfred Newton offered to raise the 1st City of London Volunteers on a scheme devised by Colonel C. G. Boxhill. Lansdowne signalled his agreement and Wolseley gave Newton unofficial permission to proceed with the raising of a contingent of a thousand men. These were formed into one infantry battalion, two mounted infantry companies and one horse artillery battery. They were despatched to South Africa in January 1900 and a further draft was sent in July. Other measures for utilising the Volunteers were put into practice. Service companies were formed to join the Army Reserve to serve at home but able to proceed to South Africa if needed. Volunteer engineer and medical units were also encouraged to offer their services. In the case of the medical corps they released doctors of the Army Medical Staff Corps for service in South Africa where they were very urgently needed. The Volunteers arrived in South Africa after Kimberley and Ladysmith had been relieved but did take part in the advance on Pretoria and fought two actions at Doornkop and Diamond Hill. Their efficiency was praised by their commander, Major-General Horace Smith-Dorrien.[73]

The Yeomanry was probably the weakest branch of the British military system. It was under-manned and under-trained and little attention had been paid towards improving this state of affairs. On 16 December Buller sent a telegram after the battle of Colenso asking for 8000 mounted men to be sent to South Africa urgently. No large units of mounted infantry existed in the British Army, so Lansdowne proposed to create a new body, the Imperial Yeomanry, out of existing Yeomanry regiments and to recruit able horsemen from the general public. Wolseley disagreed with this proposal, and on 28 December wrote to the Permanent Under Secretary:

> I am very anxious to supply the GOC in South Africa with 8000 trained men accustomed to some sort of discipline; but to go to the highways and byways and pick up any civilians who will volunteer to go to South Africa quite regardless of whether they have ever learnt even the rudiments of discipline, and to form these into companies or battalions is, according to my knowledge of war, a dangerous experiment.

Lansdowne replied that Wolseley was exaggerating the problem since Wood had drawn up a list of strict qualifications for membership of the Imperial Yeomanry. Wolseley claimed that he had no previous knowledge of the scheme, but there is evidence to suggest that he had seen Wood's minute of 23 December giving details of the recruitment and organisation of the Imperial Yeomanry.[74] The Imperial Yeomanry served efficiently on the lines of communication, thereby releasing more regulars for service at the front, but their horsemastership was appalling, and many horses suffered under their care.

Britain was also woefully short of equipment for the war in South Africa. Some shortages could be blamed on the government for refusing to spend the money essential to modernise the artillery in particular and to maintain adequate levels of stores. The responsibility for the shortage of small-arm ammunition cannot be placed on any one person or body: the 1899 Hague Conference on war had decided to ban the Dum-Dum bullet, the soft-nosed bullet Britain used in colonial warfare. Consequently 66,000,000 bullets of this type in British reserves could not be sent to South Africa. Furthermore, there was confusion created when the Boers captured boxes of ammunition marked Dum-Dum and publicised the fact. Britain argued in vain that this was normal ammunition manufactured in the Dum-Dum factory in India and not the banned bullet. The boxes had to be withdrawn.[75]

When Brackenbury was appointed Director General of Ordnance in 1899
Lansdowne asked him to undertake a thorough survey of British armaments.
On 15 December 1899 Brackenbury wrote a detailed memorandum for
Wolseley explaining the existing stores and what the ordnance factories and
trade could supply. The picture showed the consequence of years of neglect:
'we are attempting to maintain the largest Empire the world has ever seen
with armaments and reserves that would be insufficient for a third class
military Power'. Many orders were placed at home and abroad to rectify
the situation but these orders would not be filled for some time because
the order books of foreign manufacturers like Krupps and Creuzot were
already full.[76] In order to avoid such a critical state of affairs recurring in
the future, an interdepartmental committee was set up under Sir Francis
Mowatt, Permanent Secretary to the Treasury, to examine Britain's future
requirements and its ability to fulfil them.[77] The practical application of the
recommendations of this committee was postponed until after the end of
war in South Africa.

By the time Roberts and his chief of staff, Kitchener, arrived in South
Africa there were enough men there to form a fresh army corps of 40,000
men. British troops had been reinforced by contingents from Australia,
New Zealand and Canada.[78] Strategy was now clearer: Buller was to relieve
Ladysmith, and then abandon it, and Methuen was to do the same with
Kimberley. The army corps would concentrate on an advance up the railway
line towards the Boer capitals of Bloemfontein and Pretoria. On their arrival
in South Africa, Roberts and Kitchener reorganised the transport system and
caused chaos. Wolseley had always been a strong proponent of regimental
transport and this system had been in use in South Africa prior to Roberts's
arrival. The two men decided on a centralisation of the transport system,
which slowed the progress of the columns considerably. There were several
occasions when the troops, in particular the cavalry, outran their supplies.

Nor did Roberts and Kitchener prove any better than the previous commanders in the field of tactics. The great flank march on Bloemfontein was
marred by the faulty tactics of Kitchener at the battle of Paardeburg. Instead
of outflanking the Boer forces led by Piet Cronje, Kitchener adopted the
complicated procedure of a frontal assault and two flank movements. The
British ultimately won the battle because Cronje allowed the British infantry
to catch up with the cavalry. Cronje and 4000 Boers surrendered after the
battle.[79] Buller had learnt from his previous mistakes and Ladysmith was
relieved on 28 February after the British had started a series of minor battles
to clear the Boers from the high ground surrounding the town. Kimberley
had already been relieved on 15 February by a cavalry column under French.
The main column advanced swiftly northwards: on 13 March Bloemfontein

was captured and Mafeking was relieved on 17 May. Johannesburg was captured on 31 May and Pretoria surrendered on 5 June.

There was widespread rejoicing in Britain when Mafeking was relieved and its defender, Colonel Robert Baden-Powell was seen as a hero. The public and the military authorities in Britain and South Africa alike thought that the war was over. By July 13,900 Boers, 40 per cent of those mobilised, had surrendered. It had taken the services of 200,000 British and Dominion troops to reach this conclusion. Wolseley shared the general sense of euphoria: on 22 June he wrote to his brother George that the war in South Africa was over and that he was sending troops to India to replace those sent from there to China to crush the Boxer uprising.[80] Roberts also felt that the war was practically over, save the mopping up of some Boer resistance, and the last set battle was fought on 27 August when Buller defeated the Boers at Bergendal. In September Parliament was dissolved and the Unionists won the so-called 'Khaki Election' on the basis of its victory over the Boers. Yet the fighting had not stopped. The Boers now adopted guerrilla tactics and it took nearly two years and a great expenditure of money and manpower to bring them to the negotiating table.

Roberts was viewed as the victor of the war but Wolseley disagreed with this assessment. He was offended that Roberts had not written to him from the seat of the war and considered that Roberts was overrated as a commander. He was sure that since the fighting had not stopped Roberts would 'be found out as a charlatan sooner or later in all that relates to this war'.[81] Wolseley's term of office as Commander-in-Chief was due to finish at the end of October 1900. The government nominated Roberts as his successor, despite the Queen's expectations that the Duke of Connaught would be appointed.[82] On 29 September Wolseley was informed by Lansdowne of the appointment. Since Roberts could not return from South Africa to assume his new post before his retirement, Wolseley was asked whether he would consider staying on for a while[83] He replied on the following day:

Of course I shall willingly do what may be considered best for Her Majesty's Service in the matter of staying on for a few weeks longer. But I think it would be more in accordance with custom and would certainly be more agreeable to me to fix the date when I am to retire, say, either the end of November or December, I don't care which. I should not like to stay on *by the week*.[84]

He agreed to remain in office until 30 November, although Roberts did not reach Britain until 6 December.

On 1 December 1900 the military staff at the War Office gave a dinner for Wolseley to celebrate his retirement. The Queen wrote to him on

4 December thanking him for his service in the army and adding that
'She heartily joins with him in regretting the termination of his great military
career'.[85] Wolseley was actually very content to retire. He was exhausted by
recurring illnesses and relieved to escape from Lansdowne. He felt that his
post as Commander-in-Chief had been made untenable by the 1895 Order
in Council and that the events leading to the South African War demonstrated the extent to which he had been sidelined. Wolseley was also keen
to leave the War Office so that he would not have to witness the chaos he
believed Roberts would bring to the army system he had fought so hard
for. His only regret on retirement was that he would be poor. Louisa proved
an able assistant to him and 'engaged upon a most recondite exhaustive
paper of our expenses', an exercise she enjoyed.[86]

An important task remained to be undertaken before Wolseley could
relax completely. The Queen encouraged him to write a memorandum for
Salisbury on the weaknesses in the position of the Commander-in-Chief.
In it Wolseley argued that the Commander-in-Chief 'has neither the supreme
control exercised by the Secretary of State, nor the administrative functions
now conferred on those below him. Between the Ministerial Head on the
one hand and the Departmental Heads on the other, he has been crushed
out, and the Secretary of State has become the actual Commander-in-Chief
of the army'. He concluded that either the Order in Council of 1895 should
be rescinded and 'the army be again placed under a Military Commander,
who shall be responsible for its discipline and military training and
efficiency', or the post should be abolished since 'it is now merely a high
sounding title, with no real responsibility attached to it, and answers no
useful military purpose'.[87]

Lansdowne retaliated with a strongly worded memorandum in which he
listed the functions the Order in Council had placed on the Commander-
in-Chief. He noted that:

> It is remarkable that in his account of the duties which he has been performing
> during the last five years, the Commander-in-Chief has omitted all reference to
> mobilisation, to the preparation of schemes of offensive and defensive operations,
> as well as the important duties to the Department of the Director of Military
> Intelligence, who, with the Military Secretary, is placed in direct subordination
> to the Commander-in-Chief.[88]

Lansdowne's argument was that, had Wolseley performed all the functions
of the Commander-in-Chief, his time would have been so filled that it
would have been impossible for him to do more. He was keen to draw
attention to the above-quoted duty of the Commander-in-Chief because
this formed the basis for the politicians' argument that the military had not

informed them on the strength of the Boers prior to the outbreak of the war. The Under Secretary, St John Brodrick, was also drawn into the argument. He reduced his comments on Wolseley's memorandum to the level of personal criticism. He alleged that, while Wolseley had been seriously ill in January 1897, he had found sufficient energy to work on his biography of Marlborough, and that on his return to the War Office his attention to business had been 'spasmodic' and much of his work had devolved to the Adjutant General.[89]

These were the opening shots in the last battle Wolseley would have to fight, the one for his reputation. It was fought on the public stage, both in the House of Lords in 1901 and in giving evidence to the Elgin Commission in 1903. Roberts was also forced to enter the arena, as he fought to improve the status of the post to which he had succeeded.

18

The Last Years

At the end of 1900 there was a major change in the personnel of the War Office. Wolseley retired and was succeeded as Commander-in-Chief by Field Marshal Roberts. The Permanent Under Secretary was new, as was the Director of Military Intelligence, the Director of Contracts and the Accountant General. In August 1900 the Secretary of State for War, Lord Lansdowne, wrote to Salisbury suggesting that perhaps there also ought to be a new Secretary of State.[1] Salisbury agreed and Lansdowne left the War Office for the Foreign Office: his Under Secretary, St John Brodrick, was promoted to the post of Secretary of State. This drastic change in personnel was caused largely by the public criticisms of the state of the British army after its poor performance in South Africa. Indeed Evelyn Wood, the Adjutant General, was amused to recall, in his memoirs, that his deputy, General Joseph Laye, overheard two cleaning women discussing the purpose of the scaffolding covering the War Office building. One of them had concluded that it was 'to hang the old lot' who had made such a mess of things.[2]

It was widely hoped that the changes in the War Office would bring improvements but this depended to a large extent on whether there could be any agreement between the politicians and the military authorities on the value and practicability of the 1895 Order in Council. The matter was aired in several stages. First, Roberts tried to extend the functions of his office based on what Wolseley had written in his November 1900 memorandum to Salisbury. Then Wolseley took part in two spectacular army debates in the House of Lords: the first was a defence of his operation of the functions of the post of Commander-in-Chief; the second, a debate on his memorandum to Salisbury. Lastly, the government appointed a committee under the chairmanship of Clinton Dawkins, a member of the Administrative Reform Association, to examine the whole organisation of the War Office. This committee reported in May 1901 and its recommendations were incorporated in an Order in Council of 4 November 1901. The matter did not stop there though: the government made another defence of its position in the evidence of Lansdowne and Brodrick to the Elgin Commission in 1903. The unsatisfactory state of affairs at the War Office shown by this evidence and by Roberts's tenure of office led to the appointment of a committee on the War Office under the presidency of Lord Esher in 1903.

On 17 December 1900 the Director of Military Intelligence, Henry Brackenbury, wrote to Roberts warning him that: 'I do not think you will find the position of Commander-in-Chief very satisfactory under the present Order in Council', and outlined for Roberts what he thought were the defects of the system. Roberts was appalled by the weakness of the functions assigned to him. As Commander-in-Chief in India he had held much wider powers and had met less political interference from the Viceroy than he was likely to encounter from the Secretary of State. On 27 December 1900 Roberts wrote a memorandum making his position clear. Roberts disliked three parts of the 1895 Order in Council: the Commander-in-Chief was overwhelmed by minor details and red tape; he was responsible for details of mobilisation and intelligence, which should be done by the Adjutant General; and he was not ultimately responsible for the actions of those who should be his subordinate officials. He suggested that the Commander-in-Chief should be alone responsible to the Secretary of State and that the Adjutant General should be his chief staff officer.[3]

Brodrick was very disturbed by this memorandum. He saw it as an attempt to revert to the system in operation from 1870 to 1895, failing to take into account the recommendations of the Hartington Commission. He was convinced that the heads of department should remain independent of the Commander-in-Chief. Brodrick suggested the creation of a new officer, of higher status than the present Director of Military Intelligence, to undertake the work of intelligence and mobilisation: he should be named the Chief of Staff.[4] Since no agreement seemed possible between the civil and military authorities at the War Office, the government appointed the Dawkins Committee to arbitrate.

Before the committee could report, however, there was an army debate on the War Office administration in the House of Lords. The Duke of Bedford opened the debate by seeking a detailed explanation of the system of administration, since it was his impression that the functions of the Commander-in-Chief had been drastically weakened by the 1895 Order in Council. The Under Secretary for War, Lord Raglan, spoke next, arguing that there was a tendency towards decentralisation of functions as the War Office and that this trend necessarily meant a decentralisation of power. He did not mention how the Commander-in-Chief was still supposed to remain responsible for the overall efficiency of the army given this decentralisation.

Wolseley then stood up from the cross benches and made a majestic speech. He had already informed Brodrick previously that he had no intention of making a personal attack on the government or on individuals.[5] He began his speech by making this clear: 'my arguments are not directed against individuals, but against a system I have honestly tried for five years and found wanting'. His intention was to strengthen the position of his successors to the post of Commander-in-Chief, a post he described as misnamed. Wolseley then gave a brief history of War Office administration since 1870, ending with the 1895 Order in Council. The result of the alterations in the functions of senior military officers under this order was that 'there is now no one soldier to whom the country can look as directly and professionally responsible for the military efficiency of the Army it pays for'. He gave an analogy from the personal experience of converting the old farmhouse at Glynde into a country house. He had called in an architect, an expert, and told him what he wanted and left the expert to look after the builder and his men. This was how the old War Office system worked with the Commander-in-Chief being the architect. But under the new system it would be as if the carpenter had been allowed to go his own way and the plumber another. The result might have been that the house was uninhabitable. This is what had happened at the War Office. When war broke out in South Africa the team had not pulled together and the consequences of political interference, particularly in the shortage of artillery, had become apparent. Wolseley called for a reversion to the pre-1895 system but wanted the Commander-in-Chief to be empowered to make public any important area in which his opinion differed from the Secretary of State.[6]

Then Lansdowne rose to defend the system he had introduced into the War Office. Less expectedly he made a personal attack on Wolseley's tenure of the office of Commander-in-Chief. He alleged that he was pleased that Wolseley had relieved himself of 'the self-imposed muzzle which he has worn for the last five years' and was now taking part in the debates of the House of Lords. This was unjust: Wolseley had felt that he should not use his position as a peer and professional to undermine the Secretary of State. He had spoken in the Lords in 1888 only because Salisbury had directly attacked him and had invited him to speak in his defence. Beyond that occasion he was aware that several Secretaries of State, the Duke of Cambridge and the Queen had all on a number of occasions reprimanded him for publicising his differences with the government. Lansdowne then suggested that Wolseley had failed to carry out all the functions ascribed to him by the 1895 Order in Council, particularly the preparation of schemes of offence and defence. Lansdowne's argument was that it was not the office of Commander-in-Chief that had failed but the man who had held the post.[7]

Lansdowne's personal attack on Wolseley shocked the members of the Lords. When the debate was resumed on the following day, Lord Northbrook said of Wolseley that 'I do not think it would have been possible for any man to have expressed that opinion in more courteous terms, with more studied moderation, or with more entire absence of any personal allusion to the late Secretary of State for War'. The Earl of Dunraven and the leader of the Liberal opposition, Lord Rosebery, agreed that Lansdowne should not have made a personal attack on Wolseley. Rosebery was worried that the House of Lords was being turned into 'a cockpit where the ex-Secretary of State for War and the ex-Commander-in-Chief were to exhaust their personal differences in a personal discussion'. Only Earl Spencer and the Duke of Devonshire backed Lansdowne, arguing that an attack on the system was an attack on the designer.[8] Outside the Lords, the Earl of Camperdown, who had advised Wolseley not to attack Lansdowne in his speech, wrote congratulating him:

> I believe that Lansdowne was entirely misled by your not making any attack on him or on the Government, which shows how wise it was on your part to abstain from any mention of them in your first speech. He expected an attack, and could not help firing off his counter attack.[9]

The House of Lords requested to see the memorandum that Wolseley had written to Salisbury on the position of the Commander-in-Chief in November 1900.

The debate on this memorandum was set for 15 March. Louisa warned her husband to take great care with his speech:

> It is not as if you are meeting fair honest enemies in a fight. You are meeting untruthful, dishonest ones, and as their position is already shaken, and will be much more shaken, by you, they will stick at nothing to undermine you in public opinion. Yet you *must* be moderate and show no temper, or you will help them.[10]

Wolseley answered the four charges Lansdowne had made against him in the Lords on 4 March. He pointed out that to prove that he had carried out his duties fully, and not fitfully as Lansdowne had alleged, he would have to produce all the memoranda he had written over the last five years. He argued that had Lansdowne been unhappy with his performance during this period then he should have spoken to him about it at the time. Far from neglecting the auxiliary forces, Lansdowne's second charge, he had appointed two aide-de-camps from the auxiliary forces. He had been unable to persuade Lansdowne to improve the armament of the auxiliary forces and could cite the memorandum in which his recommendation had been made.

The third and fourth of Lansdowne's charges related to Wolseley's preparations for the war in South Africa. Again he cited the relevant memoranda on his recommendations for reinforcing the existing garrisons in Natal and the Cape. He also made it clear that he had always viewed the Biggarsburg as the best defensive position in Natal, not Ladysmith, and was therefore not responsible for the events that led to the siege of the town. Wolseley freely admitted that 'in common with all persons and authorities who have expressed an opinion on this question, I did under-estimate the fighting power of the individual Boer'. In June and September he had urged the mobilisation of the First Army Corps, so it was not his fault that the British were taken by surprise when the Boers invaded Natal. Wolseley was prepared to produce any paper relating to the advice he had given Lansdowne during his tenure of office.

Lansdowne then spoke, but in more moderate terms than in his previous speech. Nevertheless he continued to blame Wolseley for the reverses suffered by British troops in the first months of the war in South Africa. For example, it was not sufficient to have described the Biggarsburg as the defensive position of Natal, he should have specifically made it known that Ladysmith was an unsuitable location. Lansdowne also believed that Wolseley should have been even stronger in his demands for the despatch of the First Army Corps than he had been. Lord Northbrook voiced the sentiments of the majority of the House when he deplored Lansdowne's conduct: it is 'the more extraordinary that the noble Marquess should have departed from the course he had prescribed for himself and endeavoured to shelter himself behind the Commander-in-Chief in respect to the advice given with reference to the war in South Africa'. By placing all the blame for the government's errors onto Wolseley, Lansdowne was damaging the functioning of a parliamentary democracy.[11] It was clear that the question of the responsibility for the errors would have to be explored in depth by a royal commission after the conclusion of the war.

Wolseley was deeply distressed by the way Lansdowne had publicised their differences and unfairly tried to place the blame for his and the government's failing onto Wolseley's shoulders. He wrote to Louisa: 'Ever since that little reptile's speech in the House of Lords, I have ceased to have aspirations: their realisation would be beyond my powers at my time of life. Revenge may be sweet to those who don't believe in God, but I can't find any comfort in it'.[12] He spoke on one further occasion in the Lords, to support the Duke of Bedford's motion that recruits to the army were not paid sufficiently. Wolseley's speech was really a commentary on the reforms Brodrick was attempting to make in the army. He spoke well and was congratulated afterwards by many of his fellow peers. *The Times* also wrote a leader approving of his comments.[13] Apart from this speech, Wolseley did not comment on the changes made to the army by either Brodrick or, after 1905, by Richard Haldane.

In May 1901 the Dawkins Committee reported. It found that the War Office suffered from confusion in administration between the civil and military side, and that there was an absence of clearly defined individual responsibility. It largely vindicated Wolseley by arguing that the Commander-in-Chief should be given greater responsibility. The report did, however, criticise him for having failed to produce adequate offensive and defensive plans. The bulk of recommendations of the Dawkins Committee were incorporated in the Order in Council of 4 November 1901. This gave the Commander-in-Chief responsibility for discipline, training, mobilisation and staff planning, and the Adjutant General was placed under him.[14] The terms of the 1901 Order in Council became subject to criticism later, and the Esher Committee completely reorganised the War Office and abolished the post of Commander-in-Chief in 1904. An Army Council was established and in January 1905 a General Staff created.[15]

Queen Victoria died on 22 January 1901, the longest reigning British monarch. On 1 February her coffin was brought from Osborne, where she had died, to Windsor. There was a short funeral service in St George's Chapel and then the Queen lay in the Albert Memorial Chapel for a few days until she was buried in the mausoleum at Frogmore with her husband Prince Albert.[16] Wolseley, as Gold Stick of the Household Cavalry, was expected to be in attendance at the funeral. However, he wrote to his brother George that he could not fulfil his duty because he had no trappings and no black horse.[17] In January 1902 Wolseley thought that he might be unable to afford to attend the coronation of King Edward VII as Gold Stick because the robes and the coronet cost £150. The coronation was postponed due to the King's ill-health and, during the postponement, pressure was put to bear on him to attend the coronation. In May he wrote to George that he was going to be Gold Stick after all but he still resented the cost of the robes. After the coronation, on 9 August 1902, Wolseley was one of the first men to receive the new Order of Merit.[18]

Wolseley disliked the new King because of his notorious reliance on what was known as the 'Court Party', a group of yes-men surrounding him. He told his brother that this had earned Edward VII the derogatory title, 'Edward the Caresser, King of the Jews'.[19] He had been a victim of the Court Party earlier in his career when Edward, as the Prince of Wales, had helped to block his peerage in 1881 and later inflicted Stanley Clarke on him for the Khartoum Relief Expedition. Nevertheless, in August 1903, in his official capacity as Gold Stick, Wolseley accompanied the King on a tour of Ireland and received a diamond pin as a souvenir.

Wolseley spent much of the early part of 1902 travelling abroad. He first went on a visit to South Africa as a private citizen. A question was asked in the House of Commons about whether this visit was a special peace mission: Brodrick replied that it was not, and that Wolseley was not in communication with the War Office.[20] Following this trip he travelled to the courts of the Emperor of Austria, the Kings of Romania, Serbia and Greece, and the Sultan of Turkey to announce the accession of King Edward VII. He gained little pleasure from his visits to south-eastern Europe and Turkey but in Athens managed to watch some of the Olympic Games. He was particularly interested in the wrestling, because he was a man 'with the brutal instincts of an Englishman who loves boxing and seeing men take punishment'.[21] Following these official visits, Wolseley went on a long cruise in the Mediterranean in a yacht belonging to Sir Donald Currie, the owner of the Union Castle Steamship Company. His finances were aided by receiving £300 per annum as a paid director of the company.

The war in South Africa had not ended when Roberts left the area at the end of 1900. The remaining Boers formed small commandos and began guerrilla warfare against the British troops. Kitchener retaliated by ordering their farms to be burnt, crops destroyed, their livestock collected for British use, and their families herded into concentration camps. These unsanitary camps were extremely controversial and tarnished Kitchener's reputation. Conditions in the camps improved after Emily Hobhouse publicised the unacceptably high death rate and harsh conditions: nevertheless, approximately twenty to thirty thousand Boer women and children and even more natives died in the camps. Kitchener first tried to end the war with a series of columns sweeping across the Transvaal and Orange Free State to capture the remaining Boer commandos. This met with limited success, so a new strategy was adopted: a grid of 8000 blockhouses was built, linked by 3700 miles of barbed wire and guarded by over 50,000 troops. This strategy was more successful in capturing Boers and by April 1902 the number of armed Boers had fallen to 23,000, harried by 250,000 British and imperial troops. The harsh conditions on commando, and the fear of a Zulu uprising after a Zulu attack on Holkrantz in May 1902, led the Boers to ask for peace negotiations. These took place at Vereeniging and on 31 May 1902 the peace treaty finally was signed at Pretoria.

The war had cost over £200,000,000 and required the services of 256,340 officers and men of the regular army, 109,048 auxiliaries, 30,633 from the colonies, and 50–60,000 men raised in South Africa.[22] It was now opportune for the British to examine what had gone wrong at the beginning of the war and why it had taken so long to defeat a largely agricultural people. A Royal Commission was appointed, under the presidency of Lord Elgin, to examine the matter. At the end of November 1902 Wolseley gave evidence over two days. He argued that the government had been informed of the strength of the Boers. He had been left in ignorance of the state of diplomacy but had urged the mobilisation of the First Army Corps in ample time for it to have arrived in South Africa before the Boer invasion. It was known that the Boers would not invade until October at the earliest because before then there would not have been enough grazing for their horses and mules. The government had delayed this mobilisation and money had not been granted till too late. Wolseley defended his non-interference in the plans of the commanders in South Africa but, when asked to comment on Buller's strategy, replied that he had been wrong to go to Natal and should have stuck to his original plan to advance up the railway.[23]

Wolseley condemned the system of War Office administration instituted by the 1895 Order In Council. He made two proposals for the future. The first was that the Commander-in-Chief should

> submit to Parliament every year over his own signature certificate to say that he, on his own responsibility, certifies to the country that three Army Corps are absolutely complete in every store that is requisite in order to mobilise them at the shortest possible notice, and the same thing as regards the two Army Corps being ready for active service abroad.

The second proposal was that the King should be made the Commander-in-Chief with nominal powers and that the Secretary of State should be a soldier. Both these proposals were widely viewed as inimical to parliamentary government and were extremely unlikely to be adopted.[24]

The Elgin Commission took evidence for fifty-five days and heard 114 witnesses. As Esher reported to the King: 'the Commission have unanimously come to the sad conclusion, that the responsibility for most of the early failures must rest upon the shoulders of the late Commander-in-Chief'.[25] The commission concluded that he had not prepared adequate plans of defence and offence. Yet the previous chapter has shown that Wolseley should be largely exonerated from the blame for the failure to prepare in time. The burden of that responsibility should have been placed on Lansdowne. However, Lansdowne was still a serving minister whereas Wolseley was in retirement. It was far more convenient to blame a retired man than one in an important office, criticism of whom might bring down the government. Wolseley must be criticised for not backing up his numerous memoranda with details from the intelligence reports he received. Had he done so, Lansdowne could not have defended the failure of the government to act on the warnings from the Commander-in-Chief. Wolseley made no comment at the time about the findings of the Elgin Commission and bore the criticism with silent fortitude. His friends backed him and in 1906, when reviewing Maurice's *Official History of the War in South Africa*, William Verner wrote to him that he was going to lay stress on the fact that the military authorities were prevented by Lansdowne from making adequate preparations for political reasons.[26]

In 1903 Wolseley gave up his rooms in town and moved to the apartment at Hampton Court. He was in poor health and was often disturbed by the noise of the trams running outside. Glynde was far more pleasant and restful, particularly now that Frances had landscaped the garden with the assistance of a lady gardener.[27] In February 1903 Wolseley went on a cruise with Sir Donald Currie in the Mediterranean and up the Nile. He spent his time writing his memoirs and frequently asked Louisa for her advice on them because:

> My mind is now so military that it is difficult to know what I should say for a publication to be read by all classes. The points that interest me are very probably those about which the general public care nothing. But I think so highly of your judgement in these matters that I want you to decide what part of my scribbled story is and is not to be published.[28]

The first two volumes of Wolseley's autobiography took him to the end of the Asante War of 1873–74. The books were received well, and netted him £2494 in royalties in the first six months after publication.

Wolseley was urged to complete his memoirs but found it difficult to do so. At the end of November 1903 he confessed to Louisa that he must write them quickly because 'my memory seems to be going fast, but not regarding old events, as yet'.[29] He told this to Louisa as a secret, yet his colleagues had noticed his failing memory as early as 1897. He never did complete his autobiography: extensive notes up to the end of the Gordon Relief Expedition exist in his papers but very little on the military reforms.

Wolseley spent February 1904 in Cannes with Frances, who was convalescing after an illness. The stay was not a great success because the weather was generally very cold and windy. Wolseley toured the coast and began to think of buying a villa in the South of France where the climate would be better for his health than the dampness of London or Sussex. He and Louisa soon found a villa near the Alpes Maritimes near Menton. The move to France led a rift between Frances and her parents. Frances had opened a gardening school for ladies in Glynde: the lady gardener taught them and the two women shared any profits from the fees. Her parents intended to let the house at Glynde, since they were moving to France, but Frances needed the greenhouse there to teach the cultivation of fruit to her students. Louisa, in particular, was adamant that Frances should come to France to look after her ageing parents. She was furious when Frances raised enough money to rent the greenhouse from the new tenants at Glynde.[30]

Relations between Wolseley and Louisa on one side and Frances on the other continued to deteriorate. Although Frances tried to retain their friendship by writing weekly letters, it is clear that her parents resented her independence. The Victorian ideal of womanhood centred on marriage and the home. Indeed, in 1909, Wolseley wrote a memorandum, which he placed with his solicitors, outlining his views on the separation. He feared that after his death Frances would put forward her belief that 'her desertion of us was forced upon her by our conduct towards her'. Wolseley wanted to make it clear that Frances had made a 'self-elected desertion of her natural home'. At the same time Frances was ordered not to visit her parents unless she was specifically invited.[31]

In 1910 Frances sent a birthday present to her father, which was returned. Only now did she stop writing her parents weekly letters. Wolseley was fast becoming a recluse as his memory and health worsened. Louisa became very protective of her husband, shielding him from most of his former colleagues and his daughter. In May 1911 Wolseley admitted that his memory was so bad 'that I shirk written correspondence with any but those whom I feel will make due allowance for this terrible affliction'. When his old friend William Butler visited him he was not even recognised. A family friend, Sir Henry Bulwer, suggested to Frances that she ought to visit her parents. She duly wrote to her mother and received a reply, through Lady MacDougall, that, unless she planned to stay for a long time, she was not welcome.[32]

Frances was staying with friends in Westminster when she received a telegram of sympathy from an old friend, Sir Anthony Weldon. She had no idea to what event it referred. On her way to a tea shop, Frances 'saw a sandwich man carrying a large announcement, and to my horror saw my own surname'. Sir Garnet Wolseley had died on 26 March 1913 at Menton after a slight chill led to pneumonia. His body was brought back to London for burial but Louisa was not well enough to accompany it and telegraphed Frances to represent the family, then come to Menton. On 31 March 1913 Wolseley's coffin was borne on a carriage followed by a riderless charger to St Paul's Cathedral. Behind the carriage followed units of soldiers representing all regiments of the army in which he had either served or had commanded in war. The coffin rested in the crypt near the tomb of Wellington.[33] Frances inherited her father's title and became Viscountess Wolseley.

When Frances arrived at Menton, she was handed a piece of paper by her father's former secretary, Sir Coleridge Grove, which she was asked to sign before meeting her mother. 'It was to the effect that Lady Wolseley hoped that Frances had come to her in a humble and chastened spirit, and that she would do nothing to upset her'. She had come to share their grief, not in apology for the rift, but still signed the paper. Relations between the two ladies did not improve. In 1919 Frances heard that her mother was seriously ill and, despite making a surprise visit to Hampton Court where her mother was now living, was refused permission to see her. The two women did meet shortly before Louisa's death on 20 April 1920. Wolseley's tomb was opened in the presence of a few friends and the casket containing the ashes of Louisa were placed next to her husband.

The final shock was in Louisa's will. Frances was always under the impression that her parents had arranged for everything to pass to the surviving partner and then unconditionally to her. When the will, made in November 1919, was read the consequences of the break in relations became clear: Frances had been effectively disinherited, receiving only annuities totalling less than £1000 a year out of an estate of £55,000. All Wolseley's possessions, including Frances's patent of peerage were given to the Royal United Services Institute. Lawyers advised against disputing the will since, by her mother's will of 1912, Frances would have received nothing. Frances never married and the Viscountcy of Cairo and of Wolseley ended with her death in on 24 December 1936.[34]

19

A Victorian Hero

After the near disasters of the Crimean War and the shock of the Indian Mutiny the Victorian public bestowed hero status on any commander who could demonstrate the greatness of Britain. Newspaper correspondents followed every military campaign, applauding the achievements of the commanders. Wolseley fitted this model of the ideal soldier. His contributions to the expansion of the empire included ensuring white supremacy in South Africa by eliminating the threats posed by the Zulus and Pedi. He also conquered Egypt, which led to the country effectively becoming a British colony in all but name. His failure to rescue Gordon from Khartoum was widely blamed on Gladstone.

Yet Wolseley was not an unblinkered imperialist. He was aware that the British empire had outgrown its military resources, and consistently campaigned for politicians to recognise the fact and take some hard decisions. Opinions, naturally, were divided as to which areas were of vital strategic interest, especially where the defence of India was concerned. Wolseley himself favoured South Africa over Egypt, while in 1905 Jacky Fisher at the Admiralty made Alexandria and Cape Town two of the 'five strategic keys [which] lock up the world'.[1] He believed that India should be defended in the Middle East rather than in Afghanistan. After the First World War experts on Indian affairs, such as Curzon, argued that Britain should take a large share in the dismembered Ottoman empire in order to defend India as far away from India itself as possible.

The secrets to Wolseley's successful career were threefold: he was talented, driven by the ambition to reach the top of his profession and lucky. His inability to purchase promotions could easily have led to him remaining a lowly ranked regimental officer throughout his career. His first break came when Hope Grant plucked him out of the mass of young officers and gave him a staff job during the Indian Mutiny. Canada could have proved a backwater and stalled any prospect of further advancement had Wolseley not been on the spot when a campaign to Red River was announced. From then on his career never looked back. Later, after his period in South Africa in 1879–80, the patronage of politicians made up for the disadvantage of Wolseley's lack of social connections. This projected him into the higher administrative posts at the War Office – Quartermaster General, Adjutant General and, finally, Commander-in-Chief.

Wolseley would not have reached the heights he did had he not been extremely able. He was the master of small wars. Highly versatile, he commanded troops in a variety of climates and terrains, ranging from the wilderness of the forests of Canada to the thick bush of West Africa, the open veldt of South Africa, and the sands of Egypt and the Sudan. This variety of campaigns makes him stand out from among his contemporaries. Men like Roberts and Kitchener rested their claim to fame on one or two outstanding campaigns: Wolseley commanded six. Although the British army held the undoubted advantage of superior weaponry, it was still a great challenge to campaign in hostile environments against an enemy of whom little was known. He excelled at administration and logistics: planning each campaign before arriving at the seat of war and advancing with great care. He was respected by his troops but was too cold and distant to win their affection.

Wolseley was a man of the nineteenth century, when war was approached in a remarkably light-hearted manner. He felt most alive when surrounded by soldiers fighting a battle. Winston Churchill wrote of the typical approach to war at that time:

> Nobody expected to be killed. Here and there in every regiment or battalion, half a dozen, a score, at the worst thirty or forty, would pay the forfeit; but to the great mass of those who took part in the little wars of Britain in those vanished light-hearted days, this was only a sporting element in a splendid game.[2]

The South African War showed Britain that with modern weapons the casualty rate in warfare could be high; the First World War was to show just how high. Although small wars have remained the most common form of warfare for the British army, no wars of the twentieth century have been approached in the same carefree manner as during Wolseley's career.

The author of one of his obituaries claimed that Wolseley 'would in all probability have shown himself a great and successful leader in regular warfare'.[3] Another regretted that he 'was never pitted against any commander of importance, nor against white troops'.[4] If Wolseley was an exemplary colonial commander, he was not necessarily one suitable for European warfare. It is entirely conceivable that he would have been successful in the Second South African War, because he had the strength of character to resist the pressure to split the First Army Corps, and would have, in all probability, advanced up the railway line to the Boer capitals leaving the Ladysmith garrison to manage its extraction unaided. Furthermore he would not have made the basic tactical errors which led to Black Week: he had

already drawn attention to them in his report on the 1898 Salisbury manoeuvres. Yet European warfare, particularly the trench warfare of the
Western Front during the First World War, was an altogether different
challenge. There is evidence to suggest that Wolseley, no less than John
French and Douglas Haig, would have been prepared to accept vast losses
in attacks against fixed positions and machine guns. For example, in January
1900 he drafted a telegram to Buller urging him to renew the battle for
Ladysmith and to heliograph White to make a coordinated attack to break
out: Wolseley believed that 50 per cent losses would be acceptable.[5]

A vital ingredient in Wolseley's success was his ability to select able
subordinates. He established his 'Ring' because he believed there was a need
to push forward the claims of able officers for important staff positions
against those less talented who had gained their ranks solely by seniority.
He justified his actions to the journalist Archibald Forbes:

> I know these men of mine and they know me. I selected them originally because
> of my discernment of character, not at the behest of interest or from the dictates
> of nepotism. We have worked long together; their familiarity with my methods
> and my just reliance on them relieves me of half the burden of command.[6]

Men like Redvers Buller, William Butler, George Colley, Frederick Maurice,
Herbert Stewart and Evelyn Wood all reached high positions in the British
army largely as a result of his patronage.

The Wolseley Ring has been criticised on a number of grounds. The first
was that it was too narrow. The Duke of Cambridge often complained that
Wolseley was not bringing new men forward; a charge that he rightly denied.
The Asante campaign is usually viewed as the origin of the Ring but men
like Herbert Stewart and Baker Russell were discovered later. Young officers
encouraged by Wolseley include men, like John Adye and Spenser Childers,
who served as his aides-de-camp in Egypt and the Sudan. The Staff College
was an important step on the ladder to staff appointments and he urged
both men to apply for it. He recognised the value of the improved education
provided by the Staff College and it is noticeable that the number of men
on his staff with p.s.c. after their names rose in his later campaigns.[7]

The Ring has also been criticised on the grounds that it did not bring
the best men forward. Much of this argument rests on the careers of George
Colley and Redvers Buller, and it has some justification. Colley made a fatal
mistake by trying to take and hold Majuba Hill during the First South
African War with too few troops; he paid for this error with his life. Yet
Wolseley had wanted Colley as his successor in South Africa not because
he thought that there would be a war, but because he felt that Colley's
intelligence would serve well in what was conceived primarily as a political

crisis with the Transvaal. His support of Buller as a commander is more
suspect. Buller had proved a disappointment to him when serving as his
chief of staff on the Sudan campaign, and Wolseley must take much of the
responsibility for pressing the command of the First Army Corps on Buller
in 1899, despite this doubt as to his fitness for command. The result was
that he could only watch Buller's poor strategic decisions during the South
African War with growing dismay. Nevertheless, many of Wolseley's Ring
did great service to the British army at home. Wood and Buller together
revitalised its training; Ardagh and Brackenbury improved the expanding
Intelligence Department; Brackenbury later made urgent changes to the
Ordnance Department; and Maurice became the 'the second pen of Sir
Garnet', writing articles and books supporting the views of his chief.[8]

The Wolseley Ring was not the only one in existence. The Duke of
Cambridge had his own group of supporters. Cambridge, and the Prince
of Wales with his Court party, frequently lumbered Wolseley with senior
officers whose services he really did not want. However, it is the Ring
centred round Frederick Roberts in India, and its conflict with the Wolseley
Ring, that has been viewed as a divisive factor in the politics of the late
Victorian army. The existence of two Rings, each pressing the superior
claims of its leader, has been seen as damaging the army by not allowing
the best men to come forward. The rivalry between the two Rings was not
so much a personal conflict between Roberts and Wolseley as a competition
between the supporters of the two men. Wolseley differed from Roberts on
two grounds: their opinions on the most desirable length of service in India
and their opposite views on Indian defence. He was also jealous of the fact
that Roberts was appointed to command the forces in South Africa at the
end of 1899 instead of himself. Roberts himself was aware of this problem
and wrote to a colleague that 'Wolseley will never be a friend of mine. This
is impossible. Our aims and ambitions, views and feelings are entirely
different'.[9] Wolseley suspected that, when Roberts succeeded him as Commander-in-Chief, he would promote his followers and leave Wolseley's in
minor posts. He warned his brother, George, not to return to England
because he would be unlikely to find a satisfactory appointment.[10]

Wolseley was driven by a desire to improve the efficiency of the army
and he proved to be an extremely talented and energetic administrator at
the War Office. He was *the* defender of the newly introduced short service
system and the Army Reserve. He never questioned this system's superiority
to its long service predecessor. He believed that the quality of the army
could be improved if only the government would provide the funds for the
new system to work in toto, in particular where the size of the army was
concerned. The government was obstinate, and Cardwell principle of linked

battalions was not kept up: the army was not expanded to keep pace with the number of battalions stationed abroad permanently as a result of new conquests or threats. Ultimately, however, the validity of Wolseley's support for the Cardwell system has been demonstrated by its longevity. Short service has remained the most common term of recruitment to the British army, apart from two periods of conscription during two world wars and the early years of the Cold War. Even the linked battalion system was deemed desirable: despite the huge leap in British military commitments abroad after the First World War, the War Office attempted to reimpose this system.[11]

When parsimonious governments and the conservatism of the Duke of Cambridge blocked many of his reforms, Wolseley turned to the public to attempt to win support for his opinions. He justified his programme of educating the public on army matters on the grounds that: 'no government, Whig or Tory, has the honesty to tell the people the truth and take them into their confidence on army and navy matters'.[12] His published articles and speeches frequently offended the Duke and various Secretaries of State; yet they served a purpose, and some contemporary commentators paid tribute to his efforts. Hugh Arnold-Forster admitted that: 'There will be no real interest taken in the question of army reform in the House of Commons until the general public outside the House of Commons shows that it was in earnest, and insists upon something being done'. Leo Amery praised Wolseley for having helped 'to awaken the national consciousness out of the self-satisfied full-bellied drowsiness in which it had so long rested'.[13]

This is amply demonstrated by Wolseley's exploitation of Britain's vulnerability to invasion by France. He hoped that, once the public was aware of the danger, it would force the government's hand. He was successful: the Channel Tunnel was vetoed; and in 1889 the government voted for a large increase to the navy and a smaller sum to the army. One of Wolseley's most enduring achievements was to make the government aware that the navy alone could not be guaranteed to defend Britain: the army was needed as a second line of defence. For example, in August 1914 the Cabinet was prepared to accept the recommendation of the Secretary of State, Lord Kitchener, not to send the entire expeditionary force to France but to hold back some troops in case of invasion by Germany. Wolseley himself appears not to have realised that the German General Staff had drawn up plans for the invasion of Britain as early as 1896. Somehow the information never leaked to the War Office where France was seen as the principal enemy.[14]

Wolseley attempted to reform the army from its leading staff officers down to the rank and file. His plan for promotion by selection rather than seniority was only adopted at the end of the century, too late to influence the appointments for the South African War. The quality of junior officers did improve as they began to approach their jobs with greater professionalism, accepting Wolseley's premise that 'war is a science, and as such has its principles, and rules deducted from these principles quite as surely as every other science'.[15] He was unsuccessful in his effort to increase officers' pay: entry to the smartest regiments remained restricted to those with large private incomes. Nor was he any more successful in increasing the pay of the private soldier. He believed that only a substantial increase would attract intelligent young men of the kind needed on the modern battlefield. The South African War showed the type and size of army Britain needed to fight a modern war and conscription began to be discussed in military circles. The National Service League was founded in 1902 and Wolseley became a member. He wrote a statement in the first issue of its journal that conscription would become necessary if Britain did not begin to pay her army 'the current rate of wages obtained by able-bodied men in the labour market'. The South African War also showed the government that no large army could be recruited until housing conditions for the working classes were improved. In Manchester 8000 of the 12,000 volunteers were rejected as incapable of meeting even the extremely low physical requirements for enlistment in the British army.[16]

One of Wolseley's greatest achievements was the organisation of the British army into army corps ready for mobilisation for service at home or abroad. Historians have made the importance of his contribution clear:

> Nothing is more certain than it was Lord Wolseley, and Lord Wolseley alone, who conceived the idea of an Expeditionary Force and, when he became Commander-in-Chief he gave effect to the idea after lesser men had done all in their power to obscure the vital point at issue.

and

> But when we recall the incomparable little British Expeditionary Force of 1914 let us do justice to a great soldier, a great public servant and a great man, and, while we speak of it affectionately as the Old Contemptibles. Let us think of it as Wolseley's Army.[17]

The 1914 British Expeditionary Force was organised on the system Wolseley had drawn up in the 1880s.

The result of Wolseley's struggle to reform the British army during his service at the War Office can be summarised as the laying out of a framework on which a truly efficient army could be built when the government finally accepted the need to spend substantial sums on the military. The South African War finally convinced the government and many of his ideas were then put into practice. Indeed the Secretary of State who began this process, Brodrick, later paid this tribute. In 1918 he wrote to Evelyn Wood: 'When history is written I feel that the Army of Mons will be ascribed to Lord Wolseley, yourself and his other comrades, who first broke down the old gang'.[18] In such a way Wolseley was the father of the modern British army and fully merits the statue of him looking out over Horse Guards Parade.

Notes

Introduction

1. L. James, *The Rise and Fall of the British Empire* (London, 1994), p. 182.
2. R. Shannon, *The Crisis of Imperialism* (London, 1976), pp. 94–95.
3. Wolseley to Ardagh, 19 July 1892, Ardagh MSS, PRO, PRO 30/40/2.
4. C. E. Callwell, *Small Wars: Their Principle and Practice* (London, 1896), p. 44.

Chapter 1: Early Life and Burma

1. G. J. Wolseley, *The Story of a Soldier's Life* (London, 1903), i, p. 7.
2. Ibid., p. 8.
3. Wolseley, journal entry, 2 January 1885, PRO, WO 147/8.
4. G. Harries-Jenkins, *The Army in Victorian Society* (London, 1977), p. 75.
5. Wolseley to Raglan, 9 January 1851; Frances Ann Wolseley to Wellington, 22 September 1851, PRO, WO 31/1001.
6. C. Barnett, *Britain and Her Army* (London, 1970), p. 280.
7. For further analysis of the background of army officers, see Harries-Jenkins, *Army in Victorian Society*, chapter 2.
8. H. How, 'Lord Wolseley', *Strand Magazine*, 3 (May 1892), pp. 443–61.
9. W. Butler, *An Autobiography* (London, 1911), p. 113.
10. Wolseley, *Story of a Soldier's Life*, p. 10.
11. Wolseley to Frances Ann Wolseley, 11 June 1852, WPP, 163/1.
12. Wolseley, *Story of a Soldier's Life*, p. 16.
13. The British Army in India was divided into three Presidencies: Bengal, Madras, and Bombay.
14. W. F. B. Laurie, *Our Burmese Wars* (London, 1885).
15. Wolseley, *Story of a Soldier's Life*, pp. 36–40.
16. Laurie, *Our Burmese Wars*, p. 262.
17. Wolseley to Mr Dunn, 28 April 1853, WPP, 163/1; Wolseley, *Story of a Soldier's Life*, p. 52.
18. Wolseley, *Story of a Soldier's Life*, p. 55.
19. Ibid., p. 70.
20. Ibid., p. 81.
21. Ibid., p. 85.

Chapter 2: Crimea and Indian Mutiny

1. G. J. Wolseley, *The Story of a Soldier's Life* (London, 1903), i, pp. 86–87; Wolseley to Louisa Wolseley, 3 July 1891, WPP, W/P/20.
2. Wolseley to Duke of Argyll, 1899, in F. Maurice and G. Arthur, *The Life of Lord Wolseley* (London, 1924), pp. 31–33.
     Richard Airey (1803–1881), Quartermaster General to the Crimean Army, 1854–55; Quartermaster General, 1855–65; Governor of Gibraltar, 1865–70; created a peer in 1876; president of the commission on the short service system, 1879.
     Colin Campbell (1792–1863), served in Peninsula, 1810–13; served in India, 1846–53; commanded Highland Brigade and then First Division in Crimea, 1854–55; Commander-in-Chief in India, 1857–60.
3. Wolseley to his aunt, Dowager Lady Wolseley, 23 February 1855, WPP, 163/1.
4. Wolseley, *Story of a Soldier's Life*, pp. 118, 147–48.
     Charles Gordon (1833–1885) served in Crimea, 1855; China War, 1860–62; commanded Chinese forces against Taipings, 1863–64; Governor of Egyptian equatorial provinces, 1874–76; Governor-General of the Sudan, 1877–80; Governor-General of Sudan, 1884–85.
5. G. J. Wolseley, 'The Old Trenches before Sebastopol Revisited', *United Service Magazine*, 10 (1894), pp. 103–21.
6. Wolseley to Dowager Lady Wolseley, 11 December 1854, WPP, 163/1.
7. Wolseley, *Story of a Soldier's Life*, pp. 140–41.
8. Ibid., pp. 110–12; Wolseley to Dowager Lady Wolseley, 29 December 1854, WPP, 163/1.
9. E. Wood, *The Crimea in 1854 and 1894* (London, 1895), pp. 236–37.
10. A. W. Kinglake, *Invasion of the Crimea*, ix (Edinburgh, 1888), pp. 120, 125.
11. Wolseley, *Story of a Soldier's Life*, p. 206.
12. A. Lambert, *The Crimean War* (Manchester, 1990).
13. A captain needed to have served six years in the army before promotion to major.
14. J. Selby, 'The Third China War 1860', in B. J. Bond (ed.), *Victorian Military Campaigns* (London, 1967), p. 74.
15. Wolseley, *Story of a Soldier's Life*, pp. 240–44.
16. L. James, *The Rise and Fall of the British Empire* (London, 1994), pp. 226–27.
17. Wolseley to Richard Wolseley, 27 July 1857, WPP, 163/1.
18. Wolseley, *Story of a Soldier's Life*, p. 272.
19. C. Hibbert, *The Great Mutiny* (London, 1978), p. 338.
20. W. Forbes-Mitchell, *Reminiscences of the Great Mutiny* (London, 1894), p. 80.
21. Wolseley did manage to find Barnston before the wounded were evacuated and was distressed to hear that he died later in Cawnpore from his wounds.
22. Wolseley to Richard Wolseley, 28 November 1857, WPP, 163/1.
23. Wolseley, *Story of a Soldier's Life*, pp. 315–16.
24. Ibid., p. 318.

25. James Hope Grant (1808–1875) commanded Trans-Ghogra force in Oude during Indian Mutiny; commanded in Chinese War, 1860–61; Commander-in-Chief at Madras, 1862–63; Quartermaster General, 1865; in 1871 initiated annual army manoeuvres.

26. Wolseley to Richard Wolseley, 7 April 1858, in J. Lehmann, *All Sir Garnet* (London, 1964), p. 75.

27. G. J. Wolseley, 'Memoir of Sir Hope Grant', *United Service Magazine*, 7 (1893), p. 777; idem, *Story of a Soldier's Life*, p. 342.

28. Ibid., p. 364.

29. Wolseley to George Wolseley, 21 September 1858, WPP, 163/1.

30. Wolseley to Richard Wolseley, 23 March 1859, WPP, 163/1.

31. Thuggees were gangs who murdered travellers for the little money they carried.

32. Wolseley to Dowager Lady Wolseley, 23 February and 18 March 1855, WPP, 163/1.

33. Wolseley to Richard Wolseley, 7 August 1859, WPP, 163/1.

Chapter 3: China

1. J. Selby, 'The Third China War 1860', in B. J. Bond (ed.), *Victorian Military Campaigns* (London, 1967), p. 75.

2. G. J. Wolseley, *Narrative of the War with China in 1860* (London, 1862), p. 4.

3. G. J. Wolseley, *The Story of a Soldier's Life* (London, 1903), ii, p. 9.

4. Ibid., pp. 13–16.

5. Wolseley to Dowager Lady Wolseley, 29 April 1860, WPP, 163/2; Wolseley, *Story of a Soldier's Life*, ii, p. 21.

6. Ibid., p. 24.

7. Wolseley to Frances Ann Wolseley, 24 August, 1860, WPP, 163/2.

8. Wolseley, *Story of a Soldier's Life*, p. 78.

9. Wolseley to Matilda Wolseley, 23 October 1860, WPP, 163/2.

10. Wolseley, *Story of a Soldier's Life*, p. 86.

11. Wolseley to Matilda Wolseley, 23 October 1860, WPP, 163/2.

12. Wolseley, *Narrative of the War with China*, p. 323.

13. Wolseley, *Story of a Soldier's Life*, pp. 88–93.

14. Wolseley, *Narrative of the War with China*, p. 351.

Chapter 4: Canada

1. Wolseley to Richard Wolseley, 29 November 1861, WPP, 163/3.

2. M. Pegram, *The Wolseley Heritage* (London, 1939), p. xii.

3. Wolseley to Matilda Wolseley, undated and incomplete, WPP, 163/3.

4. Wolseley to Frances Ann Wolseley, 6 May 1860, WPP, 163/2; Wolseley to Richard Wolseley, 14 February 1863 and 20 June 1865, WPP, 163/3.

5. This was either Fanny or Matilda, since Caroline never married.

6. Cambridge to Williams, 14 December 1861, Cambridge MSS, RA, E/1/3396.

7. G. J. Wolseley, *The Story of a Soldier's Life* (London, 1903), ii, p. 113.
8. Ibid., p. 116.
9. G. J. Wolseley, 'A Month's Visit to the Confederate Headquarters', *Blackwoods*, 93 (January 1863), pp. 1–29.
10. Wolseley, *Story of a Soldier's Life*, p. 135.
11. Wolseley, 'A Month's Visit'.
12. Wolseley, *Story of a Soldier's Life*, p. 142.
13. Wolseley to Richard Wolseley, 14 February 1863, WPP, 163/3.
14. G. J. Wolseley, 'General Sherman', *United Service Magazine*, 3 (1891), pp. 97–116; 193–216; 289–309; idem, 'General Forrest', ibid., 5 (1892), pp. 1–14; 113–24.
15. G. J. Wolseley, 'General Lee', *Macmillans*, 55 (March 1887), pp. 321–31.
16. Austria-Hungary adopted conscription after her defeat by Prussia in 1866; France adopted conscription soon after the Franco-Prussian War.
17. Wolseley to R. Biddulph, 27 October 1862, in Brigadier-General H. Biddulph, 'The American Civil War: Contemporary Letters from Lieutenant-Colonel G. J. Wolseley', *Journal of Army Historical Research*, 18 (1939), pp. 38–40.
18. G. J. Wolseley, 'An English View of the Civil War', *North American Review*, 149 (July-December 1889); idem, 'General Lee'.
19. J. Luvaas, *The Military Legacy of the Civil War* (Chicago, 1959), p. 46.
20. Wolseley to Richard Wolseley, 20 February, 15 September and 20 November 1863, WPP, 163/3.
21. Wolseley to Richard Wolseley, 4 November 1863, in J. Lehmann, *All Sir Garnet* (London, 1964), p. 124.
22. Patrick MacDougall (1819–1894), joined army, 1839; served in Canada, 1844–54; Superintendent of Studies at Sandhurst, 1854–58, but served in Crimea, 1854–55; Adjutant General of Canadian Militia, 1865–69; Deputy Inspector General of Auxiliary Forces at War Office, 1871; head of Intelligence Branch of War Office, 1873–78; commander in North America, 1877–83.
23. Wolseley, *Story of a Soldier's Life*, p. 147.
24. Ibid., p. 156.
25. Ibid., p. 160.
26. Wolseley to Richard Wolseley, 8 August 1866, in Lehmann, *All Sir Garnet*, p. 130.
27. Michel to Cambridge, 1 July 1867, Cambridge MSS, RA, E/1/5528.
28. Wolseley to Frances Ann Wolseley, 22 April 1867, WPP, 163/3.
29. Wolseley to Richard Wolseley, 13 September 1867, WPP, 163/3.
30. Wolseley to Richard Wolseley, 22 January 1869, WPP, 163/3.
31. G. J. Wolseley, *The Soldier's Pocket Book for Field Service* (London, 1886), p. 1.
32. Ibid., p. 178.
33. Ibid. p. 118.
34. The Hudson's Bay Company had received its charter from King Charles II in 1670.
35. Wolseley, *Story of a Soldier's Life*, p. 173.
36. Ibid., p. 179.

37. A portage was an impassable rapid or series of rapids, past which the boats had to be dragged or carried.

38. Voyageurs were native boatmen, mostly from the Iroquois Indians, but also including some French-Canadians.

39. G. J. Wolseley, 'Narrative of the Red River Expedition', *Blackwoods*, 109 (January 1871), pp. 48–73.

40. Wolseley, *Story of a Soldier's Life*, p. 187.

41. This was a corduroy road, constructed by laying down logs of six to nine inches diameter side by side.

42. Official Diary of the Red River Expedition, 17 July 1870, PRO, WO 32/7583.

43. Wolseley, 'Narrative of the Red River Expedition', pp. 164–81.

44. Ibid.; Wolseley, *Story of a Soldier's Life*, p. 212.

45. 'Narrative of Red River Expedition' (February 1871).

46. Ibid.

47. Wolseley to Louisa Wolseley, 26 August 1870, WPP, W/P/1.

48. 'Narrative of Red River Expedition' (February 1871); in 1885 Riel attempted another rebellion, was caught, tried and hanged.

49. Wolseley, *Story of a Soldier's Life*, p. 197.

50. Ibid., p. 222; Wolseley to Louisa Wolseley, 21 August 1870, WPP, W/P/1.

51. 'Narrative of Red River Expedition' (February 1871).

52. Lehmann, *All Sir Garnet*, p. 155.

53. Ibid., p. 201.

54. I. F. W. Beckett, 'Wolseley and the Ring', *Soldiers of the Queen*, 69 (June 1992), pp. 14–25; L. Maxwell, *The Ashanti Ring* (London, 1985).

55. John McNeill (1831–1904), joined Bengal Native Infantry, 1850; served during Indian Mutiny, 1857–58; won VC during Maori War, 1864; served on Red River, 1870, and against the Asante, 1873–74; commanded second infantry brigade in the Sudan, 1885.

William Butler (1838–1910), joined army, 1858; served on Red River, 1870, and against the Asante, 1873–74; Natal, 1875, Zulu War, 1879, Egypt, 1882, and the Sudan 1884–85; commanded garrison at Alexandria, 1890; commanded brigade at Aldershot, 1893; transferred to south east district, 1896; Commander-in-Chief, South Africa, 1898–99; commanded western district, 1899–1905; prominent author.

Redvers Buller (1839–1908), joined army, 1858; served in Benares, China and Canada, 1859–62; served on Red River, 1870, and against the Asante, 1873–74; commanded Frontier Light Horse in South Africa, 1878–79; awarded VC during Zulu War, 1879; aide-de-camp to Queen Victoria, 1879; served in South Africa, 1881, Egypt, 1882, and Sudan, 1884–85; Adjutant General, 1890–97; Aldershot command, 1898–99; Commander-in-Chief, South Africa, 1899; superseded by Frederick Roberts but remained in Natal command; Aldershot command, 1901.

56. Wolseley, *Story of a Soldier's Life*, p. 178.

Chapter 5: War Office

1. Edward Cardwell (1813–1886), barrister, 1838; Liberal MP, 1842; secretary to the Treasury, 1845–46; President of the Board of Trade, 1852–55; Secretary for Ireland, 1859–61; Secretary for the Colonies, 1864–66; Secretary of State for War, 1868–74; created Viscount, 1874.

2. George, Duke of Cambridge (1819–1908), commanded a division in the Crimea and was present at the battles of the Alma and Inkerman, 1854; General Commanding in Chief, 1856–87; Commander-in-Chief, 1887–1895.

3. L. S. Amery, *The Times History of the War in South Africa* (London, 1900–9), ii, p. 14.

4. G. J. Wolseley, *The Story of a Soldier's Life* (London, 1903), ii, p. 233.

5. I. F. Clarke, *Voices Prophesying War* (London, 1970), pp. 32–65.

6. Cardwell to House of Commons 16 May 1870, *Hansard*, vol. 201. After 1878 all recruitment was to be for short service.

7. Marquess of Anglesey, *A History of the British Cavalry*, iii, *1816–1919* (London, 1982), p. 32.

8. G. J. Wolseley, 'England as a Military Power in 1854 and in 1878', *Nineteenth Century*, 3 (March 1878), pp. 433–56.

9. The net cost of compensation to officers cost the government about £8,000,000. The officers were compensated at the price close to the amount they could have hoped to receive when selling their commissions. E. M. Spiers, *The Late Victorian Army* (Manchester, 1992), p. 15.

10. Wolseley, *Story of a Soldier's Life*, p. 240.

11. Committee on the Organisation of the Various Military Land Forces, First Report, c. 493 (1872), 38; Supplementary Report of the Committee on the Organisation of the Various Military Land Forces, c. 588 (1872), 14.

12. Wolseley had been a member of the Haines Committee on War Establishments which published its report on 7 January 1871, PRO, WO 33/22.

13. The 1839 Treaty of London guaranteed Belgian independence. The infringement of this treaty forced Britain to war in 1914.

14. Cardwell to Gladstone, 23 September 1871, Cardwell MSS, PRO 30/48/8; Cambridge to Cardwell, late 1871, in W. Verner, *The Military Life of HRH George, Duke of Cambridge* (London, 1905), p. 55.

15. Cambridge to Cardwell, late 1872, in Verner, *Life of Cambridge*, p. 59; G. J. Wolseley, 'Our Autumn Manoeuvres', *Blackwoods*, 112 (November 1872), pp. 627–44.

16. Wolseley to Louisa Wolseley, 19 August 1872, WPP, W/P/2.

17. Anon., *Essays Written for the Wellington Prize 1872* (Edinburgh, 1872), pp. 191–251.

18. John Frederick Maurice (1841–1912), joined Royal Artillery, 1862; served in War Office and in Asante, South Africa, Egypt, and the Sudan, 1873–85; professor of military art and history at Staff College, 1885; commanded artillery, Woolwich district, 1895; author of a number of military books including the first two volumes of the official *History of the War in South Africa, 1899–1902* (London, 1906–07).

19. Wolseley to Louisa Wolseley, 27 August 1872, WPP, W/P/2.
20. Wolseley, *Story of a Soldier's Life*, pp. 281–82.
21. Wolseley to Dowager Lady Wolseley, 18 March 1855, WPP, 163/1.
22. Wolseley, journal entry, 16 August 1878, PRO, WO 147/6.

Chapter 6: Asante

1. J. Morris, *Heaven's Command* (London, 1979), p. 397.
2. J. Keegan, 'The Ashanti Campaign 1873–4', in B. Bond (ed.), *Victorian Military Campaigns* (London, 1967), pp. 163–78.
3. Henry Howard Molyneux Herbert, fourth Earl of Carnarvon (1831–1890), Under Secretary for Colonies 1858–59; Secretary of State for the Colonies, 1866–67 and 1874–78; resigned office over Russo-Turkish war, 1878; chairman of Colonial Defence Commission, 1879–82; Lord Lieutenant of Ireland, 1885–86.
4. G. J. Wolseley, *Story of a Soldier's Life* (London, 1903), p. 276.
5. Henry Brackenbury (1837–1914), entered Woolwich, 1854; professor of military history at Woolwich, 1868; served in Asante, 1873–74; Cyprus, 1878; Zululand, 1879; and the Sudan, 1884–85; Deputy Assistant Quartermaster General and Head of Intelligence, 1886–91; military member of the Council of the Viceroy of India, 1891–96; Director-General of Ordnance, 1899–1902; published works on military subjects.
6. Evelyn Wood (1838–1919), entered navy, 1854; transferred to army during the Crimean War; won VC in Indian Mutiny, 1859; passed through Staff College, 1862–64; served in Asante, 1873–74; South Africa, 1878–79; and Natal in 1881; Royal Commissioner for the settlement of the Transvaal, 1881; served in Egypt, 1882; first Sirdar of Egyptian Army, 1882; held Eastern command, 1886; held Aldershot command, 1889; Quartermaster General, 1893–97; Adjutant General, 1897–1901.
7. Wolseley, *Story of a Soldier's Life*, p. 280; W. Butler, *An Autobiography* (London, 1911), pp. 143–44; E. Wood, *From Midshipman to Field Marshal* (London, 1906), i, p. 254.
8. Wolseley, *Story of a Soldier's Life*, p. 317.
    George Pomeroy Colley (1835–81), joined army, 1852; border magistrate and surveyor in Cape Colony, 1857; professor at Staff College, 1873; served in Asante, 1873–74 and Natal and Transvaal, 1875; secretary to the Viceroy of India, 1875; chief of staff in Zulu War, 1879; governor of Natal, 1880; defeated by Boers and killed at Majuba Hill, 1881.
9. Wolseley, journal entry, 10 December 1873, PRO, WO 147/3.
10. B. Farwell, *Queen Victoria's Little Wars* (London, 1973).
11. H. Brackenbury, *The Ashanti War of 1873–4* (Edinburgh, 1874), ii, p. 116.
12. Ibid. i, p. 116; Wolseley, journal entry, 10 October 1873.
13. H. M. Stanley, *Coomassie and Magdala* (New York, 1874); M. Prior, *Campaigns of a War Correspondent* (London, 1912); W. Reade, *The Story of the Ashanti Campaign* (London, 1874).

14. They became known as Russell's and Wood's Regiments after their colonels. Wolseley was gazetted a Major-General in March 1874 and his promotion backdated to 6 March 1868.

15. Wood, *From Midshipman to Field Marshal*, p. 258.

16. Wolseley, journal entry, 4 October 1873.

17. Wolseley to Louisa Wolseley, 6 October 1873, WPP, W/P/3.

18. Ibid., 14 October 1873.

19. G. J. Wolseley, 'The Negro as a Soldier', *Fortnightly Review*, 44 (December 1888), pp. 689–703.

20. Wolseley to Cambridge, 3 September 1873, in W. Verner, *The Military Life of HRH George, Duke of Cambridge* (London, 1905), p. 67; Wolseley, *Story of a Soldier's Life*, p. 315.

21. Cambridge to Wolseley, 2 December 1873, in Verner, *Life of Cambridge*, p. 78.

22. Wolseley to Louisa Wolseley, 17 November 1873, WPP, W/P/3.

23. Wolseley to Louisa Wolseley, 17 October 1873 and 20 January 1874, WPP, W/P/3–4.

24. Brackenbury, *The Ashanti War*, p. 353.

25. The buggy was left at Prahsu. Wolseley reverted to the use of his chair for the trip to and from Kumasi.

26. The West India regiments had originally been raised from ex-slaves. They were stationed in climates judged unsuitable for white soldiers.

27. Reade, *The Story of the Ashanti Campaign*, pp. 366–67.

28. Glover's expedition made no contribution towards the capture of Kumasi. Later his force met the Asante in the bush and this meeting convinced King Kofi to make peace. There were few communications between Glover's column and Wolseley's before 9 February, when Wolseley ordered Glover to halt. On 12 February a detachment from Glover's force arrived at Wolseley's headquarters and from then on satisfactory communications were resumed. Glover's expedition is covered in Brackenbury, *The Ashanti War*, i, pp. 376–424; ii, pp. 98–105, 257–65.

29. Wolseley, journal entry, 31 December 1873; Keegan, 'The Ashanti Campaign', p. 187; Butler, *Autobiography*, p. 163.

30. F. Emery, *Marching Over Africa* (London, 1986), p. 49.

31. The square formation was a common tactic of Napoleonic warfare used by infantry when attacked by cavalry. It was commonly used in colonial warfare during the nineteenth century, but was totally unsuited against an enemy armed with modern breech-loading rifles. The Asante only had muzzle-loading muskets.

32. Quoted in A. Lloyd, *The Drums of Kumasi* (London, 1963), p. 109.

33. Wolseley, journal entry, 1 February 1873.

34. Brackenbury, *The Ashanti War*, p. 223.

35. Wolseley, *Story of a Soldier's Life*, p. 359.

36. Wolseley, journal entry, 9 February 1874.

37. Ibid., 16 February 1874.

38. Ibid., 13 February 1874.

39. Wolseley to Louisa Wolseley, 25 February 1874, WPP, W/P/4; Lloyd, *Drums of Kumasi*, p. 150.
40. Wolseley, journal entry, 4 March 1874.
41. Wolseley, *Story of a Soldier's Life*, p. 370.
42. Kwaku Dua, King of Asante, 1838–67, quoted in Keegan, 'The Ashanti Campaign', p. 163.
43. In September 1874 King Kofi was 'destooled' by his counsellors. Also in 1874 the protectorate at Cape Coast was raised to the status of a colony. Between 1890 and 1901 two military expeditions were despatched against the Asante which resulted in the formal annexation of their territory. Keegan, 'The Ashanti Campaign', p. 196.
44. Journal entry, Queen Victoria, in G. E. Buckle and A. C. Benson (eds), *The Letters of Queen Victoria* (London, 1926–28), second series, ii, p. 331.
45. Wolseley to Frances Ann Wolseley, 23 March 1874, WPP, 163/4.
46. J. Lehmann, *All Sir Garnet* (London, 1964), p. 282.

Chapter 7: War Office and Natal

1. Gathorne Gathorne-Hardy, first Earl of Cranbrook (1814–1906), Conservative MP; Home Secretary, 1867–68; Secretary of State for War, 1874–78; Secretary of State for India, 1878–880; Lord President of the Council, 1885–92.
2. In 1868 Wolseley was in Canada; in 1874 he was in West Africa; and in 1880 he was in South Africa.
3. Wolseley, journal entry, 11 July 1875, PRO, WO 147/5.
4. Wolseley to Bury, 17 July 1878, WOP, W38.
5. For example, Wolseley after dinner speech to the 2nd Volunteer Battalion of the Royal Fusiliers, *The Times*, 20 January 1887.
6. Memorandum on Our Army Reserve, Wolseley, 15 January 1875, WOP, W37.
7. Royal Commission on Army Promotion and Retirement, c. 1569 (1876), 15; Committee on the Reserve of Officers, 1878, PRO 33/32/690.
8. Memorandum on the eight company system, Wolseley, 6 March 1877; ibid., Ellice, 8 March 1877, both PRO, WO 33/34. The British Army adopted the four company system in 1913.
9. Carnarvon to Wolseley, 30 April 1875, Carnarvon MSS, PRO, PRO 30/6/38.
10. D. R. Morris, *The Washing of the Spears* (London, 1965), pp. 218–25; Wolseley to Carnarvon, 21 March 1875, PRO, PRO 30/6/38.
    John Colenso (1814–1883), Bishop of Natal; champion of the Zulus and wrote a Zulu grammar and Zulu-English dictionary; accused of heresy, deposed and excommunicated by Bishop Robert Grey, Metropolitan of British South Africa, 1863; appealed to the Crown and Privy Council, who ruled in his favour and reinstated him, 1865.
11. C. W. De Kiewiet, *The Imperial Factor in South Africa* (Cambridge, 1937), p. 42. Zulu men were not allowed to marry until their spears had been blooded by killing an enemy.

12. Wolseley to Carnarvon, 16 February 1875, PRO, PRO 30/6/38.
13. Wolseley to Carnarvon, 27 February 1875, PRO, PRO 30/6/38; Wolseley, journal entry, 21 March 1875, PRO, WO 147/5.
14. Wolseley to Richard Wolseley, 9 May 1875, WPP, 163/4.
15. Wolseley, journal entry, 20 March 1875.
16. Wolseley to Louisa Wolseley, 16 May 1875, WPP, W/P/5.
17. W. Butler, *An Autobiography* (London, 1911), p. 175.
18. Wolseley to Louisa Wolseley, 13 June 1875, WPP, W/P/5.
19. Wolseley, journal entries, 6 and 11 April 1875.
20. A. Preston, *The South African Journal of Sir Garnet Wolseley 1875* (Cape Town, 1971), introduction, p. 81.
21. Wolseley, journal entries, 5 April and 19 August 1875; Wolseley to Cambridge, 21 August 1875, in W. Verner, *The Military Life of HRH George, Duke of Cambridge* (London, 1905), p. 151.
22. Wolseley to Carnarvon, 8 July 1875, PRO, PRO 30/6/38.
23. Wolseley, journal entries, 4 May and 11 June 1875.
24. De Kiewiet, *The Imperial Factor*, p. 46.
25. Wolseley, journal entry, 27 August 1875.
26. Delagoa Bay remained the only non-British port in the region. Both the Zulus and the Boers imported arms through it.
27. Wolseley to Richard Wolseley, 19 November 1875, WPP, 163/4.
28. Plan for the mobilisation of the army, 25 January and 18 November 1875, PRO, WO 33/27.

Chapter 8: India Office

1. Wolseley to Richard Wolseley, 4 November 1876, WPP, 163/4.
2. G. J. Wolseley, 'Army Reform', *Macmillans*, 35 (April 1877), pp. 496–504.
3. Salisbury to Governor-General of India, 13 July 1876; Major-General T. T. Pears to Stanley, 21 March 1876; memorandum on suggestions for securing the best British troops for India at the smallest cost, Wolseley, 8 December 1876, all in WOP, W35. Soldiers of the East India Company had enlisted for life. This army was amalgamated with the British Army after the Indian Mutiny.
4. G. J. Wolseley, 'Our Coming Guest', *Blackwoods*, 108 (June 1873), pp. 712–21.
5. Frederick Roberts (1832–1914), joined Bengal Artillery, 1851; served in Indian Mutiny, 1857–58, won VC, 1858; served in Abyssinia, 1868; Quartermaster General in India, 1875–78; served in Second Afghan War, 1878–79; Commander-in-Chief of Madras Army, 1880–85; Commander-in-Chief of India, 1885–93; Commander-in-Chief of Ireland, 1895–99; Commander-in-Chief in Second South African War, 1899–1900; Commander-in-Chief, 1900–05; President of National Service League, 1905.
6. A. Preston, 'Frustrated Great Gamesmanship: Sir Garnet Wolseley's Plans for War against Russia', *International History Review*, 2 (1980), pp. 239–65.

7. General Sketch of the situation abroad and at home from a military standpoint, Brackenbury, 3 August 1886, WOP, W18.

8. A. J. P. Taylor, *The Struggle for Mastery in Europe, 1848–1918* (Oxford, 1971), pp. 228–55.

9. L. James, *The Rise and Fall of the British Empire* (London, 1994), p. 197.

10. Memorandum by Wolseley, 10 November 1876, WOP, W34.

11. Thompson to Wolseley, 30 November 1876, WPP, autograph. Benjamin Disraeli was created the Earl of Beaconsfield in 1876.

12. Memorandum by Wolseley, 7 May 1877, WOP, W34.

13. Ibid.

14. Cambridge to Hardy, 5 December 1876, in W. Verner, *The Military Life of HRH George, Duke of Cambridge* (London, 1905), p. 111; Beaconsfield to Queen, 22 July 1877, in W. F. Moneypenny and G. E. Buckle, *The Life of Benjamin Disraeli, Earl of Beaconsfield* (London, 1920), vi, p. 154.

15. Robert Napier (1810–1890), joined Bengal Engineers, 1826; served in India, 1828–59, including service in the first and second Sikh Wars and the Indian Mutiny; commanded second division in China, 1860; Military Member of Governor-General's Council in India, 1861–65; Commander-in-Chief of Bombay Army, 1865–67; commanded expedition to Abyssinia, 1867–68; Commander-in-Chief in India, 1870; Governor of Gibraltar, 1876; appointed to command British expeditionary force in event of war with Russia, 1878.

16. Beaconsfield to Queen, 27 March 1878, in Moneypenny and Buckle, *Life of Disraeli*, p. 263.

17. Napier to Cambridge, 14 March 1878, Cambridge MSS, RA, E/1/8268.

18. This decision led to the resignation from the Cabinet of Lord Carnarvon and Lord Derby.

19. G. J. Wolseley, 'England as a Military Power in 1854 and in 1878', *Nineteenth Century*, 3 (March 1878), pp. 433–56.

20. Frederick Stanley, sixteenth Earl of Derby (1841–1908), served in Grenadier Guards, 1858–65; Conservative MP; Civil Lord of the Admiralty, 1868; Secretary of State for War, 1878–80; Colonial Secretary, 1885–86; President of the Board of Trade, 1886–88; Governor-General of Canada, 1888–93; succeeded to earldom, 1893.

21. 22 July 1878, *Hansard*, vol. 241; 6 August 1878, ibid., vol. 242.

22. Wolseley to Richard Wolseley, 8 February 1878, WPP, 163/4.

23. Memorandum by Wolseley, 30 March 1878, WOP, W17.

24. Modern name Kárpathos.

25. Memorandum by Wolseley, 10 November 1876, WOP, W34; memorandum on coaling stations at the east of the Mediterranean, Lintorn Simmons, 27 April 1877, PRO, WO 33/31; Wolseley, journal entry, 19 July 1878, PRO, WO 147/6.

26. Napier to Cambridge, 9 July 1878, Cambridge MSS, RA, E/1/8368.

27. Sir F. Maurice and Sir G. Arthur, *The Life of Lord Wolseley* (New York, 1924), pp. 91–92; Wolseley, journal entry, 25 October 1878.

28. W. Butler, *An Autobiography* (London, 1911), p. 196.

29. M. Pegram, *The Wolseley Heritage* (London, 1939), p. 12.
30. Wolseley to Richard Wolseley, late March 1874; Wolseley to Matilda Wolseley, 7 August 1878; Wolseley to Richard Wolseley, 26 August 1878 and 5 February 1879, all in WPP, 163/4–5.
31. Wolseley to Louisa Wolseley, 5 August 1878, WPP, W/P/7.
32. Beaconsfield to Queen, 5 May 1878, in Moneypenny and Buckle, *Life of Disraeli*, p. 291.
33. A. F. Egerton to House of Commons, 11 July 1878, *Hansard*, vol. 241; Sir J. Goldschmid to House of Commons, 24 March 1879, ibid., vol. 244.
34. Wolseley, journal entries, 19 July, 2 November and 5 November 1878, PRO, WO 147/6; Stanley to Cambridge, 30 October 1878, in Verner, *Life of Cambridge*, p. 116.
35. Butler, *An Autobiography*, p. 197.
36. Wolseley, journal entries, 24 and 25 September, 3 October and 10 December 1878. During the First Afghan War, 1838–42, the first expeditionary force was massacred by the Afghans with only one survivor, Dr William Brydon.
37. Michael Hicks Beach (1837–1916), Conservative MP; Under Secretary for the Home Office, 1868; Chief Secretary in Ireland, 1874–78; Colonial Secretary, 1878–80; Chancellor of the Exchequer and Leader of the House, 1885; Irish Secretary, 1886–87; President of the Board of Trade, 1888–92; Chancellor of the Exchequer, 1895–1902.
38. James, *Rise and Fall of the British Empire*, p. 257.
39. Frederic Thesiger, second Baron Chelmsford (1827–1905), joined army, 1844; served in Crimea, Indian Mutiny and Abyssinia; Adjutant General in East Indies, 1869–74; Shorncliffe command, 1874–76; commanded in Kaffir War and Zulu War, 1878–79; Lieutenant of the Tower of London, 1884–89.

Chapter 9: South Africa

1. Wolseley to Frances Ann Wolseley, 29 April 1879; Wolseley to Richard Wolseley, 5 September 1879, both in WPP, 163/5.
2. Wolseley to Salisbury, 18 February 1879, Cyprus Letter Book, BL, Add. Ms 41324.
3. Journal of Queen Victoria, 26 and 27 May 1879, in G. E. Buckle and A. C. Benson (eds), *The Letters of Queen Victoria* (London, 1926–28), second series, iii, p. 24; Beaconsfield to Queen, 23 May 1879; Beaconsfield to Queen, 24 August 1879; Beaconsfield to Queen, 27 May 1879, all in W. F. Moneypenny and G. E. Buckle, *The Life of Benjamin Disraeli, Earl of Beaconsfield* (London, 1920), pp. 429–32, 435.
4. Quoted in J. Lehmann, *All Sir Garnet* (London, 1964), p. 245.
5. Diary of Hardy, 28 May 1879, in A. E. Gathorne-Hardy, *Gathorne Hardy, First Earl of Cranbrook* (London, 1910), p. 112; 26 May 1879, *Hansard*, vol. 244.
6. Notes for autobiography, Wolseley, WPP, SSL.
7. Cambridge to Wolseley, 12 August 1879, in W. Verner, *The Military Life of HRH George, Duke of Cambridge* (London, 1905), p. 164; Beaconsfield to Queen, in

Moneypenny and Buckle, *Life of Disraeli*, 19 May 1879; memorandum on the Zulu War, Ellice, 11 August 1879, PRO, WO 30/129.

8. Cambridge to Wolseley, 12 August 1879; Wolseley to Cambridge, 28 September 1879, both in Verner, *Life of Cambridge*, pp. 164, 170.

9. Wolseley, journal entry, 21 June 1879, PRO, WO 147/7.

10. Wolseley to Louisa Wolseley, 30 May 1879, WPP, W/P/8.

11. Captain Jaheel Carey, the leader of the patrol including the Prince Imperial, was court-martialled for leaving the Prince to his fate. He was found guilty and cashiered from the army. Back in Britain the sentence was overturned and Carey's commission restored.

12. Wolseley, journal entries, 23 and 24 June 1879; Wolseley to Louisa Wolseley, 24 June 1879, WPP, W/P/8.

13. D. R. Morris, *The Washing of the Spears* (London, 1966), p. 555.

14. Wolseley, journal entry, 8 July 1879.

15. Wolseley to Cambridge, 11 July 1879, Cambridge MSS, RA, M858/36.

16. Wolseley, journal entry, 17 July 1879.

17. 14 August 1879, *Hansard*, vol. 249; Cambridge to Wolseley, 12 and 18 August 1879, in Verner, *Life of Cambridge*, pp. 164–66.

18. E. Wood, *From Midshipman to Field Marshal* (London, 1906), ii, p. 5; Wolseley to Cambridge, 18 July 1879, in Verner, *Life of Cambridge*, p. 162. Wolseley wanted Wood to be promoted to the rank of Major-General because for his services in the Zulu War. The Duke of Cambridge refused because he felt it was premature and that Wood was amply rewarded with a KCB and good service pension. Wolseley to Cambridge, 18 July 1879; Cambridge to Wolseley, 26 August 1879, both in Cambridge MSS, M858/36.

19. Wolseley, journal entry, 31 August 1879.

20. Wolseley to Louisa Wolseley, 29 August 1879, WPP, W/P/8. The list was Baroness Coutts, Lady Constance Stanley, Lady Sherborne, Lady Cardwell, Miss Goschen, Miss Smith, the Miss Hennikers and the Miss Lawrences.

21. Wolseley to Cambridge, 2 March 1880, Cambridge MSS, M858/37.

22. C. W. De Kiewiet, *The Imperial Factor in South Africa* (Cambridge, 1937), p. 247.

23. Quoted in E. Unterhalter, 'Confronting Imperialism', in A. Duminy and C. Ballard (eds), *The Anglo-Zulu War* (Pietermaritzburg, 1981), p. 106.

24. Frere to Hicks Beach, 28 August 1879, in J. Martineau, *The Life and Correspondence of Sir Bartle Frere* (London, 1985), p. 347. The Zulu chiefs soon began to quarrel and in 1882 the British government recalled Cetshwayo from exile and restored him to his throne under strict conditions. Cetshwayo was attacked by some of the chiefs and was a fugitive before dying in February 1884. In 1887 the British government annexed Zululand, and in 1897 gave it to Natal.

25. Beaconsfield to Hardy, 28 September 1879, in Gathorne-Hardy, *Gathorne Hardy*, p. 122.

26. Wolseley, journal entry, 19 September 1879.

27. A zareba was a defensive structure built from wood or stone.

28. Major G. Tylden, 'The Sekukuni Campaign of 1879', *Journal of the Society for Army Historical Research*, 29 (1951), pp. 129–35.
29. Quoted in L. James, *The Rise and Fall of the British Empire* (London, 1984), p. 194.
30. Wolseley, journal entry, 28 November 1879.
31. P. Hankinson, *Man of Wars: W. H. Russell* (London, 1982), p. 246; Wolseley to Louisa Wolseley, 13 January 1880, WPP, W/P/8.
32. Wolseley to Louisa Wolseley, 30 November 1879, WPP, W/P/8; Wolseley to Cambridge, 24 November and 1 December 1879, in Verner, *Life of Cambridge*, p. 174.
33. Beaconsfield to Lady Bradford, 26 December 1879, in Moneypenny and Buckle, *Life of Disraeli*, pp. 473–74.
34. Tylden, 'The Sekukuni Campaign of 1879'.
35. Wolseley, journal entry, 18 October 1879; Wolseley to Richard Wolseley, 14 October 1879, WPP, 163/5.
36. Wolseley to Cambridge, 18 November 1879, in Verner, *Life of Cambridge*, p. 173.
37. Wolseley, journal entry, 7 January 1880.
38. Wolseley to Hicks Beach, 13 November 1879, PRO, CAB 37/1/5.
39. Wolseley to Louisa Wolseley, 15 February 1880, WPP, W/P/9; for example, journal entry, 2 February 1880.
40. Wolseley to Salisbury, 16 February 1879, Cyprus Letter Book, BL, Add. Ms 41324.
41. Notes for autobiography, WPP, SSL/8.
42. Wolseley to Louisa Wolseley, 20 March 1880, WPP, W/P/9.
43. Wolseley, journal entry, 11 January 1880.
44. Wolseley to Louisa Wolseley, 18 April 1880, WPP, W/P/9.
45. Wolseley to Richard Wolseley, 21 April 1880, WPP, 163/5.
46. Wolseley to Louisa Wolseley, 29 July 1880, WPP, W/P/9.

Chapter 10: Quartermaster General

1. Hugh Childers (1827–96), lived and worked in Melbourne, Australia, 1851–56; Liberal MP; Financial Secretary to the Treasury, 1865–66; First Lord of the Admiralty, 1868; Chancellor of the Duchy of Lancaster, 1872–73; Secretary of State for War, 1880–82; Chancellor of the Exchequer, 1882–85; Home Secretary, 1886.
2. G. J. Wolseley, notes for autobiography, WPP, SSL10.
3. C. W. De Kiewiet, *The Imperial Factor in South Africa* (Cambridge, 1937), p. 262.
4. D. M. Schreuder, *Gladstone and Kruger: Liberal Government and Colonial Home Rule* (London, 1969), p. 89; J. Lehmann, *The First Boer War* (London, 1972), pp. 115–16.
    John Wodehouse, Earl of Kimberley (1826–1902), Under Secretary for Foreign Affairs, 1852–56 and 1859–61; British Minister at St Petersburg, 1856–58; Lord Lieutenant of Ireland, 1864–66; Lord Privy Seal, 1868–70; Colonial Secretary,

1870–74 and 1880–82; India Office, 1882–85 and 1886; Secretary for India and Lord President of the Council, 1892–94; Foreign Secretary, 1894–95.

5. De Kiewiet, *The Imperial Factor*, p. 280; Schreuder, *Gladstone and Kruger*, pp. 110–17.

6. Colley to Wolseley, 21 February 1881, WPP, autograph.

7. Lehmann, *The First Boer War*, pp. 231–39.

8. I. Hamilton, *Listening for the Drums* (London, 1944), p. 139; Cambridge to Wood, 26 May 1881, in W. Verner, *The Military Life of HRH George, Duke of Cambridge* (London, 1905), p. 195.

9. Wolseley to Maurice, 1881, Maurice MSS, Liddell Hart Centre, 2/2/9; E. Wood, *From Midshipman to Field Marshal* (London, 1906), p. 112.

10. Lehmann, *The First Boer War*, p. 266; B. Bond, 'The South African War, 1880–81', in B. Bond (ed.), *Victorian Military Campaigns* (London, 1967), pp. 234–36; I. R. Smith, *The Origins of the South African War* (London, 1996), pp. 32–34.

11. Ponsonby to Kimberley, 12 March 1881, in G. E. Buckle and A. C. Benson (eds), *The Letters of Queen Victoria* (London, 1926–28), second series, iii, p. 202; Edward Hamilton, diary entry, 27 December 1880, in D. W. R. Bahlman (ed.), *The Diary of Sir Edward Walter Hamilton* (Oxford, 1972), p. 92; Wood, *From Midshipman to Field Marshal*, p. 116.

12. Wolseley, notes for autobiography, WPP, SSL8.

13. R. Robinson and J. Gallagher, *Africa and the Victorians* (London, 1961), p. 72.

14. Roberts and Stewart each received a baronetcy and a grant of £12,500. This was half the amount given to Wolseley after the Asante campaign. Roberts was not promoted for his services. D. James, *The Life of Lord Roberts* (London, 1954), pp. 174–75.

15. Cambridge to Queen, 30 August 1880; Hartington to Queen, 6 September 1880, both in Buckle, *Letters of Queen Victoria*, pp. 135, 137; Hamilton diary entries, 14 and 25 September 1880, in Bahlman, *The Diary of Edward Hamilton*, pp. 51, 57–58; S. Gopal, *British Policy in India* (Cambridge, 1965), pp. 132–33.

16. Cambridge to Wolseley, 26 August 1879, in Verner, *Life of Cambridge*, p. 166; Wolseley, notes for autobiography, WPP, SSL8.

17. Committee on the Organisation of the Army, c. 2791 (1881), 21.

18. Wolseley, memorandum on army organisation, 16 October 1880, WPP, W/W1/1.

19. Ponsonby to Cambridge, 20 December 1880, in Verner, *Life of Cambridge*, p. 213.

20. In 1880 the British Army was approximately 3700 men over-establishment.

21. G. J. Wolseley, 'Long and Short Service', *Nineteenth Century*, 9 (March 1881), pp. 558–72.

22. Idem, 'England as a Military Power in 1854 and in 1878', *Nineteenth Century*, 3 (March 1878), pp. 433–56.

23. Ponsonby to Childers, 15 May 1880, in S. Childers, *Life and Correspondence of the Right Hon. Hugh C. E. Childers* (London, 1901), i, p. 274; PRO, WO 32/6045.

24. Memorandum by Campbell-Bannerman, 9 February 1881; memorandum by Ellice, 14 February 1881; memorandum by Wolseley, 17 February 1881; memorandum by Adye, 18 February 1881, all in PRO, WO 32/8709.

25. Wolseley to Cambridge, January 1889, in F. Maurice and G. Arthur, *Life of Lord Wolseley* (London, 1924), p. 230.
26. *The Times*, 15 February 1881.
27. F. Roberts, 'The Present State of the Army', *Nineteenth Century*, 12 (November 1882), pp. 633–46.
28. Wolseley, 'Long and Short Service'.
29. C. Raleigh Chichester, 'Short Service and its Supporters', *Blackwood's Magazine*, 129 (May 1881), pp. 591–601.
30. Wolseley, journal entry, 28 December 1879, PRO, WO 147/7.
31. Hamilton diary entry, 3 March 1881, in Bahlman, *Diary of Hamilton*, p. 112; Wolseley, notes for autobiography, WPP, SSL8.
32. Gladstone to Granville, 5 March 1881, Gladstone MSS, BL, Add. MS 44173.
33. Childers to Ponsonby, 4 March 1881, Childers MSS, 5/21; Childers to Gladstone, 4 March 1881, 5/22.
34. Childers to Gladstone, 7 March 1881, 5/25.
35. Memorandum for the Cabinet, Gladstone, 24 March 1881, BL, Add. MS 44765; Hamilton diary entry, 3 April 1881, in Bahlman, *Diary of Hamilton*, p. 124.
36. Hamilton diary entry, 26 May 1881, ibid., p. 141.
37. Granville to Gladstone, 27 April 1881, BL, Add. Ms 44173.
38. Wolseley to Childers, 23 August 1881, Childers MSS, 5/37.
39. Childers to Gladstone, 28 August 1881, ibid., 5/40; Childers to Gladstone, 4 September 1881, 5/42; Childers to Gladstone, 12 September 1881, 5/47.
40. Hamilton diary entry, 28 September 1881, Bahlman, *Diary of Hamilton*, pp. 171–72.
41. Childers to Cambridge, 13 September 1881, Childers MSS, 5/48. The men were Major-General Sir C. G. Arburthnot, R. A. and Colonel Sir J. Stokes, R. E.
42. Prince of Wales to the Queen, 10 November 1881, in S. Lee, *King Edward VII* (London, 1925), i, p. 557.
43. Childers to Hartington, 4 September 1881, Devonshire MSS, 340.1115; Childers to Cambridge, 13 September 1881, Childers MSS, 5/48; Cambridge to Childers, 24 September 1881, Cambridge MSS, RA, E/1/9756; Hartington to Cambridge, 26 September 1881, RA, E/1/9761; Childers to Cambridge, 28 September 1881, 5/62.
44. Harcourt to Gladstone, 23 October 1881, Childers MSS, 5/89; Gladstone to Harcourt, 25 October 1881, in A. G. Gardiner, *The Life of Sir William Harcourt* (London, 1923), p. 416; Ponsonby to Childers, 20 September 1881, 5/55; Childers to the Queen, 12 October 1881, 5/68; Childers to Cambridge, 13 October 1881, 5/71.
45. *The Times*, 10 November 1881.
46. Wolseley, notes for autobiography, WPP, SSL8.
47. Childers to Gladstone, 12 November 1881, Childers MSS, 5/117.
48. Childers to Hartington, 12 April 1882, Devonshire MSS, 340.1142; Childers to Granville, 4 April 1881, 5/33.

Chapter 11: Adjutant General

1. See Chapters 12 and 13. This chapter will cover Wolseley's term of office until he left for the Sudan.
2. Correspondence with reference to the Proposed Construction of a Channel Tunnel, c. 3358 (1882), 17.
3. *The Times*, 24 May 1882.
4. J. F. Maurice, 'Hostilities without Declaration of War', PRO, WO 33/39.
5. Cambridge to Wolseley, 17 January 1882; Childers to Cambridge, 14, 16 and 17 February 1882, Cambridge MSS, RA, E/1/9899, 9923, 9925, 9927.
6. Lord Dunsany, 'The Proposed Channel Tunnel', *Nineteenth Century*, 11 (February 1882), pp. 288–304.
7. I. F. Clarke, *Voices Prophesying War* (London, 1966), p. 110.
8. 21 February 1882, *Hansard*, vol. 264; 31 March 1882, vol. 268.
9. Archibald Alison (1826–1907), joined army, 1846; served in Crimean War, Indian Mutiny and Asante War; commanded Highland Brigade at Tel-el-Kebir, 1882; commanded British force in Egypt, 1883; commanded Aldershot division, 1883–88.
10. Report of the Military Committee on the Channel Tunnel, 17 May 1882, PRO, WO 33/39.
11. K. Wilson, *Channel Tunnel Visions* (London, 1994), p. 37.
12. G. J. Wolseley, 'Our Military Requirements', *Macmillans*, 23 (April 1871), pp. 524–36.
13. Memorandum on the Channel Tunnel, 16 June 1882, PRO, WO 33/39.
14. Memorandum on the Channel Tunnel, 23 June 1882, PRO, WO 33/39.
15. Report of the Joint Select Committee of the House of Lords and the House of Commons on the Channel Tunnel (1883), 12.
16. Wilson, *Channel Tunnel Visions*, p. 47; memorandum on the Channel Tunnel, 2 March 1893, PRO, CAB 37/33; N. Longmate, *Island Fortress* (London, 1991), p. 360.
17. Committee on the Reorganisation of the Army, c. 2791 (1881), 21, paragraph 248.
18. Memorandum on the training of the Army Reserve, 14 April 1882, WPP, W/MEM/1; the subject was also brought up at a meeting at the War Office on 26 May 1882, PRO, WO 32/8711.
19. Wolseley to Thompson, 14 May 1883, PRO, WO 32/8713.
20. Report of the Committee on the Training of the First Class Army Reserve, 7 February 1883, WOP, W45.
21. Spencer Compton Cavendish, Marquess of Hartington and eighth Duke of Devonshire (1833–1908), Liberal MP; Under Secretary for War, 1863; Secretary of State for War, 1866; Postmaster-General, 1868–70; Chief Secretary of Ireland, 1870–74; Leader of Liberal Party, 1875; Secretary of State for India, 1880–82; Secretary of State for War, 1882–85; opposed Home Rule Bill and founded Liberal Unionist party which joined Conservative Unionists under Lord

Salisbury, 1886; chairman of Royal Commission on Administration of Naval and War Departments, 1888–90; succeeded father as Duke of Devonshire, 1891; President of the Council, 1895–1903.

22. Memoranda on the Army Reserve, 6 July 1883; 14 August 1883; 6 October 1883; 31 October 1883. All WPP, W/MEM/1.

23. Estimate as to the cost of annual training of the First Class Army Reserve, 5 January 1884, WOP, W45; memorandum on the cost of training the Army Reserve, 3 January 1884, WPP, W/MEM/1.

24. Memorandum on home establishments, Wolseley, 20 October 1883, WOP, W20.

25. E. M. Spiers, *The Late Victorian Army* (Manchester, 1992), pp. 121–23.

26. *The Times*, 5 December 1882; Wolseley to Queen, 27 December 1882, in G. E. Buckle and A. C. Benson (eds), *The Letters of Queen Victoria*, second series, iii (London, 1926–28), pp. 387–90; W. E. Montague, 'Red-Hot Reform', *Blackwoods Magazine*, 134 (July 1883), pp. 66–87.

27. Report of the Colour Committee, 25 July 1882, WOP, W45.

28. Connaught to Cambridge, 20 September 1882, in W. Verner, *The Military Life of HRH George, Duke of Cambridge* (London, 1905), p. 251.

29. Hartington to Ponsonby, 9 March 1883, Hartington MSS, 240.1338.

30. A. R. Skelley, *The Victorian Army at Home* (London, 1977), p. 62.

31. Ponsonby to Wolseley, 16 and 19 January 1884, WPP, Autograph.

32. Wolseley to Louisa Wolseley, 27 May 1883, WPP, W/P/12.

33. Louisa Wolseley to Wolseley, 31 May 1883, WPP, LW/P/9.

34. M. Pegram, *The Wolseley Heritage* (London, 1939), p. 31.

35. Wolseley to Duchess of Edinburgh, October 1883, in F. Maurice and G. Arthur, *The Life of Wolseley* (London, 1924), p. 2n.

36. Wolseley to Caroline Wolseley, 26 October 1883, WPP, 163/5.

Chapter 12: Egypt

1. Gladstone to Granville, 4 January 1882, Granville MSS, PRO, PRO 30/29/125.

2. J. F. Maurice, *The Campaign of 1882 in Egypt* (London, 1887), p. 2; M. J. Williams, 'The Egyptian Campaign of 1882', in B. Bond (ed.), *Victorian Military Campaigns* (London, 1967), p. 247.

3. Williams, *The Egyptian Campaign*, p. 251.

4. W. Blunt, *The Secret History of the English Occupation of Egypt* (London, 1907), p. 227.

5. Maurice, *Campaign of 1882*, pp. 10–11.

6. The Radical MP John Bright resigned from the government over the bombardment of Alexandria. Lawson to House of Commons, 12 July 1882, *Hansard*, vol. 272

7. Cambridge to the Queen, 20 July 1882, in G. E. Buckle and A. C. Benson (eds), *The Letters of Queen Victoria* (London, 1926–28), second series, iii, pp. 311–12; vote of credit, 24 July 1882, *Hansard*, vol. 272. Only approximately 1000 reservists

took part in the battle of Tel-el-Kebir: they acquitted themselves well. Gladstone to House of Commons, 26 October 1882, *Hansard*, vol. 274.

8. R. Robinson and J. Gallagher, *Africa and the Victorians* (London, 1961), pp. 114–19.

9. Maurice, *The Campaign of 1882*, pp. 7–8.

10. Williams, *The Egyptian Campaign*, p. 252; B. Bond, 'Mr Gladstone's Invasion of Egypt, 1882', *Army Quarterly*, 81 (October 1960), pp. 87–91; Hamilton diary entry, 25 August 1882, in D. W. R. Bahlman (ed.), *The Diary of Sir Edward Walter Hamilton* (Oxford, 1972), p. 325; Wolseley to Louisa Wolseley, 14 September 1882, WPP, W/P/11.

11. Edward Hamley, (1824–1893), joined Royal Artillery, 1843; served in Crimea, 1855; professor of military history, Sandhurst, 1859–64; published *Operations of War* (1866); commandant of the Staff College, 1870–77; British commissioner for the delimitation of the Bulgarian, Armenian and Greek frontier, 1879–81; commanded division at Tel-el-Kebir, 1882; MP, 1885–92; published many military works and important supporter of home defence measures.

12. Williams, *The Egyptian Campaign*, p. 254.

13. Wolseley to Louisa Wolseley, 26 August 1882, WPP, W/P/11.

14. Childers to House of Commons, 7 August 1882, *Hansard*, vol. 273; T. G. Fergusson, *British Military Intelligence* (Maryland, 1984), pp. 70–71.

15. S. Lee, *King Edward VII* (London, 1925), i, pp. 457–58.

16. Arthur William Patrick Albert, Duke of Connaught and Strathearn (1850–1942), third son of Queen Victoria; entered Royal Military Academy, Woolwich, 1866; joined Royal Engineers, 1868 and then transferred to Royal Artillery; served in Canada with Rifle Brigade, 1869–70; transferred to Hussars, 1874; Assistant Adjutant General, Gibraltar, 1875–76; commanded 1st Guards Brigade in Egypt, 1882; commanded at Bombay, 1886–90; Portsmouth, 1890–93; Aldershot, 1893–98; Commander-in-Chief, Ireland, 1900–04; commanded Mediterranean stations, 1907–09; Governor-General of Canada, 1911–16.

17. Cambridge to Wolseley, 18 August 1882, Cambridge MSS, RA, E/1/10134; C. Beresford, *The Memoirs of Admiral Lord Charles Beresford* (London, 1914), p. 180; Wolseley to Louisa Wolseley, 11 September 1882, WPP, W/P/11.

18. F. Maurice and G. Arthur, *The Life of Lord Wolseley* (London, 1924), p. 146.

19. Wolseley to Louisa Wolseley, 3 August 1882, WPP, W/P/11.

20. Maurice, *The Campaign of 1882*, pp. 17–18.

21. Williams, *The Egyptian Campaign*, p. 260.

John (Jacky) Fisher (1841–1920), entered navy, 1854; served at sea, 1863–69 and 1876–82; devoted himself to development of torpedo; served in war in Egypt, 1882; captain of gunnery school, Portsmouth, 1883–86; director of ordnance and torpedoes at Admiralty, 1886–90; Third Sea Lord and Controller of Navy, 1892–97; Commander-in-Chief, North America and West Indies station, 1897; commanded Mediterranean Fleet, 1899–1902; Second Sea Lord with charge of personnel of fleet, 1902–03; introduced many important administrative changes; Commander-in-Chief, Portsmouth, 1903; member of War Office Reconstruction Committee, 1903–04; First Sea Lord, 1904–10; organised redistribution of fleet to meet German menace; supported construction of Dreadnoughts; returned to Admiralty as First Sea Lord on outbreak of war, 1914; opposed naval attempt to force the Dardanelles, 1915 and resigned office.

22. Maurice, *The Campaign of 1882*, p. 33.

23. G. Dawnay, *Campaigns: Zulu 1879, Egypt 1882, Suakim 1884* (Cambridge, 1989), p. 93; Maurice, *The Campaign of 1882*, p. 36.

24. Williams, *The Egyptian Campaign*, p. 265; Maurice, *The Campaign of 1882*, p. 37.

25. W. Butler, *An Autobiography* (London, 1911), p. 226.

26. J. Lehmann, *All Sir Garnet* (London, 1964), p. 312.

27. Butler, *Autobiography*, p. 225.

28. Maurice, *The Campaign of 1882*, pp. 51–52; Wolseley to Louisa Wolseley, 26 August 1882, WPP, W/P/11.

29. Wolseley to Cambridge, 28 August 1882, Cambridge MSS, RA, E/1/10149.

30. Maurice, *The Campaign of 1882*, pp. 54–55. Wolseley's brother was now a Brevet Lieutenant-Colonel in the York and Lancaster Regiment. He held Wolseley's horse during the battle of Tel-el-Kebir.

31. Butler, *Autobiography*, p. 227; Wolseley to Louisa Wolseley, 28 August 1882, WPP, W/P/11.

32. Maurice, *The Campaign of 1882*, pp 61–64; Wolseley to Louisa Wolseley, 31 August 1882, WPP, W/P/11.

33. Major G. Tylden, 'Tel-el-Kebir', *Journal of the Society for Army Historical Research*, 19 (1953), pp. 52–57.

34. Maurice, *The Campaign of 1882*, pp. 69–70; Wolseley to Louisa Wolseley, 7 September 1882, WPP, W/P/11.

35. Wolseley to Louisa Wolseley, 10 September 1882, WPP, W/P/11.

36. Williams, *Egyptian Campaign*, pp. 271–72; Maurice and Arthur, *Life of Wolseley*, p. 157.

37. Butler, *Autobiography*, p. 229.

38. Lehmann, *All Sir Garnet*, p. 325.

39. Tylden, 'Tel-el-Kebir'.

40. P. Marling, *Rifleman and Hussar* (London, 1931), p. 63.

41. Williams, *The Egyptian Campaign*, p. 274.

42. Wolseley to Louisa Wolseley, 14 September 1882, WPP, W/P/11; Wolseley to Childers, 16 September 1882, PRO, WO 32/6096. Discipline was also good: there were only three courts-martial in Egypt. Wolseley to Ponsonby, 27 September 1882, in A. Ponsonby, *Henry Ponsonby* (London, 1942), pp. 224–25.

43. Blunt, *Secret History*, p. 421; Butler, *Autobiography*, p. 236.

44. Maurice, *The Campaign of 1882*, pp. 97–100.

45. Butler, *Autobiography*, p. 246.

46. Lehmann, *All Sir Garnet*, p. 336; Dawnay, *Campaigns*, p. 145; memorandum on parade in Egypt, Wolseley, 1882, PRO, WO 30/131; Wolseley to Louisa Wolseley, 14 September 1882, WPP, W/P/11.

47. Wolseley to Cambridge, 6 October 1882, Cambridge MSS, RA, E/1/10211.

48. Gladstone to Granville, 27 September 1882, Gladstone MSS, BL, Add. Ms 44546;

Wolseley to Louisa Wolseley, 16 September 1882, WPP, W/P/11; Wolseley to Gladstone, 10 February 1883, BL, Add. Ms 44479; idem, 22 April 1883, BL, Add. Ms 44480; memorandum on the grant of money to Wolseley, Gladstone, 23 April 1883, BL, Add. Ms 44767.

49. E. Butler, *Autobiography* (London, 1922), p. 154; Wolseley to Louisa Wolseley, 20 March 1885, WPP, W/P/14; P. Usherwood and J. Spencer-Smith, *Lady Butler: Battle Artist* (London, 1987), pp. 87–88. The fragment was displayed during an exhibition of Lady Butler's work at the National Army Museum, London in 1987.

50. Queen to Wolseley, 18 September 1882, in Buckle, *Letters of Queen Victoria*, pp. 335–36; Wolseley to Louisa Wolseley, 28 September 1882, WPP, W/P/11.

51. Connaught to the Queen, 26 September 1882, in W. Verner, *The Military Life of HRH George, Duke of Cambridge* (London, 1905), p. 255.

52. Wolseley to Louisa Wolseley, 10 September 1882, WPP, W/P/11.

53. Hamilton diary entry, 20 September 1882, in Bahlman, *Diary of Hamilton*, p. 343; Childers to Thompson, 2 October 1893, Childers MSS, 5/206; Wolseley to Childers, 11 October 1893, 5/211.

54. E. Hamley, 'The 2nd Division at Tel-el-Kebir', *Nineteenth Century*, 12 (December 1882), pp. 861–70; E. Shand, *The Life of General Sir Edward Bruce Hamley* (Edinburgh, 1895), pp. 109–10.

55. J. F. Maurice, 'Sir E. Hamley and Lord Wolseley', *United Service Magazine*, 11 (1895), pp. 414–34.

56. Dawnay, *Campaigns*, pp. 106–8; journal of Queen Victoria, 30 October 1882, in Buckle, *Letters of Queen Victoria*, pp. 354–56.

57. Queen to Granville, 17 September 1882, in Buckle, *Letters of Queen Victoria*, p. 334; Salisbury to House of Lords, 26 October 1882, *Hansard*, vol. 274.

58. M. Pegram, *The Wolseley Heritage* (London, 1939), p. 35.

59. Cambridge to Wolseley, 6 October 1882, Cambridge MSS, RA, E/1/10210.

60. John Ardagh (1840–1907), joined Royal Engineers, 1858; Deputy Assistant Quartermaster General for intelligence at the War Office, 1876; reported on defence of Constantinople, 1876; attended Congress of Berlin, 1878; Chief of Intelligence for Egypt campaign, 1882; restored Alexandria after bombardment, present at battles of Tel-el-Kebir (1882) and El Teb (1884); commandant at Cairo during Gordon Relief expedition, 1884–85; Assistant Adjutant General, 1887; private secretary to Viceroy of India, 1888–94; Director of Military Intelligence, 1896–1901; British delegate at conference to revise Geneva Convention on conduct of war, 1906.

61. Hartington to Wolseley, 30 December 1882, WPP, autograph; Wolseley to Hartington, 4 January 1883, Devonshire MSS, 340.1307; Granville to Gladstone, 9 January 1883, BL, Add. Ms 44175; Wolseley to Hartington, 20 February 1883, 340.1334.

62. Speech by Randolph Churchill, 18 December 1883, in W. S. Churchill, *Lord Randolph Churchill* (London, 1906), i, p. 280; Lord Cromer, *Modern Egypt* (London, 1908), p. 329; E. M. Carroll, *French Public Opinion and Foreign Affairs* (New York, 1931), p. 94.

63. Circular to the Powers, Dufferin, 3 January 1883, in Cromer, *Modern Egypt* p. 340.
64. Gladstone to House of Commons, 2 November 1882, *Hansard*, vol. 274.
65. Ponsonby to Granville, 2 November 1882, in Buckle, *Letters of Queen Victoria*, p. 357; Ashmead-Bartlett to House of Commons, 10 November 1882, *Hansard*, vol. 274.
66. Memorandum on measures to be taken after the defeat of Hicks Pasha's force, Wolseley, 23 November 1883, WOP, W31.
67. Hartington to Granville, 23 November 1883, in B. Holland, *Life of Spencer Compton, 8th Duke of Devonshire* (London, 1911), pp. 411–12; Dufferin to Granville, 1 December 1883, in A. Lyall, *The Life of the Marquis of Dufferin and Ava* (London, 1905), p. 56.
68. Cromer, *Modern Egypt*, p. 395.

Chapter 13: Sudan

1. Clarke to Childers, January 1884, in S. Childers, *The Life and Correspondence of the Right Hon. Hugh C. E. Childers* (London, 1901), p. 177; Granville to Gladstone, 27 November 1883, BL, Add. Ms 44176; Gladstone to Granville, 29 November 1883, BL, Add. Ms 44547; Granville to Queen, 12 January 1884, in G. E. Buckle and A. C. Benson (eds), *The Letters of Queen Victoria*, second series, iii (London, 1907–32), pp. 469–70.
2. Evelyn Baring, first Earl of Cromer (1841–1917), joined Royal Artillery, 1855; served in Ionian Islands, Malta and Jamaica, 1858–67; entered Staff College; private secretary to Lord Northbrook, Governor-General of India, 1872–76; went to Cairo in 1877 as first British Commissioner of the *Caisse de la Dette* till resignation in 1879; returned to Egypt as British controller after deposition of Ismail, 1879; financial member of Viceroy's council in India, 1880–83; British agent and Consul-General, Egypt, 1883–1907; able administrator who improved Egyptian finances and administration; supporter of evacuation of the Sudan after Gordon's death; supported Kitchener during reconquest of the Sudan, 1896–98; created Egyptian tax and education system; president of the Dardanelles Commission, 1916; author of several books including *Modern Egypt* (1908).
3. Wolseley to Gordon, 4 January 1884, Gordon MSS, BL, Add. Ms 52388.
4. J. Pollock, *Gordon* (London, 1993), p. 267.
5. Wolseley, notes for autobiography, WPP, SSL9.
6. Baring to Granville, 14 January 1884, in Buckle, *Letters of Queen Victoria*, p. 472.
7. Stephenson to Cambridge, 29 January 1884, Cambridge MSS, RA, E/1/10612.
8. Pollock, *Gordon*, p. 272.
9. Granville to Queen, 18 January 1884, in Buckle, *Letters of Queen Victoria*, p. 473; Pollock, *Gordon*, p. 272; Wolseley to Louisa Wolseley, 4 February 1885, WPP, W/P/14.
10. Pollock, *Gordon*, pp. 275–80.

11. Gordon to Dufferin, 11 March 1884, in A. Lyall, *The Life of the Marquis of Dufferin and Ava* (London, 1905), ii, pp. 57–58.

12. Gordon, journal entry, 4 April 1884, BL, Add. Ms 34478. Gordon's journals were censored twice, once by Gordon and then by an unknown hand at the War Office, before publication.

13. Hartington to Queen, 26 March 1884, in Buckle, *Letters of Queen Victoria*, p. 487.

14. Memorandum for the Cabinet, Gladstone, 9 April 1884, in J. Morley, *Life of Gladstone* (London, 1908), pp. 632–36.

15. Notes on the defence of Egypt from the southward, 1884, Ardagh, WOP, W23.

16. Memorandum on the Sudan, Wolseley, 8 February 1884, in B. Holland, *Life of Spencer Compton, 8th Duke of Devonshire* (London, 1911), pp. 425–29; Cambridge to Stephenson, 9 and 16 May 1884, Cambridge MSS, RA, E/1/10741, 10749.

17. Stephenson to Cambridge, 25 March and 5 May 1884, Cambridge MSS, E/1/10700, 10738.

18. J. Symons, *England's Pride: The Story of the Gordon Relief Expedition* (London, 1985), pp. 67, 70–71.

19. Memorandum on the Sudan, Wolseley, 8 April 1884, WOP, W26; Hartington to Gladstone, 11 April 1884 and Gladstone to Hartington, 13 April 1884, both in Holland, *Life of Duke of Devonshire*, pp. 439–40.

20. Memorandum for the Cabinet, Hartington, 15 May 1884, ibid., pp. 459–60.

21. J. Lehmann, *All Sir Garnet* (London, 1964), p. 346.

22. Hartington to Gladstone, 1 July 1884; Hartington to Granville, 15 July 1884, both in Holland, *Life of Duke of Devonshire*, pp. 464–68.

23. Memorandum on the Sudan, Wolseley, 19 July 1884, WOP, W26.

24. Memorandum on the Sudan, Wolseley, 23 July 1884, ibid.

25. Stephenson to Cambridge, 21 July 1884, Cambridge MSS, RA, E/1/10827.

26. Memorandum for the Cabinet, Hartington, 31 July 1884; Gladstone to Granville, 31 July 1884, both in Holland, *Life of Duke of Devonshire*, pp. 472–78.

27. W. Butler, *The Campaign of the Cataracts* (London, 1887), p. 12; Symons, *England's Pride*, pp. 103–07.

28. Symons, *England's Pride*, pp. 98–99.

29. Wolseley to Cambridge, 11 June 1884; Cambridge to Stephenson, 11 June 1884; Hartington to the Queen, 23 August 1884; Wolseley to Cambridge, 23 August 1884, all in Cambridge MSS, RA, E/1/10785, 10786a, 10857–58.

30. Wolseley to Louisa Wolseley, 2 and 13 September 1884, WPP, W/P/13.

31. Wolseley to Cambridge, 13 September 1884, in W. Verner, *The Military Life of HRH George, Duke of Cambridge* (London, 1905), p. 266; Cambridge to Wolseley, 19 September 1884; Wolseley to Cambridge, 26 September 1884, Cambridge MSS, RA, E/1/10901, 10915; Hartington to Wolseley, 19 September 1884, in F. Maurice and G. Arthur, *Life of Lord Wolseley* (London, 1924), p. 182.

32. Wolseley to Louisa Wolseley, 31 December 1884, WPP, W/P/13.

33. Wolseley to Louisa Wolseley, 8 January 1885, WPP, W/P/14; Cambridge to Wolseley, 14 November 1884; Wolseley to Cambridge, 8 September 1884,

Cambridge MSS, RA, E/1/10883, 10955; Wolseley to Cambridge, 11 December 1884, in Verner, *The Life of Cambridge,* pp. 273.

34. Burnaby had offended the Duke of Cambridge by his unauthorised ride to Khiva in the depth of Russian Central Asia, the Prince of Wales with personal criticism, and the government over its policy towards Gordon.

35. Charles Beresford (1846–1919), entered navy, 1859; Conservative MP, 1874–80; took part in bombardment of Alexandria, 1882; served on Gordon Relief expedition, 1884–85; MP, 1885–89; fourth naval Lord of Admiralty, 1886–88; MP, 1897–1900 and 1902–03; command of Channel Squadron, 1903; Commander-in-Chief, Mediterranean, 1905; Commander-in-Chief of Channel Fleet, 1907–09; clashed with Fisher over Admiralty policy; MP, 1910–16.

36. Charles Wilson (1836–1905), joined Royal Engineers, 1855; made surveys in Jerusalem, Palestine and Sinai, 1864–69; first director of topographical department, War Office, 1870; head of Ordnance Survey in Ireland, 1876–86; British military consul-general in Anatolia and Asia Minor, 1879–82; military attaché to British agency in Egypt, 1882–83; chief of intelligence in Gordon Relief expedition, 1884–85; Director General of Ordnance Survey of the United Kingdom, 1886–93; Director-General of Military Education, 1892–98.

37. Wolseley to Louisa Wolseley, 10 November 1884, WPP, W/P/13; S. Lee, *King Edward VII* (London, 1925), i, p. 170; Wolseley to Cambridge, 4 April 1885, Cambridge MSS, M858/47; Wolseley to Hartington, 16 August 1884, WPP, PLB/1. Valentine Baker had been forced to resign his army commission after being found guilty of assaulting a young woman in a railway carriage.

38. H. Colville, *History of the Sudan Campaign* (London, 1889), pp. 103–05.

39. Wolseley, journal entry, 9 October 1884, PRO, WO 147/8; Lehmann, *All Sir Garnet,* p. 357.

40. Hartington to Wolseley, 9 October 1884, WOP, W26.

41. Colville, *History of the Sudan Campaign,* p. 61.

42. Lehmann, *All Sir Garnet,* p. 356; Colville, *History of the Sudan Campaign,* p. 107; Wolseley, journal entry, 17 November 1884.

43. M. Prior, *Campaigns of a War Correspondent* (London, 1912), p. 207.

44. Wolseley to Louisa Wolseley, 27 September 1884, WPP, W/P/13; P. Marling, *Rifleman and Hussar* (London, 1931), p. 124.

45. Wolseley to Frances Wolseley, 12 October 1884, in M. Pegram, *The Wolseley Heritage* (London, 1939), p. 42.

46. Count Gleichen, *With the Camel Corps Up the Nile* (London, 1888), p. 33; C. Beresford, *The Memoirs of Admiral Lord Charles Beresford* (London, 1914), p. 328.

47. Butler, *Campaign of the Cataracts,* pp. 95, 204, 228; W. Butler, *An Autobiography* (London, 1911), p. 277.

48. Wolseley had heard the news of the murders when he reached Wadi Halfa but did not know about the loss of the ciphers until now. One key was 'the Christian name of his mother's father', and 'the number of "Cash" in a stated number of "Taels", with the day of the month on which he himself was born added

thereto as the key to the other'. Wolseley also told Gordon of the date on which the army should be concentrated at Debbeh, being so many days from this year's anniversary of his being made a Major-General. Wolseley, journal entry, 17 November 1884.

49. Wolseley, journal entry, 30 November 1884.

50. Ibid., 17 December 1884; Wolseley to Louisa Wolseley, 23 December 1884, WPP, W/P/13.

51. Colville, *History of Sudan Campaign*, p. 133; H. Brackenbury, *The River Column* (Edinburgh, 1885), p. 2.

52. Wolseley, journal entry, 27 December 1884.

53. Wolseley to Buller, 16 February 1885, Buller MSS, PRO, WO 132/2.

54. Wolseley to Louisa Wolseley, 31 December 1884, WPP, W/P/13.

55. Pollock, *Gordon*, p. 311; Wolseley, journal entry, 1 January 1885.

56. Gleichen, *With the Camel Corps*, pp. 129–30.

57. Beresford, *Memoirs*, p. 263.

58. Sir H. Newbolt, 'Vitaï Lampada', in L. James, *The Rise and Fall of the British Empire* (London, 1994), p. 277.

59. Colville, *History of the Sudan Campaign*, ii, p. 32.

60. Wolseley to Louisa Wolseley, 22 January 1885, WPP, W/P/14; Wolseley, journal entry, 28 January 1885. Stewart died on 16 February.

61. Marling, *Rifleman and Hussar*, pp. 137–39.

62. Wolseley to Louisa Wolseley, 28 January 1885, WPP, W/P/14; Wolseley to Hartington, 28 January 1885, Devonshire MSS, 340.1649.

63. Colville, *History of the Sudan Campaign*, pp. 33–38.

64. Ibid., p. 52; Wolseley, journal entry, 4 February 1885; Wolseley to Hartington, 4 February 1885, WOP, W26; Wolseley to Buller, 4 February 1885, PRO, WO 132/2.

65. Hamilton, diary entry, 5 February 1885, in D. W. R. Bahlman, *The Diary of Sir Edward Walter Hamilton* (Oxford, 1972), pp. 788–89; Queen Victoria, journal entry, 5 February 1885, in Buckle, *Letters of Queen Victoria*, p. 597.

66. Wolseley to Louisa Wolseley, 4 February 1885, WPP, W/P/14; Hartington to Wolseley, 6 February 1885, WOP, W26.

67. Wolseley to Cambridge, 2 March 1885, Cambridge MSS, RA, E/1/11078.

68. Wolseley to Hartington, 7 and 8 February 1885, WOP, W26.

69. Brackenbury, *The River Column*, pp. 162–69.

70. Beresford, *Memoirs*, p. 324; Colville, *History of the Sudan Campaign*, p. 56.

71. Wolseley, journal entry, 17 February 1885; Brackenbury, *The River Column*, p. 284; Wolseley to Hartington, 23 February 1884, WOP, W26.

72. Pollock, *Gordon*, p. 317.

73. Reports by Salome, 11 February and 5 March 1885, PRO, HD 3/67; Wolseley, journal entry, 23 March 1885.

74. Wolseley to Louisa Wolseley, 14 February 1885, WPP, W/P/14; Wolseley, journal entries, 4 October 1884 and 10 February 1885.

75. Wolseley, journal entry, 4 February 1885.

76. Wolseley to Cambridge, 1 June 1896, in J. A. Spender, *The Life of the Right Honourable Sir Henry Campbell-Bannerman* (London, 1923), p. 210; quoted in Lehmann, *All Sir Garnet*, p. 378.

77. Wolseley to Louisa Wolseley, 22 February 1885, WPP, W/P/14; Ponsonby, diary entry, 15 July 1885, in A. Ponsonby, *Henry Ponsonby: Queen Victoria's Secretary* (London, 1942), p. 236.

78. E. Hamley, 'Gordon, Wolseley and Sir Charles Wilson', *Blackwoods*, 137 (June 1885), pp. 872–79; C. Wilson, *From Korti to Khartoum* (Edinburgh, 1886), p. 281.

79. *Army and Navy Gazette*, 13 September 1884.

80. Butler, *Campaign of the Cataracts*, p. 261.

81. Ian Hamilton (1853–1947), joined army, 1872; served in First South African War, 1881; aide-de-camp to Lord Roberts in India, 1882–90; served in Gordon Relief expedition, 1884–85; Assistant Adjutant General, Bengal, 1890–93; military secretary to George White, 1893–95; Deputy Quartermaster General, Simla, 1895–97; Commandant of Musketry School, Hythe, 1898; served in South Africa; present at siege of Ladysmith, later commanded mounted infantry division and then Chief of Staff to Lord Kitchener, 1899–1902; Quartermaster General, 1903–04; head of military mission to Japan, 1904–05; Southern Command, 1905–09; Adjutant General, 1909–10; Mediterranean Command, 1910–14; commanded army in Dardanelles campaign, 1915.

82. I. Hamilton, *Listening for the Drums* (London, 1944), p. 176; Wilson, *From Korti to Khartoum*, p. 33

83. Gleichen, *With the Camel Corps*, p. 47; Wolseley, journal entry, 21 January 1885; Wolseley, notes for autobiography, WPP, SSL9.

84. Wolseley to Cambridge, 4 April 1885, Cambridge MSS, M858/47.

85. Smith to Wolseley, 6 August 1885, WPP, Autograph; Ponsonby to Smith, 10 October 1885; Wolseley to Smith, 13 October 1885, both in Smith MSS, PRO, WO 110/1.

86. Wolseley, journal entry, 1 March 1885; Wolseley to Hartington, 9 March 1885, 340.1677.

87. Hartington to Wolseley, 12 March 1885, PRO, WO 32/6351.

88. Wolseley, journal entries, 19 February and 6 March 1885.

89. Wolseley to Hartington, 20 March 1885, WOP, W26; Wolseley, journal entries, 13, 14 April 1885.

90. Reginald Brett, Viscount Esher (1852–1930), private secretary to Hartington, 1878–85; Liberal MP, 1880–85; Secretary, Office of Public Works, 1895–1902; succeeded father, 1899; superintended funeral of Queen Victoria and coronation of King Edward VII; member of Royal Commission on War in South Africa, 1902; chairman of War Office Reconstruction Committee, 1903; joined Committee of imperial Defence, 1904; *eminence grise* and supporter of army reform including establishment of General Staff.

91. Wolseley to Hartington, 12 April 1885; Hartington to Wolseley, 13 April 1885; Wolseley to Hartington, 14 April 1885; Hartington to Wolseley, 20 April 1885 all in WOP, W26; Brett to Wolseley, 17 April 1885, in M. V. Brett (ed.), *Journals*

and Letters of Reginald Viscount Esher (London, 1934), pp. 113–14; 20 April 1885, *Hansard*, vol. 297.

92. Wolseley to Cromer, 21 April 1885, Cromer MSS, PRO, FO 633/7; Wolseley to Hartington, 14 and 15 April, WOP, W26; Hartington to Wolseley, 17 April 1885, in Holland, *Life of Duke of Devonshire*, pp. 33–36.

93. Wolseley, journal entry, 3 May 1885; Wolseley to Louisa Wolseley, 5 and 12 May 1885, WPP, W/P/14.

94. Wolseley, journal entry, 30 May 1885.

95. Wolseley to Louisa Wolseley, 12 June 1885, WPP, W/P/14.

96. Wolseley, journal entries, 27 and 28 June 1885; Wolseley to Smith, 29 June 1885, PRO, WO 110/3.

97. Smith to Wolseley, 2 July 1885, PRO, PRO 30/6/130; Smith to Wolseley, 5 July 1885, WPP, Autograph.

98. Earl of Cromer, *Modern Egypt* (London, 1908), p. 30.

Chapter 14: Back at the War Office

1. W. Butler, *An Autobiography* (London, 1911), p. 173.

2. E. Wood, 'The Ashanti Expedition of 1873–74', *Journal of the Royal United Services Institute*, 18 (1875), pp. 331–57; Queen to Granville, 11 October 1882, in G. E. Buckle and A. C. Benson (eds), *The Letters of Queen Victoria* (London, 1926–28), second series, iii, p. 346.

3. A. Forbes, *Memories and Studies of War and Peace* (London, 1895), pp. 354–55; A. Ponsonby, *Henry Ponsonby: Queen Victoria's Secretary* (London, 1942), pp. 223–24.

4. I. Hamilton, *Listening for the Drums* (London, 1944), pp. 130, 170.

5. Wolseley to Louisa Wolseley, 15 January 1885, WPP, W/P/14; *Royal United Service Magazine*, 57 (April 1913), p. 446.

6. A. Preston, *In Relief of Gordon* (London, 1967), introduction, p. 43; J. Lehmann, *All Sir Garnet* (London, 1964).

7. Wolseley to Duchess of Edinburgh, February 1887, in F. Maurice and G. Arthur, *The Life of Lord Wolseley* (London, 1924), p. 227.

8. William Smith (1825–91), expanded father's newsagent business by opening railway bookstalls; Conservative MP from 1868; First Lord of the Admiralty, 1877; Secretary of State for War, 1886–87; First Lord of the Treasury and leader of the House, 1886.

   Henry Campbell-Bannerman (1836–1908), Liberal MP; Financial Secretary at the War Office, 1871–72 and 1880–82; Secretary to the Admiralty, 1882–84; Chief Secretary for Ireland, 1884–85; Secretary of State for War, 1886 and 1892–95; sat on Hartington Commission, 1888–90; member of committee on Jameson Raid, 1896–97; became leader of Liberal Party, 1899; Prime Minister, 1905–08.

   Edward Stanhope (1840–1893), Conservative MP; Under Secretary for India, 1878–80; President of the Board of Trade, 1885; Colonial Secretary, 1886; Secretary of State for War, 1887–92.

9. Louisa Wolseley to Wolseley, 22 April and 22 November 1886, WPP, LW/P/12.
10. Maurice and Arthur, *Life of Wolseley*, pp. 247–48; L. Edel, *Henry James: A Life* (London, 1985), p. 225.
11. J. F. C. Harrison, *Late Victorian Britain* (London, 1990), p. 170.
12. Superintendent of Royal Laboratory Woolwich to Director of Artillery, 25 February 1886; Wolseley to Surveyor General of Ordnance 2 March and 22 April 1886, both in PRO, WO 32/7068; Royal Commission on Warlike Stores (1887), 14; (1888), 25.
13. G. J. Wolseley, 'The Army', in T. H. Ward (ed.), *The Reign of Queen Victoria* (London, 1887), pp. 155–225.
14. Brackenbury, General sketch of the situation abroad and at home from a military standpoint, 3 August 1886, PRO, WO 33/46.
15. Speech by Brodrick, *The Times*, 2 February 1888.
16. Speech by Wolseley, *The Times*, 26 April 1888.
17. Salisbury to the House of Lords, 1 May 1888, *Hansard*, vol. 326; Wolseley to Salisbury, 12 May 1888, Salisbury MSS.
18. Wolseley to the House of Lords, 14 May 1888, *Hansard*, vol. 326.
19. Wolseley to the House of Lords, 29 June 1888, *Hansard*, vol. 327; Hamilton to Salisbury, 29 June 1888, Salisbury MSS.
20. Report in explanation of statements made by Lord Randolph Churchill's Wolverhampton speech, June 1887, PRO, CAB 37/20; abstract of the report on the meat, wheat and coal supply of London, 1887, WOP, W18; report of the committee to consider the plans for the fortification and armament of our military and mercantile ports, 1887, PRO, WO 33/47.
21. Memorandum on a French invasion, 8 June 1888, WOP, W18.
22. Memorandum on the defence of England, 17 April 1888, PRO, WO 33/48; memorandum on a French invasion, 29 June 1888, PRO, CAB 37/21; memorandum on the defence of London, 16 July 1888, PRO, WO 33/48.
23. Memoranda on the defence of London, 9 November 1888; 12 November 1888; 22 November 1888. All PRO, CAB 37/20; memorandum on home defence, Wolseley, 21 November 1888, Stanhope MSS, 0232/2. Two notable military men, Sir Edward Hamley and G. S. Clarke, opposed the system of permanent fortifications largely on the grounds of cost. E. Hamley, 'The Defencelessness of London', *Nineteenth Century*, 23 (May 1888), pp. 633–40; G. S. Clarke, *My Working Life*, (London, 1898), pp. 45–46. Wood and Butler also recorded the problems encountered in finding suitable sites. E. Wood, *From Midshipman to Field Marshal*, ii, p. 188; W. Butler, *An Autobiography* (London, 1911), p. 355.
24. I. F. W. Beckett, 'Edward Stanhope at the War Office, 1887–92', *Journal of Strategic Studies*, 5 (June 1982), pp. 278–307.
25. Wolseley, evidence to the Royal Commission to inquire into the Civil and Professional Administration of the Naval and Military Departments, c. 5979 (1890), 19 [Hartington Commission], Q. 77. The evidence presented to this committee was so revealing that the commissioners declined to publish the evidence along with their report. Wolseley's evidence can be found in WPP, W/MEM/3.

26. Correspondence between the Admiralty and the War Office on the invasion issue can be found in PRO, ADM 1/7046; report of the Landing Places Committee, 15 October 1894, PRO, WO 33/54. This must provide one of the few examples of a committee voting itself out of existence.

27. A. J. Marder, *British Naval Policy 1880–1905* (London, 1941); P. Kennedy, *The Rise and Fall of British Naval Mastery* (London, 1983).

28. Wolseley to Maurice, March 1897, in Maurice and Arthur, *Life of Wolseley*, p. 285.

29. Salisbury to Baring, 17 February 1888, in G. Cecil, *Life of Robert, Marquess of Salisbury* (London, 1921–32), iv, p. 95.

30. Wolseley to Cambridge, 18 February 1889, Cambridge MSS, RA, E/1/12394.

31. Cambridge to Ponsonby, 7 February 1890; Ponsonby to Cambridge, 13 February 1890; Cambridge to Ponsonby, 17 February 1890, all in G. E. Buckle and A. C. Benson (eds), *The Letters of Queen Victoria* (London, 1930–32), third series, i, pp. 563–71.

32. Dilke to Wolseley, 17 March 1887, WPP, Autograph.
    Charles Dilke (1843–1911), politician and author; Radical MP, 1868–86; leader of radical section of Liberal Party, 1880; Under Secretary at the Foreign Office, 1880–82; President of the Local Government Board, 1882–85; co-respondent in divorce suit, 1885–86 which led to his rejection by the voters and ostracism by the public; MP, 1892–1911; travelled widely and prolific author and commentator on imperial defence.

33. C. Dilke, *The British Army* (London, 1888), p. 140; cf. Wolseley to Dilke, 19 November 1887, BL, Add. Ms 43914.

34. Memorandum on the establishment of the army, 20 October 1883, PRO, WO 32/6705.

35. Memorandum on the size of the army, 12 November 1885, WPP, W/MEM/1; Campbell-Bannerman to Harcourt, 10 February 1886, in J. A. Spender, *The Life of the Right Hon. Sir Henry Campbell-Bannerman* (London, 1923), p. 101.

36. Memorandum on Indian defence, 25 August 1889, PRO, WO 33/A175.

37. Roberts to Brownlow, 9 March 1888, and Roberts to Chapman, 1 February 1889, Roberts MSS, 7101-23-100.

38. H. B. Hanna, *Can Russia Invade India?* (London, 1895); idem, *India's Scientific Frontier: Where Is It?* (London, 1895); idem, *Backwards or Forwards?* (London, 1896); analysis of General Kuropatkin's scheme for the invasion of India, Grierson and Brackenbury, August 1886, WOP, W24.

39. S. Wilkinson and C. Dilke, *Imperial Defence* (London, 1892), p. 107; meeting at the War Office, 1 April 1887, PRO, WO 163; memorandum on the defence of India, India Office, 1891, PRO, CAB 37/30.

40. Memorandum on the army, Wolseley, 8 June 1888, PRO, WO 33/48; memorandum on the army, Stanhope, 8 December 1888, Stanhope MSS, 0232/2.

41. Memorandum on the Stanhope Memorandum, 30 December 1888, WPP, W/MEM/3.

42. Speech to the 20th Middlesex Volunteers, Wolseley, *The Times*, 11 February 1889.

43. Wolseley to Richard Wolseley, 17 November 1886, WPP, 163/5; Wolseley to Louisa Wolseley, 15 February and 15 March 1887, WPP, W/P/16.

44. Maurice and Arthur, *Life of Wolseley*, p. 248.

45. Speech to 2nd Volunteer Battalion of Royal Fusiliers, Wolseley, *The Times*, 7 December 1887; speech to the Volunteers, 1st Battalion Royal Warwickshire Regiment, Wolseley, *The Times*, 28 January 1889.

46. Jowett to Wolseley, 17 February 1889, WPP, Autograph.

47. Speech to the undergraduates of Oxford, Wolseley, *The Times*, 13 May 1889; Jowett to Wolseley, 17 May 1889, WPP, Autograph.

48. Wolseley to Cambridge, June 1883, RA, E/1/10445.

49. Speech to the North London Rifle Club, Wolseley, *The Times*, 22 February 1889; Wolseley to Connaught, 30 September 1889, WPP, PLB/1.

50. Wolseley to Connaught, 30 September 1889, WPP, PLB/1.

51. Wood, *From Midshipman to Field Marshal*, pp. 198, 220–21; Bury to Smith, 4 and 6 November 1885, Smith MSS, PRO, WO 110/1. Viscount Bury, the Under Secretary, was the president of the committee on concentration.

52. Memorandum on the Army Estimates, 16 December 1889, PRO, WO 33/39.

53. H. Belloc, *The Modern Traveller* (London, 1898).

54. Wolseley to Surveyor General of Ordnance, 27 August 1885, WPP, W/MEM/1; précis of the history of machine guns, November 1886, PRO, WO 32/8901; J. Ellis, *The Social History of the Machine Gun* (New York, 1975), p. 57.

55. Ellis, *History of the Machine Gun*, pp. 57–64.

56. Wolseley to Richard Wolseley, 17 November 1886, WPP, 163/5. Wolseley also acted to improve the quality of instruction at the Staff College by sending Frederick Maurice there to teach military history.

57. Thompson to Campbell-Bannerman, 5 January 1895, BL, Add. Ms 41230.

58. Stanhope to Cambridge, 30 June 1890, RA, E/1/12619.

59. Memorandum on army expenditure, 20 August 1887, PRO, WO 33/48; Stanhope to Queen, 25 June 1889, 0250/3; memorandum for the Cabinet, Stanhope, 27 June 1889, PRO, CAB 37/25.

60. A. Haliburton, *Army Organisation* (London, 1898), pp. 83–84; B. Bond, *The Victorian Army and the Staff College* (London, 1972), p. 174.

61. Ponsonby to Stanhope, 30 November 1888, in Buckle, *Letters of Victoria*, p. 455.

62. Evidence to the Hartington Commission, Wolseley, Q. 197.

63. Ibid., QQ. 202, 205.

64. Report of the Hartington Commission.

65. Dissent to the report of the Hartington Commission, Churchill; dissent to the report of the Hartington Commission, Campbell-Bannerman; Campbell-Bannerman to Hartington, 12 January 1890, Devonshire MSS, 340.2225.

66. Memorandum on the Hartington Commission, Wolseley, 31 March 1890, Stanhope MSS, 0231/1; Wolseley to Ponsonby, 10 April 1890, in Buckle, *Letters of Victoria*, pp. 584–85.

67. Stanhope to Cambridge, 28 April 1890, Stanhope MSS, 0254/3.

68. Buller to Cambridge, 20 September 1890 in Verner, *Life of Cambridge*, p. 359.

69. Cambridge to Wolseley, 29 September 1890, in Maurice and Arthur, *Life of Wolseley*, p. 254; Stanhope to Wolseley, 28 September 1890, Stanhope MSS, 0314.
70. Wolseley to Louisa Wolseley, 3 August 1890, WPP, W/P/19.

Chapter 15: Ireland

1. In 1890 the Duke of Cambridge was seventy-one years old and had been Commander-in-Chief for thirty-six years; Wolseley was fifty-seven.
2. Wolseley to Stanhope, April 1890, in F. Maurice and G. Arthur, *The Life of Lord Wolseley* (London, 1924), p. 249. Stanhope was very angry over Wolseley's refusal to go to India. He believed it was part of a plot by the Queen to have the Duke of Connaught appointed to the Indian command. Stanhope to Salisbury, 29 April 1890, Salisbury MSS.
3. The correspondence between the Queen and Stanhope can be found in Stanhope MSS, 0250/1.
4. N. Frankland, *Witness of a Century: The Life and Times of Prince Arthur, Duke of Connaught* (London, 1993), pp. 182–84.
5. Louisa Wolseley to Wolseley, 10 August 1890, WPP, LW/P/16.
6. On this occasion the troops opened fire on an unruly crowd killing two men and injuring another twelve. A. Babington, *Military Intervention in Britain* (London, 1990), pp. 123–31.
7. E. A. Muenger, *The British Military Dilemma in Ireland* (Kansas, 1991), pp. 7–8, 73.
8. Ibid., p. 68; Morley to Wolseley, 13 April 1893, WPP, Autograph. Irish recruitment continued to fall so that by the turn of the century Irishmen formed only 13 per cent of the army, a fall of 8 per cent since 1881.
9. Irish soldiers had more than their fair share of court-martials but these were normally for relatively minor offences. P. Karsten, 'Irish Soldiers in the British Army', *Journal of Social History*, 17 (1983), pp. 31–64.
10. Wolseley to Buller, 28 May 1892, PRO, WO 32/6689.
11. Wolseley to Frances Wolseley, 6 October 1890, in M. Pegram, *The Wolseley Heritage* (London, 1939), p. 75. The 1891 census revealed that approximately 75 per cent of the population was Catholic.
12. Wolseley to Cambridge, 1 January 1893, Cambridge MSS, RA, E/1/12892.
13. Ibid.
14. The Conservative Party had been renamed the Conservative and Unionist Party after it absorbed those Liberals, such as Lord Hartington and Joseph Chamberlain, who opposed Gladstone's plans for Home Rule for Ireland.
15. Under the plans for Home Rule the new Irish Parliament would have had limited powers. Westminster would have retained control over Irish foreign, imperial and fiscal policy. R. F. Foster, *Modern Ireland* (London, 1989), p. 423.
16. Wolseley to Maurice, undated but probably 1893, Maurice MSS, Liddell Hart Centre, 2/2/18.
17. Quoted in Foster, *Modern Ireland*, p. 421.

18. Wolseley to Cambridge, 23 April 1893, RA, E/1/12945; Wolseley to Maurice, undated but probably 1893, Maurice MSS, Liddell Hart Centre, 2/2/18; Wolseley to Louisa Wolseley, 13 June 1893, WPP, W/P/22; Wolseley to Cambridge, 30 May 1893, in W. Verner, *The Military Life of HRH George, Duke of Cambridge* (London, 1905), pp. 381–82.

19. Wolseley to Cambridge, 12 March 1892, in Verner, *Life of Cambridge*, p. 366.

20. Quoted in Verner, *Life of Cambridge*, p. 365.

21. Cambridge to Wolseley, 26 November 1890, in Verner, *Life of Cambridge*, p. 363; Wolseley to Fleetwood Wilson, 26 and 28 January 1891, Wolseley MSS, National Library of Ireland, 15724.

22. Wolseley to Cambridge, 18 and 21, August 1892, Verner, *Life of Cambridge*, pp. 378–79; report of the autumn manoeuvres in Hampshire, 20 November 1891, PRO, WO 279/1.

23. Wolseley to Campbell-Bannerman, 9 February 1894, Campbell-Bannerman MSS, BL, Add. Ms 41233; Thompson to Campbell-Bannerman, 1 January 1895, BL, Add. Ms 41230.

24. Wolseley to Haliburton, 1891, in Maurice and Arthur, *Life of Wolseley*, p. 262. Haliburton was a member of the Wantage Committee; Wolseley to Campbell-Bannerman, 6 December 1892, BL, Add. Ms 41233.

25. Roberts to Gordon, 10 August 1891, Roberts MSS, NAM, 7101–23–82; Brackenbury to Roberts, 26 September 1891, 7101–23–11.

26. Roberts to Cambridge, 16 August 1891, 7101–23–100/3.

27. Summary of evidence to the Committee to Consider the Terms and Conditions of Service in the Army [Wantage Committee], PRO, WO 33/52.

28. Evidence to the Wantage Committee, Wolseley, Q. 8516.

29. Ibid., Q. 4379.

30. Ibid., QQ. 8516, 4547, 8643, 4380–81.

31. Ibid., QQ. 4674, 4454.

32. Ibid., QQ. 4467–74.

33. Ibid., QQ. 4430–38.

34. General Annual Return of the Army, c. 6722 (1892), 50.

35. Report of the Committee to Consider the Terms and Conditions of Service in the Army, c. 6582 (1892), 19, paragraph 98.

36. Ibid., underlining as in the report.

37. Memorandum on the cavalry reserve, Wolseley, 28 December 1885, Smith MSS, PRO, WO 110/3; evidence to the Wantage Committee, Wolseley, Q. 4595.

38. Report of the Wantage Committee, paragraphs 122–23.

39. Evidence to the Wantage Committee, Duke of Cambridge, Q. 2022; Wolseley, Q. 8679; report of the Wantage Committee, paragraph 102.

40. Meetings of the War Office Council, 4 and 19 March and 1 November 1892, PRO, WO 163/4b; summary of the recommendations of Lord Wantage's Committee and of the discussions thereof at various War Office meetings, PRO, WO 33/52.

41. Wolseley to Louisa Wolseley, 5 and 11 January 1893, WPP, W/P/22.

42. Wolseley to Louisa Wolseley, 26 November 1894, WPP, W/P/23.
43. Wolseley to Louisa Wolseley, 7 May 1891, WPP, W/P/20; 29 January 1892, WPP, W/P/21.
44. Wolseley to George Wolseley, 3 March and 21 September 1892, WPP, W/W4.
45. Wolseley to George Wolseley, 19 January 1893 and 13 January 1899, WPP, W/W4.
46. Wolseley to Frances Wolseley, 4 May 1894, in M. Pegram, *The Wolseley Heritage* (London, 1939), pp. 100–01.
47. Wolseley to Louisa Wolseley, 5 and 8 April, 15 September 1894, WPP, W/P/24.
48. Wolseley to Louisa Wolseley, 3 August 1892, WPP, W/P/21.
49. Wolseley to Louisa Wolseley, 13 May 1891, WPP, W/P/20.
50. Wolseley to Louisa Wolseley, 1 May 1894, WPP, W/P/24.
51. A. Forbes, 'The Recruiting Problem', *Nineteenth Century*, 29 (March 1891), pp. 398–404.
52. Wolseley to Louisa Wolseley, 1 November 1890, WPP, W/P/19.
53. R. Robinson and J. Gallagher, *Africa and the Victorians* (London, 1961), p. 313.
54. Cambridge to Queen, 4 May 1895; Queen to Cambridge, 19 May 1895, both in Verner, *Life of Cambridge*, pp. 395–96; Buller to Campbell-Bannerman, 6 June 1895, BL, Add. Ms 41212; Bigge to Campbell-Bannerman, 21 May 1895, BL, Add. Ms 41206; B. Bond, 'The Retirement of the Duke of Cambridge', *Journal of the Royal United Services Institute*, 41 (November 1961), pp. 544–53.
55. Queen to Bigge, 16 June 1895, in G. E. Buckle and A. C. Benson (eds), *The Letters of Queen Victoria* (London, 1930–32), third series, ii, p. 519.

Chapter 16: Commander-in-Chief

1. Wolseley to Salisbury, August 1895, in F. Maurice and G. Arthur, *The Life of Lord Wolseley* (London, 1924), p. 277; Wolseley to Ardagh, 5 and 12 July 1895, Ardagh MSS, PRO, PRO 30/40/2.
2. Wolseley to Wood, 11 July 1895, Wolseley MSS, Duke University.
3. Buller to Campbell-Bannerman, 18 June 1895, Campbell-Bannerman MSS, BL, Add. Ms 412212.
4. Lansdowne to Salisbury, 4 August 1895, Salisbury MSS.
   Henry Petty-Fitzmaurice, fifth Marquess of Lansdowne (1845–1927), junior Lord of the Treasury, 1869; Under Secretary for War, 1872–74; Under Secretary of State for India, 1880; Governor-General of Canada, 1883–88; Viceroy of India, 1888–94; Secretary of State for War, 1895–1900; Foreign Secretary, 1901–05; introduced the Bill to reform House of Lords, 1911; pledged Unionist party to support Liberal government on outbreak of First World War and joined first coalition administration; proponent of peace feelers towards Germany, 1916–17.
5. Memorandum by Ardagh, 6 August 1895, Ardagh MSS, PRO, PRO 30/40/13; Wolseley to George Wolseley, 7 August 1895, WPP, W/W/4.
6. Lansdowne to Queen, 7 August 1895; Queen to Salisbury, 11 August 1895, in G. E. Buckle and A. C. Benson, (eds) *The Letters of Queen Victoria* (London, 1930–32), third series, ii, pp. 545–46; further letters between the government and

the Queen, ibid., pp. 546–53; Queen to Lansdowne, 17 August 1895, in Lord Newton, *Lord Lansdowne* (London, 1929) p. 133.

7. Wolseley to Ardagh, 5 July 1895, Ardagh MSS, PRO, PRO 30/40.

8. Buller to Campbell-Bannerman, 28 June 1899; Campbell-Bannerman to Buller, 29 June 1899, Campbell-Bannerman MSS, BL, Add. Ms 41212

9. The four heads of department were the Adjutant General, the Quartermaster General, the Inspector General of Fortifications and the Inspector General of Ordnance.

10. Draft Order in Council relative to the War Department, Campbell-Bannerman, June 1895, PRO, WO 33/56; changes consequent upon the retirement of HRH the Duke of Cambridge, Lansdowne, 12 August 1895, PRO, CAB 37/40. The term of office for the Commander-in-Chief was to be limited to five years. Cardwell had wanted to impose this in 1871 but traded an unlimited term of office for the Duke of Cambridge in return for the Duke's support for the army reforms in the House of Lords. Cardwell to Cambridge, 3 June 1871, in W. Verner, *The Military Life of HRH George, Duke of Cambridge* (London, 1905), p. 9.

11. Wolseley telegram to Salisbury, 9 October 1895, Salisbury MSS.

12. Wolseley to Lansdowne, August 1895, in Maurice and Arthur, *Life of Wolseley*, p. 278.

13. Wolseley to Lansdowne, 2 and 3 October 1895, Lansdowne MSS, BL, L(5) 37.

14. Wolseley to Wood, 15 September 1895, Duke University; Wolseley to Buller, 3 October 1895, Buller MSS, PRO, WO 132/5.

15. H. S. Wilkinson, *War and Policy* (New York, 1900), p. 295. This book was a compilation of Wilkinson's articles which first appeared in the *National Review* between October 1895 and December 1897.

16. Memorandum on the Commander-in-Chief, Ardagh, 6 August 1895, PRO, PRO 30/40/13.

17. W. Hamer, *The British Army: Civil-Military Relations* (Oxford, 1970), p. 170.

18. E. Wood, *From Midshipman to Field Marshal* (London, 1906), p. 251.

19. Wolseley to George Wolseley, 6 January and 21 September 1899, WPP, W/W/4.

20. Campbell-Bannerman to Knox, 2 January 1897, Campbell-Bannerman MSS, BL, Add. Ms 41221. Both Buller and Wood were holders of the Victoria Cross.

21. Robert Baden-Powell (1857–1941), joined army, 1876; specialised in reconnaissance and scouting; served on Zululand, 1888, Asante, 1895–96, and Matabeleland, 1896 campaigns; intelligence officer, Mediterranean, 1891–93; commanded 5th Dragoon Guards in India, 1897–99; sent to South Africa in 1899 to raise two regiments; held Mafeking during siege of 217 days; raised South African Constabulary, 1900–03; Inspector-General of Cavalry, 1903–07; commanded Northumbrian division of Territorial Force, 1908–10; retired in 1910 to devote himself to the Boy Scout movement which he had inspired with its first camp in 1907 and *Scouting for Boys* (1908); later established Sea Scouts, Girl Guides, Wolf Cubs and Rover Scouts.

22. Memorandum on the establishment, Wolseley, 8 June 1888, PRO, WO 33/48.

23. Chapman to Wolseley, 25 January 1896, Ministry of Defence Library, Military

Policy 57; memorandum on the efficiency of the Regular Army, Wolseley, 22 February 1896, PRO, WO 33/56.

24. Memorandum on the increase to the establishment, Lansdowne, 10 July 1896; memorandum on the increase to the army, Wolseley, 30 October 1896, both in PRO, WO 32/6357.

25. Meeting of the Army Board, December 1896, PRO, WO 32/6357.

26. Memorandum on the strength of the army, Lansdowne, 4 December 1896, in documents submitted to the Royal Commission on the military preparations for the War in South Africa (Elgin Documents), c. 1789–92 (1904), 40–42; memorandum on the increase to the establishment, Lansdowne, 23 December 1897; reply of the Army Board, 29 December 1896, both in PRO, WO 32/6357.

27. M. Pegram, *The Wolseley Heritage* (London, 1939), p. 113; Wolseley to Cambridge, 15 January 1897, Cambridge MSS, RA, E/1/13220; Wolseley to George Wolseley, 25 February and 21 July 1897, WPP, W/W/4.

28. Buller to Campbell-Bannerman, 5 January 1899, Campbell-Bannerman MSS, BL, Add. MS 41212; N. Lyttelton, *Eighty Years Soldiering, Politics, Games* (London, 1927), p. 170; W. W. Gosse, *Aspects and Impressions* (New York, 1922), p. 289.

29. *The Times*, 23 September 1897.

30. H. O. Arnold-Forster, *Army Letters* (London, 1898), p. 5. Arnold-Forster became Secretary of State for War, 1903–05. Because Lansdowne was a member of the Lords, Brodrick was responsible for presenting the case for the increase to the establishment to the Commons. He did so ably and Wolseley wrote to Lansdowne of his approval of Brodrick's speech. Wolseley to Lansdowne, 19 February 1897, Lansdowne MSS, BL, L(5) 37.

Hugh Arnold-Forster (1855–1909), Secretary of Imperial Federation League and advocate of naval efficiency, 1884; Unionist MP; wrote much on army questions; Secretary of the Admiralty, 1901; Secretary of State for War, 1903–05.

St John Brodrick (1856–1942), Conservative and Unionist MP; Financial Secretary to War Office, 1886–92; Under Secretary for War, 1895–98; Under Secretary for Foreign Affairs, 1898–1900; Secretary of State for War, 1900–03; Secretary of State for India, 1903–05; involved in settlement of Ireland, 1921.

31. Memorandum on the increase to the establishment, Wolseley, 3 November 1897, PRO, WO 32/6357.

32. Memorandum on the increase to the establishment, Lansdowne, 3 November 1897; report of the committee on four battalion regiments, 30 November 1897; meeting of the Army Board, 24 December 1897, all in PRO, WO 32/6357.

33. Outline of army proposals, Lansdowne, 2 December 1897, PRO, CAB 37/45.

34. Salisbury to Queen, 18 December 1897, in Buckle, *Letters of Queen Victoria*, third series, iii, pp. 212–13; Wolseley to Lansdowne, 23 December 1897, L(5) 37.

35. Note on proposals made by the Chancellor of the Exchequer on the strength of the army, Lansdowne, 26 January 1898, PRO, CAB 37/46; memorandum on increases to establishment, Lansdowne, 3 February 1898, PRO, WO 32/6357.

36. Lansdowne to Salisbury, 2 February 1898, in Newton, *Lord Lansdowne*, p. 149.

37. Wolseley's evidence to the Royal Commission on the Military and Civil Expenditure of India was reported in *The Times*, 30 July 1896.
38. *The Times*, 1, 6 and 8 August 1896; Queen to Wolseley, 7 August 1896; Wolseley to Queen, 10 August 1896, both in Buckle, *Letters of Queen Victoria*, third series, iii, pp. 61–63.
39. Discussion of military prize essays, *Journal of the Royal United Services Institute*, 41 (1898), pp. 25–45; outline of army proposals, Lansdowne, 2 December 1897, PRO, CAB 37/45/42.
40. Memorandum on short service, Lansdowne, 12 January 1898; meeting of the Army Board, 24 January 1898, both in PRO, WO 32/6892.
41. Memorandum on the increase to the army and recruitment, Lansdowne, 13 December 1898, PRO, CAB 37/48.
42. Wolseley to Butler, 8 February 1899, Wolseley MSS, Dublin, 15,997.
43. Meeting of the War Office Council, 31 May and 6 November 1891, PRO, WO 163/4; Stanhope to Queen, 31 July and 10 November 1891, Stanhope MSS, 0250/4; Stanhope to Salisbury, 14 December 1891, Salisbury MSS; Rosebery to Campbell-Bannerman, 4 February 1893, Campbell-Bannerman MSS, BL, Add. Ms 41226.
44. Wolseley to Cambridge, 17 November 1896, Cambridge to Wolseley, 19 November 1896, both in Verner, *Life of Cambridge*, pp. 414–15.
45. Memorandum on the Army Reserve, Buller, 1 June 1895, PRO, WO 32/8719; the same wording was used by Lansdowne in a memorandum on 23 March 1896, PRO, WO 32/6720.
46. Meeting of the Army Board, 14 February 1896, PRO, WO 163/4b.
47. Memorandum on the army, Wolseley, 3 November 1897; memorandum by Lansdowne, 5 November 1897; memorandum by Wolseley, 13 November 1897, all in PRO, WO 32/6357.
48. Meeting of the Army Board, 6 January 1898, PRO, WO 163/4b.
49. Memorandum on the Army Reserve, Wolseley, 7 January 1899; memorandum by Stopford, 4 January 1899; Lansdowne to Wolseley, 17 January 1899, all in Elgin Documents.
50. Memorandum on selection, Wolseley, 21 January 1896, PRO, WO 32/6297; Wolseley to White, October 1896, in Maurice and Arthur, *Life of Wolseley*, p. 284.
51. Lansdowne to Salisbury, 29 October 1896, Salisbury MSS.
52. Report of the War Office Committee on selection, 20 November 1897, PRO, WO 32/6297.
53. Wolseley to Lansdowne 16 and 22 September 1898; Lansdowne to Wolseley, 29 November 1898, all in Lansdowne MSS, L(5) 37.
54. Queen to Salisbury, 9 February 1899; Wolseley to Queen, 8 March 1899; Queen to Salisbury and Salisbury to Queen, 10 March 1899; Lansdowne to Salisbury, 23 March 1899; memorandum by Queen, 15 May 1899, all in Buckle, *Letters of Queen Victoria*, third series, iii, pp. 340–65.
55. Wolseley to Lansdowne, 30 November 1895, Lansdowne MSS, L(5) 37.

56. *The Times*, 26 September 1896.

57. Report on the manoeuvres of 1898, Wolseley, 27 October 1898, PRO, WO 279/4.

58. Wolseley to Louisa Wolseley, 4 September 1898, WPP, W/P/27.

59. G. M. Sanderson, *England, Europe and the Upper Nile* (Edinburgh, 1965), pp. 244–45; Wolseley to Lansdowne, 31 March 1896, Lansdowne MSS, L(5) 37; Lord Cromer, *Modern Egypt* (London 1908), p. 106.

60. Herbert Kitchener (1850–1916), joined Royal Engineers, 1871; surveyed Cyprus, 1878; second-in-command of Egyptian Cavalry, 1882; served on Gordon Relief expedition, 1884–85; Governor-General of Eastern Sudan, 1886; Adjutant General of Egyptian Army, 1888; Sirdar of Egyptian Army, 1892–98; reconquered Sudan and Khartoum, 1896–98; Governor-General of Sudan, 1899; Chief of Staff to Roberts in South Africa, 1899–1900; Commander-in-Chief in South Africa, 1900–02, and responsible for countering Boer guerrilla warfare and for the establishment of concentration camps; Commander-in-Chief in India, 1902–09; British agent and consul-general in Egypt, 1911; Secretary of State for War, 1914–16; went down with HMS *Hampshire* on way to Russia.

61. Wolseley to Lansdowne, 10 May 1896; memorandum on the Sudan, Lansdowne, 12 May 1896, both in PRO, CAB 37/41.

62. Lansdowne to Salisbury, 20 October and 28 December 1897, Salisbury MSS.

63. Cromer to Lansdowne, June 1897, in Newton, *Lord Lansdowne*, p. 147; Wolseley to Lansdowne, 5 January 1898, PRO, WO 32/6380; Lansdowne to Grenfell and Grenfell to Lansdowne, 5 January 1898, PRO, WO 33/151; Wolseley to Kitchener, 14 April 1898, Kitchener MSS, PRO, PRO 30/57/10.

64. T. Royle, *The Kitchener Enigma* (London, 1985), p. 134.

65. Wolseley speech to the 2nd Volunteer Battalion Royal Fusiliers, *The Times*, 15 December 1898.

66. T. Pakenham, *The Scramble for Africa* (London, 1991), pp. 548–54.

67. Wolseley to George Wolseley, 3 March, 20 April, 3 and 11 May 1899, WPP, W/W/4; Maurice and Arthur, *Life of Wolseley*, p. 335.

Chapter 17: The South African War

1. Wolseley to Hicks Beach, 13 November 1879, PRO, CAB/1.

2. R. Rhodes James, *The British Revolution* (London, 1978), p. 171.

3. Cecil Rhodes (1853–1902), went to South Africa in 1870 and worked in diamond fields of Kimberley; helped to establish De Beers Mining Company, 1880; elected to Cape Legislature, 1880 and retained seat for life; in favour of local self-government in the Cape; assisted in securing large part of Bechuanaland for Cape government in 1882 and, after its annexation, in 1884 was made deputy commissioner; British South Africa Company given royal charter to administer territory north of Bechuanaland, 1889, and named Rhodesia after Rhodes; succeeded in amalgamating the diamond mines near Kimberley as De Beers Consolidated Mines and became chairman of the company, 1887–88; acquired important share in gold fields on Witwatersrand and formed corporation,

Consolidated Goldfields of South Africa; directed war with the Matabele, 1893–94; Prime Minister of the Cape, 1890–96; supported Jameson Raid and forced to resign as Prime Minister; besieged in Kimberley during Second South African War.

4. Under the 1881 Pretoria Convention the Transvaal was granted self-government subject to the suzerainty of Britain. This meant that Britain retained a degree of control over the Transvaal's foreign and internal relations. The Convention was replaced in 1884 by the London Convention in which Britain relinquished the right to interfere in the Transvaal's native policies but forbade the Transvaal to conclude a treaty with a foreign power or native tribe unless approved by Britain.

5. A. N. Porter, 'British Imperial Policy and South Africa 1895–9', in P. Warwick (ed.), *The South African War* (London, 1980), pp. 40–48; T. Pakenham, *The Boer War* (London, 1979), pp. 1–5.

Joseph Chamberlain (1836–1914), radical social reformer; mayor of Birmingham, 1873–75; became a Liberal MP, 1876; reorganised Liberal Party, 1877; President of the Board of Trade, 1880; negotiated with Parnell over Kilmainham Treaty, 1882; opposed Egyptian policy of government but advocated relief of Gordon; President of Local Government Board, 1886; resigned over Home Rule and became Liberal Unionist; Secretary of State for the Colonies, 1895–1903; resigned over government failure to support his idea of tariff reform.

6. G. J. Wolseley, journal entry, 13 October 1879, PRO, WO 147/7; Wolseley to George Wolseley, 14 January 1896, WPP, W/W/4.

7. Porter, 'British Imperial Policy', pp. 49–53.

Alfred Milner (1854–1925), called to bar, 1881; joined staff of *Pall Mall Gazette*, 1882–85; private secretary to Viscount Goschen, 1884–86; secretary to Goschen as Chancellor of the Exchequer, 1887–89; director-general of accounts in Egypt, 1889; Under Secretary of Finance, Egypt, 1890–92; chairman of Board of Inland Revenue, 1892–97, and involved in introduction of death duties; High Commissioner for South Africa, 1897–1905; along with Kitchener signed Treaty of Vereeniging, 1902 ending the Second South African War; imported Chinese labour into Rand, 1904; after his return to England, supported tariff reform and national service; opposed Lloyd George's 1909 Budget, reform of the House of Lords and Home Rule for Ireland; member of Lloyd George's War Cabinet, 1916; attended Allied Conference at Rome, 1917; reported on state of affairs following German breakthrough of March 1918; in favour of unity of command on Western Front; Secretary of State for War, 1918; Secretary of State for the Colonies, 1918–21.

8. Report of the Royal Commission on the Military Preparations and Other Matters Concerned with the War in South Africa [Elgin Commission], c. 1789–92 (1904), 40–42.

9. Wolseley to George Wolseley, 1 December 1899, Wolseley MSS, Duke University.

10. Memorandum on the Transvaal Boers from a military point of view, Ardagh, October 1896, Ardagh MSS, PRO, PRO 30/40/14.

11. Lansdowne to Salisbury, 9 April 1897, Salisbury MSS; Salisbury to Lansdowne, 21 April 1897, in Lord Newton, *Lord Lansdowne* (London, 1929), p. 145.

12. Report of the Elgin Commission, paragraph 45.

13. Lansdowne's evidence to the Elgin Commission, QQ. 21219, 21289.

14. Wolseley to Permanent Under Secretary, 20 April 1898, in Elgin Documents.

15. On the North-West Frontier British troops formed part of the field forces fighting in Malakand and Tirah, and battalions were stationed in Crete in 1898 to prevent a civil war breaking out on the island between the Turkish and Greek populations.

16. Memorandum on the defence of South Africa, Goodenough, 30 September 1896, PRO, WO 32/6369; Goodenough to Ardagh, 14 July 1897, in Elgin Documents.

17. Stopford to Wolseley, 9 December 1898; Stopford to Butler, 21 December 1898, both in PRO, WO 32/6369.

18. W. Butler, *An Autobiography* (London, 1911), p. 385.

19. Plan for the defence of South Africa, Butler, 14 June 1899, PRO, WO 32/6369; Pakenham, *The Boer War*, p. 76.

20. Quoted in L. James, *The Rise and Fall of the British Empire* (London, 1994), p. 265.

21. For details of the Bloemfontein Conference see Pakenham, *The Boer War*, pp. 61–70; evidence to the Elgin Commission, Lansdowne, Q. 21170.

22. Memorandum on the military strength in South Africa, Wolseley, 8 June 1899, PRO, CAB 37/50; Wolseley to Lansdowne, 28 September 1899, Lansdowne MSS, BL, L(5) 37.

23. Memorandum on the military strength in South Africa, Wolseley, 8 June 1899, PRO, CAB 37/50.

24. Salisbury to Queen, 20 June, 1899, in G. E. Buckle and A. C. Benson (eds), *The Letters of Queen Victoria* (London, 1930–32), third series, iii, p. 384; Wolseley to Lansdowne, 7 July 1899, PRO, CAB 37/50.

25. N. Lyttelton, *Eighty Years Soldiering, Politics, Games* (London, 1927), pp. 200–01.

26. Buller to Campbell-Bannerman, 18 June 1895, Campbell-Bannerman MSS, BL, Add. Ms 41212.

27. Evidence to the Elgin Commission, Buller, Q. 15402.

28. G. Powell, *Buller: A Scapegoat* (London, 1994), pp. 116–20; Colonel Everett to Wolseley, 3 July 1899, PRO, WO 32/6369; Buller to Lansdowne, 6 July 1899, Wolseley to Lansdowne, 7 July 1899, both in PRO, CAB 37/50.

29. Wolseley to George Wolseley, 7 July and 21 September 1899, WPP, W/W/4.

30. This committee was established on 13 July 1899 as the Commander-in-Chief's committee to consider questions relating to operations in South Africa. The membership was wider than that of the Army Board. On 11 September it was renamed the proceedings of the Army Board for mobilisation purposes, still with a wide membership. On 11 June 1900 the committee was abolished and the Army Board took over its functions.

31. Meeting of the Commander-in-Chief's committee, 18 and 21 July 1899, PRO, WO 163/612; Wolseley to Lansdowne, 19 July 1899, Lansdowne MSS, L(5) 37.
32. Wolseley to Lansdowne, 2 August 1899, in Elgin Documents.
33. Wolseley to Lansdowne, 17 August 1899, PRO, CAB 37/50.
34. Lansdowne to Wolseley, 20 August 1899, Wolseley to Lansdowne, 24 August 1899, both in PRO, CAB 37/50.
35. 'Prepared for both'. Lansdowne to Wolseley, 27 August 1899, PRO, CAB 37/50.
36. Buller to Salisbury, 5 September 1899, Wolseley to Lansdowne, 5 September 1899, both in PRO, CAB 37/50; Buller to Wolseley, 7 September 1899, Buller MSS, Devon Record Office, 2065M/SS4/14.
37. George White (1835–1912), joined army, 1853; served in Indian Mutiny; won VC in Second Afghan War, 1879–80; took leading part in ending Burmese War, 1885–87; in command at Quetta and led Zhob valley expedition, 1889; commanded pacification of Baluchistan, 1893; Commander-in-Chief, India, 1893–97; in favour of 'forward policy' which led to a succession of frontier campaigns; Quartermaster General, 1897; in command in Natal, 1899–1900; besieged at Ladysmith, 1899–1900; Governor of Gibraltar, 1900–05.
38. Pakenham, *The Boer War*, p. 91; Wolseley to Lansdowne, 8 September 1899, PRO, CAB 37/50; Wolseley to Lansdowne, 28 September 1899, Lansdowne MSS, L (5) 37.
39. Wolseley to Ardagh, 23 September 1899, Ardagh MSS, PRO, PRO 30/40/3; Lansdowne to Salisbury, 1 September 1899, Salisbury MSS.
40. Memorandum on South Africa, Lansdowne, 25 September 1899, PRO, CAB 37/51.
41. Pakenham, *The Boer War*, p. 84; see also H. S. Wilkinson, *The Lessons of the War* (London, 1900) which was a compilation of articles by Wilkinson published in *The London Letter* during the war.
42. Chamberlain to the House of Commons, 8 May 1896, in I. R. Smith, *The Origins of the War in South Africa* (London, 1996), p. 120.
43. C. E. Callwell, 'A Boer War: The Military Aspect', *Blackwoods*, 166 (August 1899), pp. 259–65. Authorship confirmed by the *Wellesley Index*. It was perhaps fortunate for Callwell's career as an intelligence officer and author of many books on military subjects that this article appeared anonymously.
44. Wolseley to Cambridge, 12 September 1899, in W. Verner, *The Military Life of HRH George, Duke of Cambridge* (London, 1905), pp. 421–22.
45. L. S. Amery, *The Times History of the War in South Africa* (London, 1900–09), ii, pp. 103, 466.
46. Evidence to the Elgin Commission, Wolseley, QQ. 8875, 8862–72.
47. Evidence to the Elgin Commission, White, Q. 14767; Wolseley to George Wolseley, 16 November 1899, WPP, W/W/4.
48. Rhodes had arrived in Kimberley just before the siege began. He made life extremely difficult for the town's military commander, Lieutenant-Colonel Kekewich, and threatened to surrender the town to the Boers if the British did not send a column to relieve it.

49. For details of these battles see Pakenham, *The Boer War*, pp. 201–42; H. Bailes, 'Military Aspects of the War', in Warwick, *The South African War*, pp. 77–84.

50. Roberts to Lansdowne, 8 December 1899, in Newton, *Lansdowne*, p. 161; Lansdowne to Salisbury, 10 December 1899, Salisbury MSS; Wolseley to Bigge, 14 December 1899, in Buckle, *Letters of Queen Victoria*, third series, iii, p. 433; Wolseley to Lansdowne, 17 December 1899, Lansdowne MSS, L(5) 37.

51. Balfour to Salisbury, 19 December 1899, in G. H. L. Le May, *British Supremacy in South Africa* (Oxford, 1965), pp. 44–45.

52. Wolseley to Louisa Wolseley, 17 December 1899 and 4 January 1900, WPP, W/P/28 and 29.

53. Wolseley to Buller, 7 September 1899, Buller MSS, Devon Record Office, 2065M/SS4/14; Wolseley to George Wolseley, 23 November 1899, Wolseley MSS, Duke University.

54. Lansdowne to Salisbury, 3 and 8 November 1899, Salisbury MSS.

55. Lyttelton, *Eighty Years Soldiering*, p. 200.

56. W. E. Cairnes, *The Absent-Minded War* (London, 1900), p. 11; evidence to the Elgin Commission, Roberts, Q. 10520.

57. Amery, *Times History*, pp. 37–38.

58. H. O. Arnold-Forster, *The War Office, the Army and the Empire* (London, 1900), p. 81. Arnold-Forster listed the previous appointments of the principal staff officers on the expeditionary force.

59. Lyttelton, *Eighty Years Soldiering*, p. 200.

60. Evidence to the Elgin Commission, Hildyard, QQ. 15973–76.

61. Memorandum on the war in South Africa, Wolseley, 30 January 1900, PRO, CAB 37/51.

62. Memorandum on the war in South Africa, Lansdowne, 30 October 1899, PRO, CAB 37/51; memorandum on the Boer War, Wolseley, 1 and 3 November 1899, both in Elgin Documents.

63. Wolseley to Lansdowne, 30 September 1899; Lansdowne to Wolseley, 12 October 1899; Wolseley to Lansdowne, 30 October 1899; Wolseley to Permanent Under Secretary, 31 October 1899; Lansdowne to Wolseley, 31 October 1899, all in PRO, WO 32/6359.

64. Records of the secret service, March 1900, PRO, HD 3/114.

65. T. H. Sanderson to Salisbury, 13 December 1899, in G. P. Gooch and H. W. Temperley, *British Documents on the Origins of the War, 1898–1914* (London, 1926), p. 83.

66. Salisbury to Devonshire, 15 December 1899, Devonshire MSS, 340.2808.

67. Wolseley to Lansdowne, 29 December 1899, PRO, CAB 37/51; Wolseley to Lansdowne, 3 January 1900, PRO, WO 32/6360.

68. Lansdowne to Clarke, 6 January 1900, PRO, WO 32/6360.

69. Memorandum by Grove, 6 January; memorandum by Wood, 8 January; memorandum by Brackenbury, 9 January; memorandum by Clarke, 9 January 1900, all in PRO, WO 32/6360.

70. Lansdowne to Wolseley, 17 January 1900, PRO, CAB 37/52; meeting of the defence committee, 20 January 1900, PRO, WO 32/6360.

71. Memorandum on the strength of the British Army, Wolseley, 23 January 1900, PRO, WO 32/6360.

72. Memorandum on the establishment, Lansdowne, 27 January 1900, PRO, WO 32/6360; Wolseley to Lansdowne, 11 February 1900, Maurice MSS, Liddell Hart Centre, 2/2/46; Bigge to Wolseley, 17 February 1900, Lansdowne to Queen, 29 January 1900, both in Buckle, *Letters of Queen Victoria*, third series, iii, pp. 489–90, 470–71.

73. I. F. W. Beckett, *Riflemen Form* (Aldershot, 1982), p. 211–14.

74. Wolseley to Permanent Under Secretary, 28 December 1899; Lansdowne to Wolseley, 30 December 1899; memorandum on the Yeomanry, Wood, 23 December 1899, all in PRO, WO 32/7866.

75. J. K. Dunlop, *The Development of the British Army* (London, 1938), p. 87; E. M. Spiers, *The Late Victorian Army* (Manchester, 1992), pp. 320–21.

76. Memorandum on the Ordnance Branch, Brackenbury, 15 December 1899, Elgin Documents; Wolseley to Lansdowne, 29 December 1899, PRO, CAB 37/51; memorandum on the Ordnance Branch, Brackenbury, 9 January 1900, PRO, WO 32/6360.

77. Memorandum on the state of the artillery, Ardagh, 20 January 1900, Ardagh MSS, PRO, PRO 30/40/14; report of the interdepartmental committee on the reserves of guns, etc., 31 March 1900, PRO, WO 33/163.

78. During the war 30,633 men from the colonies served in South Africa.

79. Pakenham, *The Boer War*, pp. 331–42.

80. Wolseley to George Wolseley, 22 June 1900, WPP, W/W/4. The Boxer uprising was an anti-foreign rebellion in China. The international legations were besieged in Peking from June to August 1900 until relieved by allied troops from Britain, France, Russia and Germany. L. James, *The Rise and Fall of the British Empire* (London, 1994), p. 243.

81. Wolseley to George Wolseley, 21 December 1900, Wolseley MSS, Duke University.

82. Queen to Salisbury, 27 September 1900 and Queen to Bigge, 6 October 1900, in Buckle, *Letters of Queen Victoria*, third series, iii, pp. 594–95 and 603; the Prince of Wales thought Roberts a better choice than his brother, S. Lee, *King Edward VII* (London, 1925), i, p. 795.

83. Lansdowne to Wolseley, 29 September 1900, Lansdowne MSS, L(5) 37.

84. Wolseley to Lansdowne, 30 September 1900, Maurice MSS, 2/2/47.

85. Queen to Wolseley, 4 December 1900, in Buckle, *Letters of Queen Victoria*, third series, iii, pp. 627–28.

86. Wolseley to George Wolseley, 5 October 1900, WPP, W/W/4; Louisa Wolseley to Wolseley, November 1900, WPP, L/W/26.

87. Memorandum on the position of the Commander-in-Chief, Wolseley, November 1900, PRO, CAB 37/53.

88. Memorandum on the position of the Commander-in-Chief, Lansdowne, 17 November 1900, PRO, CAB 37/53.
89. Memorandum on the position of the Commander-in-Chief, Brodrick, 20 November 1900, PRO, CAB 37/53.

Chapter 18: Ths Last Years

1. Lansdowne to Salisbury, August 1900, Salisbury MSS, Hatfield.
2. E. Wood, *From Midshipman to Field Marshal* (London, 1906), p. 253.
3. Brackenbury to Roberts, 17 December 1900, Roberts MSS, 7101–23–11/166; memorandum on the role of the Commander-in-Chief, Roberts, 27 December 1900, PRO, CAB 37/53.
4. Memorandum on the organisation of the War Office, Brodrick, 19 January 1901, PRO, CAB 37/56.
5. Wolseley to Brodrick, November 1900, in F. Maurice and G. Arthur, *The Life of Lord Wolseley* (London, 1924), p. 324.
6. Wolseley to House of Lords, 4 March 1901, *Hansard*, fourth series, vol. 90.
7. Lansdowne to House of Lords, 4 March 1901, *Hansard*, fourth series, vol. 90.
8. Debate on the War Office administration, 5 March 1901, *Hansard*, fourth series, vol. 90.
9. Camperdown to Wolseley, 8 March 1901, WPP, Autograph.
10. Louisa Wolseley to Wolseley, 13 March 1901, WPP, W/P/30.
11. Debate on Lord Wolseley's memorandum to Lord Salisbury, 15 March 1901, *Hansard*, fourth series, vol. 91.
12. Wolseley to Louisa Wolseley, 24 June 1901, WPP, W/P/30.
13. Wolseley to House of Lords, 28 June 1901, *Hansard*, fourth series, vol. 96; Wolseley to Louisa Wolseley, 28 June 1901, WPP, W/P/30; J. Davidson to Wolseley, 30 June 1901, Maurice MSS, Liddell Hart Centre, 2/2/36; for further details of the Brodrick's army reforms see L. J. Satre, 'St John Brodrick and Army Reform, 1901–1903', *Journal of British Studies*, 15 (1976), pp. 117–39.
14. W. S. Hamer, *The British Army: Civil-Military Relations* (Oxford, 1970), pp. 187–92; anon., 'The Position of the Commander-in-Chief', *Blackwoods*, 169 (April 1901), pp. 573–84.
15. Hamer, *The British Army*, pp. 233–45.
16. E. Longford, *Victoria RI* (London, 1964), pp. 562–64.
17. Wolseley to George Wolseley, 1 February 1901, WPP, W/W/4.
18. Wolseley to George Wolseley, 16 January, 15 May and 7 August 1902, WPP, W/W/4.
19. Wolseley to George Wolseley, 15 February 1901, WPP, W/W/4.
20. Question by Mr Tully to Brodrick, 18 March 1902, *Hansard*, fourth series, vol. 105.
21. Wolseley to Louisa Wolseley, 20 April 1902, WPP, W/P/31; Maurice and Arthur, *Life of Wolseley*, p. 336.
22. E. M. Spiers, *The Late Victorian Army* (Manchester, 1992), p. 312.

23. Evidence to the Elgin Commission, Wolseley, QQ. 8701–8927.

24. Ibid., Q. 8948, 9035–42; Esher to King, 27 November 1902, M. V. Brett (ed.), *Journals and Letters of Reginald, Viscount Esher* (London, 1934–35), pp. 363–65. Lord Esher was a member of the Elgin Commission and wrote daily to the King detailing the evidence each witness had given. On the outbreak of the First World War in 1914 a soldier, Lord Kitchener, was appointed Secretary of State for War.

25. Esher to King, 30 April 1903, in Brett, *Journals and Letters of Esher*, p. 399.

26. Verner to Wolseley, 24 July 1906, WPP, Autograph.

27. Wolseley to George Wolseley, 21 November 1901, WPP, W/W4.

28. Wolseley to Louisa Wolseley, 1 February 1903, WPP, W/P/32.

29. Wolseley to Louisa Wolseley, 26 November 1903, WPP, W/P/32.

30. M. Pegram, *The Wolseley Heritage* (London, 1939), pp. 172–84. Margery Pegram wrote this book at the express wish of Frances, who wanted her side of the story printed after her death.

31. Ibid., p. 191.

32. Wolseley to Louisa Wolseley, 3 May 1911, WPP, W/P/39; Pegram, *The Wolseley Heritage*, pp. 195–96.

33. Pegram, *The Wolseley Heritage*, p. 199; J. Lehmann, *All Sir Garnet* (London, 1964), pp. 391–92.

34. Ibid., pp. 204, 247–50.

Chapter 19: A Victorian Hero

1. The other three were Dover, Gibraltar and Singapore.

2. W. S. Churchill, *My Early Life* (London, 1930), p. 179.

3. Wolseley's obituary, *Journal of the Royal United Services Institute*, 62 (April 1913), p. 445.

4. Wolseley's obituary, *The Times*, 26 March 1913.

5. Wolseley draft telegram to Buller, 10 February 1900, Lansdowne MSS, BL, L(5) 37. Lansdowne advised Wolseley not to send this telegram.

6. A. Forbes, 'Wolseley: A Character Sketch', *English Illustrated Magazine*, 2 (May 1885), pp. 519–23; A. Forbes, *Souvenirs of Some Continents* (London, 1885), pp. 171–72.

7. p.s.c. – passed Staff College.

8. J. Luvaas, *The Education of an Army* (London, 1964) pp. 173–215; for example, J. F. Maurice, *The Balance of Military Power in Europe* (Edinburgh, 1888).

9. Roberts to Brownlow, 17 December 1888, Roberts MSS, NAM, 100/2 LXXVIII.

10. Wolseley to George Wolseley, 6 September 1900, WPP, W/W/4.

11. J. Ferris, *Evolution of British Strategic Policy* (London, 1989), p. 87.

12. Wolseley to Queen, 22 March 1885, in G. E. Buckle and A. C. Benson (eds), *The Letters of Queen Victoria* (London, 1926–28), second series, iii, p. 632.

13. H. O. Arnold Forster, *The War Office, the Army, and the Empire* (London, 1900),

p. 3; L. Amery, *The Times History of the War in South Africa* (London, 1900–09), ii, p. 24.

14. I. N. Lambi, *The Navy and German Power Politics* (Boston, 1984), pp. 118–29.
15. G. J. Wolseley, 'The Study of War', *United Service Magazine*, 2 (1890), pp. 481–93.
16. Quoted in *The Times*, 1 April 1913. Roberts became the leader of the League. See R. Adams and P. Poirier, *The Conscription Controversy in Great Britain, 1900–1918* (London, 1987); R. Rhodes James, *The British Revolution* (London, 1978), p. 222.
17. General Ellison quoted in J. K. Dunlop, *The Development of the British Army* (London, 1938), pp. 15–16; J. W. Fortescue, *Following the Drum* (Edinburgh, 1932), p. 183.
18. Midleton to Wood, 16 February 1918, Wood MSS, Duke University.

Bibliography

1. Private Papers

British Library
Campbell-Bannerman, Sir Henry
Dilke, Sir Charles
Esher, Lord
Gladstone, William
Lansdowne, Marquess of

Cambridge University Library
Childers, Hugh

Chatsworth House
Hartington, Marquess of and Duke of Devonshire

Devon Record Office
Buller, General Sir Redvers

Duke University
Wolseley, Field Marshal Viscount
Wood, General Sir Evelyn

Hatfield House
Salisbury, Marquess of

Hove Central Library
Wolseley, Field Marshal Viscount
Wolseley, Louisa

Kent Record Office
Stanhope, Edward

Liddell Hart Centre for Military Archives
Maurice, Major-General Sir John Frederick

Ministry of Defence Library
Wolseley, Field Marshal Viscount

National Army Museum
Roberts, Field Marshal Lord

National Library of Ireland
Wolseley, Field Marshal Viscount

Public Record Office
Ardagh, Lieutenant-Colonel Sir John
Brodrick, St John
Buller, General Sir Redvers
Cardwell, Lord
Carnarvon, Lord
Childers, Hugh
Cromer, Earl of
Granville, Lord
Kitchener, Earl
Smith, William Henry
Wolseley, Field Marshal Viscount

Royal Archives
Cambridge, George, Duke of

2. Parliamentary Papers

Hansard

Parliamentary Debates, 3rd and 4th series.

Reports etc., in date order

Reports of the Inspector General of Recruiting, 1871–1899.

Memoranda of the Secretary of State on the Estimates, 1887–1900.

General Annual Returns of the Army, 1874–1898.

Committee on the Organisation of the Various Military Land Forces, First Report, c. 493 (1872), 37; Supplementary Report of the Committee on the Organisation of the various Military Land Forces, c. 588 (1872), 14.

Final Report of the Committee on the Organisation of the Various Military Land Forces, c. 712 (1873), 18.

Royal Commission on Army Promotion and Retirement, c. 1569 (1876), 15.

Committee on Conditions of Service as Affected by Short Service, c. 2817 (1881), 20.

Committee on the Reorganisation of the Army, c. 2791 (1881), 21.

Reports and Documents Relating to Army Organisation, c. 2792 (1881), 21.

Committee on the Formation of Territorial Regiments, c. 2793 (1881), 20.

Colour Committee, c. 3536 (1883), 15.

Joint Select Committee on the Channel Tunnel (1883), 12.

Report of the Royal Commission Appointed to Inquire into the System under which Patterns of Warlike Stores are Adopted, First Report c. 5062 (1887), 15; Final Report c. 5413 (1888), 25.

Royal Commission to Inquire into the Civil and Professional Administration of the Naval and Military Departments, c. 5979 (1890), 19.

Report of the Committee to Consider the Terms and Conditions of Service in the Army, c. 6582 (1892), 19.

Report on the Manoeuvres Held in the Neighbourhood of Salisbury in August and September 1898, c. 9139 (1899), 53.

Committee on War Office Organisation, cd 580 (1901), 40.

Order in Council, 4 November 1901 (1902), 58.

Report of the Royal Commission on the Military Preparations and Other Matters Connected with the War in South Africa, c. 1789 c. 1790, c. 1791, c. 1 792 (1904), 40–42.

3. Official Publications

Intelligence Branch of the War Office, *Narrative of the Field Operations Connected with the Zulu War* (1989).

F. Maurice, *The Military History of the Campaign of 1882 in Egypt* (1887).

F. Maurice and M. H. Grant, *History of the War in South Africa* (4 vols, 1906–10).

4. Contemporary Newspapers and Perodicals

Blackwood's Edinburgh Magazine
Contemporary Review
English Illustrated Magazine
Fortnightly Review
Harper's New Monthly Magazine (European Edition)
Journal of the Royal United Service Institution
Macmillans Magazine
Nineteenth Century
North American Review
Review of the Reviews
Strand Magazine
The Times
United Service Magazine

5. Writings by Garnet Wolseley in Order of Publication

(Place of Publication is London)

Narrative of the War with China in 1860 (1862).
The Soldier's Pocket-Book for Field Service (5 edns, 1868–89).
The Field Pocket Book for the Auxiliary Services (1873).
The Use of Railroads in War (pamphlet, 1873).
The Life of John, 1st Duke of Marlborough 1650–1702 (2 vols, 1894).
The Decline and Fall of Napoleon (1895).
The Story of a Soldier's Life (2 vols, 1903).
'A Month's Visit to the Confederate Headquarters', *Blackwoods*, 93 (January 1863), pp. 1–29.
'Narrative of the Red River Expedition', *Blackwoods*, 109 (December 1870-February 1871).
'Our Military Requirements', *Macmillans*, 23 (April 1871), pp. 524–36.
'Our Autumn Manoeuvres', *Blackwoods*, 112 (November 1872), pp. 627–44.
'Our Coming Guest', *Blackwoods*, 108 (June 1873), pp. 712–21.
'Army Reform', *Macmillans*, 35 (April 1877), pp. 496–504.
'France as a Military Power in 1870 and 1878', *Nineteenth Century*, 3 (January 1878), pp. 1–21.
'Military Staff Systems Abroad and in England', *Macmillans*, 37 (February 1878), pp. 323–35.
'England as a Military Power in 1854 and in 1878', *Nineteenth Century*, 3 (March 1878), pp. 433–56.
'Letter from Cyprus', *Macmillans*, 39 (November 1878), p. 96.
'Long and Short Service', *Nineteenth Century*, 9 (March 1881), pp. 558–72.
'General Lee', *Macmillans*, 55 (March 1887), pp. 321–31.

'Courage', *Fortnightly Review*, 44 (August 1888), pp. 279–92.

'Military Genius', *Fortnightly Review*, 44 (September 1888), pp. 297–312.

'The Negro as a Soldier', *Fortnightly Review*, 44 (December 1888), pp. 689–703.

'War', *Fortnightly Review*, 45 (January 1889), pp. 1–17.

'Is a Soldier's Life Worth Living?', *Fortnightly Review*, 45 (May 1889), pp. 597–609.

'The French Revolution and War', *Fortnightly Review*, 45 (June 1889), pp. 780–91.

'An English View of the Civil War', *North American Review*, 149 (July-December 1889).

'The Standing Army of Great Britain', *Harper's Magazine* (February 1890), pp. 331–47.

'The Anti Slavery Campaign', *United Service Magazine*, 2 (1890), pp. 1–8.

'The Study of War', *United Service Magazine*, 2 (1890), pp. 481–93.

'General Sherman', *United Service Magazine*, 3 (1891), pp. 97–116; 193–216; 289–309.

'Field-Marshal Count von Moltke', *United Service Magazine*, 3 (1891), pp. 481–97.

'Franco-Prussian War of 1870–71', *United Service Magazine*, 4 (1891), pp. 89–100; 185–98.

'Field-Marshal Count von Moltke', *United Service Magazine*, 4 (1891), pp. 1–22.

'General Forrest', *United Service Magazine*, 5 (1892), pp. 1–14; 113–24.

'The Military Question of Today', *United Service Magazine*, 7 (1893), pp. 405–23.

'Memoir of Sir Hope Grant', *United Service Magazine*, 7 (1893), p. 777.

'Marlborough: Macaulay and Swift. A Reply', *United Service Magazine*, 9 (1894), pp. 202–15.

'The Battle of Vionville: A Discussion', *United Service Magazine*, 10 (1894), pp. 42–55.

'The Old Trenches before Sebastopol Revisited', *United Service Magazine*, 10 (1894), pp. 103–21.

Publications which include contributions by Wolseley

Anon. (ed.), *Essays Written for The Wellington Prize* (Edinburgh, 1872).

T. H. Ward (ed.), *The Reign of Queen Victoria* (2 vols, 1887).

6. Secondary Sources

Place of publication is London unless otherwise stated.

R. Adams and P. Poirier, *The Conscription Controversy in Great Britain, 1900–1918* (1987).

J. Adye, *Soldiers and Others I Have Known* (1919).

L. S. Amery, *The Problem of the Army* (1903).

—, *The Times History of the War in South Africa* (7 vols, 1900–09).

Marquess of Anglesey, *A History of the British Cavalry, 1816–1919* (4 vols, 1973–86).

H. O. Arnold-Forster, *Army Letters, 1897–1898* (1898).

—, *The War Office, the Army and the Empire* (1900).

J. B. Atlay, *Lord Halibuton: A Memoir of his Public Service* (1909).

A. Babington, *Military Intervention in Britain* (1990).

D. W. R. Bahlman (ed.), *The Diary of Sir Edward Walter Hamilton* (2 vols, Oxford, 1972–93).

H. R. Bailes, 'Patterns of Thought in the Late Victorian Army', *Journal of Strategic Studies*, 4 (1981), pp. 29–45.

—, 'Technology and Imperialism: A Case Study of the Victorian Army in Africa', *Victorian Studies*, 24 (1980), pp. 82–104.

C. Barnett, *Britain and her Army* (1970).

I. F. W. Beckett, *Riflemen Form: A Study of the Rifle Volunteer Movement, 1859–1908* (Aldershot, 1982).

—, 'Edward Stanhope at the War Office, 1887–92', *Journal of Strategic Studies*, 5 (1982), pp. 278–307.

—, 'The Stanhope Memorandum of 1888: A Reinterpretation', *Bulletin of the Institute of Historical Research*, 57 (1984), pp. 240–47.

—, 'Wolseley and the Ring', *Soldiers of the Queen* (1992), pp. 14–25.

—, 'Women and Patronage in the Late Victorian Army', *History* (forthcoming).

H. Belloc, *The Modern Traveller* (1898).

Lord C. Beresford, *The Memoirs of Admiral Lord Charles Beresford* (2 vols, 1914).

G. Best and A. Wheatcroft (eds.), *War, Economy and the Military Mind* (1976).

H. Biddulph, 'The American Civil War: Contemporary Letters from Lieutenant-Colonel G. J. Wolseley', *Journal of Army Historical Research*, 18 (1939) pp. 38–40.

R. Biddulph, *Lord Cardwell at the War Office: A History of his Administration, 1868–1874 (1904)*.

W. S. Blunt, *Secret History of the English Occupation of Egypt* (1907).

B. J. Bond, *The Victorian Army and the Staff College 1854–1914* (1972).

—, (ed.) *Victorian Military Campaigns* (1967).

—, 'Edward Cardwell's Army Reforms, 1868–74', *Army Quarterly*, 84 (1962), pp. 108–17.

—, 'The Effect of the Cardwell Reforms on Army Organisation, 1874–1904', *Journal of the Royal United Services Institute*, 55 (1960), pp. 515–24.

—, 'The Late Victorian Army', *History Today*, 11 (1961), pp. 616–24.

—, 'Mr Gladstone's Invasion of Egypt 1882: A Revelation of Military Weakness', *Army Quarterly*, 81 (1960), pp. 87–92.

—, 'Prelude to the Cardwell Reforms, 1856–1868', *Journal of the Royal United Services Institute*, 56 (1961), pp. 229–41.

—, 'Recruiting the Victorian Army, 1870–1892', *Victorian Studies*, 5 (1962), pp. 331–38.

—, 'The Retirement of the Duke of Cambridge', *Journal of the Royal United Services Institute*, 56 (1961), pp. 544–53.

K. Bourne, *The Foreign Policy of Victorian England* (Oxford, 1970).

—, and D. C. Watt (eds), *Studies in International History* (1967).

A. L. Bowley, *Wages and Incomes in the United Kingdom since 1860* (Cambridge, 1937).

H. Brackenbury, *The Ashanti War of 1873–74* (2 vols, Edinburgh, 1874).

—, *The River Column* (Edinburgh, 1885).

M. V. Brett (ed.), *Journals and Letters of Reginald, Viscount Esher* (4 vols, 1934–35).

G. E. Buckle and A. C. Benson (eds.), *The Letters of Queen Victoria*, 2nd series (3 vols, 1926–28); 3rd series (3 vols, 1930–32).

B. Burleigh, *Desert Warfare* (1884).

E. Butler, *Autobiography* (1922).

W. Butler, *An Autobiography* (1911).

—, *The Campaign of the Cataracts* (1887).

W. E. Cairnes, *The Absent-Minded War* (1900).

C. E. Callwell, *Small Wars: Their Principle and Practice* (1896).

—, 'A Boer War: The Military Aspect', *Blackwoods*, 166 (August 1899), pp. 259–65.

E. M. Carroll, *French Public Opinion and Foreign Affairs* (New York, 1931).

Lady Gwendolen Cecil (ed.), *Life of Robert, Marquis of Salisbury* (4 vols, 1921–32).

J. A. V. Chapple, *Documentary and Imaginative Literature, 1880–1920* (1970).

S. Childers, *Life and Correspondence of the Right Hon. Hugh C. E. Childers, 1827–1896* (2 vols, 1901).

Viscount Chilston, *W. H. Smith* (1965).

E. Childers, *War and the Arme Blanche* (1910).

W. S. Churchill, *Lord Randolph Churchill* (2 vols, 1906).

—, *My Early Life* (1930).

G. S. Clarke, *My Working Life* (1898).

I. F. Clarke, *Voices Prophesying War, 1763–1984* (1970).

A. Colville and H. Temperley, *Studies in Anglo-French History* (Cambridge, 1935).

H. Colville, *History of the Sudan Campaign* (2 vols, 1889).

Earl of Cromer, *Modern Egypt* (2 vols, 1908).

G. C. Dawnay, *Campaigns: Zulu 1879, Egypt 1882, Suakim 1885* (reprint, Cambridge, 1989).

P. Dennis and A. Preston (eds), *Soldiers as Statesmen* (1976).

C. W. Dilke, *Army Reform* (1898).

—, *The British Army* (1888).

A. Duminy and C. Ballard (eds), *The Anglo-Zulu War: New Perspectives* (Pietermaritzburg, 1981).

J. K. Dunlop, *The Development of the British Army* (1938).

Lord Dunsany, 'The Proposed Channel Tunnel', *Nineteenth Century*, 11 (February 1882), pp. 288–304.

J. Ellis, *The Social History of the Machine Gun* (1975).

F. Emery, *Marching Over Africa* (1986).

—, *The Red Soldier: Letters from the Zulu War* (1977).

B. Farwell, *Eminent Victorian Soldiers* (1986).

—, *Queen Victoria's Little Wars* (1973).

T. G. Fergusson, *British Military Intelligence, 1870–1914: The Development of a Modern Intelligence Organisation* (Frederick, Maryland, 1984).

J. Ferris, *Evolution of British Strategic Policy, 1919–26* (1989).

E. Fitzmaurice, *The Life of Granville, George Leveson Gower, Second Earl of Granville* (1905).

A. Forbes, *Memories and Studies of War and Peace* (1896).

—, *Souvenirs of War and Peace* (1885).

—, 'The Recruiting Problem', *Nineteenth Century*, 29 (March 1891), pp. 398–404.

—, 'Wolseley: A Character Sketch', *English Illustrated Magazine*, 2 (May 1885), pp. 519–23.

W. Forbes-Mitchell, *Reminiscences of the Great Mutiny, 1857–59* (1894).

J. W. Fortescue, *Following the Drum* (Edinburgh, 1932).

—, *History of the British Army* (13 vols, 1930).

R. F. Foster, *Modern Ireland* (1989).

N. Frankland, *Witness of a Century: The Life and Times of Prince Arthur Duke of Connaught* (1993).

A. G. Gardiner, *The Life of Sir William Harcourt* (2 vols, 1923).

A. E. Gathorne-Hardy, *Gathorne Hardy, Earl of Cranbrook* (1910).

Lord E. Gleichen, *With the Camel Corps up the Nile* (1888).

S. Gopal, *British Policy in India* (Cambridge, 1965).

G. P. Gooch and H. W. Temperley (eds), *British Documents on the Origins of the War, 1898–1914* (11 vols, 1926 –38).

J. Gooch, *The Plans of War* (1974).

—, *The Prospect of War: Studies in British Defence Policy, 1847–1942* (1981).

E. W. Gosse, *Aspects and Impressions* (New York, 1922).

J. A. S. Grenville, *Lord Salisbury and Foreign Policy: The Close of the Nineteenth Century* (1964).

J. M. Grierson, *Scarlet into Khaki* (reprint, 1988).

S. Gwynn and G. M. Tuckwell, *The Life of Sir Charles W. Dilke* (2 vols, 1917).

L. Hale, 'An Army without Leaders', *Nineteenth Century* (March 1896), pp. 357–74.

A. Haliburton, *Army Organisation: A Short Reply to Long Service* (1898).

W. S. Hamer, *The British Army: Civil-Military Relations, 1885–1905* (Oxford, 1970).

Lord G. Hamilton, *Parliamentary Reminiscences and Reflections* (2 vols, 1916–22).

I. Hamilton, *Listening for the Drums* (1944).

E. Hamley, 'The Defencelessness of London', *Nineteenth Century*, 23 (May 1888), pp. 633–40.

—, 'Gordon, Wolseley and Sir Charles Wilson', *Blackwoods*, 137 (June 1885), pp. 872–79.

—, 'The 2nd Division at Tel-el-Kebir', *Nineteenth Century*, 12 (December 1882).

H. B. Hanna, *Backwards or Forwards?* (1896).

—, *Can Russia Invade India?* (1895).

—, *India's Scientific Frontier: Where Is It?* (1895).

A. Hankinson, *Man of Wars: W. H. Russell* (1982).

A. H. Hardinge, *The Life of the Earl of Carnarvon* (3 vols, 1925).

G. Harries-Jenkins, *The Army in Victorian Society* (1977).

J. F. C. Harrison, *Late Victorian Britain* (1990).

D. R. Headrick, *The Tools of Empire: Technology and European Imperialism in the Nineteenth Century (New York, 1981)*.

C. Hibbert, *The Great Mutiny* (1978).

B. Holland, *Life of Spencer Compton, 8th Duke of Devonshire* (2 vols, 1911).

E. Holt, 'Garnet Wolseley: Soldier of Empire', *History Today*, 8 (1958), pp. 706–13.

H. How, 'Lord Wolseley', *Strand Magazine*, 3 (May 1892) pp. 443–61.

M. Howard (ed.), *The Theory and Practice of War* (1965).

E. M. Hunt, *Regional Wage Variations in Britain* (Oxford, 1973).

E. T. H. Hutton, *Five Lectures on Mounted Infantry* (1891).

P. Jackson, *The Last of the Whigs: A Political Biography of Lord Hartington, Later Eighth Duke of Devonshire (1994)*.

D. James, *The Life of Lord Roberts* (1954).

L. James, *The Rise and Fall of the British Empire* (1994).

L. J. Jennings (ed.), *Speeches of The Right Honourable Lord Randolph Churchill* (2 vols, 1889).

F. A. Johnson, *Defence by Committee* (1960).

N. E. Johnson (ed.), *The Diary of Gathorne Hardy, Later Lord Cranbrook, 1886–1892: Political Selections (Oxford, 1981)*.

P. Karsten, 'Irish Soldiers in the British Army, 1792–1922: Suborned or Subordinate?', *Journal of Social History*, 17 (1983), pp. 31–64.

P. Kennedy, *The Rise and Fall of British Naval Mastery* (1983).

—, (ed.), *The War Plans of the Great Powers, 1880–1914* (1979).

R. J. Kentish, *Maxims of the Late Field-Marshal Viscount Wolseley* (1916).

V. G. Kiernan, *European Empires from Conquest to Collapse, 1815–1960* (1982).

C. W. De Kiewiet, *The Imperial Factor in South Africa: A Study in Politics and Economics* (Cambridge, 1937).

A. W. Kinglake, *Invasion of the Crimea* (9 vols, Edinburgh, 1888).

H. M. Kochanski, 'Field Marshal Viscount Wolseley as Commander-in-Chief, 1895–1900: A Reassessment', *Journal of Strategic Studies*, 20 (June 1997), pp. 119–39.

J. P. C. Laband, *Lord Chelmsford's Zululand Campaign, 1878–1879* (1994).

A. Lambert, *The Crimean War* (Manchester, 1990).

I. N. Lambi, *The Navy and German Power Politics* (Boston, 1984).

W. F. B. Laurie, *Our Burmese Wars* (1885).

S. Lee, *King Edward VII* (2 vols, 1925).

J. Lees-Milne, *The Enigmatic Edwardian: The Life of Reginald 2nd Viscount Esher* (1986).

J. Lehmann, *All Sir Garnet: A Life of Field Marshal Lord Wolseley* (1964).

—, *The First Boer War* (1985).

G. H. L. Le May, *British Supremacy in South Africa, 1899–1907* (Oxford, 1965).

N. B. Leslie, *The Battle Honours of the British and Indian Armies* (1970).

A. Lloyd, *The Drums of Kumasi: The Story of the Ashanti Wars* (1964).

E. Longford, *Victoria RI* (1964).

N. Longmate, *Island Fortress: The Defence of Great Britain, 1603–1945* (1991).

C. R. Low, *Soldiers of the Victorian Age* (2 vols, 1880).

C. J. Lowe, *The Reluctant Imperialists: British Foreign Policy, 1878–1902* (2 vols, 1967).

—, *Salisbury and the Mediterranean, 1886–1896* (1965).

J. Luvaas, *The Education of an Army: British Military Thought, 1815–1940* (1964).

—, *The Military Legacy of the Civil War* (Chicago, 1959).

A. Lyall, *The Life of the Marquis of Dufferin and Ava* (1905).

N. Lyttelton, *Eighty Years Soldiering, Politics, Games* (1927).

G. McCourt, *Remember Butler* (1967).

R. MacGregor-Hastie, *Never To Be Taken Alive: A Biography of General Gordon* (1985).

J. W. Mackail and G. Wyndham, *Life and Letters of George Wyndham* (2 vols, 1926).

J. M. Mackenzie (ed.), *Imperialism and Popular Culture* (Manchester, 1986).

B. Mallet, *Thomas George, Earl of Northbrook* (1908).

Susan, Countess of Malmesbury, *The Life of Major-General Sir John Ardagh* (1909).

A. J. Marder, *British Naval Policy, 1880–1905: The Anatomy of British Sea Power* (1941).

P. Marling, *Rifleman and Hussar: An Autobiography* (1931).

J. Martineau, *The Life and Correspondence of Sir Bartle Frere* (1895).

H. C. G. Matthew, *Gladstone* (Oxford, 1995).

F. Maurice, *The Balance of Military Power in Europe* (Edinburgh, 1888).

—, 'Sir E. Hamley and Lord Wolseley', *United Service Magazine*, 11 (1895) pp. 414–34.

F. Maurice and G. Arthur, *The Life of Lord Wolseley* (1924).

L. Maxwell, *The Ashanti Ring: Sir Garnet Wolseley's Campaigns, 1870–1882* (1985).

R. Millman, *Britain and the Eastern Question, 1875–78* (Oxford, 1979).

A. Milner, *England in Egypt* (1894).

W. F. Moneypenny and G. E. Buckle, *The Life of Benjamin Disraeli, Earl of Beacons-field* (6 vols 1920).

G. Monger, *The End of Isolation: British Foreign Policy, 1900–1907* (1963).

W. E. Montague, 'Red-Hot Reform', *Blackwoods*, 134 (July 1883), pp. 66 87.

J. Morley, *The Life of Gladstone* (2 vols, 1908).

D. R. Morris, *The Washing of the Spears* (1986).

J. Morris, *Heaven's Command* (1979).

E. A. Muenger, *The British Military Dilemma in Ireland* (Kansas, 1991).

Lord Newton, *Lord Lansdowne: A Biography* (1929).

D. A. Nicholls, *The Lost Prime Minister: A Life of Sir Charles Dilke* (1995).

T. Pakenham, *The Boer War* (1979).

—, *The Scramble for Africa* (1991).

M. Pegram, *The Wolseley Heritage* (1939).

W. B. Pemberton, *Battles of the Boer War* (1964).

—, *Battles of the Crimean War* (1962).

J. Pollock, *Gordon: The Man Behind the Legend* (1993).

A. Ponsonby, *Henry Ponsonby: Queen Victoria's Secretary. His Life from his Letters* (1942).

A. N. Porter, *The Origins of the South African War* (Manchester, 1980).

B. Porter, *Critics of Empire* (1968).

—, *The Lion's Share: A Short History of British Imperialism, 1850–1983* (1984).

G. Powell, *Buller: A Scapegoat* (1994).

A. W. Preston (ed.), *In Relief of Gordon* (1967).

—, *The South African Journal of Sir Garnet Wolseley, 1875* (Cape Town, 1971).

—, *The South African Journals of Sir Garnet Wolseley, 1879–80* (Cape Town, 1973).

—, and P. Dennis (eds), *Swords and Covenants* (1976).

—, 'Frustrated Great Gamesmanship; Sir Garnet Wolseley's Plans for War against Russia, 1873–1880', *International History Review*, 2 (1980), pp. 239–65.

—, 'Sir Charles MacGregor and the Defence of India, 1857–1887', *Historical Journal*, 12 (1969), pp. 58–77.

—, 'Sir Garnet Wolseley and the Cyprus Expedition, 1878', *Journal of the Society for Army Historical Research*, 45 (1967), pp. 4–16.

—, 'Wolseley, the Khartoum Relief Expedition and the Defence of India', *Journal of Imperial and Commonwealth History*, 6 (1978), pp. 254–80.

M. Prior, *Campaigns of a War Correspondent* (1912).

C. Raleigh Chichester, 'Short Service and its Supporters', *Blackwoods*, 129 (May 1881), pp. 591–601.

A. Ramm (ed.), *The Political Correspondence of Mr Gladstone and Lord Granville, 1876–86* (Oxford, 1962).

J. A. Rawley (ed.), *The American Civil War: An English View* (Charlottesville, 1964).

W. Reade, *The Story of the Ashanti Campaign* (1874).

R. Rhodes James, *The British Revolution: British Politics, 1880–1939* (1978).

—, *Rosebery* (1963).

F. Roberts, *Forty One Years in India* (2 vols, 1897).

—, 'The Present State of the Army', *Nineteenth Century*, 12 (November 1882), pp. 633–46.

W. Robertson, *From Private to Field Marshal* (1921).

R. Robinson and J. Gallagher with A. Denny, *Africa and the Victorians: The Official Mind of Imperialism (1961)*.

B. Robson (ed.), *Roberts in India: The Military Papers of Field Marshal Lord Roberts* (1993).

T. Royle, *The Kitchener Enigma* (1985).

G. St Aubyn, *The Royal George* (1963).

G. M. Sanderson, *England, Europe and the Upper Nile* (Edinburgh, 1965).

L. J. Satre, 'St John Brodrick and Army Reform, 1901–1903', *Journal of British Studies*, 15 (1976), pp. 117–39.

D. M. Schreuder, *Gladstone and Kruger: Liberal Government and Colonial Home Rule, 1880–85* (1969).

A. I. Shand, *The Life of General Sir Edward Bruce Hamley* (Edinburgh, 1895).

R. Shannon, *The Crisis of Imperialism, 1865–1915* (1976).

E. Sheppard, *George, Duke of Cambridge: A Memoir of his Private Life Based on the Journal and Correspondence of His Royal Highness* (2 vols, 1905).

M. Shibeika, *British Policy in the Sudan, 1882–1902* (Oxford, 1952).

A. R. Skelley, *The Victorian Army at Home* (1977).

I. R. Smith, *The Origins of the South African War* (1996).

T. von Sosnosky, *England's Danger: The Future of British Army Reform* (1901).

J. A. Spender, *The Life of the Right Hon. Sir Henry Campbell-Bannerman* (2 vols, 1923).

E. M. Spiers, *The Army and Society, 1815–1914* (1980).

—, *The Late Victorian Army, 1868–1902* (Manchester, 1992).

E. Stanhope, *The British Army* (1892).

G. F. G. Stanley, *Canada's Soldiers, 1604–1954* (Toronto, 1954).

H. M. Stanley, *Coomassie and Magdala* (New York, 1874).

W. T. Stead, *How Britain Goes to War* (1903).

Lord Sydenham, *My Working Life* (1927).

J. Symons, *Buller's Campaigns* (1963).

—, England's Pride: The Story of the Gordon Relief Expedition (1965).

A. J. P. Taylor, The Struggle for Mastery in Europe, 1848–1918 (Oxford, 1971).

T. Travers, The Killing Ground (1987).

A. V. Tucker, 'Army and Society in England, 1870–1900: A Reassessment of the Cardwell Reforms', Journal of British Studies, 2 (1963), pp. 110–41.

G. Tylden, 'Tel-el-Kebir', Journal of the Society for Army Historical Research, 31 (1953), pp. 52–57.

—, 'The Sekukuni Campaign of November-December 1879', Journal of the Society for Army Historical Research, 29 (1951), pp. 129–35.

J. E. Tyler, The Struggle for Imperial Unity, 1868–1895 (1938).

P. Usherwood and J. Spencer-Smith, Lady Butler: Battle Artist (1987).

W. Verner, The Military Life of HRH George, Duke of Cambridge (2 vols, 1905).

H. Vogt, The Egyptian War of 1882 (1883).

P. Warwick (ed.), The South African War: The Anglo-Boer War, 1899–1902 (1980).

C. M. Watson, The Life of Major-General Sir Charles Wilson (1909).

O. Wheeler, The War Office, Past and Present (1914).

H. S. Wilkinson, The Great Alternative: A Plea for a National Policy (1894).

—, The Lessons of the War (1900).

—, The Nation's Awakening: Essays Towards a British Policy (1896).

—, Thirty-Five Years, 1874–1909 (1933).

—, The Volunteers and National Defence (1896).

—, War and Policy (1900).

H. S. Wilkinson and C. Dilke, Imperial Defence (1892).

C. Wilson, From Korti to Khartoum (Edinburgh, 1886).

J. Wilson, CB: A Life of Sir Henry Campbell-Bannerman (1973).

K. Wilson, Channel Tunnel Visions, 1850–1945 (1994).

E. Wood, The Crimea in 1854, and 1894 (1895).

— From Midshipman to Field Marshal (2 vols, 1906).

— 'The Ashanti Expedition of 1873–74', Journal of the Royal United Service Institute, 7 (1875), pp. 331–57.

P. Young and J. P. Lawford (eds), History of the British Army (1970).

Index

Lightning Source UK Ltd.
Milton Keynes UK
UKOW04n1518180816

281002UK00001B/53/P